Shakespeare's Early History Plays

Shakespeare's Early History Plays

From Chronicle to Stage

DOMINIQUE GOY-BLANQUET

OXFORD
UNIVERSITY PRESS

OXFORD

UNIVERSITY PRESS

Great Clarendon Street, Oxford OX2 6DP

Oxford University Press is a department of the University of Oxford.
It furthers the University's objective of excellence in research, scholarship,
and education by publishing worldwide in

Oxford New York

Auckland Bangkok Buenos Aires Cape Town Chennai
Dar es Salaam Delhi Hong Kong Istanbul Karachi Kolkata
Kuala Lumpur Madrid Melbourne Mexico City Mumbai Nairobi
São Paulo Shanghai Taipei Tokyo Toronto

Oxford is a registered trade mark of Oxford University Press
in the UK and in certain other countries

Published in the United States
by Oxford University Press Inc., New York

British Library Cataloguing in Publication Data

Data available

Library of Congress Cataloging in Publication Data

Data applied for

ISBN 0–19–811987–9

1 3 5 7 9 10 8 6 4 2

Typeset by Regent Typesetting, London
Printed in Great Britain
on acid-free paper by
Biddles Ltd, Guildford and King's Lynn

Contents

Abbreviations

Bullough	Geoffrey Bullough (ed.), *Narrative and Dramatic Sources of Shakespeare* (London, 1966), vol. iii
Burns	*King Henry VI, Part I*, ed. Edward Burns, Arden 3 (London, 2000)
Cairncross	*King Henry VI, Parts I, II, III*, ed. A. S. Cairncross, The Arden Shakespeare (London, 1957–64)
Cox/Rasmussen	*King Henry VI, Part III*, ed. John D. Cox and Eric Rasmussen, Arden 3 (London, 2001)
EA	*Études anglaises*
ELR	*English Literary Renaissance*
Fabyan	Robert Fabyan, *The New Chronicles of England and France*, ed. Sir Henry Ellis (London, 1811)
Foxe	*The Acts and Monuments of John Foxe*, ed. Revd George Townsend (New York, 1965) , vol. iii
Grafton	Richard Grafton, *A Chronicle at Large and Meere History of the Affayres of England*, ed. Henry Ellis (London, 1809)
1H4	*Henry IV Part 1*
2H4	*Henry IV Part 2*
H5	*Henry V*
1H6	*Henry VI Part 1*
2H6	*Henry VI Part 2*
3H6	*Henry VI Part 3*
Hall	Edward Hall, *The Union of the two noble and illustre famelies of Lancastre and Yorke*, ed. Henry Ellis (London, 1809)
Hammond	*King Richard III*, ed. Antony Hammond, The Arden Shakespeare (London, 1981)
Hattaway	*The First, Second, Third Part of King Henry VI*, ed. Michael Hattaway (Cambridge, 1990–3)
Holinshed	Raphael Holinshed, *Chronicles of England, Scotland and Ireland*, ed. Henry Ellis (London, 1807–8), ii: *1066–1399*; iii, *1399–1553*
Jowett	*Richard III*, ed. John Jowett (Oxford, 2000)
Kelly	Henry A. Kelly, *Divine Providence in the England of Shakespeare's Histories* (Cambridge, Mass., 1970)
Knowles	*King Henry VI, Part II*, ed. Ronald Knowles, Arden 3 (Walton-on-Thames, 1999)
Lull	*King Richard III*, ed. Janis Lull (Cambridge, 1999)
Mirror	*The Mirror for Magistrates*, ed. Lily B. Campbell (Cambridge, 1938)
MLR	*Modern Language Review*
More	Thomas More, *History of Richard III*, Latin and English, in *Complete Works of St. Thomas More*, ed. Richard S. Sylvester, Yale Series (New Haven, 1963), vol. ii
R2	*Richard II*

R3	*Richard III*
RSC	Royal Shakespeare Company
SD	stage direction
ShS	*Shakespeare Survey*
ShSt	*Shakespeare Studies*
SQ	*Shakespeare Quarterly*
TLS	*Times Literary Supplement*
Vergil	*Three Books of Polydore Vergil's English History, Comprising the Reigns of Henry VI, Edward IV, and Richard III*, ed. Henry Ellis (London, 1844)

Il y a plus haut, plus essentiel que l'art: la vérité n'est pas ni ne peut jamais être d'ordre esthétique seulement. L'art est une médiation nécessaire mais approximative.

(Jacques Darras, *Nous sommes tous des romantiques allemands*)

'IF WE OFFEND, IT IS WITH OUR GOOD WILL'

There are things in this book that will never please, I know. It runs counter to the current notion that authors are dead, a fashionable murder often imputed to Roland Barthes who was too fine an artist himself for such a crude assassination of the creative mastermind. It deals with 'that most dreary precinct of Shakespeare studies, source studies'.[1] And it approaches the early histories as a continuous work in progress. Most recent editors of *1, 2,* and *3 Henry VI* work on the hypothesis that they are things of shreds and patches put together by several hands, in haphazard order where last written came first, and signed Shakespeare for want of a better name in the team.[2] Their long introductions generally conclude that the question remains unanswered. I do not mean to quarrel with their expertise, but whatever the process used, by one or several pen-and-scissors holders, I think and I hope to show that there is a method in this apparent disorder, that it bears the mark of a conscious artist, and that he is the same artist who wrote *Richard III, Macbeth,* and *Hamlet.* For want of a better name, failing all contrary evidence, I will call him Shakespeare.

---

[1] Hugh Grady, 'Falstaff: Subjectivity between the Carnival and the Aesthetic', *MLR* 96 (July 2001), 611.

[2] On signature practices, see Brian Vickers, *Shakespeare Co-author* (Oxford, 2002), 5–6, 10–18. In the case of *1 Henry VI,* 'the identity of the sharer(s) is still shadowy', 'scholarship has yet to provide convincing candidates', pp. vii, 145.

Introduction

The Mysteries of *Henry VI*

1. CRITICAL WAVES

E. M. W. Tillyard brought Shakespeare's first tetralogy into prominence at the end of the Second World War with his rousing treatment of the histories as the grand epic of Tudor England, but it was undoubtedly the rebellion against his theses, in the 1960s, which won them the largest measure of interest since their creation.[2] No scholarly work was more radically demolished, with the consequence that 'the book's detractors have made its fortune much more than its admirers'.[3] Once that particular bogey was laid, the plays fell back into their limbo, and inspired only three scholars to treat them at length in the last decade of the century.[4] My object here being their sources, the critical history of the early plays will be pared down to its dramatic turning points since the first and almost final onslaught executed by Robert Greene against the 'upstart crow' before his own demise in 1592. Although Heminge and Condell had guaranteed the authenticity of *1, 2*, and *3 Henry VI* by including them in the 1623 Folio, Greene's *Groatsworth of witte* at the expense of the young 'Shake-scene' caused Edmond Malone in the eighteenth century to bring in a charge of plagiarism which stuck until the beginning of the 1920s. Peter Alexander then argued that two Quartos generally thought to be the originals of *2* and *3 Henry VI*—*The First Part of the Contention betwixt the two Famous Houses of Yorke and Lancaster*, and *The True Tragedy of Richard Duke of York*—were in fact memorial reports of them, destroying most of Malone's case.[5] Yet even their attribution to Shakespeare did not ensure a noticeable improvement in their critical or theatrical popularity. Theories of composite authorship continued to flourish,

---

[2] E. M. W. Tillyard, *The Elizabethan World Picture* (London, 1943); *Shakespeare's History Plays* (London, 1944).

[3] Paola Pugliatti, 'Shakespeare's Historicism: Visions and Revisions', 339, in J. Bate, Jill Levenson, and Dieter Mehl (eds.), *Shakespeare and the Twentieth Century* (Newark, Del., 1998), 336–49.

[4] Phyllis Rackin, *Stages of History: Shakespeare's English Chronicles* (Ithaca, NY, 1990); Donald Watson, *Shakespeare's Early History Plays: Politics at Play on the Elizabethan Stage* (London, 1990); Nina Levine, *Women's Matters: Politics, Gender, and Nation in Shakespeare's Early History Plays* (Newark, Del., 1998). E. A. Pearlman, *William Shakespeare: The History Plays* (1992) deals summarily with the early plays; Jonathan Hart, *Theater and World: The Problematics of Shakespeare's History* (1991), Eric Sterling, *The Movement towards Subversion: The English History Play from Skelton to Shakespeare* (1996), Albert Rolls, *The Theory of the King's Two Bodies* (2000), and Tim Spiekerman, *Shakespeare's Political Realism: the English History Plays* (2001) all concentrate on the second tetralogy.

[5] Alexander, *Shakespeare's 'Henry VI' and 'Richard III'* (Cambridge, 1929). Malone, 'Dissertation on the Three Parts of *King Henry VI*' (1790), in *Plays and Poems of William Shakespeare*, Boswell's Variorum edition (1821), vol. xviii.

until Hereward T. Price in 1951 pointed out their unity of design, the mastery of which none but Shakespeare could have achieved at the time, and went on to discuss the plays without further ado. Andrew Cairncross took his cue from him for the Arden Shakespeare.[6] Like most critics of his generation, he was also strongly influenced by Tillyard, who was then at the height of his authority. Assuming, then, that the trilogy of *Henry VI* and *Richard III* were all written by the same hand, in the natural order, at some time between 1589 and 1592, a majority of researchers felt free to turn to other subjects of debate.

Tillyard's reading of the histories as a dramatization of the 'Tudor myth' continued almost unchallenged into the early 1960s. Then the same year, 1961, A. P. Rossiter and Philip Brockbank expressed some doubt about Shakespeare's political orthodoxy, opening the way to a new wave of critics who began to tear Tillyard's theories to pieces with great gusto.[7] Taking stock of those eventful years, Raymond Utterback observed that Tillyard had provided a useful conceptual frame of argument throughout the period. The quarrel raged for a whole decade, culminating in 1972 with Robert Ornstein's fierce attack against Tillyard's school of mindshrinkers, followed by Moody E. Prior's subtler balance of power between St Augustine and Machiavelli.[8] Peace prevailed after this Yalta, along with a noticeably cooling interest for the history plays and their historical concerns.

Stating that the shapeless material of the chronicles could not throw any light on the genesis of their dramatic offspring, critics like Emrys Jones and Paul Dean invited scholars to study the literary matrices of the histories, Euripides' drama, romance, rhetorical exercises, and the great mystery cycles which had so far received less attention than the moralities as sources of the new genre.[9] Their followers concentrated on the formal aspects that tied the early to the later plays, celebrating their timeless quality, and denying Shakespeare any historical consciousness, on the ground that 'the pastness of the past' had not been invented yet by modern history.[10] John Wilders's opinion in this regard is most representative: whether Shakespeare is portraying Antiquity or Agincourt, 'his imagination is, I believe, governed by a view of human nature which he held irrespective of the historical period he chose to depict'.[11] At that point, Paul L. Siegel called attention to the dangers of anti-historicism, a tendency he detected in the new generation of critics.[12]

---

[6] Price, 'Construction in Shakespeare', in *Contributions in Modern Philology*, XVII (Ann Arbor, 1951). Cairncross, *King Henry VI, Parts I, II, III* (London, 1957–64).

[7] Rossiter, *Angel with Horns* (London, 1961). Brockbank, 'The Frame of Disorder: *Henry VI*', in *Early Shakespeare* (Stratford-upon-Avon, 1961).

[8] Utterback, 'Dramatic Perspectives on Shakespeare's History Plays: A Review Article', *Studies in the Literary Imagination*, 5 (Atlanta, 1972). Ornstein, *A Kingdom for a Stage* (Cambridge, Mass., 1972). Prior, *The Drama of Power* (Evanston, Ill., 1973).

[9] Dean, 'Shakespeare's *Henry VI* Trilogy and Elizabethan "Romance" Histories: The Origins of a Genre', and Jones's review of K. Muir's *Sources of Shakespeare's Plays*, both in *SQ* 33 (1982). Jones, *The Origins of Shakespeare* (Oxford, 1977).

[10] L. C. Knights, 'Shakespeare and History', *Sewanee Review*, 86 (1978), 380–95.

[11] Wilders, *The Lost Garden: A View of Shakespeare's English and Roman History Plays* (London, 1978), p. ix.

[12] Siegel, 'Tillyard Lives: Historicism and Shakespeare's History Plays', *Clio*, 9 (1979), 5–23.

A firing of 'Invisible Bullets' at the dawn of the 1980s signalled the return to hard politics.[13] The next decade saw the parallel emergence of cultural materialism, a phrase and practice borrowed from Raymond Williams's works, and new historicism. Both currents argued for a radical contextualization of literature, and confirmed the rejection of Tillyard, whose most grievous fault was in their eyes the invention of a unified collective 'Elizabethan mind', as if his work still wanted debunking. Both schools of followers have since been employed in tracking the dominant ideologies of the Early Modern period and the various forms of resistance, dissent, transgression, that Power aimed to suppress. This meant shifting the weight of attention from so-called 'major works' to weaker voices silenced by the dominant discourse, i.e. all the marginal texts that had been reduced to the status of 'minor' literature by mainstream criticism.

The main divergence between schools concerns the degree of success such subversive threats achieved in undermining the dominant social order. The cultural materialists have faith in the disruptive force of popular transgression, but in Greenblatt's view, all struggle against dominant ideologies is in vain: the ideological process of containment is so effective that the subversion of authority actually comforts its power. In Shakespeare's histories, 'the subversive voices are produced by the affirmations of order, and they are powerfully registered, but they do not undermine that order'.[14] Shakespeare was a conservative, whether willingly or not, and his own opinions are immaterial. This pessimistic appraisal of man's freedom opened increasingly sceptical queries on the liberty of the poet, on his control over meaning and intention, as well as on the creative act itself and the very notion of author. On the same grounds, the critic's independence of judgement and objectivity were illusions, and his claims to knowledge, sheer vanity. As in Heisenberg's uncertainty principle, whatever he observed, he altered beyond reprieve.

The theorists' extreme positions raised, as they still do, violent hostility, the most frequent complaint being that the new historicists simply ignored the alternative groups or movements that did not fit their theories.[15] David S. Kastan, who declares admiration for new historicism, notes it has appropriately challenged the largely unexamined categories of literary analysis, but failed to offer convincing alternatives. It is no surprise if new historicism would and did replace new criticism: its name unwittingly reveals their similarities. In Kastan's measured appraisal, these alternative histories tend to behave just like the official one: 'The aberrant, the marginal, the local, the particular are appropriated and homogenized into a unitary culture.' In fact, 'they are not properly historical at all but rather formalist practices, discovering pattern and order, unity and coherence, in the culture.' The claims of theory cannot be demonstrated at the level of theory: 'we need to produce not more theory but more facts.'[16]

[13] Stephen Greenblatt's essay originally appeared in *Glyph 8, Johns Hopkins Textual Studies* (1981).

[14] Greenblatt, 'Invisible Bullets', in J. Dollimore and A. Sinfield (eds.), *Political Shakespeare: New Essays in Cultural Materialism* (Manchester, 1985), 38.

[15] James Holstun, 'Ranting at the New Historicism', *ELR* 19 (1989), 189–225.

[16] *Shakespeare after Theory* (New York, 1999), 30, 31.

In his survey of the century's work, Michael Taylor observes a hectic prolifera-
tion of texts and criticism in the Shakespeare industry: 'All this frenzy spawns and
has been spawned by a myriad competing theories,' he remarks.[17] The fear that
excess of theory might kill its object, suppress pleasure, and obliterate the texts is
palpable in today's scholarship. A growing awareness of this peril appears sympto-
matically in the timid comeback of various traditional categories, author, meaning,
intention, character, and so on, with nuances acquired thanks to the vigorous
airing they took in the revisionist process. To Leah Marcus, we should recuperate
some tools of the 'old historicism' and primarily 'an idea called the Author's intent
or putative intentionality', although in the revised form of a construct.[18] 'Author
retrieval' appears in various programmes, Paola Pugliatti notes, but when we
examine the theoretical statements on what the construct should be, 'we find not
only that the critical tools are more or less the same', but that the author as cultural
construct 'is, in the final analysis, a "person" very much like the person of traditional biographism'.[19]

In his review of *French Essays on Shakespeare*, Bruce Boehrer notes with surprise
that the French critics are not attracted to any of the topics currently popular
among Anglo-American scholars, for instance 'questions of queer theory', 'feminist analyses', 'the notions of misrule and Bakhtinian theory', or 'the problematics
of dramatic authorship foregrounded by the New Textualism'.[20] It is no less surprising, for a French observer, to see Anglo-American scholars fuel their arguments
with authorities like Althusser, Foucault, and various formalists, Propp, Bakhtin,
whose influence declined in continental Europe as the frailties of their systems were
exposed by a large range of thinkers. The critics of Shakespeare's histories might
find it more rewarding to concentrate on the remarkable work on historiography
produced by the École des Annales since its foundation in 1929 by Marc Bloch and
Lucien Febvre. Around the Annales, a rich galaxy of scholars constantly strive to
discuss with adjacent disciplines, to check theory against practice; most of them
have been translated and commented on by Anglo-American historians, less so by
Shakespearian scholars.[21]

My own Pantheon would include along with those the works of Ernst Curtius,
Kantorowicz, Étienne Gilson, Erich Auerbach, and, closer to my area of research,
Jean Jacquot, Richard Marienstras, Edward Berry's *Patterns of Decay*, Wilbur
Sanders, Henry A. Kelly, David Riggs, all of whom were formative guides; since then
I have learnt much from others like David S. Kastan, Wolfgang Iser, or Ian
Moulton, whom I read at a later stage.[22] I belong to a generation who rejected

---

[17] *Shakespeare Criticism in the Twentieth Century* (Oxford, 2001), 17, 24, 168.

[18] *Puzzling Shakespeare: Local Reading and its Discontents* (Berkeley 1988), 42.

[19] 'Shakespeare's Historicism', 341–2.

[20] Boehrer, in *SQ* 47 (1996), 348–50, reviews J.-M. Maguin and Michèle Willems (eds.), *French Essays on Shakespeare and his Contemporaries: 'What would France with us?'* (Newark, Del., 1995).

[21] Among the most renowned, Paul Ricœur, Louis Marin, Jean-Pierre Vernant, Marcel Détienne, Paul Veyne, François Hartog, Pierre Nora, Jacques Le Goff, Henri-Irénée Marrou, Fernand Braudel, Georges Duby, Carlo Ginzburg, Robert Mandrou, Jacques Revel, Roger Chartier, Michel de Certeau, Florence Dupont . . . and Foucault himself.

[22] Parts of the present essay are updated versions, translated with the generous help of Catherine

dictatorial ideologues, and although I believe the new historicists did salutary work in operating a general shift of static habits, their arguments have a strong element of circularity, which Phyllis Rackin implicitly recognizes when she writes that 'the questions with which we approach the past—and therefore, the answers we seem to hear—are inevitably shaped by our own historically specific concerns'.[23] This circularity appears for instance in feminist works which identify misrule or tears with women, and draw the conclusion that unruly males and tearful fathers are constructed as feminine—a fallacy efficiently exposed by Ian Moulton.[24]

There is also, I fear, a perverse corollary to the postulate that history is essentially fictive, that there is no coherence or sense in 'facts' other than the construction we impose on them, that truth is impossible to reach and therefore of no consequence. Graham Holderness takes the example of young Richard of York's tales about his uncle to argue that the substance of history lies not in remains or documents, but in myth, legend, oral tradition: 'when the reliability of his source is questioned, the validity of the story is authenticated by reference to those most generalized of sources, popular memory and oral tradition. The point is that the truth the story contains is in no way dependent on its historical accuracy.' Holderness does not quote Derrida, but is guided by his reference to Socrates' *akoè*, an ancient tradition very like this 'popular memory'.[25] To pronounce little York's story as 'authenticated' by anonymous rumours is to erase authorship as insignificant and give critics full licence for irresponsibility. Edward Said is certainly right when he defines the intellectual as someone who attempts to tell the truth at all times and to the best of his abilities. What is the point of conducting research that gives up on the question of truth?

Even as he refuses the initial confusion between historical fact and remembrance of a real event, the philosopher Paul Ricœur stresses the need to resist the temptation to dissolve the fact into the narration, and the narration into a literary piece of writing indiscernible from fiction. The claim that we cannot be objective in our reconstruction of the past confuses different levels of analysis, 'la phase documentaire avec la phase explicative et compréhensive, et au-delà de celle-ci avec la phase littéraire de la représentation', i.e. first we collect documents, then analyse and understand them, and only after that do we put them through the literary phase of mimesis. His study is 'haunted' by Derrida's notion of the *pharmakon*, and the open crisis in belief which turns historical knowledge into a school for scepticism: is documentary evidence a remedy or a poison for the weaknesses inherent to testimony? Can history break all its ties with declarative memory? 'Il dépendra de

Lisak, of *Le Roi mis à nu: Histoire d'Henry VI, de Hall à Shakespeare* (Paris, 1986), *Shakespeare et l'invention de l'histoire* (Brussels, 1997), and *William Shakespeare: Richard III* (Paris, 1999).

[23] *Stages of History*, 39.

[24] Richard II or Falstaff in Marcus, *Puzzling Shakespeare*, the Duke of York in Rackin, 'Engendering the Tragic Audience: The Case of *Richard III*', in Deborah Barker and Ivo Kamps (eds.), *Shakespeare and Gender: A History* (London, 1995). Moulton, '"A Monster Great Deformed": The Unruly Masculinity of Richard III', *SQ* 47 (1996).

[25] Holderness, *Shakespeare: The Histories* (New York, 2000), 100. See Jacques Derrida, *Dissemination*, trans. Barbara Johnson (London, 1993), 74, on *Phaedrus*, 274c.

l'explication et de la représentation d'apporter quelque soulagement à ce désarroi, par un exercice mesuré de la contestation et un renforcement de l'attestation.'[26] The object of phases two and three of the process is to alleviate this mental distress, by exercising contestation moderately and fortifying the part of attestation. It is the programme I aim to follow here.

2. CLASSICAL SHADES

The writing of history

To the question, 'What is history?' Paul Veyne replies that the answer 'has not changed over the 2,200 years since the successors of Aristotle found it: historians tell of true events in which man is the actor; history is a true novel.' Facts do not exist in isolation, he further notes, in the sense that 'the fabric of history is what we shall call a plot, a very human and not very "scientific" mixture of material causes, aims, and chances'. This plot may be 'a transversal cut of different temporal rhythms' and still 'always be a plot because it is human, sublunary; because it will not be a piece of determinism.' In history as in the theatre, it is impossible to show everything, not because that would require too many pages, but 'because there is no elementary historical fact, no eventworthy atom'. History is what the historian chooses to tell. If his choice is subjective, it is by no means arbitrary. The main phrase of the historical genre is 'It is interesting.' What is 'interesting', hence worth writing about, boils down to 'two archetypes: "this action is worthy of living on in our memory" and "Men are different from each other".' Heroic events, singular events. Whatever kind of history the historian aims to write, 'unfortunately, if the norm of truth is driven out through the door, it comes in again through the window'.[27]

St Augustine's question, 'What is time?', revolutionized historiography. Time in *The City of God* is the actualization of a providential design; the transientness of the world is that of a work in progress, the writing in the present tense of man's salvation.[28] Political Augustinism, gradually emptied of all historicity, survived to fuel the endless quarrel between *regnum* and *sacerdotum*, spiritual against temporal power.[29] The Catholic Church ruled almost unchallenged over the Middle Ages, victoriously fighting all the scientific advances that might threaten to upset it. Empirical knowledge and technique progressed nonetheless; the urban time of business began to challenge church bells and agrarian rhythms, to use Le Goff's telling image, as facts increasingly rebelled against traditional authorities. The

[26] See Ricœur, *La Mémoire, l'histoire, l'oubli* (Paris, 2000), 224–30. Derrida's 'Plato's Pharmacy', in *Dissemination*, 63–171, is ostensibly a commmentary on the *Phaedrus*, but in fact, n. 20 discloses, a reading of *Finnegans Wake*. All translations from untranslated works are mine.
[27] Veyne, *Writing History: Essay on Epistemology*, trans. Mina Moore-Rinvolucri (Manchester, 1984), pp. x, 32–3, 47–8, 54, 51–2.
[28] Augustine, *Confessions*, trans. Henry Chadwick (Oxford, 1991) xi. xiv. 230. *The City of God against the Pagans*, Latin and English, ed. W. MacAllen Green (Cambridge, Mass., 1957–72).
[29] See C. A. Patrides, *The Phoenix and the Ladder: The Rise and Decline of the Christian View of History* (Berkeley, 1964). Robin G. Collingwood, *The Idea of History* (Oxford, 1946).

Church still demanded that reason bow to faith, but the spirit grew intractable, no longer assured that the sole end of this transitory life was to prepare salvation in the next world.[30] Before they could devise satisfactory protocols, the Early Modern historiographers must escape this double yoke, Christian teleology and the superiority of the Ancients. To set history free, they had to find a proper value for earthly life, proclaim that its quality could be improved by knowledge, and establish science on the strong basis of nature's unvarying laws. These conditions were only fully met in the long run of the seventeenth century.[31] Even then, most scientists did not yet realize the implications of these developments until the early eighteenth century, when Malebranche asked aloud what was the point of praying to God if He could not change the order of nature.

The seeds of modern history all appear at some point in the course of the English Renaissance, but at the height of Elizabeth's reign the process was far from complete. Many writers were still unaware of radical incompatibilities between old and new doctrines, either striving to reconcile them, or happily fusing them without great concern for consistency. The most common way of writing history was a year-by-year account of events in the form of chronicles or annals, reproducing earlier relations, suitably enriched with original details. It prevailed until the historians felt it was ill adapted to their higher designs, and turned to the Classics for more rational modes of composition. The most popular chroniclers of the Tudor age—Polydore Vergil, Hall, and Holinshed—were 'transitional figures not yet alert to the limitations of their scissors-and-paste methods':[32] they studied larger sections of national history than did their predecessors, whose interests seldom went beyond the replacement of one dynasty by the next, but the scope of their vision was still framed by the medieval thought structures, while they strove to extract some sort of perennial truth from the teachings of the past. The next generation, William Camden or John Selden, would leave out Providence from their commentaries, without openly denying its existence. In Sir Walter Ralegh's phrase, 'to say that it was thus because God was pleased to have it so were a true but an idle answer'.[33]

It took civilized Europe 300 years to mature from the medieval to the modern world. Several features herald the dawn of modernity:

- The trend towards secularization, initiated by the humanist historians, who were the first to steer away from Augustinism; with Machiavelli and Giucciardini, this trend led to a complete division between history and theology, proclaimed the autonomy of human history, and placed public government outside the realm of private morals.
- The progress of experimental methods, evidenced in various areas by a

[30] Jacques Le Goff, *Time, Work, and Culture in the Middle Ages,* trans. Arthur Goldhammer (Chicago, 1980), 29–52.

[31] See J. B. Bury, *The Idea of Progress* (New York, 1932), 65–80.

[32] Frank S. Fussner, *The Historical Revolution: English Historical Writing and Thought, 1580–1640* (Westport, Conn., 1976).

[33] *The History of the World,* III. II. xix, in *The Works of Sir Walter Ralegh,* ed. William Oldys and Thomas Birch (Oxford, 1829), v. 570.

preference for original documents over traditional authorities, a more consistent recourse to archives, scientific tests of evaluation, comparatist studies, and critical reassessments of sources. Symbolic images of the social body could not long survive the dissection of human bodies that was becoming regular practice, not a hundred miles from Palladio's *teatro olimpico*, in the *teatro anatomico* of Padua.

- A new sense of historical development, and of context, which showed up the discontinuities between ages, disqualifying the analogy between past and present, and the validity for all times of history's lessons. Gradually, the French and English humanists came to realize that learning about old customs and institutions was pointless unless one first re-created the society which had produced them and might have died out altogether.
- The division into specialized fields of research. Having established its own finality, history was no longer pressed to please or convince, but to devise a suitable form of presentation. The more scientific methods involved greater technical difficulties, leading the historians to define a specific area for their enquiries, distinct from philosophy, literature, or philosophy.

At the dawn of the seventeenth century, Walter Ralegh and Francis Bacon stand side by side like the two poles of historical consciousness, a medieval providentialist and a herald of modern science. Actually they have more in common than first meets the eye. Both are open to new ideas, but their mode of writing belongs to an earlier age of historiography; the contributions of these two notorious stylists are literary masterpieces, not decisive advances in historical knowledge and methodology. In 1614, Ralegh's *History of the World* exhibits all the indexed features of an obsolescent genre: the symmetry of past and present, the enduring value of history's moral and political teachings, a providentialist design, logical and doctrinal incompatibilities, and a plain lack of interest for the developing methods of documentary research. It is 'a superb expression of the baroque style. Not a scholarly one,' in the opinion of Fussner, who dismisses it as 'a rich jewel of medievalism'.[34] Ralegh sees history as the repetition of old scenes by the same actors who return on stage with new costumes but no clearer judgement than in the past, and ascribes its writing to God, 'author of all our tragedies'. The mutability of fortune is such that the same man will play the prince and the beggar in one day:

Certainly there is no other account to be made of this ridiculous world, than to resolve, that the change of fortune on the great theatre is but as the change of garments on the less: for when, on the one and the other, every man wears but his own skin, the players are all alike.[35]

A vision more akin to Spenser's allegorical 'Cantos of Mutabilitie' than to any modern definition of history.

Compared with Ralegh's, Francis Bacon's philosophy is resolutely secular.[36]

---

[34] Fussner, *The Historical Revolution*, 11, 210.

[35] *History of the World*, preface, p. xliii.

[36] In Bury's view, *The Idea of Progress*, 49–63, Bacon's novelty lies less in his theory of scientific progress than in his recognition of its practical utility.

Without expressly denying the role of Providence, Bacon obviously finds it out of place in a lay history, just as he thinks that the proper end of knowledge is to serve man in this world rather than help him to the next. He firmly rejects the dogma of the Ancients' superiority: an excessive respect for traditional authorities is the first obstacle to the progress of science. Yet if Bacon in some regards qualifies as a modern, whose contradictions may be thought a sophisticated medium of historical consciousness, it is now established that his fame as a model of scholarly research was largely usurped.[37] He took rather less care with his sources than the predecessors he had mocked, often copied their assertions without troubling to check if they were true, and relied on his own sense of probability to write speeches for his characters, in the authorized Classical and humanist traditions. In this respect, the movement from Vergil to Bacon is one of regression rather than progress.

The truth of poetry

Polydore Vergil raised indignant protests in England when he turned a critical eye on the line of British kings and their Arthurian offspring. This amounted to questioning the official story of origins favoured by the monarchy.[38] The question would open a fierce argument between supporters of history and of poetry, ending by a clear division between history and legend, but no one, including Vergil, could yet fully appreciate its implications.[39] To Aristotle, history was a 'particular statement' saying 'what, for example, Alcibiades did or suffered', whereas 'the poet's function is to describe not what *has* happened, but the kind of thing that *might* happen'. Interpreting Aristotle's view that 'Hence poetry is something more philosophic and of graver import than history,' Sidney defended the imaginative truth of literature against the restrictive truth of history, with an urgency suggesting that many disagreed with his militant views.[40] In the *Defence of Poesie*, he wonders 'why England the Mother of excellent mindes should be growne so hard a stepmother to *Poets*', and claims that the historian's access to truth hardly justifies his arrogance. History, which depends on hearsay, is often less than truthful. 'Now for the *Poet*, he nothing affirmeth, and therefore never lieth.'[41] He writes of universal, not particular,

---

[37] Wilhelm Busch, *England under the Tudors, King Henry VII*, trans. Alice M. Todd (London, 1895), concluded after a sentence-by-sentence examination of Bacon's *History* that he had not the least concern for historical truth. Modern researchers take a more positive view of his contribution to the advancement of political consciousness, while confirming his inaccuracy as a historian. See Henry Weinberger's introduction and interpretative essay in *The History of the Reign of King Henry the Seventh* (Ithaca, NY, 1996), 8–16, 213–52.

[38] See Denis Hay, *Polydore Vergil, Renaissance Historian and Man of Letters* (Oxford, 1952), 157–8. Holinshed and Camden betrayed scepticism but did not reject the legend explicitly. Bacon was one of the first after Vergil to deny it.

[39] Michel Foucault, *The Order of Things: An Archeology of the Human Sciences* (London, 1970), 39–40, recalls the original meaning of *legenda*, things to be read 'when one is faced with the task of writing an animal's *history*'.

[40] *Poetics*, in *The Basic Works of Aristotle*, ed. Richard McKeon (New York, 2001), 51^{b}5. Sidney, *The Defence of Poesie*, in *The Complete Works of Sir Philip Sidney*, iii, ed. Albert Feuillerat (Cambridge, 1923).

[41] Sidney, *Defence*, 28–35.

matters. Today's historians, who have learnt to recognize the vanity of any pre-
tension to objectivity, are closer to the humility advised by Sidney. History no
longer claims to be a science; historians catch but faint traces of reality and have to
fall back on their imaginations to fill in the blanks.

Tudor history was predominantly a collection of heroic deeds, and poetic licence
but a means of lending weight to its lessons in a desperate fight against 'Obliuion the
cancard enemie to Fame'.[42] The custom of inventing speeches for historical characters, authorized by the examples of Thucydides and Tacitus, was one way of solving
the problems of causality. Hobbes's defence of Thucydides' method would still
refer to the traditional couple of truth and rhetoric: 'For in *truth* consisteth the *soul*,
and in *elocution* the *body* of history. The latter without the former is but a picture of
history; and the former without the latter, unapt to instruct.'[43] Yet despite their
faultless antiquity, the allurements of style inspired growing reticence in Sidney's
own time; interpolated speeches especially were regarded as unwelcome distor-
tions. Jean Bodin, one of the first historians of the century, advised a rugged
simplicity and plain grammar as best suited to the purpose: it was impossible to
please readers and to serve truth at the same time.[44] Camden would follow his lead
and help to set a norm of austere clarity in historical writing. Historiography bade
farewell to literature at the precise point where historical drama resurrected 'brave
Talbot', inviting audiences to emulate virtuous heroes. What the two traditions had
in common were the rhetorical modes used to specify the qualities of great men.
Works like *A Mirror for Magistrates*, Shakespeare's plays, or Daniel's *Civil Wars*
tended to stress rather than soften the differences: they not only used material that
historians were coming to reject, 'but could use it with a freedom, and twist it to a
function, that those who cared for truth abhorred'.[45]

The contribution of history to the Elizabethan theatre was to operate a lively
renewal of its heroic stereotypes. The recourse to famous British figures helped
build up a new tension between the timeless quality of heroic virtue and the
evolving codes of behaviour. In the wake of the *Mirror* and *Gorboduc*, a crowd of
chronicle playwrights, led by Marlowe and Shakespeare, turned away from nebu-
lous orients to medieval England, from Titus or Tamburlaine to Henrys and
Edwards, with a didacticism that fully deserves the label 'moralities of state' delivered by the critics.[46] Reviewing the themes of Shakespeare's first histories against a
background of high moral tone and bellicose humour will show their natural links
with the dominant trends: foreign war, popular rebellion, civil strife, among other

[42] Hall's dedication, p. v.

[43] Thomas Hobbes, 'Of the Life and History of Thucydides', Preface to his translation of *Eight Books
of the Peloponnesian War*, in *The Collected English Works of Thomas Hobbes*, ed. Sir William Molesworth
(London, 1843), viii, p. xx. See also his considerations on *The Whole Art of Rhetoric*, vi, 419–536.

[44] Jean Bodin, *Method for the Easy Comprehension of History*, trans. Beatrice Reynolds (New York,
1945). For his influence on historiography, see J. W. Allen, *A History of Political Thought in the Sixteenth
Century* (London, 1957), 405–7.

[45] Herschel Baker, 'The Truth of History', in *The Race of Time: Three Lectures on Renaissance
Historiography* (Toronto, 1967), 80.

[46] See David Bevington, *Tudor Drama and Politics: A Critical Approach to Topical Meaning*
(Cambridge, Mass., 1968). The phrase 'morality of state' is Rossiter's.

ingredients prominent in the three parts of *Henry VI*, happen to be the main topics of the London stage at the time. The topicality of Henry Tudor's victory in *Richard III* goes without saying.

The recent religious division, haunted by fearful memories of the late civil wars, made it a necessity to re-create a large consensus.[47] With danger threatening the old order, the fear that a vital structure was about to disintegrate was sufficient urge to reassert its basic principles. The Tudor propagandists drew persuasion as well as images from an extant system of beliefs, obsolete perhaps but still very much alive in set patterns of thought and phrases. Successive governments thus gained support for their more daring innovations by appealing to time-honoured practices, in which Henry VIII figured as the true restorer of medieval kingship.[48] This sometimes required delicate juggling with the archives: 'expediency demanded that where accepted legal precedent was inadequate, acceptable legal precedent had to be found.'[49] It was no mean task, nor were the apologists of the regime ordinary sycophants. Their eagerness to serve the state often went with a deep-seated belief in the validity of the cause they fought for. Hard as we find it now to reconcile such an attitude with the integrity of historical research, official Tudor historiographers and other practitioners of history felt no qualms about dividing their service of truth with an equally worthy cause.

In this regard, the treatment of history inside the theatre was probably no worse than outside, nor would artists have been thought to prostitute their art by applying it to a task of propaganda. In Heywood's *Apology for Actors*, plays were enrolled, as were the chronicles by the homilists, to teach subjects 'obedience to their king' by representing 'the untimely end of such as have moved tumults, commotions and insurrections'.[50] As David Bevington points out, writers like Shakespeare or Ben Jonson would not have kept aloof from the political debates of their time, nor agreed to the modern dichotomy between utility and poetic vision: 'They still believed in the power of art to guide and reform.'[51] But an artist of Shakespeare's talent may be thought to have influenced intellects more than he was bound to absorb the prejudices of his age. The contemporary brew of Machiavellian providential Calvinism is at best a downgraded version of the arguments exposed in *Richard III*, or *Macbeth*, not the other way round.[52] The same modern historians who are unimpressed by Machiavelli's efforts loudly praise Shakespeare, whose 'subtlety about history was worth more at the time than Hall's facts, or even the best historian's interpretation'.[53] In their paradoxical way, the plays contributed to the evolution of historiography, which Shakespeare eased into its modern age.

[47] See C. S. L. Davies, *Peace, Print and Protestantism, 1450–1558* (London, 1995).

[48] See G. W. Zeeveld, 'Richard Morison, Official Apologist of Henry VIII', *Publications of the Modern Language Association of America*, 55 (1940), 406–25.

[49] Zeeveld, *Foundations of Tudor Policy* (Cambridge, Mass., 1948), 112.

[50] Thomas Heywood, *An Apology for Actors* (London, 1841), 53.

[51] Bevington, *Tudor Drama*, 4.

[52] See Wilbur Sanders, *The Dramatist and the Received Idea: Studies in the Plays of Marlowe and Shakespeare* (Cambridge, 1968).

[53] Fussner, *Tudor History and the Historians* (New York, 1970), 305, 230.

3. CYCLICAL STORMS

Are the three parts of *Henry VI* and *Richard III* independent plays or do they form a cycle? The place of *1 Henry VI* in the sequence is linked with the problem of dating, which cannot reconcile the evidence or the scholars. As the anti-Tillyardian wave set in, the notion of 'cycle', 'sequence', or, worse still, of 'tetralogy', with its Wagnerian echoes, raised increasing objections and various alternative hypotheses. It is worth noting that the word was first applied to these plays in Weimar, of all places, to celebrate Shakespeare's tercentenary.[54] It is also worth recalling what it meant originally in Ancient Greece: three tragedies on connected subjects, concluded by a satyrical drama, performed by the same actors, which debunked the heroic figures by placing them in a playful or derisive context.

Against totalitarian oppression, the anti-Tillyardians generally insisted on the autonomy of each play. The critics who connected them with the mystery cycles agreed that they form sequences but imagined a variety of combinations: groups of two, three, four, or even eight parts. F. W. Brownlow found the unity of design evidence enough that the two tetralogies were planned as a whole, whether by Shakespeare alone or by a committee of writers, though he did not explain why the second half was composed before the first.[55] Moody E. Prior and Emrys Jones, among others, questioned the dramatic continuity between *Henry VI* and *Richard III*, but inclined to Brownlow's reading of the last play as a compulsory piece, clearly a regression on the trilogy despite its enduring popularity: cutting off the last play would establish the independence of *Henry VI* from *Richard III*'s offensive providentialism. A position completely reversed today by the Oxford editor of *Richard III*, John Jowett, who rejoices that with his new Quarto-based text, '*Richard III* is breaking free from the *Henry VI* trilogy.'[56]

Many upheavals have taken place between these two symmetrical rejections of embarrassing pieces. Cairncross in Arden 2 had opted for the order of the Folio, the date 1590 for Part 1, and the notion that the four plays formed an epic cycle. The Oxford editors reopened the whole quarrel by relegating *1 Henry VI* after Parts 2 and 3, adopting their Q titles, plus a number of passages and readings usually excluded from edited texts, and again querying Shakespeare's sole authorship.[57] Michael Hattaway summed up the argument over *1 Henry VI* exhaustively without bringing

---

[54] When the Arden 3 editors write that Frank Benson's production of the trilogy in 1906 'was the first known performance of *3 Henry VI* since the 1590s' (Cox/Rasmussen 16), they mean in England, presumably. In 1864, Frank Dingensteldt directed a production of the eight plays, which he described as two tetralogies, performed in chronological sequence, at the Weimar Court Theatre. See Robert K. Sarlos, 'Dingelstedt's Celebration of the Tercentenary: Shakespeare's Histories as a Cycle', *Theatre Studies*, 5 (1964), 117–31.

[55] *Two Shakespearean Sequences: 'Henry V' to 'Richard II' and 'Pericles' to 'Timon of Athens'* (London, 1977).

[56] Introd. 132.

[57] Stanley Wells and Gary Taylor (general eds.), *The Complete Works* (Oxford, 1986); *William Shakespeare: A Textual Companion* (Oxford, 1987), 177. Taylor, 'Shakespeare and Others: The Authorship of *Henry VI Part One*', *Medieval and Renaissance Drama in English*, 7 (1995), 145–203, concludes it is partly Nashe's, and approximately 20% Shakespeare's.

it nearer to a solution. I cannot hope to improve matters and do not mean to try. Hattaway is 'inclined to believe that the play was written before the other two parts of the sequence at some date between 1589 and 1591', and that since no analysis he has read so far 'makes an indisputable case for dual or multiple authorship', he does not 'feel inclined to dispute the implicit claim' of Heminge and Condell.[58] As to his next query—'even if it could be proved that the play was in whole or in part not by Shakespeare, should that affect the way in which we read or direct it?'—I am inclined to believe that even if it should not, it does.

The attitude towards dramatic texts has changed radically in one generation. Plays were treated by academics like any other literary text, novel, or piece of poetry, until the 1950s, when the pioneering works of Jean Jacquot called attention to stage conditions, theatrical history, and the variety of iconographic sources that could document them.[59] This not only marked a considerable advancement in the understanding of Elizabethan dramaturgy, it also called for a thorough rereading of the plays in this new light; in 1986, the Oxford editors took a radical turn from earlier practice and gave preference to the texts produced by the theatre. All editions of Shakespeare now include a section on performance history, though few will pause to weigh the implications of designing theatrical scripts for readership. Yet there is some risk in applying the conditions of the stage to the book. Imagine printers editing Beethoven's scores on the basis of a performance possibly adapted in some unknown year for a children's tea party or classroom ballet. Although I agree with Muriel Bradbrook that 'all drama, being an art of performance, is collaborative', a reader is not bound by time as a spectator is: he can begin at the end, pause when he likes, go back several pages, read the same passage twice, skip the next, and should be allowed to prefer Shakespeare's original to an actor's rephrasing. From arrogant ignorance of what made 'pure' poetry unpure—the theatre—scholarship has shifted to thoughtless acceptance of rules derived from another medium without its necessities.

The debate on authorial or theatrical authority hides another larger issue, which is the question raised by genetic criticism when faced with several versions of the same text, all equally genuine but reflecting different states of mind, at different stages in life: which one is it most proper to print? the earliest, crudest, and most spontaneous draft, or the pentimento, the repented one, more reflexively composed for posterity? How far is an author allowed to correct his own copy, his self-conscious self-portrait? The solution adopted in a crucial case like Ezra Pound's *Cantos*, to print all versions side by side on facing pages, is ethically impeccable but practically unreadable.[60] When the text is a play, and its ultimate destination the stage, it is clearly impossible. A director has to choose whether he favours youthful untaught energy or mature knowledge, the solitary artist or the technical team,

---

[58] *1H6*, introd. 35–41. See Vickers's answer, *Shakespeare Co-author*, 206.

[59] Jean Jacquot's Groupe de Recherches Théâtrales et Musicologiques, CNRS, created in 1954, produced the innovative volumes of various series, Le Chœur des Muses, and Les Voies de la Création théâtrale.

[60] *A Variorum Edition of The Cantos of Ezra Pound*, ed. Richard D. Taylor, 'a computer-assisted collation of all published texts' (1981–   ).

eventful prose or static poetry. The Oxford Shakespeare is an excellent tool for readers who know the issues involved, and have a specific reason for using this text among the many available.[61] If it is meant as a guide for stage use, directors are unlikely to repeat some one else's performance, even Shakespeare's. They are no more tied to a didascalic text than he was to his sources; the original stage directions are not Bible truths, Daniel Mesguich claims, only instructions to directors to use their imaginations, and the resources of modern technique, at places in the text clearly requiring some stage business. Their first commitment is not to the author—no misguided performance will lastingly damage a good play, and even unsophisticated spectators soon understand they are watching something else than Shakespeare's original. The editor's responsibility is not to a passing audience, but to a generation who will know Shakespeare through his editing.

What a scholar learns from the stage is unique, but cannot supply a methodology for research. A director's choice will inevitably reflect the values of the society it was made for, and adapt to its limits. Today's theatre still operates under the combined influence of Brecht and Artaud. Shakespeare was head of the list when Artaud declared war against masterpieces: 'Written poetry is valid once and then ought to be torn up. Let dead poets make way for the living.'[62] A view loudly endorsed by Peter Brook: 'Of course nowhere does the Deadly Theatre install itself so securely, so comfortably and so slily as in the works of William Shakespeare.'[63] He claims not to have read more than three books about Shakespeare, which is probably wise if they offer him no more than his own reflection. Brook's shrewd understanding of texts and of audiences' receptive qualities is so far above the rest that he is often described as a directors' director. Now is it well advised to make him a scholars' director as well? He explained the heavy cuts of his latest *Hamlet* with the raw statement that 'what we have removed is what is no longer necessary'.[64] Does it mean that a great deal of what Shakespeare wrote is useless to us, now and for ever after, or that only a limited portion of the play can be taken in by audiences in far distant parts of the world? Thanks mainly to Adrian Lester's performance, the show was a joy to watch. For those who will not have a chance to see it, should this *Hamlet* lite be the authorized version in print for the twenty-first century?

Editorial politics involve more than a preference for the collaborative over the isolated work of art. When it comes to choosing an edition for reference, it appears that textual studies, though at first glance a more sedate area of research than politics, are no less conflictual, and far more subversive. Most editors advertise a preference for texts weathered in the theatre, 'the complex of author/ book-keeper/ actor/prompter and others',[65] but few actually refrain from correcting the team's 'mistakes' or deviations from unspecified norms. Arden 3 and Cambridge insert

---

[61] It has succeeded so well that it is the basis of many editions for the public at large, including foreign ones—Laffont Bouquins and Ellipses in France, Norton in the United States—which do not all give advance warning of what readers are in for.

[62] 'No More Masterpieces', in *The Theatre and its Double*, trans. Victor Corti (London, 1993), 55–63.

[63] *The Empty Space* (London, 1968), 12.

[64] Interview with J. P. Thibaudat, *Libération*, 30 Nov. 2000.

[65] Hammond, introd. 49.

unwarranted stage directions, and punctuate the verse as they would have the lines spoken. Both tend to bring the texts in conformity with the chronicles when they detect 'errors' in their copy. All recent editions reject the name 'Falstaff', as he is consistently called in the Folio, in favour of the 'correct' Fastolfe, which Shakespeare 'would have read in Holinshed'.[66] Since no one knows who renamed the historical character, nor when or why, one could equally argue that the name of this cowardly knight naturally came to mind when Sir John Oldcastle had to be rechristened. Arden 3 turns the 'base Walloon' of Act I into a 'villain', because the Walloons at that time fought on the side of England. Historically the editor is right, but he does not stop to consider that it was the reverse when the play was created, and that the 'base Walloon' would have gone down very well with an Elizabethan audience.

As to which chronicle Shakespeare 'would have read', there is no agreement either. Tillyard's *Shakespeare's History Plays* stressed the influence of Hall, as Charles Kingsford and W. Gordon Zeeveld had done before him.[67] After Tillyard, 'received opinion for a long time was that Hall was the main source', says Michael Hattaway, who turns the scale in favour of Holinshed, on the grounds that the scholars who argue for Hall do so 'from their own political inclinations'. Though he quotes Brockbank's measured conclusion—'"that Shakespeare used more than one chronicle is demonstrable, but to which he referred and at what points in the preparation of the plays, are questions which can only be imperfectly decided from the evidence"'—he gives priority to Holinshed, thus following his own political inclinations to read Shakespeare's plays as 'a much more modern, secularist, and sceptical kind of history' than those prejudiced scholars would have us believe.[68]

Before we turn to the evidence, I must state my own inevitably prejudiced views. I began with no opinion on any of the litigious points above, discovered as I went how far they could affect reading, and strove to stick to hard facts, hard copy in this case, i.e. the printed texts of plays and sources.[69] After reading the two chronicles through, I came out fairly assured that they had no regular pattern to speak of, but an equal spatter of providential judgements; that if Shakespeare could create sense out of the chroniclers' profusion of anecdotes, he was no less able to weave his fellow playwrights' contributions into a meaningful design, and gradually learn to take no one else's aesthetic judgement, like today's most eminent producers who learnt to grow from democratic consensus to solitary despotism, as the only way to impose their artistic designs on shapeless materials. The plays may or may not have been designed originally as a cycle, but they grow to something of great constancy

---

[66] Hattaway, n. to I. i. 131. See G. W. Williams, 'Fastolf or Falstaff', *ELR* 5 (1975), 308–12.

[67] Kingsford, *English Historical Literature in the Fifteenth Century* (Oxford, 1913), 264–5, 424. Zeeveld, 'The Influence of Hall on Shakespeare's English Historical Plays', *Journal of English Literary History*, 3 (1936), 317–53.

[68] Hattaway, *1H6*, 56, quoting from Brockbank's unpublished Ph.D. dissertation (Cambridge, 1953). His own system of references gives the impression that Holinshed is the source of Hall instead of the reverse.

[69] D. Goy-Blanquet, 'De Hall à Shakespeare: Quelques glissements idéologiques opérés par la drama-tisation', in M.-T. Jones-Davies (ed.), *Théâtre et idéologies: Marlowe, Shakespeare* (Paris, 1982).

when they are shown in sequence, as in Michael Boyd's highly applauded RSC production. Granted that Shakespeare did have some share in them, as everyone agrees
even if the attributions differ, what matters most is not whether he composed the
tetralogy chronologically, or incorporated odd pieces in a collage, whether it is the
expression of one continuous dramatic impulse, or an original patchwork playing
up the variety of textures: these are but two different artistic ways towards an
accomplished work of creation. Even if the pieces are uneven, at some stage in the
patching-up process, an artist of no mean talent created this collage.

National Unity and Military Honour

1. THE MATTER OF 1 HENRY VI

If the three parts of *Henry VI* and *Richard III* are dramatically autonomous, they form a sequence through the continuity of historical facts and characters, the development of themes and images, the dramatic links tying present to past and future events.[1] Chronology is often disregarded in these carefully contrived transitions—the royal wedding, Talbot's death and the loss of France, the five-year truce between York and Lancaster, or Richard III's greedy haste which swallows up most of his brother's reign. Of course the inconsistencies of the historical material will be explained differently according to the textual theory adopted: if an old Talbot play was revised to fit into a sequence dealing with the rivalry between York and Lancaster, the death of his hero reduced the author to searching the chronicle for matter with which to pad his original plot and tie it with the tragedy of Duke Humphrey. Conversely, if a cycle was in project from the start, the carving of the material must be the result of a division of themes between Part 1 and its sequel, the loss of France being the first stage in the long tragedy of England.

The Arden 3 editor defines *1 Henry VI* as 'a "prequel", a dramatic piece that returns for ironic and challenging effect to the narrative roots of an already familiar story'. In contrast with the two other plays, 'here moments of decision are opened up to the spectator with a sense of the farcically unpredictable, of the self-aggrandizing littleness of individuals manufacturing for themselves and for their nations a "fame", a heroic identity'.[2] Talbot appears 'divided and indecisive' before Orleans, 'an index of his bathetic collapse of control'. Yet our modern sense of derision cannot easily be reconciled with Nashe's tale of his contemporaries' vibrant reception. The evidence of the sources also contradicts Burns, for the play uses Hall's moving story of the hero's last stand instead of Holinshed's shorter and drier account. Concerning the order, the strongest argument for putting *1 Henry VI* last, that there is no trace nor memory of Talbot in Parts 2 and 3, actually cuts both ways. How is it that the war with France is absent from those plays if they were written first? The answer in both cases may be the same Aristotelian one: the 'missing' element would have upset the designed *sustasis*. The French war in Part 2 is

---

[1] Unless otherwise stated, quotations are from Arden 3 for *1, 2*, and *3 Henry VI*, and New Cambridge for *Richard III*; references to Qs and F follow their divisions in acts and scenes.

[2] Burns 4–5.

clearly relegated to the past, while Part 1 oversteps its historical boundaries to close this account.

Even if 'relative maturity of character, style and design' are held to be weak arguments, it is hard to believe that Part 1 was written after two far more sophisticated plays.[3] Had a maturer Shakespeare taken any hand in the writing, at any time, would he have left raw this rather crude piece instead of giving it 'perspectivism'[4] with a few extra touches, as he does elsewhere? Again, the answer depends on his degree of involvement in the whole scheme. My own belief, and working assumption, is that whatever part he had in it must have been done at an early stage in the writing of the trilogy, and contributed to the maturing of technique and historical consciousness displayed in 2 *Henry VI*. Not only is it more coarsely put together, it also builds on a very simplistic moral and political rule. This may be why it is so effective on stage, where the subtlety of Part 2 is often less successful. *Henry VI Part 1* shows an artistic will in the masterly selection of material from the chronicle, but also an unquestioning acceptance of its conventional creeds. History appears at first a fund of spectacular plots, then becomes a matter for meditation, as its inner works are exposed to the audience.

Genealogy

The induction to *Henry VI* is the meeting of two independent sets of circumstances, some fortuitous and others more deeply rooted in the past; the ambitions released by the premature death of Henry V around his infant son are heightened by their dubious dynastic title. The claims of the rival branches are explained twice during the trilogy, when Richard Plantagenet is informed of his rights by his dying uncle, the last of the Mortimers, and again when, having been restored to his inheritance, he explains them to his supporters.[5] Edward III had seven sons. The eldest, Edward, the Black Prince, was the father of Richard II. The next, William of Hatfield, had no heirs. The third, Lionel, Duke of Clarence, had a daughter, Philippa, who married Edmund Mortimer. The fourth, John of Gaunt, Duke of Lancaster, was the father of Henry Bolingbroke. The fifth, Edmund, Duke of York, was grandfather to Richard, Earl of Cambridge, who was beheaded for revolting against Henry V with his wife's relations, the Mortimers. There were two more sons, Thomas of Woodstock, ancestor of the Buckingham branch, and William of Windsor, who died issueless. In the play, Richard Plantagenet learns that he is heir to Edward's third and fifth sons by his mother and father, while Henry VI holds the throne from the fourth son of their common ancestor. The weakness of the King's title is made worse by the weakness of his nature: a kind and charitable man ill suited to his task. While the French rally around Joan of Arc, the quarrels dividing his nobility will

---

[3] Knowles 113.

[4] A notion defined by Hattaway 2 as 'a dramatic cross-examination from differing points of view' of the issues raised, and reformulated by Pugliatti, *Shakespeare the Historian* (New York, 1996), 8, as active criticism.

[5] *1H6*, II. v. 63–92, and *2H6*, II. ii. 10–52.

cause the defeat of the valorous Talbot. Henry's marriage to Margaret of Anjou costs him two more provinces and introduces an ambiguous foreigner at court. The loss of France which concludes Part 1 is only the beginning of disaster.

Most of this material comes from the sixteenth-century chroniclers Hall and Holinshed, neither of whom lays consistent stress on dynastic rewards or punishment. Rather than the workings of God's will, Hall aims to understand the main factors of unrest, and the best foundations of political stability. This view of history leads him to endorse a succession of antagonistic theses. He is constant only in his horror of rebellion, save in the case of Richard III, when it becomes an act of public duty, ratified by the success of the conqueror. With Raphael Holinshed, the difficulties of assessment have been much increased by the interference of his editors. The first version of the *Chronicles of England, Scotland and Ireland,* a collective work directed by him, is probably closest to his original plan. The posthumous edition of 1587, which is established as the one Shakespeare used, is seasoned with the comments of his publishers John Hooker and Abraham Fleming who censored or rewrote a number of passages.[6] Holinshed draws on a large variety of sources, whose incompatible theories often land him in patent contradictions, though he manages better than most of the earlier chroniclers to unify his materials, and build up the events of the century into a logical sequence.

Holinshed sometimes copies, sometimes paraphrases Hall's narrative, with corrections, cuts, marginal notes, and moral or philosophical comments. After a close analysis of *1 Henry VI,* Brockbank concludes that 'of the twenty-seven scenes into which modern editions divide, thirteen could derive from either, two are quite independent of both, and five offer evidence too trifling to permit a decision'. When the same material appears in both chronicles, my own task is not so much to decide which of the two served the purpose, but what purpose it served. Shakespeare clearly does not adhere to Hall's reading of history, any more than he adheres to Holinshed's, which shows a similar mixture of providential and practical views. Apart from these two, other chroniclers like Robert Fabyan or John Foxe occasionally provide details that will be dealt with in the relevant scenes.

A mention must be made here of the popular Elizabethan best-seller *A Mirror for Magistrates.* Initially designed as a sequel to Boccaccio's *De Casibus Virorum Illustrium,* which had enjoyed great success in Lydgate's translation, *The Fall of Princes,* it made original use of Boccaccio's formula by drawing a chain of 'Tragedies' from episodes of national history, borrowed from Hall's chronicle. Six editions augmented with new stories followed the original nineteen Tragedies that were published in 1559. The seventh, in 1587, went back to the Conquest of Julius Caesar and included thirty-four Tragedies on the period treated by Hall. The heroes of the *Mirror* return as the main protagonists of Shakespeare's drama, and no doubt contributed to the shaping of the first histories, though probably less than Lily

---

[6] See Henry A. Kelly, *Divine Providence in the England of Shakespeare's Histories* (Cambridge, Mass., 1970), 138–60, for a comparison of the two editions, and Vernon F. Snow, 'The Printing History of Holinshed's *Chronicles*: An Introduction to the Reprint Edition', in *Holinshed's Chronicles* (New York, 1976).

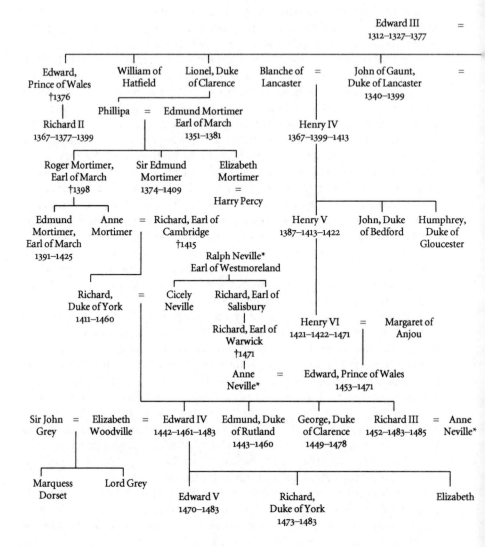

Edward III
1312–1327–1377   =

Edward,   William of   Lionel, Duke   Blanche of   =   John of Gaunt,   =
Prince of Wales   Hatfield   of Clarence   Lancaster   Duke of Lancaster
†1376   1340–1399

Phillipa   =   Edmund Mortimer

Richard II   Earl of March   Henry IV
1367–1377–1399   1351–1381   1367–1399–1413

Roger Mortimer,   Sir Edmund   Elizabeth
Earl of March   Mortimer   Mortimer
†1398   1374–1409   =
                              Harry Percy

Edmund   Anne   =   Richard, Earl of   Henry V   John, Duke   Humphrey,
Mortimer,   Mortimer   Cambridge   1387–1413–1422   of Bedford   Duke of
Earl of March   †1415   Gloucester
1391–1425
                    Ralph Neville*
                    Earl of Westmoreland

Richard,   =   Cicely   Richard, Earl of
Duke of York   Neville   Salisbury
1411–1460
                    Richard, Earl of   Henry VI   =   Margaret of
                    Warwick   1421–1422–1471   Anjou
                    †1471
                    Anne   =   Edward, Prince of Wales
                    Neville*   1453–1471

Sir John   =   Elizabeth   =   Edward IV   Edmund, Duke   George, Duke   Richard III   =   Anne
Grey   Woodville   1442–1461–1483   of Rutland   of Clarence   1452–1483–1485   Neville*
                                        1443–1460   1449–1478

Marquess   Lord Grey
Dorset   Edward V   Richard,   Elizabeth
                    1470–1483   Duke of York
                              1473–1483

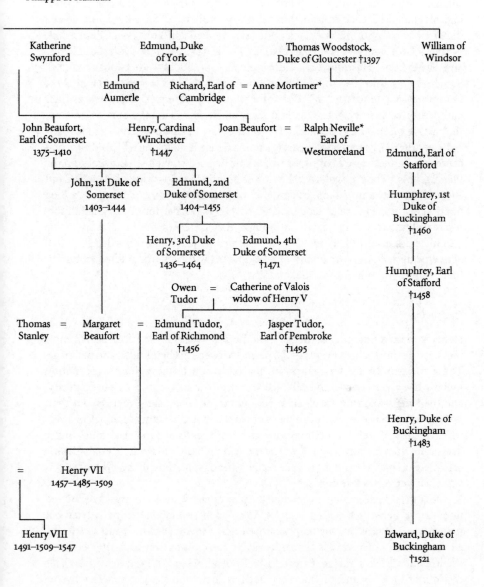

Philippa de Hainault

Katherine Swynford

Edmund, Duke of York

Thomas Woodstock, Duke of Gloucester †1397

William of Windsor

Edmund Aumerle

Richard, Earl of Cambridge = Anne Mortimer*

John Beaufort, Earl of Somerset 1375–1410

Henry, Cardinal Winchester †1447

Joan Beaufort = Ralph Neville* Earl of Westmoreland

Edmund, Earl of Stafford

John, 1st Duke of Somerset 1403–1444

Edmund, 2nd Duke of Somerset 1404–1455

Humphrey, 1st Duke of Buckingham †1460

Henry, 3rd Duke of Somerset 1436–1464

Edmund, 4th Duke of Somerset †1471

Humphrey, Earl of Stafford †1458

Owen Tudor = Catherine of Valois widow of Henry V

Thomas Stanley = Margaret Beaufort = Edmund Tudor, Earl of Richmond †1456

Jasper Tudor, Earl of Pembroke †1495

Henry, Duke of Buckingham †1483

= Henry VII 1457–1485–1509

Henry VIII 1491–1509–1547

Edward, Duke of Buckingham †1521

Campbell argued.[7] Her presentation, which follows the order of publication, is slightly misleading, since it does not reflect the authors' will to observe a chronological sequence in each edition: thus Salisbury, the hero of 'Tragedie 9', is followed in her edition by Suffolk (11), Jack Cade (12), the Duke of York (13), Clifford (14), Warwick (16), Henry VI (17), Clarence (18), Edward IV (19), Woodville, Lord Rivers and Scales (20), Hastings (21), Buckingham (22), Richard of Gloucester (24), Somerset (25), and last, among the additions of 1578, the Duchess (28) and Duke Humphrey of Gloucester (29). The authors quote a variety of chroniclers as their authorities, yet history, at least as we understand it now, is not their prime concern: the past is explored for adequate lessons on the ways to master fortune, and suitably reduced, altered, or recast to illustrate a point. There is no telling which edition first came into Shakespeare's hands, or which one he used when he began work on the Plantagenets.[8] The 1587 volume, the closest in time to the writing of *Henry VI* and *Richard III*, draws up a table of contents with dated events, and is in fact a long poetical history of the relevant period. As such, it may have done more than supply discrete items to the plays, by outlining a raw sketch in the huge mass of the chronicles. It seems likely that before he ever opened Hall or North's Plutarch, Shakespeare read the *Mirror* and other popular favourites which directed him to their sources for more substantial matter.

Chronology

Henry V died in August 1422 leaving a son born in November 1421. *Henry VI Part 1* picks up the most salient events of the period between his heir's birth and marriage. The victories and defeats in France, the quarrels at court, young Henry's coronation in Paris, the desertion of Burgundy, Talbot's death, Joan's capture, the peace treaty, and the King's wedding are all close enough to the chroniclers' reports, but their order of appearance owes little to the original sequence. Whether 'prequel' or overture, *1 Henry VI* rehashes chronology and reshapes Hall's material much more drastically than the next two plays. The movement back and forth through historical time and space is enough to make readers' heads spin, though the effect of all this activity is perfectly clear on stage.

The court is in deep mourning when the play opens. The ceremony is interrupted by a quarrel between the King's uncles, followed by several reports of bad news. A first messenger raps out the names of the French towns they have just lost to the enemy, a series of reversals that historically took place over a quarter-century: Rheims and Orleans in 1429, Paris in 1436, Rouen in 1449. And yet, we witness later the loss of Orleans and of Rouen, as well as their unhistorical recovery by the English. The Parisians' uprising and the loss of Paris are mentioned at Act V. The

---

[7] *Shakespeare's 'Histories': Mirrors of Elizabethan Policy* (London, 1947). The original spelling of the 1559 edition—*Myrroure*—often varying in the next ones, I adopt her neutral *Mirror*.

[8] Bullough only refers to the 1559 edition for *Henry VI*, and 1563 for *Richard III*. See Wolfgang Iser's analysis of the *Mirror* in *Staging Politics: The Lasting Impact of Shakespeare's Histories* (New York, 1993), 39–43.

chronology is so wild that 'Poictiers', the last name on the messenger's list, might stand for either Poitiers or Patay, which have the same spelling in the Folio.[9] The English did take a beating at Patay, near Orleans, in 1429, whereas the battle of Poitiers had been fought and won a century earlier by Edward III. It was in Poitiers, however, that Charles VII was proclaimed King of France in 1422, when his father died.

A second messenger brings news of the Dolphin's coronation in Rheims.[10] When the proclamation was made in Poitiers, Rheims still belonged to the English, and Charles was crowned there only in 1429, once the road to Rheims had been reopened, as fame has it, by the Pucelle's endeavours, but the dramatic chronology does not allow her any part in this sacred act, her most renowned achievement, which Hall attributes to the tales of her shameless admirers. A third messenger announces the defeat and capture of Talbot, ascribing it to Fastolfe's desertion. These events occurred at the battle of Patay, but the date given by the messenger, 10 August, appears neither in Hall nor Holinshed, and is incorrect. Patay was fought on 18 June 1429. In a later battle, on 10 August 1432, the Duke of Bedford was beaten by French troops before Lagny, which he had been besieging for a long time.

The conflict between Gloucester and Winchester is derived from an episode dated September 1425 by Fabyan. Hall and Holinshed also report the incident, but it is Fabyan who mentions that the Londoners fought with stones and that the Mayor had to interfere.[11] This is but the beginning of a fight to the death that will come to conclusion in *2 Henry VI*. Here comes in another source: John Foxe's popular 'Book of Martyrs', in its determined assault against all popish priests, makes Winchester the chief destroyer of Duke Humphrey, whereas in Hall he is only an accomplice in the plot.[12] The play's audience surely know that Winchester is a cardinal, after many mentions of his state, hat, and red dress, or Gloucester's insult, 'scarlet hypocrite!' Yet at Act V, his 'cardinal's degree' surprises Exeter.[13] In fact, he was made a cardinal in 1427, after the fight with Gloucester's men, but long before the marriage negotiations of 1443. Fabyan might be the source of this discrepancy, for he reports successively Gloucester's bill of complaint and Winchester's elevation to cardinalship.

The noblemen's quarrel is sandwiched between two scenes near Orleans where the Dolphin is encamped, unable to raise the siege, and forced to retire by Salisbury, when Joan of Arc makes her entrance. The historical siege began in September 1428;

---

[9] *1H6*, I. i. 61; IV. i. 19. Since Holinshed draws abundantly on Hall, it seems logical to refer primarily to Hall when both give the same material. References to Holinshed, when he does not significantly differ from Hall, will henceforth be given after Hall's in italics, thus: on Patay, see Hall 149–50 *(165)*.

[10] He is called 'Dolphin', never Dauphin, by Hall and Holinshed until his coronation. Both narratives then refer to him as 'Charles the French king', 157 *(158)*. In the Folio he remains the Dolphin throughout the three parts of *Henry VI*, but the Arden 3 editors did not see fit to harmonize their decisions on this point: he is 'Dolphin' in Part 1, and 'Dauphin' again in Part 2.

[11] I. iii; III. i. 80, 89. Fabyan 596. Hall 130 *(146)*.

[12] In the second edition (1570) of his *Actes and Monuments of these latter and perilous dayes, touching matters of the Church*, Foxe 709–11 gives a retroactive account of their quarrel when narrating Gloucester's fall.

[13] I. iii. 56, SD 57; v. i. 28–33.

Salisbury was dead by the time Joan arrived at Chinon the following March. Hall dates the episode of the master-gunner which cost him and Gargrave their lives two months after the beginning of the siege, that is around October 1428. Talbot was captured in July 1429, and released in exchange for Xaintrailles 'without delay' after the battle of Patay according to Hall and Holinshed, actually two years later, in 1431.[14] Joan raises the siege at I. iv, as she did in May 1429. The honours promised to her for her victory may be echoes of her official rehabilitation in 1456, which Holinshed records after the account of her trial and execution in 1431.[15] Talbot's heroic recovery of Orleans at II. ii has no historical basis, but borrows details from the siege of Le Mans in 1428. His ensuing visit to the Countess of Auvergne is generally accepted as Shakespeare's invention. So is the quarrel in Temple Garden, even if the idea of opposing red and white roses was not. It is repeatedly used by the Burgundian chronicler Molinet, but applied to the later rivalry between the Houses of York and Tudor, when he reports Perkin Warbeck's claim: 'Ainsy, appert clèrement que l'englentier, par qui j'entengz Engleterre, estoit chargiét en ce temps de doubles roses, aucunes vermeilles que portoit le roy, aultres blances que portoit Richart d'Yorcq, et comment les espines d'icelles s'entrepoindoyent.'[16]

The interview between young Richard Plantagenet and his uncle in the next scene raises the much discussed question of the Mortimers. The dying man who transmits his rights to Richard is a conflation of two, perhaps three, different historical characters: Edmund Mortimer, fifth Earl of March, who had been declared heir presumptive to the crown in 1398 at the death of his father the fourth Earl, rebelled against Henry V, but nevertheless died a free man in 1425; his cousin Sir John, who was sent to jail in the Tower for having supported his claim, and executed in 1424; and his uncle Sir Edmund Mortimer, who was taken prisoner by Owen Glendower, married Glendower's daughter, and died in 1409. The stage character's 'mother' Philippa was the mother of Sir Edmund, his 'sister' Anne was the sister of Earl Edmund and the mother of Richard Plantagenet, whom he calls 'nephew'. Whether deliberate or not, the confusion follows Hall's, unless 'mother' here simply means 'female forebear', as Michael Hattaway argues, in which case the character is a fusion of Earl Edmund and his cousin John, who struck an alliance to claim the throne.[17] But more on the Mortimers later.

[14] Hall 174 (164).
[15] After defending the justice of the verdict, Holinshed 170–1 notes that it was reversed twenty-six years later.
[16] *Chroniques de Jean Molinet*, ed. Georges Doutrepont and Omer Jodogne (Brussels, 1935), ii. 420: 'Thus it is clear that the Eglantine, by which I mean England, carried at the time double roses, the ones vermeil, borne by the king, the others white, borne by Richard of York [Perkin Warbeck], whose thorns interlaced and wounded each other.' See Charles Ross, *The Wars of the Roses: A Concise History* (1986), 11–15, and Sydney Anglo, *Spectacle Pageantry*, 36–8, on the roses and the Lancastrian connection in Tudor propaganda. Molinet's chronicle, which runs from 1474 to 1506, and was finished by 1514, never discusses the earlier wars, nor mentions the name Lancaster, but when Warbeck is executed (ii. 467), he concludes: 'Ainsy fut la blance rose, qui tant avoit fait de travail tant à la rose rouge comme au bouton vermeil, pendue au vent et seschie au soleil.'
[17] Hattaway, II. v. n. 74. Warwick does use 'grandfather' in this way at II. iv. 83—in a short speech stressing the nobility of Richard's descent, though, not in a detailed pedigree as in II. v. Holinshed 226 gives the genealogy correctly.

Gloucester's indictment of Winchester in Parliament took place in 1426. The quarrel staged at III. i, where Winchester is again a bishop as he actually was at the time, uses both this episode, transferring the Parliament from Leicester to London, and another list of accusations addressed in 1441 to the King by Gloucester. We saw that the stone fight between their servingmen belongs to the first period, as do their forced truce and Richard's reinstatement in his dukedom, which occurred during a feast held on Pentecost day to celebrate the end of the division among the nobles.[18] The perils of their discord are heightened by the situation abroad, a point made by Bedford who, in this Parliament, 'openly rebuked the Lordes in generall, because that they in the tyme of warre, through their priuie malice and inwarde grudge, had almoste moued the people to warre and commocion'.[19] After the fake reconciliation at court, the scene returns to France, where Rouen is treacherously won by the French, and recovered the same day. Joan enters the town disguised, but she cannot resist Talbot's assault, supported by the undaunted spirit of Bedford. Invoking Uther Pendragon as his model, Bedford is carried sick to the battlefield and dies once victory is secured.[20] The historical Bedford died in 1435, four years after Joan of Arc but long before Rouen was lost, and never recovered, in 1449. It was Le Mans which Talbot reconquered in 1428, after its inhabitants had opened their gates to the French and 'shewed a burnyng Cresset out of the steple' as a warning signal. Joan's stratagem was actually used in 1441, long after her demise, when Cornill castle was entered by 'four soldiers dressed as husbandmen, carrying sacks, and speaking French', says Fabyan—English soldiers, in that case, whose ruse is saluted by Holinshed as 'An excellent finesse in warre'.[21]

To this complex of events must be added Fastolfe's doubled flight, which has no basis in the chronicles, and creates a new discrepancy. It is hard to understand Talbot's fury in the following act, where he upbraids Fastolfe for his first defection, as if he had not met him again since Patay, unless one considers that this second betrayal, much less decisive since Talbot won the day, reawakens his indignation at the first, which caused his defeat. More significantly, Fastolfe's desertion is part of a larger design, a prelude to Burgundy's, whom Joan must entice 'To leave the Talbot and to follow us'. Burgundy's sudden reversal again makes havoc of the chronology. It was a long-drawn-out process, concluded in 1435, years after Joan's death. The argument she uses in the play, that the English freed the Duke of Orleans to spite him, disagrees with the chroniclers' report that Burgundy ransomed Orleans himself in 1440 to placate his former enemy.[22]

Burgundy's breaking-off letter to the King of England adds its jarring note to the coronation scene, celebrated in Paris as it was indeed in 1431. The setting conflicts

[18] Hall 130–8 (146–54).
[19] Hall 130 (146).
[20] 1H6, III. ii. 93, 108–9. Hall 178 (184). Bullough 29, 78–80, gives Monmouth's *Historia Regum Britanniae* as a direct source for this passage. The story of Pendragon is also reported in Holinshed's *History of Scotland*, but ascribed to Uther's brother.
[21] Fabyan 615. Holinshed 198. Hall 197 mentions six soldiers and does not say if they spoke French. On Le Mans, Hall 142 (159).
[22] III. iii. 69–73. Hall 194 (195–6).

with the news heard at the funeral of Henry V [1422] that the town was lost, but agrees with the later news of the Parisians' revolt [1436], given at v. ii. Neither Talbot, still a prisoner, Exeter, dead in 1426, nor Gloucester, then in England, attended the ceremony. But Bedford did; he still had some four years to live, and figures in the chroniclers' lists of those present. His early disappearance from the stage makes room for a new Regent in France.[23] In fact York had to wait until 1435 for this dignity, and Talbot until 1443 for the earldom of Shrewsbury. The Talbots did die near Bordeaux, but this only happened in 1453, a few months before the end of the Hundred Years War.

This to-and-fro movement through the chronicles continues in the final act, where the Pope and the Emperor are said to work at promoting peace between France and England. Winchester, 'newly' made a cardinal, will represent England at the peace conference. We see him at v. i paying the Pope's legate for his cardinal's hat, and taking part in the negotiations at v. iv, where Suffolk arranges a marriage for the King to Reignier of Anjou's daughter, and the ambassadors sign a truce. The conference called by the Emperor Sigismund and Pope Eugenius IV met at Arras in 1435, with no result, and the following year, Paris welcomed the French King's army. It was at Tours in 1444 that the parties agreed on an eighteen-month truce, renewable. The marriage with Margaret was part of the arrangement. Joan of Arc had been executed under the regency of Bedford, not York, before Henry VI's coronation in Paris, but Shakespeare keeps her alive until Margaret makes her entrance. Was Suffolk corrupted with bribes, Hall wonders, when he so far exceeded his commission to arrange this unprofitable alliance, which Holinshed labels in the margin 'An ominous mariage'? The play ends on an equally sombre note: Suffolk returns home with a new Helen to bring war and destruction to his land.[24]

Thirty years of anecdotes, unrelated facts, side remarks scattered through heavy volumes have thus been jammed into the racy two-hour traffic of a well-run stage. This violation of all speed limits could be added to Northrop Frye's casualty list of 'fair copies, foul papers and drunken compositors' to explain away minor incoherences. Other anomalies—events reported before they are shown on stage, or others duplicated—are still waiting to be satisfactorily explained away.[25] Theories of revision or collaborative authorship which were the norm in the early twentieth century are again back in fashion, as today's editors still invoke them to account for various 'unconformities' in the play. The order of certain scenes may well have been altered in either process, whether by accident or to answer practical needs. One could also find dramatic justifications for these anomalies: a cumulative effect of disasters, the oscillations of victory, and a concentration of events on haunting names.

It appears from Hall's piecemeal account that a number of French towns constantly change hands in the course of the Hundred Years War: they turn to the King

---

[23] Hall 160, 178 (*173, 185*).

[24] Hall 204 (*205*). Holinshed 208. *1H6*, v. v. 103–6.

[25] They formed the basis of Kristian Smidt's argument in favour of revision, *Unconformities in Shakespeare's History Plays* (London, 1982).

of England to escape an oppressive domination, but fall back into the hands of the French, the English lacking men to defend them, until they are reconquered, then lost again, and so on. Or the reverse: the inhabitants of Le Mans complain that they are vassals under the English yoke and revert to the French party. The town of Saint-Valéry suffers 'many calamities and euill chaunces, beyng twoo tymes besieged by the Frenchemen, and thryse recouered by thenglishe nacion', but they are not the only ones to be thus affected.[26] On the death of the Earl of Arundell at the siege of Gerborie, Hall notes that

suche is the chaunce of warre, thus Lady Fortune daily turneth her whiele, and mightie Mars, often varieth his countenaunce, so that one tyme the Englishemen gat by assaut and yieldyng, diuerse strong tounes, Castles, and piles. At another season, the Frenche people, somtyme by bargain, somtyme by assaut, obteined thesaid citees and fortificacions again, or other in their stede.[27]

Hall wisely omits a number of these daily attempts, for 'he, which should write the negligent losses, and the pollitique gaines, of euery citee, fortresse, and turrett, whiche were gotten and loste in these daies, should fatigate and wery the reader'.[28] More wisely still, Holinshed omits Hall's verbose plea for brevity, though he no less dutifully reports the loss of many a small castle. Both leave the reader with a dreary sense of wasted labours. On stage, the long-drawn-out war and the obscure place names boil down to a few fighting episodes, mostly concentrated around the three towns emerging from the reduction, Orleans, Rouen, Bordeaux. These names attached alternately to victories and defeats make sensible the movement which structures the play. By having them lay siege repeatedly to the same strongholds, Shakespeare shows the English heroes painfully adding up victories that never win them the war.

2. BORROWING MATERIAL

The chronicle offers not only facts but characters, themes, and writing modes. Hall's phrases often turn up in the dialogue, though his narrative is never 'simply' adapted to the stage: the historical material is thoroughly reshaped by its insertion into a new form.

Conversion

The news from France at the opening of 1 *Henry VI* is culled from many points, but the messenger's report on Patay follows the chronicles, to the point of incoherence: Talbot, he tells us, was attacked as he was retiring from the siege of Orleans, which is historically true but conflicts with the next scenes where the siege is represented.

---

[26] Hall 170 (not in Holinshed 178).
[27] Hall 173. Holinshed 180 has the same comment, amputated of Lady Fortune and mighty Mars.
[28] Hall 173 (*180*).

However, Talbot will be freed in time to share in the fight. The sources also relate the charge of the French cavalry, the confusion among the English archers, their attempt to protect themselves behind pitched stakes, the length of the fight, the valiance of all except Fastolfe, the base wounding of Talbot in the back and his capture, and the loss of 1,200 men. As to the size of the British troops, they numbered 5,000 men according to Hall, 6,000 in Shakespeare as in Holinshed, who pinpoints Hall's inaccuracy with a marginal note, 'Fiue thousand saith *Hall.*'[29]

All the details of the scene where Salisbury loses his life—action, setting, characters, motives, movements—appear in both narratives:

the sonne of the Master gonner, perceived men lokyng out at the wyndowe, toke his matche, as his father had taught hym, whiche was gone doune to dinner, and fired the gonne, which brake & shevered ye yron barres of the grate, wherof one strake therle so strōgly on the hed, that it stroke away one of his iyes and the side of his cheke. (145)

In *The Mirror for Magistrates*, the ghost of Salisbury makes no mention of the master-gunner but records that he was hit 'as I busily talked with my frend', the only detail that contributed to the scene, where he is killed while conversing with Talbot. The stage version heightens the suspense by having the audience warned of the trap laid for the characters, and adds Talbot's pathetic cry to the list of Salisbury's wounds: 'One eye thou hast to look to heaven for grace.'[30]

The end of Mortimer collects elements from various places in Hall and Holinshed. When reporting his death under Henry VI's reign, both write that his sole heir is Richard Plantagenet, son of the Earl of Cambridge who was beheaded at Southampton. Hall, but not Holinshed, adds that Richard will claim the crown thirty years later in open Parliament. He has already exposed the Mortimer titles at the beginning of his work, 'An Introduccion into the History of Kyng Henry the Fourthe', and will do so again via York's speech to Parliament in 1460. Holinshed follows Hall's wording closely but corrects his genealogy of the Mortimers, and concludes independently that, owing to his descent from Edward III's third son, to this Richard the royal title 'perteineth and belongeth afore anie issue of the said Iohn of Gant, the fourth sonne of the same king Edward'.[31] The point will be more fully developed in *2 Henry VI*, where Edward III's descent is again unrolled by Richard of York. Here Shakespeare anticipates, as Hall does at the time of Mortimer's death, to introduce an element that has no immediate dramatic impact: the Yorkist claim prepares the future, 'as herafter shal more manifestly appere'.

The last battle, which Talbot's death makes final, takes place before the truce negotiations of Act V. Historically the defeat of Castillon did bring the Hundred Years' War to a close, but only some twenty years after Joan's death. The losing fight of Talbot, his vain attempts to spare his son, and their heroic end together are all very close to Hall's two-page account, which Holinshed cuts down to two terse

---

[29] Hall 149. Holinshed 165. *1H6*, I. i. 112; IV. i. 20.

[30] Hall 145 *(161–2)*. I. iv. 82. In the *Mirror*, ix. 270, the shot is said to come 'fro the towne'.

[31] Hall 2, 128, 245–8. Holinshed 262–3, 266, is more outspoken than Hall in his condemnation of the Lancasters' usurpation.

paragraphs. Shakespeare gives an added touch of nobility to his hero by having him rescue his heir from Dunois's sword, and suppresses his illegitimate son, Henry Talbot, whose death on the same day is recorded in the chronicle.[32]

The material collected often serves in scenes other than the original episodes. The events in Le Mans, which surrendered to the French and was recaptured by Talbot, lend some striking details to the unhistorical recoveries of both Orleans and Rouen: a burning torch to show the way into Rouen, the cry of 'sainct George, Talbot', which sends the French leaping in their shirts over the walls of Orleans, 'leuyng behynde theim all their apparell, horsses, armure and riches'.[33] The ensuing quarrel between the French leaders takes its inspiration from their division after the failed attack against Saint-Jacques-de-Beuvron in 1425, 'the one laiyng to the charge of the other, the losse of their men and the cause of their fliyng'.[34] Hall's comment that 'when the battaill is loste, the faulte is assigned to the beste, and not to the wourste' is followed by the account of 'a greate diuision in the realme of England, which, of a sparcle was like to growe to a greate flame': the enmity between Winchester and Gloucester broke out publicly in the fourth year of the new reign. The play shows it erupting even earlier.

By a similar process, some stage characters are given the benefit of others' actions. For instance, where King Lewis XI protected Bedford's monument from desecration by his noblemen in the chronicle, Charles does the same in the play for Talbot's remains.[35] In Hall, it was Bedford 'in a great anger', not Talbot, who tore off Fastolfe's Garter and George, though Hall adds that he was later restored to the order 'against the mynd of the lorde Talbot'. As for the original Exeter, 'the sadde, wise and wel learned coūsailer' who died within five years of Henry V, he could not have remained so long on stage as to conclude each act with wise maxims and sombre prophecies for England.[36] The title remained vacant until 1444, when Henry VI gave the dukedom of Exeter back to the son of the first Duke, whom Henry IV had had executed in 1400.

The conversion of Burgundy illustrates yet another aspect of Shakespeare's technique. The dramatic dialogue contracts in one brief speech, spoken by a character who had no part in the actual events, a sum of details scattered over some fifty pages of the chronicle, but paradoxically, this abundant material contributes only meagre elements to Joan's vibrant hymn to national feeling. Far from being sudden, the breach between Burgundy and England was the end of a relationship that had slowly deteriorated over the years. The main steps of this process are related at various points in the chronicles:[37]

[32] IV. vi. 16–24. Hall 229. Holinshed 235–6.

[33] III. ii. 25–32; II. i. 38, SD 77. Hall 142–3 (*159–60*).

[34] II. i. 49–71. Hall 129 (not in Holinshed).

[35] IV. iv. 161–2. Hall 178 (*184*).

[36] F. M. Powicke (ed.), *Handbook of British Chronology* (London, 1939), 307–8. Hall 138. In Holinshed 155, Exeter is 'a right sage and discréet councellor'.

[37] Hall 147, 154, 161, 167, 173, 174, 176. Holinshed gives the same information in shorter and plainer style at 163, 168, 173, 176, 181, 183, 184.

- 1428, Bedford rejected the offer of the Orleans people to deliver their city to Philip of Burgundy, seeing no reason why 'the kyng of Englande should beate the bushe and the duke of Burgoyne should haue the birdes', to the great displeasure of the Duke.
- 1430, in an attempt to break Burgundy's league with England, King Charles sent him ambassadors 'not onely requiryng hym, of concord, peace, and amitie, but also promisyng golden mountaines'.
- In 1431, Philip of Burgundy is listed among those present at Henry VI's coronation in Paris.
- But in 1433, when Bedford remarried barely a year after the death of his first wife Anne, sister to Burgundy, the love between them 'began to waxe fainte and colde'. After a last meeting at Saint-Omer which failed to reconcile these two proud lords, 'all loue, betwene theim ceased, all affinitie was forgotten'.
- By 1435, Burgundy was so dissatisfied with the poor benefits of his alliance to England that he decided 'to take part, and ioyne with his awne bloud and nacion', and at the Council of Arras signed a peace treaty with Charles VII.
- After this, he sent a letter to the English King, explaining why he had made his peace with Charles, and advising him to do the same.
- Five years later, by way of retaliation, the King of England's council considered delivering the Duke of Orleans 'to do displeasure to the duke of Burgoyn', but Burgundy sensed the trap and paid his former enemy's ransom himself to conciliate him. Here Holinshed recalls the history of the enmity between Orleans and Burgundy, which lends no extra detail to the scene.[38]
- Having reported the growing discord between Bedford and Burgundy, Hall reflects that 'in all Christendome, no Region was more vnquiete, more vexed, more poore, nor more to be pitied, then the coūtrey of Fraūce', then proceeds to describe the pitiful state of its cities and towns, the wasted cornfields, meadows, and woods. Holinshed does not reproduce this country scene but briefly evokes the sufferings of poor people and soldiers 'for warre seldome beareth anie other fruit'.[39]

In fact, it took seven years of mounting grievances and cooling affection between old friends to bring France and Burgundy back together again, a process dramatized in one short scene through an encounter which actually never took place. The frame of Joan's plea, and some of her arguments, can be found in the various narrative passages listed above. Like Charles's ambassadors in the chronicle, Joan reminds the Duke that he is fighting on the side of his ancestral enemies against his own country. Like the Duke himself when he decided to make his peace with Charles, she points out that he can gain nothing from this unnatural situation: the English are merely using him to make Henry VI sole master of France, at the expense of his own power. Her clinching argument, that they released his personal foe the Duke of Orleans, is also taken from the chronicle where it is a consequence,

[38] Hall 194 *(195–6)*.
[39] *1H6*, III. iii. 44–51. Hall 174. Holinshed 181.

not a cause, of the breach. Only the hostile intent of the release is common to both versions.

This list of elements is still far from complete. For instance, Hall reports much later, in the ninth year of Edward IV's reign, a secret meeting between Clarence and an anonymous 'damosell' who worked to win Clarence back into the family camp and who, like Joan, stressed the unnatural character of his quarrel with his own blood. She too argued that he would win little honour and less benefit by joining forces with the enemies of his house. Besides, if Hall and Holinshed allow Joan of Arc no part in the rallying of Burgundy, the French sources tell another story: according to various Burgundian chroniclers, they met once when she was a prisoner in Compiègne, but the tenor of their interview remains unknown.[40] She actually wrote to the Duke on the very day of Charles's coronation, exhorting him to sign a good, long peace with the French King, 'et s'il vous plaist à guerroier, si alez sur les Sarrasins'—if he wishes to wage war, let it be against the Saracens.[41] Here Shakespeare knows better than the English chroniclers, for the Duke did not attend Henry VI's coronation in Paris, and even abstained from visiting the young King during his sojourn in France, to the great displeasure of the English court.[42] Five days before the ceremony, Philip the Good wrote to Henry telling him he had been forced to sign a truce with France because the English council had not paid the wages due to his troops, and recalled the many occasions when he had asked England in vain for men and money.[43]

Another troubled relationship in the play builds up on a somewhat similar technique. Like the peace negotiations in Act V drawn from two distinct conferences, the conflict between Gloucester and Winchester contracts features from various episodes and various chroniclers, mainly Fabyan and Hall. In 1425, the upset created by their partakers' quarrels was such that Bedford had to return in haste from France to restore order. Gloucester presented a list of accusations to the Parliament of Leicester. Both parties were heard at great length and formally reconciled by arbitrators. Then in 1441, Gloucester's displeasure with the Cardinal's behaviour inspired him again to send a list of his misdeeds to the King, but the only outcome of this letter was to excite resentment against himself, in which Hall reads the origin of his downfall. The two sets of articles make up one scene in Parliament at Act III, but the enmity between the two men is made clear from their first entrance, where their bickering over Henry V's coffin draws on the itemized

[40] Monstrelet claims he was present at the interview but cannot remember what words were exchanged, *La Chronique d'Enguerran de Monstrelet, 1400–1444*, II. LXXXVI, ed. L. Douët d'Arcq (Paris, 1857–62), iv. 388. According to another Burgundian, Jean Jouffroy, the Duke refused to see her. See *Revue historique*, 19 (1882), 65–6.

[41] Jules Quicherat (ed.), *Procès de condamnation et de réhabilitation de Jeanne d'Arc dite la Pucelle* (Paris, 1841–9), v. 126.

[42] He spent twenty months in Paris, from April 1430 to January 1432, without paying a visit to young Henry VI, and was blamed for his absence by the poet Lydgate in 'A songe made of the duke of Burgundy'. See C. A. J. Armstrong, *England, France and Burgundy in the Fifteenth Century* (London, 1983), 368.

[43] See J. Stevenson, *Letters and Papers Illustrative of the Wars of the English in France during the Reign of Henry VI*, Rolls Series (London, 1864), ii. 1, 164–5.

grievances, as does their men's endless fighting. After the staged reconciliation and Exeter's sombre prophecies, their conflict fades into the background unresolved, to be replayed by a new aristocratic rift. The supporters of York and Somerset stand ready to violate the solemnity of Henry's coronation in the next act. Before these two currents of enmity unite, in *2 Henry VI*, to strike at the royal family, Talbot will be the first victim of their division.

Invention

On the other hand, one random word in the chronicles will inspire a whole affair. Suffolk 'the Quenes dearlynge', a much quoted instance, deserves a closer look. Though the chronicler has little more to say on the matter, the very words he uses here and elsewhere are suggestive enough to have inspired Suffolk's illegitimate feelings. The French deputies at the Tours conference, 'perceiuyng the ardent affeccion of the erle, toward the conclusion of mariage', were quick to take advantage of it, and so, we may infer, was Shakespeare. Suffolk's 'affeccion', we understand, was doubly material, for he, 'by the meanes of the Quene, was shortely erected to the estate and degree of a Duke, and ruled the Kyng at his pleasure', just as he plans to do in the play. Cruder still, he achieved this distinction 'by greate fauor of the kynge, and more desire of the Quene'. That she 'entierly loued the Duke', while he was 'the Quenes chefe frende & counseiler', dramatic evidence will show later.[44]

The narrative says no more about the couple's feelings, though it shows well enough that they were ruling in the King's place, while Henry slowly divested himself of his responsibilities. On stage, their meeting is straightaway marked by seduction. The similarities of Suffolk's designs with Richard's have often been commented; as to his words,

> She's beautiful, and therefore to be wooed:
> She is a woman, therefore to be won ...   (v. ii. 99–100)

they may well be a commonplace of the dramatic repertory, as the Arden editor claims, but one that returns definitely improved in Richard's rephrasing:

> Was ever woman in this humour wooed?
> Was ever woman in this humour won?   (*R3*, I. ii. 231–2)

The other illegitimate pair formed by Joan and the Dolphin relies on even flimsier material, although the terms used by the chroniclers are again suggestive. In Hall, Bedford charges the newly crowned King with having usurped his title, 'onely alured and intised by a deuilishe wytche, and a sathanicall enchaunterese'. Holinshed reports that Joan, hoping to save her life, did not hesitate 'to confesse hir selfe a strumpet'—the name York gives her in the play—but does not endorse the insult himself, and confirms that she was a virgin. When he mentions 'hir louers', he

---

[44] *1H6*, v. iv. 107–8. Hall 219, 204, 206, 207, 210, 218, 219. Holinshed 206, 209, 220 keeps only three of these mentions, with less innuendoes.

means the French chroniclers who have turned her into a legendary heroine. Neither he nor Hall ever suggests an affair, even a platonic one, with Charles, whereas in the play Joan takes her place in a line of French charmers, all harmful to England. If Talbot escaped the trap set by the Countess of Auvergne, he cannot destroy Joan, whose eventual defeat will be but temporary: the witch's exit as a captive makes way for Margaret, as if her final curse calling mischief and despair upon England had immediately conjured up another enchantress in her stead. Leslie Fiedler was the first to note that Joan actually claimed as putative father of her unborn child 'Reignier, King of Naples', moments after Margaret's presentation of herself as daughter to 'the King of Naples'.[45] Naturally there is no such link between the two characters in the chronicles, where Margaret appears some fifteen years after Joan's capture. Shakespeare imagines her entrance as Suffolk's prisoner, making it soon obvious who holds the other enthralled, and how much this prize will cost the English King.[46]

In a similar way, two brief sentences concerning the historical Talbot contributed to build up the stage hero. Hall informs us 'that his only name was, and yet is dredful to the Frenche nacion', and again later, in his funeral encomium, that it was so 'spitefull and dreadfull to the common people' that the French women, 'to feare their yong childrē, would crye, the Talbot commeth, the Talbot commeth'.[47] But this is not enough to raise him above other English champions. Hall uses almost identical words about Salisbury, 'by whose wit, strength and pollicie, the Englishe name was muche fearfull and terrible to the French nacion'. In the *Mirror for Magistrates*, whose authors repeatedly quote Hall as their authority, Talbot is not even entitled to a 'Tragedie' of his own.[48] The reasons why he is elected to his pre-eminent position on stage (and with what success, Nashe's comment well records) must be sought elsewhere—Hall's Homeric account of 'thys English Hector', his famed exploits and awe-inspiring name, his death in the last losing battle of the war. Although the Countess of Auvergne uses the term derisively, saying she had expected 'a second Hector', not this 'silly dwarf', his allies see in him a reincarnation of the Trojan hero, an ideal combination of public and private virtues.

In the play, Talbot's name rings several times, evincing at first the derisive comments of the people:

> 'Here', said they, 'is the terror of the French,
> The scarecrow that affrights our children so'.   (1. iv. 41–2)

It sounds again, more awesomely, after Salisbury's death, when he threatens: 'Wretched shall France be only in my name.' Next, in burlesque mode, when a

---

[45] v. iii. 78; v. ii. 73. Fiedler, *The Stranger in Shakespeare* (London, 1973), 48.

[46] A point often treated since Bevington's 'The Domineering Female in *1 Henry VI*', *ShSt* 2 (1966), 51–8, for instance by Gabriele B. Jackson, 'Topical Ideology: Witches, Amazons, and Shakespeare's Joan of Arc', in *Shakespeare and Gender*, 142–67; Leah Marcus, *Puzzling Shakespeare*, 53–91.

[47] Hall 141, 230, 144. Holinshed 158, 160 has only the first comment on Talbot's name, and the one on Salisbury.

[48] Salisbury is their model of valour in Henry VI's reign, *Mirror*, ix, as the stage Talbot records in his address: 'How far'st thou, mirror of all martial men?' 1. iv. 73.

scavenging soldier scares off Charles and his friends simply by crying 'A Talbot! A Talbot!' When the Countess of Auvergne asks if this is the man whose name stills the babes, her irony is short-lived, and Talbot's men enter to embody the legend. Sir William Lucy's posthumous tribute tries to maintain the legend beyond the grave: Talbot's ghost, or his picture, 'were enough to fright the realm of France'. The hero vanquished by 'Triumphant Death, smeared with captivity' escapes her 'insulting tyranny' and flies to immortal glory. The ambivalence of the theme recalls Henry V's funeral, where Hall's banal comment 'that helth was ouercome and had lost the victory' inspires the Petrarchan image of Death's dishonourable victory, glorified by captives bound to her triumphant car. Joan punctures Lucy's inflated praise with a few derisive words and buries the legend: the great warrior is dead flesh and will not be reincarnated.

The metaphors born from a chance expression thus spread from one scene to another. Reporting Talbot's last battle, Hall evokes the 'subtile labirynth, in the which he and hys people were enclosed', initiating a rich network of images in the play.[49] The French General warns Talbot that he is lost, showing him their squadrons pitched 'to wall thee from the liberty of flight', a point Talbot takes up in his monologue, 'How are we parked and bounded in a pale', comparing his troops to 'a little herd of England's timorous deer'. These deer turn war into a hunt and initiate a string of words, 'kennel of French curs', 'desperate stags', 'bloody hounds', 'heads of steel', 'at bay', down to the bravura of the final pun:

Sell every man his life as dear as mine
And they shall find dear deer of us, my friends.　　(iv. ii. 53–4)

A parallel series of associations develops from the phrase 'in a pale', itself a punning echo of the 'pale destruction' promised to Talbot. Coloured blood and livid corpses alternate with images of the quarry and fuse in the last line, 'Prosper our colours', which rings in defiant answer to the sombre fate threatened by the Captain:

These eyes, that see thee now well coloured
Shall see thee withered, bloody, pale and dead.　　(iv. ii. 37–8)

A third series unfolds gradually in the following scenes, also suggested by Hall's 'subtile labirynth'. The English are 'mazed', surrounded by a wall of enemy squadrons which leaves no way out. Young Talbot firmly refuses the escape offered by his father, 'To fight I will, but not to fly the foe', leading them to imagine another form of flight, 'And soul with soul from France to heaven fly', 'Two Talbots, winged, through the lither sky', both senses of the word recalling the flight of Icarus and his father, 'thy desperate sire of Crete', the unnamed author of the 'subtile labirynth'. With the inevitable fall, 'in that sea of blood' of 'My Icarus, my blossom, in his pride'. These old shades return in *3 Henry VI*, when the burial of a son unites commoner and King in a shared tragedy—a point neatly stressed in Michael Boyd's production, where they re-entered to play the parts of anonymous father and son.

Talbot's election to the role of hero was dictated in part by his valour, by the

---

[49] Hall 229 (not in Holinshed).

tragic circumstances of his and his son's death, but above all by the neat coincidence of his rise and fall with the success and reversal of England's fortune abroad. His place at the centre of a mosaic of images reflects his role in the dramatic contruction. The texture of the play is made up of several such networks, a fine web that ties theme to structure and gives a strong artistic coherence to the whole construction. This metaphoric microstructure is at once self-contained and part of a sustained development through the sequence of plays. Long after Talbot's death, the theme of the hunt continues to illustrate war, while Mortimer's review of his own decaying body, both reality and image, communicates his disease to the commonweal as part of his nephew's inheritance. The cancer of discord grows like vegetation in various emblematic gardens, until the bloody harvest of Bosworth clears the ground of its anarchic surfeit of Plantagenets.

3. THE THEME OF UNION

The enemy within

A reading of the chronicles shows how close the playwright kept to his material, and how independent he was in rearranging facts, compressing or expanding details, and most of all infusing historical episodes with meanings his sources had never imagined. For instance, York's appointment as Regent of France in 1435 stirred the jealousy of Somerset, who took every opportunity to defeat his efforts, 'till Paris and the floure of Fraunce, were gotten by the Frenche kyng', Hall tells us, adding that their enmity would see the destruction of these two princes and their offspring.[50] In the play their rivalry is the direct cause of Talbot's death. Sir William Lucy repeats Hall's theme,

> Thus, while the vulture of sedition
> Feeds in the bosom of such great commanders,
> Sleeping neglection doth betray to loss
> The conquest of our scarce-cold conqueror,   (IV. iii. 47–50)

before directing more specific accusations at Somerset:

> The fraud of England, not the force of France,
> Hath now entrapped the noble-minded Talbot.
> Never to England shall he bear his life,
> But dies betrayed to fortune by your strife.   (IV. iii. 89–92)

There is no such link, of course, in the chronicles, where Talbot still has another twenty years to live.

The next example is even more telling. The chroniclers have several reasons for the defeat of Patay—unequal numbers, the effect of surprise, the capture of Talbot—and add in a later paragraph, as an afterthought, that 'Frō this battaill, departed without any stroke striken, sir Ihon Fastolffe.' It is the Burgundian

[50] Hall 179 (185).

chronicler Monstrelet who explains that the flight of 'Jehan Fastocq' enabled the French to encircle and capture Talbot, and reports their subsequent quarrel, followed by the removal of Fastolfe's Garter. On stage, we hear that despite the large difference in numbers, the English army valiantly withstood the assault of the French cavalry and rushed against them:

> Here had the conquest been fully sealed up
> If Sir John Fastolfe had not played the coward.

It was Fastolfe's flight, the messenger insists, which caused the whole disaster:

> He, being in the vanguard, placed behind
> With purpose to relieve and follow them,
> Cowardly fled, not having struck one stroke.　(i. i. 130–5)

By leaving their rear undefended, he allowed the English troops to be encircled, and Talbot to be hit, significantly, 'into the back', where neither chronicler specifies the nature of the wound.[51]

The point made in the first scene is the focal point of the play: Talbot is never vanquished by foreign enemies, but always betrayed by his own side. Fastolfe's defection causes his capture, York and Somerset's bickerings send him to his death. From the very beginning, the divisions among the nobility are held responsible for the disaster abroad. To Gloucester who wonders what treachery caused so many losses, the messenger puts the matter straight:

> No treachery, but want of men and money.
> Amongst the soldiers this is muttered:
> That here you maintain several factions:
> And while a field should be dispatched and fought,
> You are disputing of your generals.　(i. i. 69–73)

The rout at Patay confirms the diagnosis. Defeat must not be imputed to the superiority of the enemy, not even their superiority in numbers, be it five or ten to one. The French themselves admit that they cannot win by their own forces alone, and pay reluctant homage to English valour. For both chronicler and playwright, England loses only when divided against itself.

Division is the leitmotiv of the play. Henry V is no sooner dead than his relatives exchange insults over his coffin. Each ceremony after this is interrupted by violent outbursts. The hatred between factions is such that young Henry must plead with tears to recall his peers to a proper respect of the place, while Exeter's premonitions dissipate any hope of lasting concord. Where both Joan and the Countess of Auvergne have failed, Margaret will succeed, having turned the heart of the King into a battle ground,

> I feel such sharp dissension in my breast,
> Such fierce alarums both of hope and fear,
> As I am sick with working of my thoughts ...　(v. iv. 84–6)

---

[51] i. i. 138. Monstrelet, *Chronique*, LXI (iv. 330–2). Hall 150 (165).

an intimation of the fires she is about to light, more destructive than his 'passion of inflaming love'.

These scenes of discord alternate with episodes celebrating the virtue of union. Hall stresses the solidarity of Talbot's troops who had to cross the Somme under enemy fire: 'where the lord Talbot passed, his men went in the water vp to the chinne, so glad wer the men to rescew their felowes,' and soon won the bastille opposite.[52] The unhistorical encounter with the Countess of Auvergne shows her powerless against the united force of Talbot's army. But the quarrel in Temple Garden opens a new division at court and soon cancels the benefits of the war effort. The roses picked by the young noblemen, blood red and death white, prefigure the colours of Talbot's bloodless corpse.

Ironically, the theme of union is defended adversely by the despicable Joan and her 'fickle, wavering nation'. When they lose Orleans, the French show themselves quite as vulnerable to discord, deflecting the responsibility onto each other, but their quarrelsome humour is firmly quenched by Joan, who suggests a better way to retaliate: rally their troops, and make new plans to harm their enemies. Indeed her companions seem to improve under her tuition, for the loss of Rouen creates no further disagreement, while Charles confirms their faith in her: 'One sudden foil shall never breed distrust.' It is Joan who exalts national feeling to win Burgundy on their side, pleading France's woes and his natural bond with his countrymen. Her cynical appraisal of his conversion does not pre-empt the force of her arguments, although Graham Holderness probably goes too far when he reads her 'Turn and turn again' as an admiring tribute to conversion, homecoming, not to be mistaken for an ironic aside.[53]

Hall's main theme is systematically illustrated on stage by contrasting pictures, at the cost of a few liberties with facts. The episodes, circumstances, and historical roles selected are vigorously reshaped, and eked out by unhistorical elements to design the allegorizing tableau of discord and concord. The constraints of theme over naturalism are particularly obvious in the treatment of characters. They are cut to demand and distributed between two camps to illustrate one side of an idea, with few nuances and no psychology to speak of, on a downward scale of merit. This is done with or without the original features supplied by the chroniclers, which do or do not fit the pattern. The antithetic traits of Joan and Talbot play up the conflict of values they represent, and extend the meaning of their acts beyond their own limited range of consciousness.

Around the central antagonists, most of the cast are reduced to something less than their historical roles. Bedford and Exeter, whom Henry V left in charge of France and his infant son, are powerless to execute his last will. The order they stand for is threatened, and they the survivors are but weak memories of the late King's glory. Bedford's part is shortened to much less than his actual share of life. Exeter's is extended beyond his lease to the end of the play, but he can only bewail the present state of discord, and prophesy sad days ahead for England. Gloucester,

[52] Hall 188. Holinshed 192 reports the crossing without mention of Talbot.
[53] *Shakespeare: The Histories*, 126–33.

another defender of the late King's inheritance, is at the same time a threat to this order. Hall portrays him as both impulsive and shrewd, prudently administering the realm with the help of well-chosen counsellors, 'least paraduenture he might herafter repent his actes and doynges, as a man remembryng other and forgettyng hymself'; his worse weakness is a tendency to unsuitable marriages, which will cause his downfall, and eventually that of Lancaster. His first union, 'either blynded with ambicion or dotyng for loue', is not mentioned in the play but may have inspired young Henry's plea to 'censure me by what you were | Not what you are', and allow his own foolish marriage to Margaret.[54] Gloucester's Duchess does not appear in this play, but Winchester's ominous insult, 'Thy wife is proud', points to the weak spot in his armour.

Henry VI's well-meaning attempt to keep peace places him with the defenders of the commonweal, but also shows him unequal to the task, praying and begging where he should command. The ambitious York begins to tower over him as a more kingly figure, with a possibly stronger title to the crown. York's prowess on the battlefield enables him to share in the chorus of protests against the infamous peace settlement with France, but not from selfless motives, as his rivalry with Somerset and thirst for power amply show: civil war is in his view a reasonable price to pay for the crown. Lower still on the scale stands Winchester, of whom Hall tells us that he was 'surnamed the riche Cardinall of Winchester, and nether called learned bishop, nor verteous priest'. The stage character has no spark of virtue to redeem his greed, cynicism, and maliciousness, and adds debauchery to Hall's long list of faults.

The French are figures of fun, providing the only light relief of this heavily moralistic play. They have all the usual ugly traits so pleasing to English audiences, though the caricature is mild, compared with Hall's declared acrimony, or contemporary plays like the hysterical *Massacre at Paris*. The comedy turns to sour black around Joan's ambiguous figure. Alençon the anachronistic Machiavel stands out as craftier still than the rest of his wily countrymen, while Reignier is far more present than in the chronicles, and marked as England's constant enemy, in preparation for the ominous entrance of his daughter Margaret.

The critics' attempts to force subversive innuendoes on the text of 1 *Henry VI* offer subtle readings of the lines but cannot bend or disguise its gross structure. The play is crude, let us face it, and efficiently built around two major oppositions, public/private, inside/outside, concentrated on two sets of enemies: France, and selfish greed. These pairs of opposites do not quite overlap, which saves the morality pattern from raw simplicity. Harmony and union are extolled through realistic quarrels between characters who, even if they lack depth, are not bound to a single idea or theme, but alternately play actors in a tragedy or choric figures, agents or victims of discord. The faint-hearted, deceitful French use witchcraft and stratagems to defeat an army of gentlemen, yet the vision offered avoids Manicheism by showing them united, and contrasting their vulgar common sense with their enemies' obsolete elegance. At this stage, the ugliness of vice causes no one to doubt

---

[54] v. iv. 96–9. Hall 115, 116 *(136, 137)*. Hall's dire premonitions, 128–9, are omitted in Holinshed 145.

the quality of virtue, which even unpleasant characters like the Dolphin are some-times moved to celebrate. Against this citadel, Joan leads the first assault.

The theme of witchcraft runs through the whole sequence of plays, from the first charges against 'the subtle-witted French | Conjurers and sorcerers' to Richard's cunning slurs on his own victims in the final phase. Joan's appeal to 'substitutes | Under the lordly monarch of the north' heralds Richard's entrance in the next play, while her usurpation of masculine dress initiates the sexual inversion that Margaret will carry to extremes. The mode of inversion goes one dramatic step further than the symmetrical conflicts of good and evil, for it does not end with the destruction of the positive heroes, it strikes at the codes of the institutions they defend. Following in Joan's wake, Jack Cade's commonwealth, Margaret's sacrilegious parody of the coronation, pending its absolute subversion at Richard III's hands, are increasingly radical attacks on the monarchic order.

France and England

Where Holinshed departs from Hall, he provides little significant material to the play, except on a few points, most of which concern Joan. Hall's account of her is less detailed than Holinshed's, and more inaccurate: he places Joan's birth in Burgundy, and, though he correctly terms her a shepherd's daughter, turns her into 'a chamberlein in an hostrie', a tale he got from Monstrelet, who explains thus her ability with horses.[55] Hattaway suggests that the choice of making Joan a shepherdess was designed to establish a parallel with Tamburlaine, a 'Scythian shepherd'. Actually it was Jean Gerson who first made her a shepherdess in his vindication, *De quadam puella*, written in 1429, but she herself insisted at her trial that she had never kept her father's sheep.[56]

In a few instances, we already noted, Shakespeare is better informed than chron-icler or critic. None of the narratives he is known to have used reports the insults hurled at Joan by the English soldiers at the siege of Orleans, very similar to those in the play.[57] Intriguingly, these parallels all have some link with France, or present unexpected analogies with French affairs, for instance the coronation of Charles VI with that of his infant successor Henry VI, both perturbed by a violent quarrel between their uncles.[58] Shakespeare obviously went to other sources of informa-tion, perhaps one of Holinshed's authorities, unless he heard stories brought back from the continent.[59] The Burgundian chroniclers Monstrelet and Jehan de

---

[55] Monstrelet, *Chronique*, LVII (iv. 314). Hall 157. Holinshed, 163, writes that her father, 'a sorie sheepheard', brought her up to keep cattle.

[56] 'Jean Gerson's Theological Treatise and Other Memoirs in Defence of Joan of Arc', trans. H. G. Francq, *Revue de l'Université d'Ottawa*, 41 (1971). *Procès de condamnation de Jeanne d'Arc*, ed. Pierre Tisset (Paris, 1970), 45, 64.

[57] They are first reported in the *Journal d'un bourgeois de Paris*, ed. Colette Beaune (Paris, 1990), 258, and have no equivalent in Monstrelet, Wavrin, Vergil, Hall, or Holinshed.

[58] Régine Pernoud, *Jeanne d'Arc* (Bourges, 1959), 60.

[59] Holinshed 163 quotes 'W. P, Jehan de Tillet, *Les chroniques de Bretaigne*, *Le Rosier*', and '*Les grandes chroniques*'. On the second hypothesis, see G. Lambin, 'Here Lyeth John Talbot', *EA* 24 (1971), 371–6.

Wavrin, largely and wrongly held to be the sources of the English prejudiced view of Joan, would have told him even less than Hall, for they report no wondrous details about her. Hall drew those from Fabyan's biased reading of Robert Gaguin, one of Joan's 'French lovers'.[60]

Historical accuracy is visibly not Shakespeare's prior concern. Joan's tale of pregnancy, told by Holinshed but omitted by Hall, was a late invention, probably forged at the time of her rehabilitation. Apart from this piece of slander, Holinshed is milder than Hall in his appraisal of Joan, and has more knowledge to impart, but his extra learning is not used to improve the stage character. Shakespeare keeps the worst that is told of the Pucelle. Where the sources disagree, their divergences are put to more profitable use than accuracy. Hall suggests that if Joan remained chaste, it was perhaps 'because of her foule face', whereas Holinshed reports that 'of favour was she counted likesome'. On stage these conflicting views of her charms are fused to imply that her power is unnatural, when she recounts her vision of Our Lady:

> And, whereas I was black and swart before,
> With those clear rays which she infused on me,
> That beauty am I blest with which you may see.   (i. ii. 84–6)

This tallies with Hall's statement that 'she declared suche priuy messages from God, our lady, and other sainctes, to the dolphyn'.[61] It proves to be the Devil's beauty when her spirits abandon her in Act V, and York sends 'the ugly witch' off to be burnt.

As for the wondrous signs surrounding her progress, the miraculous discovery of her sword and recognition of the Dolphin, Holinshed reports what 'French stories saie', but gives no credit to the legends told by 'hir louers (the Frenchmen)'. Hall is even more outspoken: her fables were so 'full of blasphemy, supersticiō and hypocrisy, that I maruell much that wise men did beleue her, and lerned clarkes would write suche phantasies'.[62] Both chroniclers mock the credulousness of her supporters in one sentence, then declare she practised sorcery and fully deserved her fate in the next. In their views, the French have proved their baseness by choosing such a disreputable ally and trying to pass her off as a saint. Hall gives the full text of a letter sent by Bedford to all the courts of Europe, according to which Joan had confessed that she was beguiled by evil spirits. It is this letter, designed to justify her execution, from which all later accusations were derived, although in fact she was not condemned for sorcery, but as a relapsed heretic, as Holinshed properly notes. He abstains from reproducing Bedford's letter, never mentions her evil spirits, and

---

[60] Wavrin, *Croniques et anchiennes istories de la Grant Bretaigne a présent nommé Engleterre, from A.D. 1422 to A.D. 1431*, ed. William Hardy, Rolls Series (London, 1879). Gaguin, *Compendium super Francorum Gestis, a Pharamundo usque Annum 1491* (1495). See D. Goy-Blanquet, 'Shakespeare and Voltaire Set Fire to History', in *Joan of Arc: A Saint for All Reasons* (Aldershot, 2003), 8–22.

[61] Hall 148. Holinshed 164 says nothing of her visions at this stage, but later at her trial, 171, he mentions our Lady, along with 'saint Katharine, and saint Annes' who are not cited in the play. The saints she did name at her trial were Katharine, Margaret, and Michael.

[62] Holinshed 163, 170. Hall 148.

has her simply confess 'hir iniquities', but entertains no more doubt than Hall that she was 'possest of the feend'.[63]

Shakespeare divides his chroniclers' accounts and their side remarks on the French writers equitably between Joan's admiring compatriots and their English foes. The rescue of Orleans causes her to be hailed as 'Divinest creature, Astrea's daughter'.[64] To Charles's court, who express gratitude for all the wrong reasons, she 'shall be France's saint', a vow confirmed by Alençon's blasphemous promise, and more prophetic than even Shakespeare could know:[65]

> We'll set thy statue in some holy place
> And have thee reverenced like a blessed saint.   (III. iii. 14–5)

Meanwhile insults pour from the English side, more numerous still and more varied than their models. In the chronicles, as in the charges held against her by her judges, her debauchery is restricted to wearing masculine dress and leading the life of a soldier. Holinshed reports that her virginity was confirmed at the trial, and that the Regent—Bedford, not York—patiently waited nine months before her execution to disprove her tale of pregnancy. In the play she is called 'witch', 'damned sorceress', 'vile fiend and shameless courtezan', 'fell banning hag, enchantress', and last, 'foul accursed minister of hell' as an early forerunner of Richard III.

Joan is at best a dubious kind of saint in her friends' eyes, a devil in her enemies' opinion, which is vindicated by the end of her adventures. The origin of her mysterious power is made clear when her familiar spirits abandon her to her fate, in conformity with the terms of Bedford's letter in Hall:

she opēly confessed, that the spirites, whiche to her often did appere, were euill and false, and apparant liers, and that their promes, which they had made, to deliuer her out of captiuitie, was false and vntrue: affirmyng her self, by those spirites to bee often beguiled, blynded, and mocked. (159)

Here Holderness denounces 'the "official" critical judgements which have accepted the play's closure as its final judgement on Joan of Arc'. In his remarkably ingenious reading, her rejection of her father is a stance against 'the restrictive parameters of patriarchal normality': those who take for fact her sexual promiscuity 'miss the crucial symbolic idea of a child, fathered collectively by the French aristocracy, and born from the superhuman femininity of the French saint and national heroine'. That the Bard could so grossly abuse the Maid has long been a thorn in the critics' flesh. George Bernard Shaw, one of Joan's most eminent supporters, imagined that Shakespeare began writing the part as a beautiful romantic heroine, and was recalled to his senses by his scandalized company.[66]

---

[63] Hall 157–9. Holinshed 171. Monstrelet, *Chronique*, cv (iv. 442–7), and Wavrin 397–403 reproduce Bedford's letter without any comment.

[64] I. v. 43. On her possible identification with Elizabeth, see Marcus, *Puzzling Shakespeare*, 88.

[65] Jeanne was rehabilitated in 1456, but canonized only in 1920.

[66] Holderness, *Shakespeare: The Histories*, 133. Shaw, preface to *Saint Joan*, in *Collected Plays with their Prefaces* (London, 1973), vi. 39.

Whatever the cause—and speculation on this point cannot but be inconclusive—Joan claims to be pregnant as in Holinshed, but meets with no leniency from the Regent, and is immediately led to the stake, cursing all in sight. On the other hand, Joan's rejection of her father has no basis in the chronicles. Stranger still, her bragging that she is of royal blood coincides with a tale which modern historians unfamiliar with *1 Henry VI* consider a nineteenth-century invention. Having found no trace of such a rumour in the earlier accounts of Joan, I came to the conclusion that Shakespeare invented it himself, to suit his design.[67]

Knights and villains

Joan's claim to nobility enhances her symmetrical opposition to the noble Talbot.[68] The parallelism between the alleged 'scourges' is pointed enough to suggest that Shakespeare may have attached no more credit to the rumours concerning either, and only sacrificed to convention, as Shaw believes, in exposing her at last unambiguously as a witch. It is Talbot himself who underlines their very similar roles as useful scarecrows rather than divine instruments:

> A witch by fear, not force like Hannibal,
> Drives back our troops and conquers as she lists: (I. v. 21–2)

just as the Countess exclaims on seeing 'the Talbot, so much feared abroad' that 'report is fabulous and false'. Shakespeare's French characters are nearly as violent in their abuse of the awesome warrior as the English are of Joan, and quite close to believing that he too is endowed with monstrous powers. 'I think this Talbot be a fiend of hell', confesses Dunois after their humiliating defeat. These antagonistic views contrast Talbot, 'the Frenchmen's only Scourge', with Joan, 'the English scourge', but fame speaks for him, while she is a self-appointed heroine. She thinks of her own end as a national catastrophe, but in the end it makes no great difference to the fortunes of France, which are on the mend. Much more than her satanic strength, the divisions in the English camp ensure the success of the French party, who keep the advantage after the loss of their champion.

Yet unlike Joan's, Talbot's death is an irreparable loss to his country. Two different passages equate it with victory for the French. Charles's confident hope that 'All will be ours now bloody Talbot's slain' is confirmed by Burgundy: 'Now he is gone, my lord, you need not fear.' His part in the play, we saw, far exceeds his historical role. Hall grants an equal importance to Salisbury, after whose death 'fortune of warre began to change, and triumphant victory began to be darckened', and to Bedford: 'After the death of this noble prince, and valeaunt capitain, the bright sunne, that commonly shone in Frāce faire and beautifully vpon the

---

[67] Pierre Caze, in *La Mort de Jeanne d'Arc* (1805), and *La Vérité sur Jeanne d'Arc* (1819), defended the thesis that she was the Dauphin's half-sister. Most historians believe he invented this story, but he probably found the hint of her royal birth in Shakespeare.

[68] David Riggs, *Shakespeare's Heroical Histories: 'Henry VI' and its Literary Tradition* (Cambridge, Mass., 1971), 104–7, sees in Joan a deliberate parody of the Marlovian hero.

Englishmen, began to be cloudie, and daily to waxe darker.'[69] The war, however, did not end with Salisbury, giving Talbot leave to succeed him in this symbolic function.

The glorious age of chivalry dies on stage with the old knight, who wields his sword bravely in the open field, when the French are not ashamed to use artillery and shelter behind their battlements. The chronicles give many instances of the French soldiers' wiles and cowardice.[70] In fact, the English could be as crafty as any Frenchman, for instance using the moment when their enemies were at church to launch an attack: 'In the masse time, thenglishmen entered by subtiltie into the gate & so gat the dongeon.' Both sides, it appears, used gunpowder and war engines.[71] During the siege of Le Mans, the English 'shot against their walles great stones out of great gonnes (which kynd of engines before y^t time, was very litle seen or heard of in Fraunce' and quickly forced the town to surrender. At the battle of Castillon where Talbot was killed, it was the reverse: the French camp was defended by '.iii. C. peces of brasse, beside diuers other small peces, and subtill Engynes to the English-men vnknowen'; Talbot was overcome despite his valiance, 'his enemies hauyng a greater company of men, & more abūdaunce of ordinaunce then before had bene sene in a battayle'.[72] On the chroniclers' evidence, the two camps used the same weapons, and both resorted to subterfuge, but the play keeps them neatly opposed in this regard. Not so much to enhance English valour, perhaps, as to show them fighting a losing war against vulgar modernity. Alençon at the beginning of the play recalls how the French chronicler Froissart wrote, 'England all Rolands and Olivers bred,' a reference, as Edward Burns notes, already pointing to 'the decline of hero-ism', but one that reflects at the same time on the unchivalrous carriage of his own camp. The phrase is used also by Hall and Holinshed, in an even less heroic context, when the Earl of Armagnac, who would like 'to haue a Rowland to resist an Oliuer', wants an ally against the French King and offers Henry the hand of his daughter, 'promisyng hym silver hilles, and golden mountains with her'.[73]

Among other points in favour of Talbot's election as the hero of the piece was the fact, reported by both chroniclers, that his heir died on the same day, having manfully resisted his father's plea to save himself: 'But nature so wrought in the sonne, that neither desire of lyfe, nor thought of securitie, could withdraw or pluck him frō his natural father.' The death of his illegitimate son is suppressed, as we saw above, a piece of editing which allows the old gentleman some withering comments on Dunois's vile birth. Dunois's nobility is praised earlier on in the narrative, when he prefers the honour of being known as the bastard son of the Duke of Orleans to the Coucy inheritance; the point will serve in *King John*, but here, Talbot's bastard is out of place, no matter how bravely he shared his father's fate. The Talbots' heroic

[69] Hall 146, 178 *(185)*.

[70] Hall 122, 129, 140, 142, 149. Holinshed 142, 145, 157, 159, 164 cuts most of Hall's scornful comments except the last, at Orleans, that the French fled back into the city like sheep before the wolf.

[71] Hall 140, 126, 129, 139, 142, 146, 149 *(157, 143, 146, 156, 159, 162, 164)*.

[72] Hall 126, 229. Holinshed 143 omits the second comment in his account of Castillon at 235.

[73] I. ii. 29–30. Burns, n. 30. Hall 202. Holinshed 205 is content with 'great summes of money'.

stance confirms the traditional links between birth and deeds, as do *a contrario* the base-born Dunois and Joan, who prove vile in every sense of the word.[74] They are the essence of aristocratic merit, conveyed not by birth alone but by the transmission of moral rules they were bred to defend. Like Talbot, Joan is the champion of national unity, a scourge to her enemies, a successful and popular leader, but there the likeness ends. Talbot is governed by codes that she flouts with audible glee; her efficiency lies in her disregard for all the traditions he stands for.

The heroine emulates the virtue of the hero, while corroding his values with derision and blasphemy. The cynicism and cowardice of the Dolphin's party do not leave their opponents wholly immune. Talbot's scornful challenge to meet the French soldiers in the field is drawn from an inglorious episode near Orleans, possibly inspired by Holinshed whose terms here are more suggestive than Hall's: Talbot wanted to leave the siege without seeming to fly before the enemy. He and his captain 'assembled together in councill' and after some debate, decided 'to assemble in the plaine field, and there to abide all the daie, to see if the Frenchmen would issue foorth to fight with them'. The Frenchmen 'durst not once come foorth to shew their heads', and the English left in good order.[75] On stage this is just the prelude to their recovery of Rouen, and Talbot's challenge sounds far more dashing, but then so does Joan's retort:

> Belike your lordship takes us then for fools,
> To try if that our own be ours or no.   (III. ii. 61–2)

Railing Hecate or no, her low common sense draws blood. Confronted with the Talbots' golden legend, her truculence evokes a more sordid reality, a base world where heroic worth is still admirable but hopelessly archaic.

The structure of the play thus systematically contrasts the English chivalry and their medieval weapons to the French leaders who depend on gunpowder, deceit, and the services of a low hussy. The valour inherited with the family name becomes a test of the Talbots' legitimacy, as the son reminds his father when pressed to flee:

> Is my name Talbot? and am I your son?
> And shall I fly? O, if you love my mother,
> Dishonour not her honourable name,
> To make a bastard and a slave of me.   (IV. iv. 12–15)

If merit alone cannot emulate true aristocracy, honour cannot be simply inherited, as Talbot specifies when he tears off Fastolfe's Garter: the felon knight should, for his cowardice

> Be quite degraded, like a hedge-born swain
> That doth presume to boast of gentle blood.   (IV. i. 43–4)

How to prove worthy of a desired inheritance, still a minor theme in Part 1, becomes increasingly problematic as Henry VI begins to doubt his own legitimacy, ultimate-

---

[74] Hall 229 (236).
[75] Holinshed 164–5. Hall 149. *2H6*, III. ii. 59–62.

ly driving his own son to make amends for his father's weak spirit and prove himself heir of Henry V on the battlefield.

The opposition noble/ignoble epitomized by Joan and Talbot explores current tensions between aspiring individuals and a rigid society that allowed little scope for vulgar energy. The claim to heroic stature through high deeds and spirits rather than by virtue of any birthright was in phase with 'the peculiar fluidity of Tudor society' after the many upheavals that left the ruling classes depleted.[76] Henry VIII's apologists, often members of the middle class themselves, defended learning and personal worth as legitimate ways of advancement, but these progressive views were dangerously close to revolutionary theories of levelling. When faced with rebellious attempts to upset traditions, the official doctrine relayed by the homilists promptly reasserted its hostility to social change.[77] Against a background of rapid ascension, the old aristocratic family of Talbot represent genuine nobility; at the same time, their chivalrous values, no matter how admirable, begin to appear anachronistic, and potentially destructive. The point will be made more clearly still, and more painfully, in the losing duel fought by Hotspur against Hal. The hero, when no longer required by a worthy cause, becomes a threat to the community that dubbed him. Talbot is the last of his class to fight for the common weal. The warlords of the Hundred Years War will take the lead in the approaching civil struggle, and serve themselves before they preserve widows or orphans.

The dismembered body

Talbot's name—both patronym and reputation—makes him a link in the transmission of heroic virtue, through a long glorious line recalled in the family 'name'. He stands at the crossroads of an old chivalric succession and a living collective organism. The ancestral valour comes alive in the tightly knit body of head and limbs, the 'substance, sinews, arms, and strength' of soldiers led by a charismatic captain. Together, they prove 'so great a warrior' that his name spells terror to his enemies. If severed from them, Talbot is sapped of all his vigour: 'Where is my strength, my valour, and my force?' he cries, when they have been routed by Joan. Bedford maintains the same organic tissue when he animates his soldiers' hearts with his own dying spirit. That Talbot cannot leave his men just to save his life is a matter of course shared by his son, who in turn refuses to flee:

> No more can I be severed from your side
> Than can yourself yourself in twain divide.   (IV. iv. 48–9)

The body military would prove invincible if they were not being literally starved through the selfishness of the body politic. A chance expression in Hall, allied with

---

[76] D. M. Palliser, *The Age of Elizabeth: England under the later Tudors, 1547–1603* (London, 1983), 84. Historians of the period generally agree on its unprecedented mobility, even if they explain it by radically different factors.

[77] *Certaine Sermons or Homilies Appointed to be Read in Churches in the Time of Queen Elizabeth I (1547–1571): A Facsimile Reproduction of the Edition of 1623*, ed. M. E. Rickley and T. B. Stroup (Gainesville, Fla., 1968).

his many references to the difficulties of victualling besieging troops, develops into a consistent picture. At Compiègne, the English besiegers attempted to 'famishe' those within the town. At Pontorson, it was an English company returning with full carriages who 'like gredy Lions, together in an vnpeaceable fury, set on their enemies'. On stage the positions are reversed, and transferred to Orleans. While the first scene shows the noblemen at court too busy quarrelling to send them vital supplies, we hear from Reignier that the 'famished' soldiers 'faintly besiege us one hour in a month'; the French believe themselves safe as long as Talbot is kept prisoner, but Salisbury's troop of pale ghosts rise up 'like lions wanting food' to tear down the walls with their teeth.[78] Talbot's concern for his men's stomachs contrasts with the indifference of his compatriots at home, as with the Frenchmen's heavy banqueting.

The death of Salisbury is soon revenged, contrary to Hall's pessimistic view, and victory smiles again on the English camp. But the disease in the body politic spreads to the limbs. Its army, though a healthy organism, cannot be regenerated, nor replace its dead leaders. In the natural order, Talbot would have been reborn in his son and buried by him: 'Now my old arms are young John Talbot's grave' not only pinpoints a significant inversion, it stresses the finality of the hero's death. Indeed the French need not fear, for the extinction of Talbot's house puts an end to the heroic succession:

> In thee thy mother dies, our household's name,
> My death's revenge, thy youth and England's fame.   (IV. iv. 93–4)

Joan's persona mirrors the pattern of Talbot's, the better to prove them worlds apart. Her union with her soldiers is charged with sexual undertones, and their selfish gluttony at Orleans is contrary to any thought of common interest.

Talbot's dual aspect presents similarities with the image of royal perenniality elaborated by Tudor lawyers, the King's two bodies. The hero's natural body is subject to disease and death, his other body transmigrates from one carnal envelope to another, saluted by funeral rites which celebrate both the triumph of death and the triumph over death. Dynastic succession ensures immortality to the king, who will be reborn in his son, like the phoenix from his ashes, a privileged emblem of monarchy. But when Sir William Lucy warns the French that a phoenix shall be reared from the Talbots' ashes, all know this to be an empty threat. These two notions of the collective body, organic and dynastic, actually never coexisted. Historically, the rites of royal burials took on different meanings in time. The hereditary principle replaced the image of the king united to his subjects by the union of predecessor to successor, turning the royal figure into a *corporation sole*, a community of one.[79] Talbot, who reconciles both definitions, interprets the collective body on the two axes of time and space, organic like St Paul's image of the Christian community,

---

[78] Hall 140, toned down to 'like couragious persons' in Holinshed 156, who does not use the word 'famishe' either. *1H6*, I. ii. 7–12, 27–8, 38–40.

[79] See Ernst H. Kantorowicz, *The King's Two Bodies: A Study in Mediaeval Political Theology* (Princeton, 1957), 310–20, 415–36.

successive like the Tudor lawyers'. He belongs to past and present, a character both normative and obsolete.

'How can these contrarieties agree?' the Countess of Auvergne wonders. The answer may be in Pendragon's exploit, drawn from Geoffrey of Monmouth.[80] The warrior kings of *Historia Regum Britanniae* embody an ideal, unchallenged down to the fourteenth century: God's lieutenant on earth who, like Christ, can sacrifice his life for his fellows. Decay has begun to set in when *1 Henry VI* begins. The corpse of the warrior King occupies centre stage in the opening scene. The political and military functions once naturally united in his person, as Gloucester recalls, are split between five men whose separate powers and interests immediately clash. Before the King is even buried, the body of the commonweal is dismembered. Exeter's vision of England is a picture in negative of the glorious body military:

> As festered members rot but by degree,
> Till bones and flesh and sinews fall away,
> So will this base and envious discord breed.   (iii. i. 194–6)

Hall used the same image to evoke the decline of English prosperity,

which thing although the Englishe people like a valiant & strong body, at the first tyme did not perceiue, yet after yᵗ they felt it grow like a pestilēt humor, which succesciuely a litle and litle corrupteth all the membres, and destroyeth the body.[81]

The body military survives for a while on its own resources, nourished by the memory of high deeds. The Countess of Auvergne is the last to harbour and feed it properly. After this pause, all the corporal images in the play record the progress of disease. The first case of gangrene, both literal and symbolic, is Mortimer, who details the decrepitude of his limbs before he gives his nephew 'one fainting kiss'. Unlike Talbot, the dying Mortimer leaves behind a spiritual son who inherits his title to the crown. The ailing body is now identified with the commonwealth, whose bowels are gnawed by the 'viperous worm' of civil dissension, threatening to 'slay your sovereign and destroy the realm'. The disease thrives on putrefied flesh: moral rot is strong, persistent, dynamic, and unhindered by distance. The corrupted body of the commonweal answers limb for limb to the glorious body of the hero, showing the solidarity principle at its most lethal.

The oft derided Elizabethan World Picture looms behind these images of starved, fighting, rotting bodies.[82] Whether or not the Middle Ages believed in this view of the universe as an organic whole, its symbolic associations still lend tragic form to the collapse of an ordered system of beliefs. These images are fossils of an ideal world of continuum, not sensuous perceptions of its tissue-like texture. At odds with Foucault's system of analogies, *1 Henry VI* dramatizes the historical breach between words and things. Its organic pictures of the commonweal are

---

[80] *The History of the Kings of Britain*, trans. Lewis Thorpe (Harmondsworth, 1966), 208–11.

[81] Hall 146. Holinshed 162 simply notes that after Bedford's death the luck of England 'began to decline' and their glory 'fell in decaie'.

[82] See Mikhail Bakhtin, *Rabelais and his World*, trans. Helene Iswolsky (Cambridge, Mass., 1968), 399–435.

metaphors shored up against the fragments of a collective body, not so much the effort of the poet 'who, beneath the named, constantly expected differences, rediscovers the buried kinships between things, their scattered resemblances', as the characters' desperate efforts to articulate and resist the fragmentation of their universe.[83] The breach is shown as a process: the resilience of the military corps, the physical pain inflicted on the King by his relatives' quarrel, the link both material and symbolic between political rifts and military famine, all show off the solidarity between related organisms as a biological fact, not a political commandment. If the fragmented body of *1 Henry VI* is the result of a collective effort, the limbs assembled begin to look like a proper body of work.

The thin veneer of contemporary science imperfectly covered persistent ancient beliefs. The model of the universe was still Lucretius' cosmology, relayed by Boethius, and integrated in the teleological Christian pattern: the contrary qualities of elements at war with each other would inevitably lead to chaos if they were not held in check by God's love for mankind. With the progress of experimental methods, the analogy between microcosm and macrocosm, the theory of nature's decline, and the providentialist doctrine would each be abandoned separately, but at the end of the sixteenth century these beliefs were inextricably mixed, while direct observation seemed to support apocalyptic pessimism.[84]

In Bakhtin's view, the microcosm was a triumphant assertion of man's ascendancy over the rest of nature, for his body held the key to all its mysteries.[85] The exaltation of man may have been a common theme among humanists, but Calvinism soon doused it down to more pessimistic views. In England especially, far from proclaiming the victory of man, the microcosm took on tragic overtones in the apocalyptic visions of twilight Renaissance. Preachers of the late sixteenth century read signs of decline everywhere, and exhorted the faithful to repent before it was too late. Solar spots, bad crops, the debasement of coinage or the corruption of manners, the loss of ten summer days in the Julian year, the late religious divisions, unemployment, were all unmistakable signs that the world was growing old.[86] The tragic fate of Talbot, which leaves the world depleted, draws on current images of nature's decay. As in the contemporary theories of decline, the cancer grows more virulent with each new transgression. But its inscription in history works contrary to the doctrine. Far from dissolving human time into myth like other literary works of the period, the first Henriad confronts the workings of God's providence with the facts of England's past.

---

[83]   *The Order of Things*, 49.

[84]   See Bury, *The Idea of Progress*, 59–90.

[85]   Bakhtin, *Rabelais*, 362–7, 404–8, quotes the supporting evidence of Pico della Mirandola, Giordano Bruno, Campanella, and of course Rabelais.

[86]   Victor Harris, *All Coherence Gone* (Chicago, 1949), 40–5, notes that with the notorious exception of Bacon, very few at the time rejected those beliefs.

4. SPACE AND TIME

Thematic coherence dictated many readjustments of the original material; stage necessities explain a number of others. To contract into two hours and a few square yards thirty years of events occurring in various countries was to ask of the public precisely the kind of tolerance which turned Sidney's stomach: Shakespeare's infant grows into adulthood, gets married, and travels at ease, if not from Affrick to Asia, at least from England to France. The characters cross back and forth, move from court to battlefield, from Orleans to Rouen, Paris, or Bordeaux, and do often begin by telling you where they are, else the plot could not be conceived. These names are hammered on with dramatic value added, 'Rouen' for instance, 'lost—and recovered in a day again!'

The positions on stage highlight the pattern of rivalries: '*Enter Talbot and Burgonie, without: within, Pucell, Charles, Bastard, and Reignier, on the Walls.*' Talbot and his men enter Orleans '*with scaling ladders*', causing the French to '*leape ore the walles in their Shirts*'. Worse still, in London, '*Glosters men rush at the Tower Gates, and Woodville the Lieutenant speakes within*'.[87] In some of these cases, the occupation of the space '*within*' may be signified by the appearance of one or several characters '*on top*' or '*on the wall*', as Joan does from inside Rouen to provoke Talbot. In other scenes where the opposition within/without is also heavily stressed, the characters change places within sight of the public. The stage is frontally divided between two rival groups fighting for possession of the space, like Gloucester's and Winchester's men before the closed doors of the Tower.

Other scenes imply movements that are trickier to account for. Joan is directed to '*enter the Towne with Souldiers*', after her fight with Talbot before Orleans, yet she addresses another four lines to him, presumably from 'within' before she does exit. Unless she lags behind while her soldiers make the directed move, the 'entrance' may just be a crossing to the other side of the stage through a practicable or symbolic division, instead of behind the tiring-house wall.[88] Such a partition would make the Frenchmen's leap over the wall in the next scene less perilous than a ten-foot drop from the balcony. The specialists generally agree that the balcony only served for short scenes requiring little space and few characters. By their standards, some of the scenes supposedly played on the balcony must have been quite crowded, and the one '*on the Turrets*', where Salisbury stands '*with others*', is relatively long—ninety lines—compared with the average thirty-seven of Gurr's computation.[89]

These various difficulties are no deterrent to modern directors, who can construct a practicable 'wall' more easily than researchers, or invite audiences to 'piece

---

[87] SD (at III. ii. 40; II. i. 8, 39; I. iii. 14), *The First Folio of Shakespeare*, Facsimile, ed. Charlton Hinman (New York, 1968).

[88] In Cairncross, she goes from lower to upper stage. Hattaway suggests that '[*she pauses before entering*] *the town*'. Burns, SD I. v. 14, inserts '[*Charles passes over the stage and*] *enters the town*'.

[89] Andrew Gurr, *The Shakespearean Stage, 1574–1642* (Cambridge, 1992), 135. T. J. King, *Shakespearean Staging, 1599–1642* (Cambridge, Mass., 1971), thinks that some ascents or descents were executed in front of the public on a practicable staircase, which Joan possibly did while speaking her four lines.

out' some device for themselves. With the evolution of dramaturgy, it is easier now to visualize the persistent polarization of the stage in Part 1, French against English, 'blue coats to tawny', red rose versus white rose. The recently excavated remains of the Rose, which saw the creation of 'harey the vj', suggest a wide shallow stage that would have been especially apt for this design.[90] The antagonistic structure of *1 Henry VI* was well served anyway in the Elizabethan theatre by the two upstage doors, which allowed symmetrical entrances and open rivalries. Conflict is visibly all the matter of the plot, the stakes fought for being audibly defined by characters who alternate between active parts and choric comments explaining them. Though rooted in medieval practice, the symbolic division of space no longer has the medieval fixity that assimilated stage left and right with acts sinister or righteous. Heaven and Hell still fight for empire, but they are not rigidly located nor identified with any permanent area of the stage.[91] Talbot and Joan appear indifferently left side or right, above or below, exchanging positions in a way free from any predetermined moral value. The essence of the drama lies in the clash between opposite forces, not in the distribution of space.

The Elizabethan stage, while retaining the medieval freedom to abolish distance, has opened up to the third dimension. Sidney's fastidious disapproval of crude stage practices is in part vindicated, kingdoms no longer figuring side by side, but the question of verisimilitude is not a priority. Sidney's is a bookish notion, derived from Aristotle's Italian commentators, and quite disconnected from the public's response. An Elizabethan audience would have no difficulty in following the wildest motions on a stage clearly redefined every time it was emptied of characters. A warning like the Prologue in *Henry V* served both to answer the learned fraction who were interested in new Italian modes, and to escape such restrictive rules by renewing its contract with audiences brought up on medieval stage conventions. Recent productions have shown that even without the help of explicit rules, dramaturgies of the Elizabethan type were easily accessible to an untutored audience. Ariane Mnouchkine's *Richard II* and *Henry IV*, set in an imaginary feudal Japan, and enacted on a large carpeted platform before a silk backdrop, held audiences of schoolchildren spellbound. Denis Llorca had the assembled cast set fire to Joan's funeral pyre by waving little red flags around her.[92] Michael Boyd's actors did everything with ropes; *1 Henry VI* proved especially successful with its exciting mixture of athletic leaps, enchantments, hard fighting, and visual fireworks.

Thanks to various writing devices, the dramatist avoids gross unlikelihoods. The problem of the King's age (he grows from infancy to manhood in the course of the play), is partially solved by his delayed entrance, after several vague allusions to his youth. The memory of his father's words blurs the fact that he was a babe when Henry V died:

---

[90] 'If it is Shakespeare's *Henry VI, Part 1*', as Carol C. Rutter cautiously notes, *Documents of the Rose Playhouse* (Manchester, 1999), 22.

[91] See Élie Konigson, *L'Espace théâtral médiéval* (Paris, 1970).

[92] Mnouchkine, 'Les Shakespeare', at the Cartoucherie de Vincennes, 1981 and 1984. Llorca, *Kings, ou les adieux à Shakespeare*, Festival de Carcassonne, 1978.

When I was young—as yet I am not old—
I do remember how my father said
A stouter champion never handled sword.   (III. iv. 17–19)

At the beginning he is too young for the actions he is credited with, at the end it is the reverse. He and his counsellors repeatedly refer to his 'tender youth'—''Tis much when sceptres are in children's hands'. At the time of the Armagnac proposal, when he finds himself too young for marriage, the King was actually 21, quite an advanced age for a bridegroom by the standards of the time.

The ghost of Henry V, 'That ever-living man of memory', hovers over the play, spanning the time from past to future, for his reign is constantly contrasted with his son's, and the prophecies of his time are frequently recalled. The role of the prophet is usually held by Exeter, whose hindsight feeds on a premonition attributed by Hall to the great King himself: 'My lorde, I henry borne at Monmoth shall small tyme reigne & much get, & Henry borne at Wyndsore shall long reigne and al lese, but as God will so be it'. The comparative lengths of their reigns inspire the lamentations of Act I, 'Henry the Fifth, too famous to live long'. Exeter, again, when he sees Winchester in his cardinal's robes, recalls another prophecy of Henry V, which in the chronicle was no prophetic vision but plain prudence when the King withheld this title from ambitious Winchester, 'meanyng that cardinalles Hattes should not presume to be egall with Princes'.[93]

From the first funeral onward, dire forebodings form a leitmotiv of the play, as the characters' pessimistic views of the future alternate in a Cassandra-like chorus. All predict sad days for England. Not only Exeter, but Bedford turns prophet: 'now that Henry's dead | Posterity, await for wretched years.' The peace negotiations cause York to 'foresee with grief | The utter loss of all the realm of France'.[94] Some previsions are inevitably contradicted by events. Joan may be equated with the nine sibyls of Rome, but when she and York both predict at the same time the defeat of their own camp, he is right and she is wrong. Although she is several times called a prophetess, she makes little use of her visionary powers after she has flaunted them at her first interview with the Dolphin:

I know thee well, though never seen before.
Be not amazed, there's nothing hid from me.   (I. ii. 67–8)

The other oracles of the play make few announcements that need higher divining powers than common sense. Warwick solemnly predicts that the quarrel in Temple Garden will lead thousands of souls to their graves. As Exeter acknowledges, 'no simple man that sees | This jarring discord of nobility', 'But that it doth presage some ill event'. Like Henry V's 'prophecy' concerning Winchester, these owe more to worldly wisdom than to any supernatural gift, but they create a climate of expectations and dramatic symmetries. Just as the prophecies of Henry V's reign are being averred, the omens, premonitions, and forebodings unveil the fate of England as surely as if it was already written, which, in the chronicles, of course, it

---

[93] III. i. 200–1; IV. iii. 51; I. i. 6; V. i. 28–33. Hall 108, 139 *(156)*.
[94] I. i. 47–8; V. iii. 111–12.

is. Indeed, the device is similar to Hall's, whose narrative often anticipates events, to depict their long-term effects or to stress the ironies of Fate.

Intimations of the supernatural lie elsewhere. Just as they are occasionally inspired by the spirit of deep prophecy, the characters feel invested with a mission. Joan, 'ordained', 'assigned', 'to be the English scourge', vows that she is sent by Heaven to free her native land. Talbot, who makes no such claim, is famed to be 'the Frenchmen's only Scourge', 'black Nemesis'. Both are resolved to make the enemy nation rue, and identify their own fate with their country's.[95] Their feats of arms, reported and swelled by a living legend, seem superhuman to witnesses who wonder about their extraordinary powers. However, the French do not truly believe in Talbot's devilish nature:

> *Bast.* I think this Talbot be a fiend of hell.
> *Reig.* If not of hell, the heavens sure favour him.   (II. i. 46–7)

His successes are 'explained' to us by the charismatic union of the leader with his men, whereas Joan is a 'real' witch. The epithet 'holy' is used ironically by her own supporters, as is her nickname 'Pucelle', or the Dolphin's advice to 'enchant' Burgundy with her words. Were there any doubts left concerning her true nature, they would be allayed by the appearance on stage of her familiars.

The point is made insistently that the French benefited from devilish practices, while the English had no magic to help them other than sacred union. English defeats are ascribed both to Joan's witchcraft *and* to discord among the nobility. The play maintains a double system of interpretation throughout, of which Burgundy gives the example when converted by Joan:

> Either she hath bewitched me with her words,
> Or nature makes me suddenly relent.   (III. iii. 58–9)

The characters explain successes and reversals by supernatural causes, in which they believe if we do not. However, the interference of superior powers in human affairs, always to be reckoned with as a likely possibility, does not exclude the more prosaic reality of facts. From the outset, the death of Henry V and all the ensuing catastrophes are imputed to the 'comets', 'bad revolting stars', 'planets of mishap', 'bad mischance', and to the treachery of French 'conjurers and sorcerers', a comforting illusion which the first messenger soon dispels: 'No treachery, but want of men and money'.

The next scene demonstrates the same dual system of explanation on the opposite side. The Dolphin, after thanking the planets for his recent success, confirms the English messenger's point of view: Talbot is a prisoner, and as for Salisbury, 'Nor men nor money hath he to make war'. Nevertheless, Salisbury soundly beats him. Joan then enters, sent from above, or is it below, to lead them to victory, but her charms are not potent enough to spare them reversals in fortune. Her spirits' desertion at the end does not alter the face of the world, only hers, which is again

---

[95] I. ii. 129–37; I. iv. 96. Unlike Joan's, v. iii. 45–50, Talbot's belief that his death must imperil England, IV. iv. 85–96, is amply confirmed by what follows.

that of an 'ugly witch'. As for the next enchantress, the origin of her power is even more obscure.

Against the holy alliance of 'God and Saint George, Talbot and England's right', a league of planets and devils brings support to very human traitors. Though York deplores that his fortune can do no more for the hero, he and Somerset are jointly held responsible for Talbot's end, who 'dies betrayed to fortune by your strife', while Talbot himself accuses the 'malignant and ill-boding stars' as well as the treachery of men. The play does not explain the misfortunes of England by any simple cause. The premature death of the King, the void thus temptingly opened to his relatives' ambitions, and the weak basis of his colonial plantation all conspire to help the new French national spirit, momentarily reinforced with satanic help. Against this mysterious conjunction of forces, the valiant armies cannot summon providential help or win on their own merits. None of these factors alone, either human or supernatural, is shown as being decisive: the import of dramatization is to send them each to their relative place, and expose them to the course of time.

The supernatural in the play does not shape events so much as it does perspective, extending the limited scope of the characters, who pursue narrow aims without guessing the consequence of their acts. It gives the measure of all that lies beyond us in the natural world, of what human strength cannot govern, nor rational exertion explain away. The chronicler who anticipates what is to come makes retroactive use of his learning for a clearer view of a 'now' gone by. Historical drama endows this knowledge with special powers of divination, overstepping the bounds of Part 1 to establish links with the rest of the sequence. It opens the present to the depth of historical time, and beyond the triviality of human concerns, allows us a glimpse of transcendence. The sum of Hall's influence is both more and less than is reported; more precisely, it does not so much reflect his 'providential theme'—never rigorous at its best—as his attempt to cast the progress of disaster into moral shape, through a laborious conjunction of human factors which includes spirituality.

Most of the themes dramatized are already in the sources: the hesitations of victory, the perils of dissension, the national tragedy of the hero's death. In the chronicles, after the repeated announcements that 'all' is lost in France, it becomes unclear which particular episode was decisive: the decision is left to Shakespeare.[96] Hall, followed by Holinshed, declares that Henry's marriage will bring nothing but unhappiness to England. It is also the burden of their laments over Gloucester's quarrel with Winchester, 'thorowe whiche vnhappie deuision, the glory of thenglishemen within the realme of Fraunce, began first to decaye, and vade awaie in Fraunce', and it is repeated again when York and Somerset are at odds: 'This cancard malice, and pestiferous diuision, so long continued, in the hartes of these twoo princes, till mortall warre consumed theim bothe, and almoste all their lynes and ofsprynges'. At this point, although it follows hard upon the death of Bedford, it does not greatly affect English fortunes in France as it does in the play. Two paragraphs later, however, Hall notes that

---

[96] Hall 197, 146, 178 (*180, 162, 185*).

either the disdayne emongest the chief peres of the realme of Englande, (as you haue hearde,) or the negligence of the kynges counsaill, (whiche did not with quicke sight, forese and preuent thynges for to come) was the losse of the whole dominion of Fraunce (179)

for instead of sending abroad 'thousandes of men, apte and mete for the warre', as they were wont, they sent only 'hundredes, yea scores, some rascall, and some not able to drawe a bowe, or cary a bill'. Last but not least of the momentous events that divide young Henry's realm comes his decision to follow Suffolk's choice of a bride against Gloucester's advice, 'Whiche facte engendered suche a flame, that it neuer wente oute, till bothe the parties with many other were consumed and slain, to the great vnquietnes of the kyng and his realme.'[97] Hall, like Shakespeare, sees discord as a fire or a contagious disease, spreading to the whole of the country, devouring all the protagonists and their lineage. But where the chronicler stresses the link between interior division and exterior peril throughout his narrative, whenever the occasion permits, Shakespeare centres the first Part around this theme, following its logical development up to the final defeat. After which disaster the foreign theme fades out of the action, and reappears only in bitter memories of the glorious past. In Hall's view, Gloucester's death, the main event of 2 *Henry VI*, is again a cause of setbacks in France, owing to the divisions it creates among the nobility. On stage, where everything has been said on the subject, it initiates a new set of variations.

In Shakespeare's construction, the numerical inferiority of English troops abroad is a consequence of political division; even when they manage by their valour to overcome this handicap, the benefits of victory are always cancelled by dissensions at home. Margaret brings a new source of conflicts that will overthrow the Protector and leave her party exposed to their own forces of destruction. The selection of matter has extended beyond the royal wedding to collect the threads related to the loss of France. Henry's ill-advised marriage seals the defeat, displaces the fighting to the home front, and is anything but a happy end, indeed hardly an end at all: the French leaders do not mean to respect the treaty, and one of their agents is inside, manipulated by yet another ambitious upstart.

[97] Hall 204 (not in Holinshed 207).

2

Plotters and Plot

1. REFASHIONING HISTORY

Between Parts 1 and 2, the turning of chronicle into drama moves from extensive to microsurgery. Shakespeare still borrows, cuts, contracts, displaces material, but the design becomes far more intricate. *Henry VI Part 2* exhibits the most brilliant construction of the sequence, and the most frequently mutilated on the modern stage, where its slower, subtler developments seem more dispensable than the activity of the other plays. Where Part 1 wanders wildly through the records of thirty years, Part 2 covers the decade following the King's marriage, using less than thirty pages in Hall's chronicle—forty in Holinshed's—against a hundred for the first play, and adapts the narrative so closely that one might indeed be tempted to mistake the chroniclers' narrow views for the playwright's own. Far from the moral comforts of Part 1, where good behaviour appeared the best way to prosperity, *2 Henry VI* shows Shakespeare's shrewd political judgement taking shape, as he comes to assess the benefits of virtue, and its chances of success in a fallen world.

The historical pattern of 2 Henry VI

The opening scene reports the main stages of the Tours marriage negotiations, often with the very words of Hall's chronicle, in which Suffolk, *as procurator* to King Henry, *espoused* Margaret, in *presence* of the *kings* of France and *Sicil, the Dukes of Orleans, Calaber, Bretagne,* and *Alençon, seven earls, twelve barons,* and *twenty* reverend *bishops*. After which, in execution of the contract, Anjou and Maine must be *released* and *delivered* to poor King Reignier whose large *style* ill agrees with the leanness of his *purse*. Holinshed duly repeats Hall's words, except that the two provinces are just 'deliuered'.[1] The terms of the agreement read on stage include other historical details, Margaret's lack of dowry and travelling at the King's expenses, Suffolk's fee, the truce of eighteen months, the date of the Queen's coronation, and Gloucester's hostility to the whole deal. York's exposition of his flawless title to his friends, the *commotion* in Kent, the macabre parade of heads made to kiss by Cade's order, and the *striking off* of Suffolk's, on the *side* of a *boat*, likewise paraphrase the narrative.[2]

[1] I. i. 1–9, 49–50, 108–9. Hall 205 (*207–8*). My italics.

[2] II. ii. 10–50; III. i. 29, 357; IV. vii. 122–8; IV. i. 68–9. Hall, 2, 23, 246 (*265–6*), 221 (*225*), 219 (*220*), uses the term 'commotion' half a dozen times about Cade's rebellion or whenever popular agitation threatens, against Holinshed's three (*220, 230*).

   The stages of the conspiracy against Gloucester, which occupy the first three acts, develop the chroniclers' suggestion that the indictment of his wife was part of a larger plot aimed at himself: 'for diuers secret attemptes wer aduaūced forward this season, against the noble Duke Hūfrey of Glocester, a farre of, whiche in conclusiō came so nere, that they bereft hym both of lyfe and lande.' In this first attempt, years before Henry's marriage, the Queen could have had no part. But being a woman of 'haute stomacke', she soon resented the authority of the Protector and plotted his downfall with the help of 'suche, as of long tyme had borne malice to the duke', namely Suffolk and Buckingham, with the assistance of Winchester and the Archbishop of York. Hall reports, along with Gloucester's faith in his innocence and the King's justice, the summons before Parliament, his arrest, followed the next morning by the discovery of his corpse in bed, and the anger of the Commons.[3] Neither chronicler is very clear as to how the trap for the Duchess was set, nor how it advanced the attempts against her husband, whose downfall occurred several years later. Eleanor's alleged designs on the crown, the charges of witchcraft, the names and qualities of her accomplices, the sentences pronounced against them, are all in conformity with the chronicles. All, except for the fate of the three men sentenced to death. Only one actually suffered the penalty; one died the night before the execution, while the third was pardoned, for reasons unexplained.

   Shakespeare advances Suffolk's end, while retaining the original setting, Dover sands, as well as the destination of the exiled Duke, France, the fight at sea, his capture and decapitation, and the opinion of the people who read God's punishment in his miserable end. The chroniclers make no such connection with the death of Winchester, though it followed hard upon Gloucester's murder. What they do see, however, and in this again they agree with the popular judgement, is that this untimely death encouraged sedition abroad. On stage, the order of events is reversed. The news that all is lost in France comes just before the attack on Gloucester. In both source and play, this setback coincides with a period of unrest in Ireland, which York is sent to appease.

   Cade's rebellion takes place during the Irish campaign. For this episode, Shakespeare uses other accounts besides Hall and Holinshed's, though he takes many details from theirs, namely the stirring up of a commotion in Kent by York's supporters, Cade's lofty promises to the people, the rebels' threat to the nobility, their supplication to the King, the defeat and death of the Staffords, the King's flight to Killingworth, Cade's anarchic rule, ended by the surrender of his troops in exchange of a royal pardon, the thousand marks' reward set on his head, and his capture by Alexander Iden, squire of Kent.

   The last act is wholly dedicated to York's activities until the battle of St Albans. Thanks to his first soliloquy, the audience have long been aware of his underground dealings, whereas Hall and Holinshed only mention his secret plans after the death of Gloucester, which leaves the throne unprotected, and makes him heir presumptive. The historical York made two vain attempts to remove Somerset,

---

[3] Hall 202, 208, 209 (*203, 210–11*).

separated by a three-year interval; he marched twice against London at the head of an army to demand his arrest, before the Yorkists actually took arms against the royal troops and finally disposed of Somerset, whose death was thought to fulfil an old prophecy, as it does in the play.[4]

A more exhaustive list of details and verbal parallels borrowed straight from the chronicles would further confirm Shakespeare's precise knowledge of his sources, and his close reading of Hall especially. Sometimes these words are lent to characters other than the original speakers, suggesting certain affinities between them: for Hall it was 'the Quene, whiche then ruled the rost and bare the whole rule'; in Shakespeare it is 'Suffolk the new-made Duke that rules the roast', the only instance of this phrase in the whole canon; Holinshed simply writes 'the quéene (which then bare the chiefe rule)'. The chroniclers' commonalty berate the rule of the Queen 'with her minions', while on stage it is Margaret who complains that Eleanor ''mongst her minions' queens it over her. Margaret again, who resents the King's 'fond affiance' for Gloucester, unwittingly echoes Hall's comment on the Protector's innocent trust: 'suche affiaunce had he in his strong truthe'. When York sees in Gloucester 'the shepherd of the flock', he repeats a compliment Hall had paid to Henry V in his funeral oration.[5] These associations make dramatic sense, although they may simply be faint memorial traces of the chroniclers' views on their own characters.

The order of events on stage follows the original chronology with only minor alterations. These, though less conspicuous than the rehashings of *1 Henry VI*, can inflect the facts so sharply that they deserve as careful attention as the events themselves. Why Shakespeare chooses to dramatize some anecdotes rather than others, why he should prefer an armourer's servant to those who murder a bishop in Edington, and why waste time on peasants but none on the sale of cereals which so preoccupied Parliament, may throw some light on the patterns of his design. Whole episodes irrelevant to the purpose are ignored, whole pages of narrative are reduced to a single line. The Norwich citizens who rebelled against exactions 'contrary to their auncient fredomes and vsages' provide Jack Cade with the phrase 'ancient freedom' but leave no other trace in the play.[6] Suffolk's long self-promotion in Parliament after his Tours embassy lends but a touch of vanity to the dramatic character, who finds himself raised directly to the dukedom instead of going through the intermediate stages of earl and marquess, with years of waiting in between.

The most drastic cuts affect the situation on the continent, the main concern of the twenty-sixth, -seventh, and -eighth years of the reign. The loss is dealt with in two lines halfway through the play, without prior warning that the truce is broken, or news of military operations. In the chronicles, the defeats in Normandy and Aquitaine follow identical patterns: domestic dissensions lead to rebelliousness abroad, an opening which the French King is quick to seize, while poorly defended

---

[4] I. iv. 34–7; v. ii. 67–9. Hall 233 *(240)*.

[5] I. i. 106; I. iii. 85; III. i. 74; II. ii. 73. Hall 232, 217, 209, 112 *(238, 218, 211, 133–4)*.

[6] IV. viii. 26. Hall 208 *(210)*.

towns turn to the enemy or surrender without fight. In *2 Henry VI*, the only allusion to this state of affairs is York's, who recalls that Somerset kept him waiting for supplies 'Till Paris was besieged, famished, and lost', but it is obviously a thing of the past. The end of the war, Hall tells us, marked the renewal of inner divisions

for when the care of outward hostilitie (whiche kept the myndes of the Princes in the realme occupied, and in exercise) was taken awaye and vanished, desire of souereigntie, and ambicion of preeminence, sodainly sprang out so farre, that the whole Realme was diuided into twoo seuerall faccions, and priuate partes. (231)

He then evokes the descent of Henry IV, 'first aucthor of this diuision', and of the York branch, whose rival claims brought great ruin to the country, 'For while the one part studied to vanquishe and suppresse the other, all commō wealth was set aside, and iustice and equitie was clerely exiled'. This thought appears in the chronicles shortly before St Albans, whereas Shakespeare sows the seed in his opening scene and allows it to mature until the fifth act, between the foreign wars of Part 1 and the civil fights of Part 3.[7]

The seasonal repetitiveness of Parliament sessions or the Commons' endemic grievances are cut down on stage to singular events. Instead of being summoned half a dozen times, as it actually was during the period dramatized, the Parliament meets for one decisive session at Bury St Edmunds where Gloucester's arrest, the Commons' complaint, and Suffolk's banishment each take place in quick succession. Three popular rebellions reported in the chronicles combine into one: the rising of the Norwich citizens for the restoration of their ancient liberties, an insurrection led by a Captain Blue Beard after the Commons' vain indictment of Suffolk, and Cade's rebellion, which soon followed Blue Beard's but only began after Suffolk's death. In Hall, the anger against Suffolk unites 'the commons of the neither house' who draw articles of treason against him, and 'the commons in sundry parts of the realme' who followed Captain Blue Beard. 'After this little rage was asswaged, . . . the cōmōs of the lower house' again require the King to punish Suffolk, along with others they hold responsible for the loss of Anjou and Maine. If Hall finds them 'mutable', it is because he had noted earlier that they had thanked Suffolk 'in open Parliament' for his part in the King's marriage and the ensuing truce, then 'within foure yeres . . . in thesame place', accused him 'of many treasons'.[8] When Warwick enters the stage with 'with many Commons', announcing that he has 'calmed their spleenful mutiny', it may be a trace of these earlier uprisings, which become fused with Cade's in the Lieutenant's list of Suffolk's faults.[9] More significantly, it is a deliberate confusion between the parliamentary and the rebellious forms of protest.

Of the two armies originally sent against Jack Cade, only one remains in the play. Cade had gone to Sevenoaks when the King's soldiers reached Blackheath, but the

---

[7] Hall 231 *(237)*. *2H6*, III. i. 83–5; I. iii. 169–73.

[8] Hall 217–19 *(218–20)*, 207. Holinshed 209 omits Hall's comment anticipating their variability, and substitutes 'the people' for the 'mutable commons'.

[9] Hall 208, 219 *(210, 220)*. *2H6*, III. ii. 128; IV. i. 100–3.

Queen, mistaking this tactical retreat for a flight, sent the Staffords after him with a company of gentlemen who were soon defeated. Shakespeare's one army goes to Blackheath under command of the Staffords, and meets with the same fate. This greatly simplifies Cade's progress, a confused sequence of dubious moves and skirmishes, which Shakespeare straightens out into a regular advance of the rebels against the London strongholds of law and order, making it appear all the more scary.

Part models

Among other iterative patterns in the chroniclers' reading of history, the careers of Suffolk and Somerset followed somewhat similar courses. To satisfy the discontented Commons, the Queen sent Suffolk to the Tower, then released him after a month, believing their ill humour appeased, instead of which they rose in various parts of the kingdom under the leadership of Blue Beard. Four years later, Somerset, whom the people hated quite as heartily, was committed to the Tower but soon released by the King's favour, or the Queen's, causing York to march against London. Shakespeare avoids repetition by shortening Suffolk's fall, as he had abridged his ambitious careering to dukedom some years before. Likewise, York's two successive attempts against Somerset are treated as one.[10] In 1452, York failed to obtain his rival's arrest, and was taken to London virtually a prisoner after he had obediently dismissed his army. His second attempt in November 1454 was more successful: Somerset was sent to spend Christmas in the Tower, and came out the following February, to be killed three months later at St Albans. The Folio stage direction, '*Enter Yorke and his army of Irish*', ignores the chroniclers' statements that on both occasions he collected his men in the marches of Wales, but follows York's declared plan to find troops in Ireland, and the messenger's news in Act IV that he has returned with an army of kerns. After negotiations with the King's emissary, York dismisses his soldiers on the assurance that Somerset is in prison, then flies into a rage when he finds him at liberty in the King's tent, and is arrested for treason, as in the first episode. Nevertheless, as his soldiers were appointed to meet him the next day in St George's Field to receive their pay, a detail of Shakespeare's coinage, they are ready to fight at St Albans, and spare York the need to summon a second army, or wait another three years to claim the crown. Holinshed completes Hall's account of these two episodes with the full texts of the messages exchanged between York and the King, adding that a letter which might have preserved the peace was kept from the King's knowledge by Somerset. Shakespeare speeds up Hall's more concise version further by omitting all peace offerings or shows of reverence.

The characters provided by the sources are similarly cut to size. In Part 1, the Mortimers are 'a constant source of confusion' to the critics. It is thought that Hall is at the origin of the tangle, for he visibly confused Edmund the fifth Earl with his

---

[10] Hall 231, 232 (*237, 238*).

uncle Sir Edmund: Glendower, he writes, took the Earl prisoner 'and feteryng hym in chaynes, cast hym in a depe and miserable dongeon', from which Henry IV refused to ransom him because he was heir presumptive to Richard II. Hall however twice gives the genealogy of the Earl and his dynastic title correctly, but Shakespeare confuses these two men further still by endowing his Mortimer with the mother of one, Philippa, and the sister of the other, Anne.[11] To conclude with the Mortimers, Hall reports that during the Parliament of 1425, 'Edmonde Mortimer, the last Erle of Marche of that name (whiche long tyme had been restrained from his liberty, and finally waxed lame) disceased without issue' and that during the same Parliament 'Sir Ihon Mortimer cosin to the said erle was attainted of treason and put to execution'. Part 1 staged the end of the last Mortimer, a lame man who died a natural death like the Earl, after a long captivity 'within a loathsome dungeon' like Sir Edmund, in the Tower like Sir John.

Matters get rather worse in Part 2. The genealogy of the Earl is mended: he is now correctly the grandson of Philippa, but he has been made to exchange a life sentence with the Lancasters for one with Glendower 'who kept him in captivity till he died'. Overscrupulous editors understood that Shakespeare, again 'from an imperfect reading or recollection of Hall 23', was confusing his Mortimers with yet a fourth individual, Lord Gray of Ruthvin, whom Glendower forced to marry his daughter, promising to set him free as a reward.[12] For these critics knew a detail which Shakespeare kept from his audience, but must have known from Holinshed, namely that the ubiquitous Mortimer, 'prisoner with Owen Glendower', had 'agréed to take part with Owen, against the king of England, and tooke to wife the daughter of the said Owen'. The confusion between Glendower's sons-in-law should be obvious to anyone familiar with the chronicles. Hall, however, makes no such confusion: the Welsh terror kept Lord Gray 'with his wife still in captiuitee till he died. And not content with this heynous offence, made warre on lorde Edmond Mortimer erle of Marche . . . and toke hym prisoner.'[13] Hall says nothing of Mortimer's nuptials, Holinshed nothing of Lord Gray's, and Shakespeare nothing of either marriage here, though we meet Mortimer's Welsh bride in *1 Henry IV*.

The public have the scholars to thank for giving the alarm and filling a gap they might never have suspected. Indeed only those anxious to identify the genes of the stage characters could fathom the mess. Stuart Seide's 1993 production of the trilogy in Poitiers raised shouts of ignorant laughter with the punchline of York's genealogy: 'What plain proceedings is more plain than this?' Perhaps Shakespeare expected just this reaction from his own audience. The stage Mortimer displays a convincing set of features culled from a whole family whose claims on the crown made them a constant threat to the House of Lancaster. His name, which Cade will briefly resurrect, has more dramatic weight than the various individuals who

---

[11] Knowles, II. ii. n. 39, thinks as Cairncross did, that this abundance of historical Mortimers 'led to a confusion in the chronicles which reappeared in Shakespeare'. Cf. Hall 2–3, 21, 28, 128, 246 (265–6). *1H6*, II. v. 61–92. *2H6*, II. ii. 10–58.

[12] Hattaway, II. ii. n. 42, continues the argument with Cairncross n. 38, who announces further confusions in *1 Henry IV*.

[13] Holinshed 21. Hall 23

flourished it in their time, before the self was invented. Shakespeare's contemporaries would have shared the Senecan view, that a family was jointly answerable for the acts of its members.

The case of the Mortimers is often dismissed as a misreading of the sources, but no such suspicion is attached to the make-up of Warwick, unquestioningly accepted as a deliberate conflation of two historical characters: Warwick the Kingmaker and his father-in-law Henry Beauchamp, whose title he inherited. Hailed as 'victorious Warwick' in the opening scene, he is endowed with the glorious past of the first, and with the housekeeping talents of the second, directly derived from Hall's account of his 'plentifull house kepynge' which won him 'suche fauor and estimacion, emongest the common people'.[14] Somerset's treatment is probably quite as deliberate. The Duke of Somerset holds the stage from the death of Henry V to his own at St Albans, although two different men wore the title during the period dramatized, from 1422 to 1455. John, the first Beaufort elevated to this dignity, died in 1444 and was succeeded by his brother Edmund, Earl of Mortain, who became Regent of France in 1447. This succession, which would roughly coincide with the end of Part 1, is nowhere recorded on stage, nor is any change of character indicated, while the enmity between York and Somerset continues unchecked into the next play.

In this case, the conflation was partly done by the chroniclers, who advanced John's death and his brother's accession to 1431, and attributed to the latter the rivalry with York for the regency in 1435:

Although the Duke of Yorke, bothe for birthe and corage, was worthy of this honor and preferment, yet he was so disdained of Edmond duke of Somerset, beyng cosin to the kyng, that he was promoted to so high an office, (whiche he in verie deede, gaped and loked for) that by all waies and meanes possible, he bothe hindered and detracted hym, glad of his losse, and sory of his well dooyng, causyng hym to linger in Englande, without dispatche, till Paris and the floure of Fraunce, were gotten by the Frenche kyng. (179)

In 2 *Henry VI*, York upbraids Somerset for the loss of Paris in similar terms, which could also apply to the loss of Bordeaux in Part 1, as does Warwick's accusation of 'traitor'. In each case it is Edmund who is named in the narratives, Edmund who, as Earl of Mortain, stood by the coffin of Henry V, fought with the first Warwick in Bedford's army, and was present at Henry VI's coronation in Paris, while his elder brother John, the first Duke, is only mentioned twice during the whole of the period. Actually they were successive rivals of York's authority in France, John in 1442 during York's regency, and Edmund in 1447, when he was named Lieutenant of France in preference to York.[15] All Shakespeare had to do was follow Edmund's early career as Earl of Mortain and anticipate the chroniclers' anticipation of his access to dukedom.

[14] Hall 232 (238).
[15] John, Earl of Somerset, was appointed captain-general of Guienne in 1442. His brother Edmund was created Marquess in 1443 when John was elevated to the dukedom. John died in May 1444, but Edmund only became Duke in 1448. See Sir James H. Ramsay, *Lancaster and York: A Century of English History, A.D. 1399–1485* (Oxford, 1892), II. 7, 47–54, 82, 85, 620.

Somerset, who was not among Gloucester's enemies, nevertheless joins them on stage, instead of the Archbishop of York, who shared in the conspiracy, but played no other part in the relevant years of the narrative. Other legates drop out, leaving their diplomatic missions to Buckingham or Clifford, who bring in the rebels' supplication, receive their surrender, and go to enquire the reason for York's rising. These transfers have practical advantages besides the economy of minor parts. Clifford is allowed a short scene as the spokesman of the King's party before his death at St Albans introduces the revenge theme that will develop in the next play. As for the bishops banished from the stage in favour of military men, a trace of their original presence remains in Henry's well-meaning plan: 'I'll send some holy bishop to entreat', an indication of his ineffective goodwill. Or of drastic cuts in the company's budget?[16]

Economy is practised also on Matthew Gough's contribution, restricted to a stage direction at the opening of IV. vii: '*Alarums. Matthew Goffe is slain, and all the rest.*' The hero of the French wars disappears without further ado, his name is never mentioned again in the play, and why he was cast in it at all is not clear, unless as a bathetic reminder of the glorious past. As in Hall's final eulogium, 'it is often sene that he, whiche many tymes hath vanqueshed his enemies in straūg countreys, and returned agayn as a conqueror, hath of his awne nacion afterward been shamfully murdered, and brought to confusion'.[17] The play allows him no funeral oration; he is just one more protective figure of the realm to be idly destroyed, a casualty less significant than the death of Lord Saye who enters next.

2. PLAYING WITH TIME

The suppression of repetitive episodes or bit parts mends the stutters of history without sensibly affecting the original material, and avoids the return of issues discussed in the first play. Most of the above cuts are self-explanatory. Other alterations, mainly of the time-sequence, though never so spectacular as those of Part 1, create more significant changes.

Intervals

The first scene treats as one continuous sequence the royal wedding, the end of York's regency, Suffolk's accession to dukedom, and the conspiracy against Gloucester, thus linking in time as in facts the first ruinous effects of the King's improvident marriage. By a similar suppression of intervals, the Duchess's indictment immediately leads to her husband's disgrace, though the chroniclers place it four years before Margaret's arrival at court, six before Gloucester's death. But in this instance, Shakespeare was taking a leaf from the *Mirror for Magistrates*, where

---

[16] IV. iv. 8. See William Montgomery, 'The Original Staging of *The First Part of the Contention* (1594)', *ShS* 41 (1988).

[17] Hall 222. Not in Holinshed 225.

the jealousy between the Queen and the Protector's wife causes Gloucester's fall.[18] In the *Mirror*, the Duchess swears she never intended any harm to the King; she is guilty of prophesying, as in the play, whereas in Hall and Holinshed she is accused of having made a wax figure of him. Foxe's *Actes and Monuments*, which provided parts of Gloucester's itinerary, presents her fall as the first phase of a plot against her husband, like the *Mirror*, and names the Cardinal as the most likely suspect because he was a mortal enemy of the house of Gloucester. Besides, Foxe notes that one year after Humphrey's death, 'it followed also that the cardinal, who was the principal artificer and ringleader of all this mischief, was suffered of God no longer to live', where neither Hall nor Holinshed connects the two events.[19]

Foxe's narrative through the first eighteen years of Henry VI's reign is wholly dedicated to religious fights and persecutions on the continent, which lead him into home politics with the trial of 'Margaret Jourdeman, the witch of Eye'. In his enlarged edition of 1570, he explains that his earlier one was 'so hastily raked up' that he wrote only a short note on the events to exemplify 'this rage of persecution', but now he will expose the whole plot in a 'Brief answer to the cavillations of Alan Cope's concerning Lady Eleanor Cobham'. His authority is Grafton's *Continuation* of John Hardyng, which he offers to send as evidence to the wrangling Master Cope in Louvain. The charge against the Duchess was in his opinion a forgery, one of the possible reasons being that she and Bolingbroke 'seemed then to favour and savour of that religion set forth by Wickliff; and therefore it is like enough that they were hated of the clergy'; another is 'the grudge kindled between the cardinal of Winchester and duke Humphrey, her husband', which began before, not after, her impeachment for plotting the King's death. As corroborative evidence, Foxe observes that the town of Eye is close to Winchester, 'and in the see of that bishop'. Actually none of his suspicions is implemented with data. The only clue to the framing of the Duchess is the fact that one of her accomplices, John Hume, was pardoned, although the deed was 'so heinous, that neither any durst ask his pardon, nor, if it had been asked, had it been likely to be granted', while her own penalty was very light for a deed of high treason. But the mechanism of the trap is nowhere exposed, nor does Foxe explain why it took six years to close on the Duke. It was Shakespeare who designed it, suppressed all religious implications, and gave verisimilitude to the innuendoes of his sources by contracting the interval between the trials of the couple.[20]

The interval is also narrowed in the dramatic conjunction of crime and punishment. Hall and Holinshed, who named Cardinal Beaufort among the conspirators, do not allude to the plot when he dies, a bare two months after Gloucester. Their funeral portraits stress his large cupidity and small religion, and Hall's, the harsher

---

[18] *Mirror*, xxviii. 78–81. To Lily Campbell, *Shakespeare's 'Histories'*, 109–10, the anachronism served to draw a contemporary parallel with the fall of Protector Somerset during the minority of Edward VI.

[19] Foxe 707–8, 716. In the *Mirror*, xxviii. 257–61, Eleanor repents having caused the Duke's death, but does not explain how.

[20] Foxe 704–8. See R. A. Griffiths, 'The Trial of Eleanor Cobham: An Episode in the Fall of Duke Humphrey of Gloucester', *Bulletin of the John Rylands Library*, 51 (1968–9), 381–99.

of the two, includes a dying speech devoid of remorse or confession.[21] When Suffolk's turn comes three years later, both report that many saw in his violent death the execution of divine justice for the murder of Good Duke Humphrey, although this accusation did not appear in the list of articles drawn against him by the Commons. The main grievance of the Lower House was his responsibility in the loss of Normandy. The murder of Gloucester and its providential punishment were widely held popular opinions, which the chroniclers report without expressly adopting them as their own. Gloucester's sudden death at a most convenient time for his enemies naturally gave rise to suspicions of foul play and various hypotheses as to the method of his murder, including an opinion reported by Holinshed 'that he died of verie gréefe', but the names of the murderers were left for everyone to guess.

In the play, Suffolk and Winchester openly claim responsibility for the deed. The Cardinal dies immediately after his victim with hallucinated admissions of guilt, but no sign of hope, his awful agony being evidence of 'a monstrous life' to all present. As for Suffolk, the time interval is again contracted on stage where, disregarding the sources, his banishment is pronounced in righteous anger by the King even before the news arrives of his accomplice's agony. His execution in the next scene rounds off a chain of events which, depending on their degree of scepticism, both witnesses and audience can read as an act of divine justice or a logical outcome of violence. Suffolk might be said to reap what he has sowed, but no medical cause is offered for Beaufort's abrupt seizure. God's hand strikes more swiftly on stage than was suggested in the narratives.

In such cases, the compression of time introduces correlations unthought of by the chroniclers. In others, their causal systems are ignored and the borrowed episodes reinterpreted. In Hall's account, the loss of France, which soon followed the Protector's fall, was partly due to it, 'for the Frenche kynge and his counsaill began now to perceyue and smel, that the affayres of Englande, by the death of the duke of Gloucester, were sore minished and decayed'. In the play the news that 'all is lost' in France comes during the Parliament at Bury, along with other threats against the Crown: a rebellion in Ireland, York's ambitions, and the rising planned in Kent. These later events are also held to be a consequence of Humphrey's death in the chronicles, 'for if this Duke had lyued, the Duke of Yorke durst not haue made title to the crowne'. Shakespeare follows them in making the Protector the last stronghold of the dynasty, brought down by the very ones he was protecting. York sees Gloucester as an obstacle:

> For Humphrey being dead, as he shall be,
> And Henry put apart, the next for me.   (III. i. 381–2)

He even joins the conspiracy, though the chroniclers never suggest he took part in it. It was only after Gloucester's death that Richard of York 'began secretly to allure to his frendes of the nobilitie, and priuatly declared to thē, his title and right to the

---

[21] Cf. *2H6*, III. iii. 1–18. Hall 210–11. Holinshed 212–14 omits the speech but adds two pages on the religious activities of his successor, which include the foundation of Magdalen College, Oxford.

Crowne'. Shakespeare's character is shown to harbour such designs as soon as he inherits Mortimer's claim in Part 1, and proves a much more resolute pretender than his model, two points which sensibly alter his original progression.

At the beginning of the play, York is endowed with past exploits in Ireland, where he first met Jack Cade, though historically he has not been there yet. Cade comes from Kent, as in Hall, while Holinshed, in making him an Irishman, may have suggested the meeting in Ireland. York thus plans the Kentish rebellion himself before leaving, instead of the chroniclers' unidentified Yorkists, who 'began to practise the gouernaunce of his title' in his absence, and thought it expedient 'to cause some great commociō and rysyng of people to be made against the King'. The dramatic character generally reacts more speedily than his model, who had two separate consultations with the Nevilles, one on his return from Ireland, another preceding his second attack against Somerset, before he undertook any decisive action to seize the crown.[22]

Part 1 shows York's military record somewhat tarnished by his responsibility in Talbot's death. In the opening scene of Part 2, the unhistorical trip to Ireland and his hostility to the French marriage give him a voice among the supporters of the commonweal, but he soon reveals the true motive of his concern for the welfare of the realm: France and Ireland, like England, belong to him by right. Besides, this early meeting with Cade heightens the impression that he has long been scheming and, like a proper Machiavel, waited for the most opportune moment to strike. The second trip to Ireland provides the army he needs to make good his claim, a foresight Hall had not thought to grant him. He is even less determined a pretender in Holinshed, who omits several of Hall's references to the Yorkist underground dealings.[23]

The chroniclers accuse York of deviousness, but if one judges by their accounts, their suspicions must have been retroactive, for his behaviour during those long years was unimpeachable:

his humble submission, his reasonable requestes, and profitable peticions, for the pore commons, wer iudged no pointes of a man, that desired souereignetie, or rule aboue other which thinges he did onely for a cautele, (as afterward openly appeared). (227)

When York ruled the realm as Protector with the Nevilles, even their faultless government earned them but a grudging tribute: 'New Lordes, new lawes: suche lippes, suche lettice. And yet in all their rule, I finde no mencion made, of differyng Iustice, or of their pollyng, or their bribery, as was openly proued by such as gouerned before their tyme'.[24] By all accounts, the historical Duke of York showed little haste in conquering the coveted crown: apparently it was the death of Gloucester in 1447, the twenty-fifth year of the reign, that stirred his ambition by erecting him to the position of heir presumptive in rivalry with the base-born

---

[22] Hall 225, 231 (229, 237).

[23] Holinshed 212, 220, 229, 233, 238. Cf. Hall 210, 219, 225, 227, 231.

[24] Hall 233. Holinshed 233, 243, omits 'cautele', 'lippes', and 'lettice'. See R. A. Griffiths, 'Duke Richard of York's Intentions in 1450 and the Origins of the Wars of the Roses', *Journal of Mediaeval History*, 1 (1975), 187–209.

Beauforts, but York did not make any public claim of his dynastic rights at that stage. His friends did it for him, by stirring up a rebellion in Kent while he was busy pacifying Ireland. York's movements on his return are contracted into one scene of Act V, but took place in fact over a period of several years. He landed in 1450, two months after Cade's defeat, then waited a year and a half to raise an army, which he was naive enough to dismiss, and another five before he actually took arms, perhaps spurred on by the birth of the Prince of Wales, the enmity of the Queen, or the King's mental illness, which must have had greater impact than is inferred by Hall's brief note that 'The kyng at this time was sicke at Clarendon.'[25] Whatever the immediate cause, a full eight years passed between York's secret intent, quite a late one at that, and the deed itself. To these Holinshed adds his humble letter attempting to save the peace, which Somerset and his allies maliciously suppressed—as did Shakespeare.

The chronicler takes a breath after St Albans. The King's army has been dispersed. Buckingham and Wiltshire, 'seyng fortunes loweryng chaunce, left the kyng poste a lone & with a great numbre fled away'. The victorious York who has always claimed to fight for the good of the kingdom abstains from all violence against the King and takes him back to London with all due honours. Parliament rehabilitates the Duke of Gloucester, clears the Yorkists of all charges of rebellion, and names York Protector of the realm. Salisbury is made Chancellor and Keeper of the Great Seal, Warwick becomes Captain of Calais. Between the three of them, the confederates hold all the power:

and so emongst them, it was agreed, that king Henry should still reigne, in name and dignitie, but neither in deed nor in aucthoritee: not myndyng either to depose or destroy thesaid kyng, least they might sodainly prouoke and stirre the fury and ire of the common people against theim. (233)

The two parties observe a watchful truce until 1459, when they take up arms again.

These five eventful years disappear between Parts 2 and 3, leaving *2 Henry VI* with no denouement to speak of. The first and third parts of *Henry VI* end with a fragile peace, but Part 2 does not even mark a pause. Young Clifford's threats announce that personal revenge will soon prevail over the common weal. Instead of taking a disordered flight, the King's followers fall back in good order to regain London and summon Parliament. The Yorkist victory is far from decisive, as Salisbury reminds his party:

Well, lords, we have not got that which we have:
'Tis not enough our foes are this time fled,
Being opposites of such repairing nature.   (v. iii. 20–2)

York must consolidate his advantage, and pursue the King 'ere the writs go forth'. Unlike his historical model, he will not rest until he has gained the crown or met his

---

[25] Hall 230, 232 (*236, 238*). B. P. Wolffe, 'The Personal Rule of Henry VI', in S. B. Chrimes et al. (eds.), *Fifteenth-Century England 1399–1509* (Manchester, 1972), points out that York urged the need to find a way out of this *impasse*, from which the nobility was unable to rescue the kingdom.

death. Even Hall admits that he was a competent Protector, who never attempted anything against the King, although he could easily have disposed of him. Whatever motives York may have harboured, his conduct during those years appears blameless. It was the Queen who harried him with her hostility, and tried by every means to unseat him.

The conclusion of 2 *Henry VI* shows the family of York rushing to London in pursuit of the Lancasters. Parts 2 and 3, linked up by York's resolution, follow one another like Parts 1 and 2, without any break or time gap. At the opening of Part 3, York has failed to overtake the King's party, his son Richard enters carrying the head of Somerset, and York demands the crown, though by historical counts he should wait another five years to put forth his claim. The Parliament following St Albans in 1455, when York contented himself with the title of Protector, is fused with that of 1459, when he expounded his hereditary rights but eventually agreed to let Henry reign for his lifetime.

It appears from the chronicles that the Queen resented York's authority quite as strongly as she had Gloucester's, for similar reasons: Somerset, Buckingham, and others of the King's party pointed out to her 'that it was not honorable, but a reproche and infamy to the Kyng, to haue one to bee a Protecter and gouernor of hym and his Realme', as if he were a child in need of a nurse or a tutor, and 'that the Duke of Yorkes only intent was, vnder the colour of this protectorship, sodainly to destroy & depose the kyng'. Here Holinshed simply notes that, 'perceiuing whereto the courtesy of the duke of Yorke did draw', they consulted with her for a remedy. Whereupon, in both accounts, she called a great council at Greenwich, where the Duke was discharged of his protectorship. This was soon followed by a hunting party at Coventry, 'where were diuers ways studied priuely, to bryng the quene to her hartes ease, and long expectate desire: which was the death & destruccio of the duke of Yorke, the erles of Salisbury and Warwycke'.[26] By making York's progress more resolute and indefensible than in the sources, Shakespeare gives much stronger ground to the chroniclers' suspicions. The seeds sown by the dying Mortimer have matured into a full project, which is signalled by an aside in Act I. The time intervals between York's successive steps to open rebellion, from Kent to Ireland to St Albans, are all erased. His designs take some time in maturing, as in the chronicles, but he begins earlier and is a cleverer opportunist than his model, stirring up one popular revolt, then taking advantage of another to reach for the crown, as Hall's would-be Machiavel never did.

Inversions

The relation of Cade's rising is no less significantly altered by changes in the order of events. Failing other virtues, Hall's Cade seems quite a good tactician; he hides his real plans by sending a petition to the King, simulates a flight that ensures his victory at Sevenoaks, forbids—temporarily—murder, rape, and robbery 'by

---

[26] Hall 234, 236 (243, 245).

whiche colour he allured to hym the hartes of the common people'. He is found 'sober in communicacion, wyse in disputyng' by the King's emissaries, while Hall describes him as 'A certayn yongman of a goodely stature, and pregnaunt wit'. Of this wit, all that remains on stage is a certain gift for cynical banter, for instance, this aside in answer to Lord Stafford's brother:

> *Bro.* Jack Cade, the Duke of York hath taught you this.
> *Cade.* He lies, for I invented it myself.   (IV. ii. 144–5)

Stafford's accusation may have been inspired by a remark in Hall: 'This capitayn not onely suborned by techers, but also enforced by pryuye scholemasters, assembled together a great company.' On stage the King asks whether Cade has been taken or if he made a strategic retreat, the only remaining trace of his dodge. In the narratives, Cade's letter to the King, asking him to dismiss his false counsellors, was sent before, not after, the battle of Sevenoaks; the King's flight to Killingworth anticipated the rebels' arrival in Southwark, not the reverse; and Lord Saye was killed before Matthew Gough. The chroniclers who distrust the rebellious mob have not the least doubt that Cade's 'humble supplicacion' to the King was only devised to hide his real plans. Though Holinshed gives the full text of this complaint, he is hardly less severe than Hall's dismissal of it as full of 'malicious entent'. The two differ slightly about its reception: in Hall 'this proude byll, was both of the kyng, and his counsaill, disdainfully taken', in Holinshed it was 'well perused', both points being made on stage where Henry reads it over twice while the rest of his court ignore it. In both accounts, however, the result is the same: although the Kentishmen have not committed any criminal offence so far, the King's council decides that one must answer these presumptuous rebels by force rather than by fair promises. The King's army find them already fled, and the Queen's company of gentlemen who thought to cut off their retreat are utterly defeated.[27]

From this time onwards, things take a different turn in the play. The Staffords' apostrophe to Cade's troops,

> Rebellious hinds, the filth and scum of Kent,
> Marked for the gallows, lay your weapons down . . .   (IV. ii. 113–14)

betrays as much arrogance as the royal counsellors' in the narrative, but it comes after several hasty executions ordered by Cade, and before any mention of a letter to the King, hypocritical or not. The supplication does arrive, after we have just seen Cade parading in Stafford's armour, determined to march on. There would be little point in his using guile to hide intentions which, by now, must be plain to all. The scene is more credible if one takes the rebels' supplication for what it purports to be, a fearful request from Cade's less hardened recruits, not a crafty attempt by their leader to fool the authorities. On rereading the letter, the King finds that Cade has sworn to take Lord Saye's head, which agrees with Cade's own earlier announcement but would be out of place in a humble suit originating from him. Again, it

---

[27] Hall 220 (221, 224).

makes better sense if this anonymous plea prepares the final reversal of Cade's uneasy followers.

Despite the chroniclers' strong prejudice against the rabble, at least they show some reasons for the people's discontent. It is Shakespeare who erases all extenuating circumstances: the explosion in Kent has no rational motive, no link with the commons' anger at the death of the Protector. Their resentment was found legitimate, and answered with Suffolk's banishment, whereas the Kentishmen's rising is the cold scheme of a nobleman who banks on their potential violence to advance his ambitious designs. The escalation of popular anger thus proceeds by nice degrees from the courteous petitions of Act I to the Commons' less courteous but still justified wrath after their Protector's demise, to the mad demands of Cade's lawless crowds. Shakespeare shows them as an obtuse and cruel mob, and surpasses even the hostile Hall in the staging of their vacillations.

The scenes of bloodletting excesses have a carnivalesque humour devoid of any political justification. The popular revolt has no other fuel than the appetite of the Duke of York, who turns to profit the anarchic leanings of a misgoverned people.[28] Hattaway's attempts to exculpate them from mindless savagery, and Shakespeare from class prejudice, work against the evidence. Richard Wilson's comments on the 'venomous fourth act of 2 *Henry VI*' seem more convincing. He notes the significant change of the rioters from medieval peasants into Renaissance artisans, and brilliantly interprets the play's spinning of textile metaphors by the light of the clothiers' protests in 1592, in which Shakespeare 'aligned himself squarely with the empire and free market in timely opposition to London's small masters'. Wilson bases his argument on Born's theory that Parts 2 and 3 were finished by early August 1592, which to him 'remains unchallenged', despite Ann Patterson's attack.[29] It may be excessive, though, to view Cade's uprising as 'the blue print for all his later crowd scenes'. In *Coriolanus*, if not until then, popular protests and grievances will receive a more sympathetic hearing.

If Shakespeare's rebels appear even blacker than Hall's 'vngracious cōpany', their opponents generally improve on the performance of their models. Thus Lord Saye nobly refuses Henry's offer to go with him, for fear of endangering the King; his trust in his innocence, which recalls Gloucester's, prepares the audience for what is to come. As Treasurer of England, he was most unpopular. The chroniclers do not dwell on his execution by the mob, which serves primarily to illustrate Cade's cruelty, and save their concern for the wasteful death of the war hero Matthew Gough. But the order and importance of these two episodes are reversed in the play. We saw earlier how Matthew Gough was shown out in one terse stage direction. The death of Lord Saye, the last on a list of senseless crimes, occupies a whole scene,

---

[28] IV. ix. 8–9. Hall 220–2. Holinshed 220–7 gives more details, plus the full texts of Cade's bill and the royal proclamation.

[29] Hattaway, 'Rebellion, Class Consciousness, and Shakespeare's 2 *Henry VI*', *Cahiers élisabéthains*, 33 (1988), 13–22. Wilson, *Will Power: Essays on Shakespearean Authority* (New York, 1993), 26–34. R. H. Born, 'The Date of 2 *Henry VI*', *SQ* 25 (1974), 323–34. Ann Patterson, *Shakespeare and the Popular Voice* (Oxford, 1989), 34–7.

heightened in pathos by his plea, 'These cheeks are pale with watching for your good,' the echo of Gloucester's,

> So help me God, as I have watched the night
> Ay, night by night, in studying good for England!   (III. i. 110–11)

which moves even his executioner to remorse.

In both Lord Saye's and Gloucester's case, the expansion of source material contrasts with the various techniques of abbreviation we have just examined. The chroniclers deal in one page with the sad fate of Duke Humphrey, which takes three acts to develop on stage, while York's plans slowly mature at the back. During this long prelude, the action marks time with indications absent from the narratives: Horner's duel will be fought at the end of next month, York's dinner party is planned for 'tomorrow night', the King will leave for London the day after the hunt, and summon his Parliament the following month. It appears from the news brought in Parliament that the eighteen-month truce with France announced in Act I is over. York, on his way to Ireland, awaits his soldiers at Bristol within a fortnight.

Then the tempo accelerates, and events happen all at once. Suffolk is given three days to leave the kingdom; his accomplice dies, and Kent is up in arms, before he attempts to sail. The length of Cade's rule remains unspecified. He keeps in hiding for five days before he is killed. Just as his head is brought into court, York enters, pretending he came back to fight the rebels, only to defy the King and claim the crown for himself moments later. Gloucester's death is the turning point between the slow incubation period and the eruptive phase.

3. PIECING OUT FACTS

Town and country

The action in Part 1 constantly crosses the Channel, a motion driven by the central theme—losses abroad caused by division at home. In Hall's chronicle, this to and fro motion persists after the King's wedding, whereas the action of 2 *Henry VI* remains in England, alternating between unspecified and precise locations. The scenes introduced by flourishes of trumpets, like those treating of state affairs, presumably take place within the palace precincts. Others of a more domestic nature suggest the home of a protagonist, or his garden. The conjuring scene where Mother Jourdain is told to 'grovel on the earth' is placed 'in an Orchard' by the Q text, which directs the Duchess 'vp to the Tower'; F simply sends her 'aloft'.

From these conjuring tricks we move on to St Albans, as dialogue and directions repeatedly inform us, for a hunt where Duke Humphrey catches a petty rogue before discovering he is cast as the main quarry. The scene draws on two different events: a hunting episode which took place several years later in Coventry, and Gloucester's exposure of a bogus blind man at St Albans. This story, originally told by Thomas More, is reported in the 'Book of Martyrs'.[30] Foxe's location of the fake miracle in St Albans adds dramatic weight to the occasion. The name of the saint is invoked many times as caution for a false prodigy before it is involved in the still more dubious cause of the civil war. We return to London after the hunt, to the privacy of York's garden, for his genealogical conference with his friends, then to a place which harbours diverse forms of justice, the Duchess's trial and the ordeal of the armourer's servant. The Duchess is condemned to do open penance in the streets of London, and there bids farewell to her husband, just as he receives his summons to the Parliament of Bury St Edmunds.

Act III stages the arrest of Gloucester, soon followed by his murder, in Bury historically, on stage or off depending on the didascalias of Q or F, though both versions meet on the discovery of his body in bed behind curtains. Winchester's body is shown moments later, possibly in the same bed and behind the same curtains as that of his victim, the same props anyway, which link the two deaths even more effectively by this simple device. The air is purged by a waft of sea breeze from the next Folio direction, '*Alarum. Fight at sea. Ordnance goes off,*' which Q interprets more modestly as '*Alarums within, and the chambers be discharged, like as it were a fight at sea,*' located by the dialogue in the Downs.

Cade's rising takes us through Kent all the way to Blackheath, Southwark, and several raids on London in the wake of his rebel troops, ending in a confused fight for the possession of London Bridge and their surrender in Southwark. Their progress in the play suppresses all the waverings, retreats, or long cuts of Cade's original itinerary. They take the direction of London, but their position on the map remains undefined until we learn that they have reached Southwark; the only locations are of the various places these characters come from, 'the tanner of Wingham', 'the clerk of Chartham', 'the butcher of Ashford', craftsmen all, practising in the vicinity of Canterbury. 'The filth and scum of Kent' swiftly eliminate the Staffords in an indeterminate area, and proceed towards the capital.

The news of Cade's arrival in Southwark sends the King off to Killingworth, and Matthew Gough to Smithfield for a fatal encounter with the rebels. Cade, who is master of the city, orders raids against London Bridge, the Tower, the Savoy, and the Inns of Court, then gives commands to strike off the heads of Lord Saye and his son-in-law, which the Q text decorates with two geographical references found in the chronicles, the Standard in Cheapside and Mile-end Green. A retreat and a parley are sounded while Cade directs his troops 'Up Fish Street! down Saint Magnus' Corner!', which would place them north of London Bridge, though a few lines later he upbraids them for leaving him stranded 'at the White Hart in Southwark'. Editors who attempt to locate these scenes have difficulties reconciling the indications of the dialogue with the chronicles. The routing of Matthew Gough did not give a clear victory to the rebels, who met with the citizens' resistance:

---

[30] The anecdote, told in More's *Dyaloge . . . on the veneracyon and worshyp of ymages and relyques,* I. xiv. 25, inspired both Grafton's *Chronicle at Large* and Foxe's *Actes.*

for some tyme the Lōdoners were bet back to the stulpes at sainct Magnes corner, and sodaynly agayne the rebelles were repulsed and driuen backe, to the stulpes in Southwarke, so that both partes, beyng faynte, wery and fatigate, agreed to desist from fight, and to leue battail til the next day, vpon condicion: that neither Londoners should passe into Southwarke, nor the Kentishmē in to London.[31]

If the Elizabethan imagination could accept 'Rome and Alexandria on the same stage', Ronald Knowles argues, then 'perhaps the breadth of the Thames hardly matters'. But in this particular case, the side on which they stand changes the face of the battle: north they win, south they lose. Whatever the audience could accept, the fighting area was literally round the corner from the theatre. The only other scene in the whole sequence so to defy topography is that of the parallel tents on Bosworth field, where the supernatural interferes as it does not in Cade's progress.

There is no easy way out of this deadlock. Either we must infer that Cade recalls the glorious beginning of their epic at Southwark to urge his troops on, or we must piece out the missing phases of the fight ourselves. Frustratingly, the concise stage directions leave room for doubt. It is clear from neither whether Cade's men beat a retreat. When Cade cries out: 'Dare any be so bold to sound retreat or parley, when I command them kill?', it is in answer to a request of the royal emissaries. In fact the suggestion comes from the chronicle. In Hall, the rebels are exhausted after a night of indecisive fighting, and they surrender with relief to the offer of a pardon. On stage, Cade has just ordered his men to wait for the night before they sack the city. Here the Folio notes an '*Exeunt*', but the Quarto allows no break between this command and the next: 'Up Fish Street!'[32] If we take the dialogue on trust without appealing to external data, Cade's men, far from being half-beaten and scared, have taken possession of the city. In the two chronicles, they return home without demanding their pay, for they are in no position to dictate terms. There is no basis for their double turn-about on stage, where they acclaim the King, then Cade, then once again the King after each speech.

Cade's last-ditch move after this inconclusive battle was to break open the King's jails with the hope of making fresh recruits—a brilliant plan that comes to him much earlier in the play—but all in vain because his company, somewhat subdued after their beating back, gladly gave in to the offer of a general pardon:

Lorde how glad the poore people were of this Pardone (ye more then of the great Iubile of Rome) and how thei acepted thesame, in so muche that the whole multitude, without biddyng farewel to their capitain, retired thesame night, euery man to his awne home, as men amased, and strikē with feare. (222)

Cade's flight to Sussex ended in a garden, where Alexander Iden found and killed him. Holinshed, who calls the squire Eden, adds to Hall's account that Cade was slain 'at Hothfield' and brought to London 'in a cart'. On stage, Iden kills the rebel in his own peaceful plot and leaves the body to the crows, bringing the severed head

---

[31] Hall 222 (225–6). Bullough 97. Knowles, n. iv. viii. John Dover Wilson located the scene north of the Thames, and Cairncross south, following Theobald.

[32] Knowles puts a scene break at SD iv. vii. 128, and has Cade re-enter at iv. viii. 1.

to London. He arrives there just as York appoints his army of Irishmen to meet him the following day in St George's Field, an open space near Southwark not mentioned in the sources, though the ensuing fight with the royal party is located at St Albans, as in the sources. The play ends with the Yorkists' victory, and their declared intention to march against London.

The characters' constant movement gives impetus to the action. Not all the places they visit are named, but the dialogue mentions enough of those to broaden the scope. Some of the locations are precise—Killingworth, the Downs—others remain vague, like Kent, or the roads to London. These place names are used to various dramatic effects. Ireland and France, though never shown, are often bitterly evoked by the characters. The names of Anjou and Maine return obsessively; Maine especially rings a bitter psalmody of puns. Some English names are also repeated insistently: those associated with famous historical events, bloody ones usually, are sounded with ominous echoes long before the event actually takes place, like St Albans. Others, less notorious, add a touch of local colour, as for instance in the scenes of Cade's rebellion: the names of Kentish towns, Wingham, Chartham, or areas of London, Pissing Conduit, Fish Street, contribute to a vivid image of popular crowds swarming in from the surrounding countryside to infiltrate every last corner of the town.

Shreds and patches

In a number of cases where Shakespeare closely follows Hall's plot, he has to reconstruct events from fragments scattered over large sections of the chronicles, but he also at times makes a new whole out of independent elements collected at random. Thus, at the beginning of the play, Gloucester bitterly laments the unfortunate marriage of his nephew. To give substance to his bitterness, Shakespeare gleans from various parts of the chronicle:

- The Duke's objections during the bargaining at Tours—'Humfrey duke of Gloucester, Protector of the realme, repugned and resisted as muche as in him laie, this new alliaunce and contriued matrimonie,' says Hall, while to Holinshed, he 'was much against it'.
- The people's hostility—'This marriage semed to many, bothe infortunate, and vnprofitable to the realme of England' and their complaint that 'for the fetchyng of her, the Marques of Suffolke, demaunded a whole fiftene'.
- Divine displeasure—'But moste of all it should seme, that God with this matrimony was not content', as appeared from the catastrophes which followed the wedding up to the deposition of the King.
- Hall's funeral eulogy of Henry V—'No colde made him slouthfull, nor heat caused him to loyter,' which is echoed on stage by the memory of his difficult campaigns, 'In the winter's cold, and summer's parching heat'.
- His sarcastic comments on Reignier's legendary poverty.[33]

[33] I. i. 78. Hall 204–5, 112 (*207, 208*).

Shakespeare uses a similar technique for the first concerted assault against Gloucester, collecting and redistributing the accusations among the plotters. The attack is launched by the Queen, as in Hall: 'And although this inuēciō came first of her awne high mind, and ambicious corage, yet it was furthered and set forward by suche, as of long tyme had borne malice to the duke', and pursued by Gloucester's enemies, the conspirators enumerated by Hall minus the Archbishop of York, who is replaced by Somerset. As to the accusations raised against him—various extortions and misuse of public money—the conspirators did advise the Queen to examine the Protector's accounts, for 'she should euidently peceiue, that the Duke of Gloucester, had not so muche aduaunced & preferred the commō wealth and publique vtilitie, as his awne priuate thinges and peculier estate'. They also accused him of disregarding the law, though his alleged fault was a lack of severity, whereas, in the play, Buckingham charges him with 'cruelty in execution'.[34]

Other reproaches addressed to Gloucester on stage appear in various places in the chronicle, but, in the majority of cases, concern the accusers themselves, Suffolk first, who in Hall 'ruled the Kyng at his pleasure', and whom the Commons accused of having helped the French King to reconquer his realm:[35]

> Since thou wert king—as who is king but thou? -
> The commonwealth hath daily run to wrack,
> The Dauphin hath prevailed beyond the seas . . .   (I. iii. 125–6)

Winchester's charge,

> The commons hast thou racked; the clergy's bags
> Are lank and lean with thy extortions . . .   (I. iii. 129–30)

is precisely the way he made his own fortune: 'Of the getting of this mannes goodes both by power, legantye or spirituall bryberie I will not speake.' Having obtained a cardinal's hat 'to his greate profite, and to the empouerishyng of the spiritualitie', he 'gathered so much treasure, that no man in maner had money but he, and so was surnamed the riche Cardinall of Winchester'. The Queen's accusation, 'Thy sale of offices and towns of France', should probably also be put down to Winchester's account. A few years before, Gloucester's list of twenty-four offences included the sale of charges to the highest bidder, in England as well as in France. Next and last, Somerset accuses him of living sumptuously off the public treasury, where rumour had it that Somerset lost Normandy because he only kept half of the soldiers assigned to him and pocketed the pay of the rest. Thus the various marks of hostility towards Gloucester all combine to build up the case for the prosecution; even the popular rumours circulating against his enemies in the narrative become his imaginary faults on stage. It is immaterial whether these slanders carry weight: as Hall says, though the Duke defended himself well against the attacks of his enemies, 'yet because his death was determined, his wisdom little helped, nor his truth smally auailed'.[36]

---

[34] Hall 208–9. 2H6, I. iii. 133.
[35] Hall 207, 217–18 (209, 218–19). Cf. 1H6, v. v. 107–8.
[36] I. iii. 131–2. Hall 211, 139, 201, 216, 209 (212, 156, 203, 218, 211).

The entrance of the indignant Commons at Act III has been prepared by the preceding scene. The Cardinal wants some legal justification for Gloucester's death, but Suffolk points out to him the risks of a court trial: the King may try to spare him or 'The commons haply rise to save his life', which agrees with Hall's narrative: 'But his capitall enemies and mortal foes, fearyng that some tumulte or commocion might arise, if a prince so well beloued of the people, should bee openly executed, and put to death, determined to trappe & vndoo hym'. There was no disorder following the assassination of the Duke, apparently, but some loudly voiced discontent. Gloucester's servants, at first condemned to death like Duncan's in *Macbeth*, were grandly pardoned by Suffolk, 'but this doyng appeased not the grudge of the people, whiche saied that the pardone of the seruauntes, was no amendes for murderyng of their master'. The discontent persists, if Hall is to be believed, and finally erupts three years later, causing the fall of Suffolk. For the numerous charges made by the Commons, Shakespeare substitutes the popular one of being 'the chief procurer of the death of the good duke of Gloucester', but suppresses Suffolk's arrest and quick release, which caused their burst of anger. After the entrance of the Commons, the body of Gloucester is exposed on stage, as in Hall's narrative: 'The duke the night after his emprisonement, was found dedde in his bed, and his body shewed to the lordes and commons.' The cause of his death remained unknown, Hall writes, though no one doubted that it was murder, possibly by strangling. It is also Warwick's diagnosis in the play, after a lengthy description of the stigmata found on the body.[37]

In the chronicle the King only banishes Suffolk under pressure from the Commons, reported with a reproving tone as 'the furye of the mutable commons', 'the continual clamor of the importunate cōmons', 'the furious rage of yͤ outragious people', and it is decided to recall him as soon as they have calmed down.[38] These harsh judgements on the populace do not imply any sympathy for Suffolk, whom Hall plainly holds in even lower esteem. When on stage Salisbury makes himself the spokesman of the commons, his speech is inspired by their reaction after Suffolk's release: 'it was a shame to all the Realme, to se such a persone, infected with so many misdedes, either to rule about a prince or be had in honor.' In the play, Henry VI echoes Hall's 'infected' with his pronouncement, 'He shall not breathe infection in the air', and is easily convinced by Salisbury that the Commons' sole concern is to protect him from the serpentine Suffolk, since he shares their opinion. It is left to Suffolk to mock the elegance of Salisbury's report and accuse him of demagogy, a trace of Hall's repeated allusions to the Yorkists' courting of popular favour. And in truth the brutal invasion of the Commons, 'An answer from the King or we will all break in!' appears to deserve Suffolk's scorn for the 'rude unpolished hinds', more than Salisbury's oblique praise.[39] The popular delegation, halfway between these

[37] III. ii. 160–78. Hall 209, 217, 218 (*211, 218, 220*). See Samuel M. Pratt, 'Shakespeare and Humprey Duke of Gloucester: A Study of Myth', *SQ* 16 (1965), 201–16.

[38] Hall 218, 219, which Holinshed 220 sums up as 'the peoples furie'. To Hattaway, introd. 24, their 'furious rage' is legitimately directed against those responsible for the loss of Anjou, but his reading of 'outrageous' as '[i.e. outraged]' is not supported by the general tenor of Hall's comments.

[39] III. ii. 241–88. Hall 218, 219.

representations, puts in dialectical perspective two opposite views of their virtues and vices, just as ethics waver at all levels of the social scale.

To institute proceedings against Suffolk, Shakespeare draws on several appearances of the character in the chronicle, and invents a Lieutenant-prosecutor to collect the articles of impeachment, but still follows Hall's narrative on the circumstances of the execution. After the royal marriage, Suffolk, 'somewhat infected with the sede of vainglory', gave a long speech in the House of Commons 'omittyng nothyng, that might sounde to his glory, nor openyng any thyng, whiche might redound to his dispraise', features recalled in the arrogance of the dramatic character. His self-proclaimed merits—'This hand of mine hath writ in thy behalf'—are no less spurious, as the petitioners of Act I could testify.

The Lieutenant's indictment of Suffolk combines the Commons' charges, the rumours that were rife at the time of his fall, and the report of his earlier role in the negotiations at Tours, plus a few extra touches absent from the chronicle. The first reproach, 'swallowing the treasure of the realm', fits the popular opinion of him as 'the moste swallower vp and consumer of the kynges treasure'. The second, 'Thy lips that kissed the Queen', echoes rumours of his liaison with Margaret, and 'emong the commonaltie, disdain of lasciuious souereigntie whiche the Queene with her minions, and vnprofitable counsailers daily toke and vsurped vpō them'. There is more than enough in Hall to substantiate the Queen's misconduct, for instance the gossip he reports at the time of the birth of the Prince of Wales:

> whose mother susteyned not a little slaunder and obloquye of the commō people, saiyng that the kyng was not able to get a chyld, and that this was not his sonne, with many slaunderous woordes, to the quenes dishonor, whiche here nede not to be rehersed. (230–1)

A model of preterition.[40]

Suffolk, long since dead, could not be the guilty one in this instance, but the rumours specifically attached to him, with Hall's strictures, all find their way into the mouth of the Lieutenant. One grievance at least is original: 'By devilish policy art thou grown great.' In the chronicle Suffolk owes his ascension solely to royal favour. Like the Lieutenant, the chroniclers impute to him the loss of Anjou and Maine. He is also held responsible, twice over, for the loss of Normandy. The Lieutenant does not explain how, but Hall does: indirectly because the French cities revolted on learning of Gloucester's death, and directly because Suffolk so racked the English that they were burdened with domestic worries, 'by reason whereof men of warre were vnpayed, and no armye for resistēce was either gathered or assēbled together'. Shakespeare does not take up Hall's leitmotiv on the causes of the revolt in France, and omits a large number of the Commons' charges, for instance that of conspiring with the enemy, but adds an uprising in Picardy for good measure: Suffolk has a share in all the evils that afflict England, the cumulative effect taking precedence dramatically over the establishment of his guilt. The reproach of thrusting aside good counsellors to promote evil men, enemies of the public good, has just been demonstrated with the murder of the last good counsellor.

[40] IV. i. 74, 75. Hall 206, 217, 230–1 (206, 218, 236).

Other scenes likewise connect elements unrelated in the chronicle. The tale of the Duchess's disgrace is combined with a vague prophecy about Somerset, reported years later, at the time of St Albans—two totally independent episodes.[41] The chronicles mention no other prophecies, nor any link between the different destinies announced on stage to the Duchess. Gloucester's enemies take advantage of a hunting party, probably suggested by a 'Hawking and Huntynge' which took place at Coventry, ten years after his death.[42] The setting is different—St Albans, where Foxe locates the false miracle—and so is their motive: in the chronicle the Queen hopes to destroy York and the Nevilles, and uses this pretext to lure them out of London. Yet in both texts the hunters pursue human game rather than the ostensible prey of the outing. The combination of two separate events and the references to St Albans, which will harbour the first battle of the civil war, link up the play's two major themes.

After Gloucester's assassination, Margaret interrupts the King's laments with memories of the tempest that nearly prevented her landing in England:

> Was I for this nigh wrecked upon the sea
> And twice by awkward wind from England's bank
> Drove back again unto my native clime?   (III. ii. 82–4)

In the chronicle, she faces a similar tempest much later, under the reign of Edward IV, when she tries to return after seeking the help of the French King:

> but the Wynter was so sore, the wether so stormie, and the wynde so contrariant, that she was fain to take land again, and defer her iorney till another season. Her enemies saied, that it was Goddes iuste prouision, that she whiche had been the occasion of so many battailes, and of so much manslaughter in Englande, should neuer returne thether again, to doo more mischief. Her friendes on the otherside, said, that she was kept awaie, and her iorney empeched by Sorcerers and Necromancers: (286–7)

'thus as mennes immaginacions ranne, their toungues clacked', Hall disdainfully concludes, borrowing his examples of conflicting interpretations and his mockery of sign readers from the French chronicler Commynes.[43] The theatrical character, like the chorus of rumours in Hall, finds a providential explanation to the unleashing of natural forces: the wind warned her to flee this unkind shore but she cursed the gentle gusts, and sacrificed to the waves, as a propitiatory offering, a heart-shaped diamond. Although occurring in different contexts, the two tempests merge in opposing the Queen's wishes, and summoning obscure forces against human destinies.

---

[41] Hall 202, 233 *(204, 240)*. *2H6*, I. iv. 33–7.

[42] Hall 236 *(245)*.

[43] Hall 286–7. *Memoirs of Philippe de Commynes*, ed. Samuel Kinser, trans. Isabelle Cazeaux (Columbia, SC, 1973), IV. x. 283. Holinshed 302 records the storm up to 'season', and omits the interpretations.

Beasts of England

The dramatic text often provides an unexpected sequel to a minor anecdote, or elaborates a network of images from a single word. Touching the hunt at St Albans, the term 'hawkyng', supplied by the chroniclers, starts a string of metaphors which punctuates the unfolding of Gloucester's fall. It is Suffolk who sets it off in revealing to the Queen the trap set for the Duchess:

> Madam, myself have limed a bush for her,
> And placed a choir of such enticing birds
> That she will light to listen to their lays
> And never mount to trouble you again.   (I. iii. 89–2)

At the hunt, the image of the hawk's imperial rise gives an opening for the charges of ambition directed against the Protector, whose emblem was a hawk. Gloucester's glory reaches its summit with the exposure of the bogus blind man, and soon falls again with the announcement that the Duchess stands accused of treason: fortune's wheel has turned full circle for him. His enemies will not rest

> Till they have snared the shepherd of the flock,
> That virtuous prince, the good Duke Humprey . . .   (II. ii. 73–4)

where the term 'snared' spins the metaphor of the bird caught in birdlime. The Duchess, now captive, warns her husband that the same fate awaits him: Suffolk, York, and Beaufort

> Have all limed bushes to betray thy wings;
> And fly thou how thou canst, they'll tangle thee.
> But fear not thou until thy foot be snared. . . .   (II. iv. 54– 6)

Once the bird is caught, the animal images multiply, some of them drawn from Hall, who calls the Duke's enemies 'venemous serpentes, and malicious Tygers'. Holinshed's more sober narrative omits or abridges most of his similes, as well as the moral saws they suggest, though he often compensates with original ones of that ilk. The Queen borrows Hall's image of discord, 'thys cācard crocodryle and subtile serpēt', to declare Humphrey as false 'as the mournful crocodile . . . Or as the snake', where Holinshed replaces the reptiles by 'goodlie apples corrupted at core' and 'rotten walles new plastered without'.[44]

Shakespeare's characters crush Gloucester under metaphors—deceitful fox, raven decked in the plumes of the dove, wolf in a lamb's skin—firing back the images used by the King in defence of the innocent lamb or harmless dove. Animal names are tossed back and forth; hunter and prey, protector and predator exchange places as each speaker casts himself in the role of innocent victim and aims to unmask his opponent. It is in vain that Gloucester denounces the deceivers:

> Thus is the shepherd beaten from thy side,
> And wolves are gnarling who shall gnaw thee first.   (III. i. 191–2)

---

[44] III. i. 226–8. Hall 208, 239. Holinshed 249. See James L. Calderwood, 'Shakespeare's Evolving Imagery in 2 *Henry VI*', *English Studies*, 53 (1972).

The King, though dismally unfit for the role of keeper, now sees his uncle as the calf led to the slaughter-house, and himself as the doe weeping the loss of her fawn. The conspirators retort with a new batch of wild game, and bind up the two series of images with a double meaning: the wild beast in a shepherd's hide, the bird of prey caught in the trap. Eagle, vulture, fox, he must be destroyed 'by gins, by snares'. As elsewhere in the play, they unwittingly give us a glance of the future:

> Weren't not all one an empty eagle were set
> To guard the chicken from a hungry kite,
> As place Duke Humprey for the King's Protector? (III. i. 248–50)

A clear indication of what the King's new protectors have in store for him.

After Gloucester's death, the animal images are thrown back to their proper recipients who catch them on the bounce. Now it is the King who accuses the murderers: Suffolk, the crow disguised as wren, snake, basilisk. Margaret counter-attacks:

> What? art thou, like the adder, waxen deaf?
> Be poisonous too and kill thy forlorn Queen. (III. ii. 76–7)

Yet the wind had warned her when she tried to land: 'Seek not a scorpion's nest.' Against his enemies, the reptilian Suffolk conjures up 'murdering basilisks', 'lizards' stings', 'the serpent's hiss', 'And boding screech-owls'. Neither is aware of a truth that surpasses them in their hypocritical postures. In his delirium, the Cardinal is haunted by the memory of his victim:

> Comb down his hair; look, look, it stands upright
> Like lime-twigs set to catch my winged soul! (III. iii. 15–16)

The circle of metamorphoses comes to a close with this image of the hunter's soul as the bird limed and barred from Heaven. The Cardinal's delirious vision unveils the trap that Gloucester's enemies have set for themselves.

Through the play of images, Gloucester's death releases disorder at all levels. After their skirmish with the royal troops, Cade congratulates one of his recruits, butcher by trade: 'They fell before thee like sheep and oxen, and thou behaved'st thyself as if thou hadst been in thine own slaughter-house.' The literal and metaphorical meanings merge, recalling Gloucester's arrest, dragged like a calf 'to the bloody slaughter-house'. York's fit of anger picks up the thread of images, fulfilling the Protector's anxiety for the flock deprived of its shepherd:

> And now, like Ajax Telamonius,
> On sheep or oxen could I spend my fury. (v. i. 26–7)

Gloucester's death, the first to occur in the play, opens a series of violent executions. Four heads thus make their appearance on stage as a result of four beheadings reported by the chronicle. When Suffolk's head is brought to the Queen, two other characters are threatened with a similar fate:

> *King.* Lord Saye, Jack Cade hath sworn to have thy head.
> *Saye.* Ay, but I hope your highness shall have his. (IV. iv. 18–19)

A double wish that will be promptly fulfilled, as both heads fall before the end of the act. Before losing his own, Cade, as in Hall, parades the heads of Lord Saye and his son-in-law, Sir James Cromer, in the streets of London. Those of Suffolk and Cade, after being cut off as the chronicle prescribes, suffer unwarranted adventures. The 'capitayne' who captured Suffolk 'caused his head to be stryken of, and left his body with the head vpon the sandes of Douer', to be later discovered and buried by Suffolk's chaplain. On stage, Q and F differ slightly, but in both cases the Queen is in possession of the head at Act IV.[45] Concerning Cade's remains, Hall reports that Alexander Iden 'brought his ded body to London, whose hed was set on London bridge', whereas in Shakespeare's version, it is now the King's turn to receive this macabre present.

The unforeseen appearance of the two heads creates telling contrapuntal effects. In the first case, Margaret's laments alternate with Henry's more altruistic concerns, until he gently points out to her the unseemliness of her tears. While the helpless King worries over the salvation of souls, the Queen has only vengeance in mind, recalling not only her guilty affection for Suffolk, but also their recent disdain for the people's petitions. The gift of Cade's head fulfils a similar function but of converse meaning. Framed by the confrontation between York and the King, this episode makes a last incongruous show of chivalry and degree before the civil war takes over. The contrast is amply prepared for by the preceding scene, which develops the few details provided by the chronicle: Cade fled and hid in Sussex, where he was hotly pursued because of the reward promised to whoever caught him, 'til one Alexander Iden, esquire of Kent found hym in a garden, and there, in his defence, manfully slewe the caitife Cade'. Shakespeare sends him to Kent, and ends the hunt in Iden's personal garden, an ideal plot in the disordered kingdom:

> Lord, who would live turmoiled in the court
> And may enjoy such quiet walks as these?   (IV. x. 16–17)

In Holinshed, this 'gentleman of Kent named Alexander Eden awaited so his time that he tooke thesaid Cade in a garden', and slew him without further ado. To Hall's praise of the country squire—he killed Cade 'manfully' in self-defence—Shakespeare adds further qualities fast disappearing from the landscape: proud of his paternal heritage, deprived of ambition or envy, satisfied with his lot, generous to the poor, and loyal to the Crown.

Iden rules over 'a monarchy', 'my state', as will the sagacious gardeners of Richard II.[46] His arrival at court follows York's pretence that he took arms to oust Somerset and fight the rebel Cade. York has dispersed his army on assurance that Somerset was held prisoner, so the audience are prepared for his angry outburst when he sees Somerset lording it as ever, but Shakespeare suspends the scene to confront the noble rebel with the loyal squire, an emblem of allegiance in the heart of the revolt. The contrast is reinforced by York's show of loyalty:

---

[45] Hall 219 (220). 2H6, IV. i. 144–9; SD. IV. iv. 1. He is called 'Lieutenant' in the speech-headings, but addressed as Captain by Whitmore, IV. i. 65.

[46] Hall 222. Holinshed 227. The Queen's garden in 2H6 (III. i. 31–3, 88–90) is already threatened by weeds and caterpillars.

> In all submission and humility
> York doth present himself unto your highness   (v. i. 58–9)

To the reward announced by Hall, Shakespeare adds a knighthood which is straightaway given to Iden on stage. As in the ceremonies of *1 Henry VI*, the much flouted code is briefly evoked at the height of insurrection.

Signs and portents

It is Gloucester who first harps on the *de casibus* theme in his reprimand to his wife,

> And wilt thou still be hammering treachery
> To tumble down thy husband and thyself
> From top of honour to disgrace's feet?   (I. ii. 47–9)

before he has the same warning delivered to himself via the flight of his hawk at St Albans. The Protector's fall leads Hall to ponder the uncertainty of fate:

So all men maie openly se that to men in aucthoritie, no place no not the courte the cheif refuge of all, nor the dwellyng house, nor yet a mannes priuate Castle, or his bed ordeined for his quietnes, is out of daungier of deathes dart. (209)

So does the Queen's marriage, and its disastrous consequences: the King deposed, her son killed, she will leave as wretched as she arrived glorious, 'suche is worldly vnstablenes, and so waueryng is false flattering fortune'. As to the honours bestowed upon Suffolk, he lost them within four years: 'Here a man maie beholde, what securitie is in worldly glory, and what constancie is in fortunes smilyng.' Yet he might have escaped his fate, 'if he had remembred the counsail of the popyngay, saiyng: when thou thynkest thy self in courte moste surest, then is it high tyme to get thee home to rest.'

In the *Mirror*, the story of Suffolk is a warning to princes 'to abhorre untroth', for, the author concludes,

> Was never prince that other did oppresse
> Unrighteously, but died in distresse.   (xi. 181–2)

In the play, the comparison between past fortune and present misery creates various dramatic effects other than moral lessons. When Suffolk recalls his former glory, it is without remorse or reflections on fortune's uncertainty, but with a haughtiness meant to crush the commoner who dares lift his hand against him. Gloucester, when arrested, is still more concerned with politics and the future of the kingdom than with philosophy; for Margaret, the gap between yesterday and today will be nourishment for her curses. On stage, the movement of fortune inspires revolt more often than soul-searching and repentance.

With these meditations on the vagaries of fortune, Hall leaps ahead in time to link distant effects with initial causes, foretell the outcome of an episode at the onset, or create suspense by promising unexpected developments. 'As the experience afterward did declare', 'as you shall hereafter bothe lament and heare', 'as you shall here after heare', 'as in the sequele of this story, you shall more plainly perceyue' are frequent devices, used to stimulate the curiosity of his readers, edify them with moral teachings, or outline a process in the course of events.[47] His reflection on the movement of history usually carries a moral, as with the long-term effects of discord between the King's allies, 'Whiche facte engendered suche a flame, that it neuer wente oute, till bothe the parties with many other were consumed and slain, to the great vnquietnes of the kyng and his realme'. The hostility between York and Somerset proved no less harmful:

This cancard malice, and pestiferous diuision, so long continued, in the hartes of these twoo princes, till mortall warre consumed theim bothe, and almoste all their lynes and ofsprynges, as within few yeres you shall perceiue and se. (179)

Anticipation plays a major role in the dramatic structure of *2 Henry VI*, mainly through prophetic visions. The misfortunes in store are preceded by dark forebodings. Each character involved foresees part of what is to come. Gloucester, the Duchess, Buckingham, York all turn prophetic. Even the King, a new Epimetheus, at the moment of banishing Suffolk, has a premonition of impending disaster:

For sure, my thoughts do hourly prophesy
Mischance unto my state by Suffolk's means. (III. ii. 283–4)

These sombre feelings follow Hall's anticipations fairly closely. The tragic destinies of all the characters concerned are prepared for well in advance, in both chronicle and play.

On stage, the future is unveiled as through a glass, darkly, by misleading dreams or sibylline predictions, admitting several interpretations that the would-be diviners usually ignore. The irony reaches its peak when they turn prophets in spite of themselves. Gloucester concludes his last judgement with the words 'This is the law, and this Duke Humprey's doom'. The irony is even more sinister when he parries his enemies' attacks with the complaint that 'Virtue is choked with foul ambition', an apt picture of his impending death by strangulation.

Dreams and forebodings share the same dangerous ambiguity. The only prophecy in the chronicles retroactively touches the death 'vnder the signe of the Castle' of Somerset, 'who long before was warned to eschew all Castles'. Shakespeare invents the others, as well as Gloucester's dream, to link the destinies of Lancaster. Gloucester sees in his sleep the heads of Suffolk and Somerset fixed on the broken pieces of his Protector's staff: a vision which announces at one and the same time the fate of the three men, the entrance on stage of the two heads later in the play, and those that will be paraded on Jack Cade's pikes. With Somerset's decapitation, unhistorically charged to his account, the young Richard is from his first entrance the executant of a fate prophesied to his victim. Duke Humphrey does not understand the meaning of his nightmare, which Eleanor interprets correctly— those who attack the Protector will lose their heads for it, as the future will confirm—but incompletely: they will first succeed in destroying him. Her own

---

[47] Hall 210, 213 (212, 215), 204 (not in Holinshed 207).

dream is the only one that finds no sort of accomplishment, a fact so rare in the canon that she can be thought to have invented it, as a guarantee given from above to her ambitions. Her husband does not lend credence to her story that she saw herself crowned at Westminster, the King and Queen kneeling before her.

The prophecies of the conjured spirit are even more cryptic than the premonitory dreams. No matter how dubious the sorcerer, the spirit he raises speaks the truth, which the victim discovers only when the prediction is fulfilled. Suffolk dies 'by water', doubly so, by the sea and by the hand of Walter Whitmore. By naming himself, his adversary tears away the veil: 'Thy name affrights me, in whose sound is death.' As for Somerset, 'castles mounted' suggested a castle on high but he dies bathetically under the sign of an inn, 'The Castle in Saint Albans'.[48] Each character hastens to read the destiny of the others but fails to decipher his own future. The spirit's contorted syntax—'The Duke yet lives that Henry shall depose; I But him outlive and die a violent death'—receives two interpretations: the Duchess understands one, that seems to comply with her wishes; York detects a double meaning, the death of the King after that of Gloucester, and misses the third: he will depose Henry but die before him. Only the public perceives the dramatic irony and the triple fate of Gloucester, the King, and York himself in this hermetic formulation.

Gloucester's death is the pivotal point in the play's system of anticipations. It is preceded by a number of signs and ill omens. This prophetic vein ends with his death, as the promised future comes into being. His own sombre intuitions also have a double meaning:

> But mine is made the prologue to their play;
> For thousands more that yet suspect no peril
> Will not conclude their plotted tragedy.   (III. i. 151–3)

Here the theatrical metaphor stresses the vanity of human efforts against the flow of history; the historical matter of the plot enables the audience to decipher the messages from beyond, and savour the ironies of fate.[49] As in the chronicle, the hermeticism of the oracle combines with the Christian view of God's mysterious ways. Divine will and Fortune's caprice mix happily in Hall's lesson: 'But if men wer angels and forsaw thynges to come, they like beastes would not ronne to their confusion: but fortune which gideth the destiny of man, will turne her whele as she listeth, whosoeuer saith nay'. Had the Queen and her faction been able to foresee the future, they would have spared the Duke of Gloucester: 'This is the worldly judgement, but God knoweth, what he had predestinate & what he had ordained before, against whose ordenaunce preuayleth no counsaill, and against whose will auayleth no stryuinge'. The chroniclers constantly waver between two conflicting articles of faith: men would escape misfortune by avoiding certain faults, yet they are powerless to control destiny. The elimination of York's brood would no doubt have prevented the civil war, 'But the necessitie of destinie, can not by any mans

[48] I. iv. 34–7; v. ii. 67–9. Hall 233.
[49] See John W. Blanpied, 'History as Play in *Henry VI, Part II*', *Susquehanna University Studies*, 9 (1972), 83–97.

deuise, be either letted or interrupted.'[50] On the face of it, nothing happens that was not willed by God, yet everything that happens is the result of human actions.

Hall's determinism stops short of predicting the form taken by divine will to treat earthly affairs. He does not hide his contempt for superstitions, and often mocks those who see supernatural phenomena everywhere, especially when Commynes gives him the hint. Amateur prophets foresaw a change of dynasty when a crown fell to the ground during York's presentation of his claim in Parliament: 'This was the iudgement of the cōmon people, whiche were neither of Gods priuitie, nor yet of his priuie counsaill, and yet they wil say their opinions, whosoeuer saie nay'.[51] The medieval chroniclers made much use of such signs to support their theses, Yorkist or Lancastrian, according to their allegiances. The Tudor God, especially Hall's, is as impenetrable as the Greek oracle, as whimsical as Fortune's wheel:

But se the chaunce, what so euer man intendeth God sodainly reuerseth, what princes will, god wil not, what we thinke stable, God sodainely maketh mutable, to the entent that Salomons saiyng might be found trewe, which wrote that the wisdome of men is but folishnes before God. (45)

The only opinions voiced in the play touching the dynastic rivalry are York's, who naturally considers the Lancasters as usurpers. When the Lieutenant who arrests Suffolk evokes 'the house of York, thrust from the crown | By shameful murder of a guiltless king', it simply means that he is a Yorkist himself. The Lancaster claim is not presented, nor is the murder of Richard II a dramatic issue; the only expiatory punishment follows Gloucester's assassination. When misfortunes begin to fall on the House of Lancaster, they all result from the Protector's death. York may well have a right of primogeniture, but his scorn of the public weal hardly recommends him for the exercise of power.

At this stage of the dramatic cycle, Providence does not interfere between York and Lancaster, but hovers around Winchester's anguished agony, and seems to unite with wine in a parodic transubstantiation to ensure the victory of David over Goliath in the armourer's duel. The false miracle of St Albans makes an even more problematic appeal to the supernatural. 'Miracles are ceased', at least none indisputably occurs in the play.[52] The healed beggar was never blind, the traitor is floored by alcohol, and the Cardinal's conscience is sufficiently burdened to torture him with hallucinations. God refrains from showing his hand in human affairs. His presence is nevertheless felt in a foreknowledge of events suggested throughout the play: all the prophecies, visions, dreams come true, all the visionaries foretell the future correctly. Men are allowed to weave their destinies alone, no miraculous immanence comes to upset their projects, to reward or punish them, yet none survives long enough to enjoy the benefit of their crimes. The only intimation of the supernatural comes from this sense of a superior power and knowledge constantly focused on their actions.

[50] Hall 147 (not in Holinshed 163), 210, 226 (212, 233).
[51] Hall 248 (not in Holinshed 264).
[52] Cf. Foxe, 73–5, 'Why true miracles shall cease under the Antichrist' and 'Cause why the church now worketh not miracles'.

3

Grammatical Laws

1. FROM NARRATIVE TO DRAMATIC SYNTAX

Although 2 *Henry VI* stays very close to its sources, in comparison with Part 1, several minute changes transform the sense of the episodes dramatized. Shakespeare recycles every detail of the chronicle, emphasizes or plays them down, combines scraps of information, produces keys to explain them, or motives to lend them credibility. Some major changes are effected without significant alteration of the original event, as we saw, simply by omitting intervals, merging episodes, or connecting independent facts. Others see their meaning radically altered by methods that we will now explore. For this we must return to key episodes at nodal points of the plot

The causal system

The popular uprising undergoes several revisions in the play. The dramatization erases Cade's few positive features in the same way that it suppresses all rational explanation for the rebels' behaviour. Conversely, the King behaves more nobly than the fearful suspicious creature of the sources, who fled London as soon as he had news of Cade's approach, 'doubtyng asmuch his familiar seruauntes, as his vnknowen subiectes', without a thought for those he left behind, and reappeared only when order was restored. In the chronicle, Cade summoned him to come in person to discuss the conditions for a peace, in vain, of course; on stage Henry is ready without any summoning to go and parley with Cade himself if this would save the simple souls in his keeping. His flight to Killingworth is made less shameful by the arrival of the rebels at the gates of the city. Instead of mistrusting his entourage, he seeks to protect them, and invites Lord Saye to share his retreat. The King plays hardly any part in Hall's version of the episode; it is the Archbishop of Canterbury, Chancellor of the Realm, who undertakes to negotiate with the rebels. Shakespeare's Henry pardons everyone, thanks Heaven, and gracefully honours the rebels with the name of soldiers:

> Soldiers, this day have you redeemed your lives,
> And showed how well you love your Prince and country. (IV. ix. 14–15)

A little earlier Cade had urged his men not to put any faith in the promises of the King's emissary. Judging by the chronicle, he was probably right: although the promise guaranteed 'a general pardon vnto all the offendors', the King himself went to Kent to pass judgement, 'and so punished the stubburne heddes, and deliuered the ignorāt & miserable people, to the greate reioysyng of his subiectes'. The chroniclers find nothing to criticize in the procedure; indeed, the King showed uncommon goodness in being content with a few heads: 'if he had not mitigated his iustice, with mercie and compassion, more than fiue. C. by the rigor of his lawe, had been iustely put to execucion'.[1] The stage character has little more political grasp than his model in the chronicle, but a far superior moral stature.

Another episode noticeably enhances the royal figure. Shakespeare omits the five-year lull that followed St Albans, and turns York's conflict with Somerset into the first public statement of his claim. In the chronicle, Somerset accuses the Duke of intentions that have never been publicly declared but agree with Hall's suspicions. York's designs on the crown remain dormant for a few more years, and when he does speak up before Parliament he sets forth his titles with rigour and method, as the dramatic character does to his Neville friends at Act II. Parliament takes time to reflect before delivering its judgement and gains a few more months of armed peace by naming York heir apparent, while Henry VI keeps the throne for his lifetime—an episode dramatized in Part 3 of the trilogy. On stage the quarrel immediately spills over to the battlefield. York offers no reasoned appeals to justice and demands the crown, thus clearing the King of any hint of arbitrariness.

The Queen's suggestion to take York's sons by way of surety for their father has no exact equivalent in Hall, where Somerset wants to imprison them 'to the intent that by the losse of this onely Prince and his sequele, all ciuill warre, and inward diuision might cease and be repressed'. The chronicler shares his feeling that this measure would have avoided civil war, 'But the necessitie of destinie, can not by any mans deuise, be either letted or interrupted: for many thynges (to common judgementes) declared the duke of Yorkes thought and innocēcye in this case'.[2] In the play, it is Clifford who expresses a similar desire to destroy the whole family, here justified by the menacing attitude of the York sons, unlike Somerset's politic plan to exterminate the yet unguilty brood. Instead of one more phase in the waverings of the pretender York, we see the camps form and divide along the lines of clannish rancours: on one side the King, the Queen, the Cliffords, Somerset, and Buckingham, on the other York, his sons, and his Neville friends.

Hall's chronicle teems with anecdotes apparently unrelated to the main thread of his narrative. Some of his correlations are purely stylistic. Thus when he relates, one after another, Suffolk's death and Cade's uprising:

But the death of this froward person, and vngracious patron, brought not the Realme quyete ... For allthough Rychard duke of Yorke, was in pryson, (as the kynges deputie) in ye Realm of Irelande, continually resyaunt there, yet his breath puffed, and his wynde blew dayly, in many partes of the Realme. (219)

Here he recounts the disturbance unleashed in Kent. Despite the form 'But / For',

---

[1] Hall 222 (227).   [2] Ibid. 226 (233).

there is no connection between these two episodes, only the mark of a sporadic desire to find a transition between two sets of events.

On the other hand, facts recorded in sequence without a co-ordinating tag are not always unconnected. Cade's misrule and the chronicle of the eighteenth year end thus: 'Dvryng this commocion aboute London, Raufe bishop of Salisbury, was by his awne tenantes, & seruaūtes, murdered at Edyngton, and so from thensefurth daily succeded, murder, slaughter, & discencion'.[3] At first sight the murder appears an isolated item, unrelated to what precedes it—the judgment given by the King against the Kentish rebels. Holinshed's longer and gorier account of the crime has no visible impact on the play either. Yet coming after Cade's reign of anarchy, the murder of a man of God by his servants points to the enduring effects of disorder, even once it seems eradicated. More often than not, tales designed to entertain, surprise, or horrify the reader serve first to illustrate the chroniclers' leitmotivs.

Such exemplary anecdotes may be associated with the major themes of the play by causal links absent from the chronicle, like Cade's alias. Hall explains that by dressing him in this borrowed identity, the Yorkists hoped to rally the Mortimer family to their cause. On stage Cade threatens death to those who remember his true identity, but the motive as revealed by the Duke of York is quite different:

> This devil here shall be my substitute;
> For that John Mortimer, which now is dead,
> In face, in gait, in speech, he doth resemble.
> By this I shall perceive the commons' mind,
> How they affect the house and claim of York.   (III. i. 370–4)

Incidentally, it seems clear that Shakespeare does not 'confuse' John Mortimer with the two Edmunds: if confusion there be, it is deliberate. The 'pretender' Cade becomes the first to make public York's claim. His pretensions are subsequently reported to the King:

> Jack Cade proclaims himself Lord Mortimer,
> Descended from the Duke of Clarence' house
> And calls your Grace usurper, openly...   (IV. iv. 27–9)

Cade's claim echoes the Yorkist thesis set forth earlier to his friends by the Duke: 'The third son, Duke of Clarence, from whose line | I claim the crown.' The Lancastrians are taxed with usurpation, as in the Lieutenant's tirade to Suffolk:

> And now the house of York, thrust from the crown
> By shameful murder of a guiltless king
> And lofty, proud, encroaching tyranny,
> Burns with revenging fire...   (IV. i. 94–7)

Finally, before giving battle to the royal army, Cade offers to let Henry reign in memory of his noble father on condition that he, Cade, be named Protector. Of course the chroniclers' reports on Cade show no trace of this generous compromise, but some years later it is the Duke of York who pays homage to the great

---

[3] Ibid. 222–3 (227).

Henry V in Parliament, is made Protector, and agrees to let the King reign. The popular revolt is but a curtain raiser, compared with the exploits of the knightly crew, who are better armed for destruction than the fiercest mob.

Besides the liabilities of his writing style, Hall is inclined to take the antecedent for the cause or, in Roland Barthes's terms, consecution for consequence: *post hoc, ergo propter hoc*.[4] Thus the misfortunes following the King's marriage become consequences of it. The paralogism disappears behind the action of Providence. Other correlations are barely explained, or left obscure, like the origin of the plots against the Protector. Gloucester presented a list of accusations against Winchester before the royal council, 'wherof the most parte were spiritual persons', wholly in vain:

But venyme will once breake oute, and inwarde grudge will sone appeare, whiche was this yere to all men apparaunt: for diuers secret attemptes were aduaūced forward this season, against the noble duke Hūfrey of Glocester, a farre of, whiche in conclusiō came so nere, that they bereft hym both of lyfe and lande, as you shall hereafter more manifestly perceyue. For first this yere, dame Elyanour Cobhā, wyfe to the sayd duke, was accused of treason . . . (202)

Presumably this anonymous rancour is the Cardinal's, but it is difficult to decide whether the 'secret attemptes' are done by Winchester alone or the whole cohort of the Duke's enemies. Of the mechanism set in motion, we will know nothing more. The 'For' which connects the fall of the Duchess with the attempts against her husband may be just a stylistic device joining his wife's disgrace to his other worries without any clear causal link, as in our first example.

Where Hall's system of correlations is flawed by the gaps in his logic, Shakespeare provides independent clues without touching the facts themselves. Like Hall's narrative structure, Part 1 depends on parataxis to hold together a set of loosely joined illustrative episodes; Part 2 articulates Hall's rough joints into a far subtler causal system, and covers up the solid thematic underpinning with an apparently natural flow of events. In the play, Gloucester's enemies make use of the Duchess's ambition—an element furnished by Hall's report of the charges against her, namely 'that she, by sorcery and enchaūtmēt, intended to destroy the kyng, to thentent to aduaūce and to promote her husbande to the croune'. One Hume is employed as 'Suffolk and the Cardinal's broker' to set a trap, through her, for her husband:

Hume's knavery will be the Duchess' wrack,
And her attainture will be Humphrey's fall.   (i. ii. 105–6)

By the same roundabout route, York makes Jack Cade his instrument against the King. The rule of the game is set in the opening scene, where the court are assembled to welcome the new Queen. As each character exits, groups form to seal alliances, and progressively disclose their separate designs. When the royal couple leave with Suffolk, Gloucester immediately expresses his feelings on the marriage to those who remain. Once he has left, Buckingham invites Somerset to join him in bringing

---

[4] See his 'Introduction to the Structural Analysis of Narratives', in *A Barthes Reader*, ed. Susan Sontag (London, 1982), 266–75.

down the Protector, and Winchester goes to inform Suffolk of the plan, enabling his two associates to tell each other that they distrust him even more than they detest Gloucester. As soon as they are gone, the Nevilles tell York that they three must unite against those four to defend the public good. Alone at the end of the scene, York reveals that he counts on their common enemies to rid him of Gloucester, and will make use of the Nevilles to win the crown. Suffolk recommends similar tactics to Margaret:

> Although we fancy not the Cardinal,
> Yet must we join with him and with the lords
> Till we have brought Duke Humprey in disgrace.
>
> . . . .
>
> So, one by one, we'll weed them all at last,
> And you yourself shall steer the happy helm. (1. iii. 95–101)

The Duchess's fall, the first step, sets off the mechanism that structures the play. Through the interlocking of rival ambitions, she brings down in her wake her husband, Suffolk and the Cardinal, then Somerset, the House of Lancaster, and finally her last antagonist, York, who has patiently let them kill each other to clear the ground, but who will not escape either. Shakespeare strengthens the connection, asserted by Hall, between Gloucester's death and the fall of Lancaster, first playing up the Protector's talents and virtues, then the dire consequences of his demise. Margaret's jealousy of the Duchess gives her a credible motive to enmesh herself in the plots against Humphrey. The links between the fates of the Lancastrians are further tightened by the prophecies made to the Duchess, prophecies intelligible only to those in the audience who know what is in store. The three-fold meaning of the prophecy concerning the King reinforces the unity of the play and overspills into the next Part, where it comes to completion with the death of York.

The judicial system

In the twenty-fourth year of the reign, perhaps to fill up a rather uneventful season, Hall and Holinshed report an incident unconnected with any political process or moral teachings. 'This yere, an Armerars seruant of London, appeled his master of treason, which offered to bee tried by bataill.' The story is told in a few lines and has no other visible purpose than to pad out an uneventful year. On the given day the armourer, having absorbed a great deal of drink brought by his friends, loses his powers: 'and so he beyng a tall and a hardye personage, ouerladed with hote drynkes, was vanqueshed of his seruante, beyng but a cowarde and a wretche, whose body was drawen to Tiborne, & there hanged and behedded'.

Hall sheds no light on this unexpected denouement. Holinshed is slightly more explicit: the armourer, put out of action by the drink, 'réeled as he went, and so was slaine without guilt. As for the false seruant, he liued not long vnpunished; for being conuict of felonie in court of assise, he was iudged to be hanged, and so he was, at

Tiburne'. A marginal note sums up the lesson: 'Drunkenese the ouerthrow of right and manhood.'[5]

Although they are sure of the armourer's innocence, neither chronicler questions the reliability of the ordeal. On stage, the conclusion of the duel is the same, save that the armourer, named Horner, is truly guilty, and confesses his treason before dying. The victory of his servant, Peter, is even more wonderful: he does not know how to fight, and believes himself lost because his master is a practised fencer. The dialogue offers two explanations for this victory: for the cynics it is the effect of wine, for the pious it is the workings of Providence:

> Go, take hence that traitor from our sight,
> For by his death we do perceive his guilt.
> And God in justice hath reveal'd to us
> The truth and innocence of this poor fellow . . .   (II. iii. 101–4)

If wine takes the part of divine justice, it is plain that Providence employs natural means to accomplish its designs. But there is more to it, for Providence thus vindicated unmasks more than one guilty man. Neither Hall nor Holinshed specifies the nature of the supposed treason. In the play Horner is accused of having declared

>   that Richard, Duke of York
> Was rightful heir unto the English crown,
> And that your Majesty was an usurper.   (I. iii. 184–6)

For his trouble he is insulted by York himself who demands the head of the traitor. The armourer protests his innocence but the accusation carries. Unimpressed by York's virtuous indignation, the wise Gloucester gives his double verdict: a trial by combat, and the regency for Somerset 'Because in York this breeds suspicion'. A doubt supported by the duel, which confirms the truthfulness of the servant.

In the play, Gloucester proves an exemplary judge in two instances, the incident of the armourer and Simpcox's false miracle. When it comes to the sentence against his wife, he bows to the decision that banishes her:

> Eleanor, the law, thou seest, hath judged thee:
> I cannot justify whom the law condemns.   (II. iii. 15–16)

Modern wives might find him a contemptible husband, but Eleanor's complaints that her rank should protect her from a shameful penalty awake no sympathy, nor do they seriously challenge the virtue of Gloucester's scruples. His honourable restraint sets down the norm, like Gaunt's when he puts the law before fatherly love, and recalls the hierarchy of duties before it is disrupted. Hall's comment that 'the duke of Gloucester, toke all these thynges paciently, and saied litle' pays homage to his Christian forbearance. When he is summoned shortly after to give up his office, he complies, with dark forebodings that fit in the play's pattern of anticipation:

> Farewell, good King. When I am dead and gone
> May honourable peace attend thy throne.   (II. iii. 37–8)

---

[5] Hall 207–8. Holinshed 210.

It is then that the outcome of the Horner duel upholds the wisdom of his verdict. Gloucester forbids his men to free the Duchess by force on her way to the pillory, and reiterates his faith in the law. But when he is arrested in the following scene, no other man of integrity presents himself to defend the right, and justice dies with him. Like brave Talbot, he will not be replaced.

The armourer's treason, which anticipates York's, echoes Hall's report on the rumours spread by the Yorkists, that 'the Kynge was not the true enheritor to the crowne, or that he or his counsaill was not able of wit, pollicie, and circumspeccion, to rule and gouerne so noble a Realme', given which, the Duke of York's friends 'began to practise the gouernaūce of his title: Infusyng and puttyng into mens heades secretely his right to yᵉ crown, his pollitique gouernaūce, his gentle behauior, to all the Iryshe nacion'. The murmurs increase after the defeat of the Staffords, 'some wishing the duke of Yorke at home, to ayde the capitayne his cosyne: some desiryng the ouerthrow of the kyng and his counsaill: other openly cryeng out on the Quene, and her complices'. Years later, when York leaves Ireland to make good his titles before Parliament, 'the cōmon people babbeled, that he should be Kyng, & that king Henry should no lōger reigne'. Holinshed, who omits all these rumours, reports 'the great indignation of manie' at the 'presumptuous attempts' of the Duke.[6] In the play, the voice of justice having been silenced with Gloucester, no one remembers his reservations about York, nor signals a link between Peter's innocence and the Duke's guilt. Incidentally, it is York who attributes the triumph of the truth to the virtues of liquor rather than to a Providence that would brand him as suspect: 'Fellow, thank God, and the good wine in thy master's way.'

The duel thus plays a pivotal role in the dramatic structure. Peter's complaint against the armourer is one of the petitions addressed to Gloucester in I. iii. These petitions which annoy the Queen impeach, directly or indirectly, the Cardinal, Suffolk, and York, and call on Gloucester as the last barrier against ambition, cupidity, rebellion. The puns on his title underline the threats to his position, 'Protector, see to't well, protect yourself.' Along with these signs of his power and weakness, the Horner incident links up the Queen's alliance with his enemies, the dynasty's dubious legitimacy, the popular discontent, the Yorkist rumours, the appointment of Somerset, and the divisions at court. The choice of a Regent opposes two factions, York's and Somerset's, with the King unable to choose in the middle:

> For my part, noble lords, I care not which;
> Or Somerset, or York, all's one to me. (I. iii. 102–3)

In Temple Garden, two clans formed around the same characters; the point of the quarrel seemed so slight then that the King did not believe he was making a decisive choice in picking a red rose. Here again the conflict is still peripheral and serves above all as a pretext for a concentrated attack on Gloucester. The loss of France is announced just as he goes on trial, and the play turns against him the accusation aimed at Somerset in the source:

[6] Hall 219, 220, 245. Holinshed 261–2.

> 'Tis thought, my lord, that you took bribes of France,
> And, being Protector, stayed the soldiers' pay;
> By means whereof his highness hath lost France.   (III. i. 104–6)

Now the national rout serves only to score points against an enemy of the same blood. None but the common people are left to deplore what happens abroad.

The supreme irony is that the Duke's enemies destroy themselves in bringing him down. As in the *Mirror* and in Foxe's *Actes*, Suffolk and the Cardinal soon follow their victim into the grave. It may be Foxe who suggested this quick succession of deaths, for he narrates them in one shot with a marginal note: 'Judgement of God upon those who persecuted the duke'—the principal enemies of Gloucester being, in order, the Cardinal, Suffolk, and the Queen—and imputes Winchester's death to divine justice. Hall draws no such conclusion from the proximity of the two demises, nor does he make Winchester the main culprit of the crime. He does, however, contribute to the scene of his agony, tortured not by Gloucester's ghost but the shadow of older sins: 'Why should I dye hauīg so muche ryches, if the whole Realme would saue my lyfe, I am able either by pollicie to get it, or by ryches to bye it. Fye, will not death by hyered, nor will money do nothyng?'.[7] These last words, a common theme of Tudor moralities, are echoed and amplified by the stage character:

> If thou be'st Death, I'll give thee England's treasure,
> Enough to purchase such another island,
> So wilt thou let me live and feel no pain.   (III. iii. 2–4)

'England's treasure' is not only the price of the kingdom but its rightful property, as the chroniclers imply: 'for his hiddē ryches might haue wel holpen the king, and his secrete treasure might haue releued the cōmonaltie, whē money was scante.' Another of their comments, 'His couetous insaciable, and hope of long lyfe, made hym bothe to forget God, hys Prynce and hym selfe, in his latter daies', inspires the messenger's report of him 'Blaspheming God, and cursing men on earth'. Rumour had it that Gloucester was smothered between two featherbeds. On stage, he is taken prisoner to spend his last night in the house of Winchester, whose agony in bed satisfies dramatic justice.[8] Suffolk survived his accomplice by several years, but in his case Hall notes that many attributed his death to divine wrath:

This ende had Williā de la pole, first duke of Suffolke, as men iudge by Gods punyshmēt: for aboue all thinges he was noted to be the very organ, engine, and diuiser of the destruccion of Hūfrey the good duke of Gloucester, and so the bloudde of the Innocente mā was with his dolorous death, recompensed and punished. (219)

Although Hall's syntax is as usual ambiguous, here he seems to share the common feeling, instead of passing judgement on naive superstitions. Holinshed is even more assertive: 'Gods iustice would not that so vngratious a person should so

---

[7] Foxe 714–17. Hall 210.
[8] III. i. 137–8, 186–8. Hall 209–11. Holinshed 210–12 omits Winchester's dying speech.

escape', and proceeds to tell the end of Suffolk, 'as men iudge by Gods prouidence, for that he had procured the death of the good duke of Glocester'.

The play does not need providential help with Suffolk's death, which is the direct result of his crime, whereas in the case of Winchester, the witnesses have no doubt that God has dealt swift punishment. There could be a medical explanation for his sudden death but none is offered. Thus the fate of the two men proceeds from their crime, where the chronicle establishes a distant link between the act and the penalty for the one, and for the other no link at all. Suffolk's end combines several independent strands of the historical narrative, as the Lieutenant indiscriminately reproaches him with all the ills affecting the realm, from the loss of the French provinces to the murder of an innocent king, arbitrarily concluding his list with the accusation, 'And all by thee'. Suffolk cannot seriously be held guilty for the death of Richard II, but he has invited this amalgamation by flaunting his Lancastrian blood, hence allowing associations between his fate, the destiny of the House of Lancaster, and the state of the kingdom.[9] Providence is primarily an agent of dramatic cohesion.

A similar coherence is worked into the dramatic chain with the arrest of the Duke of York. The designs he is charged with in the chronicle are confirmed a posteriori according to the same logic that confuses cause and effect. Shakespeare backs up the chronicler's suspicions with the accused's own confession. York had meant to bide his time—'I must make fair weather yet awhile | Till Henry be more weak, and I more strong'—but the sight of Somerset makes him forget his recent resolutions, and he noisily demands the crown. His first act of rebellion, for which Hall keeps us waiting another three years, shortens by the same stroke Somerset's career. Shakespeare, like Hall, recalls at the moment of his death the prophecy which advised him to shun castles.[10] In Hall's tale, it is reported as a curiosity; on stage it plays its role in the unfolding of the Lancastrian destinies.

2. THE APPEAL TO THE SOURCES

Blind man's bluff

The thematic structure of *2 Henry VI* is as strongly built as that of Part 1, and shows equal mastery in the choice of significant episodes, but none of its demonstrative character.[11] The ingenuity of the ramifications disappears behind an apparent logic of events. The play shows traces of many readings apart from Hall, and the use at specific points of several chronicles.[12] These may be confined to small details. For

[9] IV. i. 50–2. 'A false claim' says Cairncross, n. 50. Suffolk's mother was a distant cousin of the King.

[10] I. iv. 34; v. ii. 67–9. Hall 233. The Q and F texts differ slightly on his death, but both recall the prophecy.

[11] See Larry S. Champion, 'Prologue to their Play: Shakespeare's Structural Progress in *2 Henry VI*', *Texas Studies in Literature and Language*, 19 (1977), 294–312.

[12] The discussion here will be confined mostly to historical sources, and references to Holinshed (to vol. II on the Peasant's Revolt in 1381, to vol. III everywhere else) restricted to the points where he significantly differs from Hall.

instance, Shakespeare borrowed the phrase 'the keys of Normandy', but little else, from Fabyan's account, to which Hall and Holinshed send the reader for more details on the royal wedding.[13] The Duchess's accomplice is called 'Hume' in the Folio, a spelling special to John Foxe. It is spelt 'Hum' in Hall, who has furnished most of the details to the episode (including the name, erroneous, of Sir John Stanley).[14] This spelling may have been adopted to avoid confusions with Humphrey of Gloucester, whose exit is notified by the stage direction 'Ex. Hum.', ten lines before the entrance of Hume. Touching Gloucester, both Foxe and Shakespeare use the expression 'condign punishment', but Hall, writing of wrong-doers whom the Duke had to judge, says that he attracted the hatred of 'such as feared to haue condigne reward for their vngracious actes'. It is difficult to assert whose phrase the play borrowed.[15]

The *Mirror for Magistrates*, with its broad patterns, had paved the way from chronicle to dramatic form: its arbitrary ordering of events, and elimination of all matters not essential to the purpose, anticipated several dramatic requirements. Just as Gloucester's fall is linked to the errors of his wife, the 'Tragedie' of Suffolk links his end to his crime. He arranged the Anjou match against the wishes of Gloucester, who had already concluded an agreement with Armagnac, and whose hostility to the marriage caused the Queen's resentment. She instructed Suffolk to rid her of the Duke, and richly rewarded him for his services, but he was banished by popular pressure, taken prisoner by a captain, and led to Dover,

> Where whan he had recounted me my faultes,
> As murdring of Duke Humfrey in his bed,
> And howe I had brought all the realme to naughtes
> In causing the King vnlawfully to wed,
> There was no grace, but I must loose my head. (*Mirror*, XI. 169–73)

In the play, the Lieutenant is moved to a similar though more specific indignation, whereas Hall tells us nothing of the captain's feelings nor the motives for his act. Each link of this strong chain from initial cause to final expiation is present in the chronicle, but often lost in a tangle of motives: the promise to Armagnac is but one cause of Gloucester's opposition, which is but one of Margaret's grievances. The Duke has many other enemies, and many factors contribute to his elimination. The Anjou marriage has more disastrous consequences than his death, which is but one motive of the commons' hatred. With the *Mirror*'s selection, one exchanges the complexity, the uncertainty, of historical matter for a clear and highly pedagogic concatenation of deeds, a skeleton on which the history plays add new flesh.

Holinshed's chronicle, though more detailed than Hall's on certain relevant episodes, furnished only a few significant elements to the play, and none where its diverging points serve to build up contrary views as in Part 1. In addition to Hall's account, Holinshed notes that the Duchess of Gloucester 'was inioined to go

---

[13] I. i. 113. Fabyan 617. Hall 224 uses the expression 'the very keys of Guyen' about the city of Fronsac.
[14] Sir John Standly in Foxe 711. Hall 205. Holinshed 208 refers to Fabyan, 423–7.
[15] III. i. 30. Foxe 217. Hall 209.

through Cheapside with a taper in her hand' for her public penance, a detail preserved in the two versions of the play. In F, '*Enter the Duchesse in a white Sheet, and a Taper burning in her hand.*' In Q, '*Enter Dame Elinor Cobham bare-foote, and a white sheete about her, with a waxe candle in her hand, and verses written on her backe and pind on.*' Her complaints evoke two of these items—'with papers on my back' and 'The ruthless flint doth cut my tender feet', while the other two, sheet and candle, must have been visible enough. The variant of 'taper' to 'wax candle' suggests a description of what was shown rather than consultation of a written source. Foxe records 'a taper and banisment', like most accounts of the episode, but only the *Mirror* mentions at once 'Taper burning', 'sheete', the penitent's walk 'bare foote', 'Three dayes a row, to passe the open streate', her 'shame' and 'cruel banishment' to 'The yle of Man'.[16] Besides, Foxe believes her innocent, while in the *Mirror* she recalls her rivalry with the Queen, and confesses to the same degree of guilt as in the play. Since the 'Tragedie of Dame Elianor Cobham' first appeared in 1578, this helps clarify two or three points in one go: Shakespeare drew more on the *Mirror* than the official quota, he definitely used a later edition than the original one, and he had no need of Holinshed's extra lights in this particular scene.

Concerning the regency and the rivalry between York and Somerset, Holinshed again diverges a little from Hall's narrative. Both chroniclers report Somerset's attempts to oppose York's first appointment, at the death of Bedford, but only Hall explains his hostility by the promotion of York to an office which he 'gaped and loked for'. Some two years later, York is divested of his functions and replaced by Warwick, for reasons unspecified. On the death of Warwick, York exercises the regency again until 'the duke of Somerset, was appointed Regent of Normandy, and the Duke of Yorke thereof discharged'—the episode represented in Act I.[17] Here Holinshed adds two paragraphs: according to a register belonging to the Abbey of St Albans, the Duke of York acquitted himself so well of his task that on his return to England at the end of his mandate, he was reappointed to the regency; but Somerset interfered, always jealous of his rival's successes:

> he likewise now wrought so that the king reuoked his grant made to the duke of Yorke for enioing of that office the terme of other fiue yeeres, and with helpe of William marquesse of Suffolke obtained that grant for himself. (208–9)

These two paragraphs supply several elements to the dramatic episode: the double movement leading Gloucester to reconsider his choice of York after the armourer's tale, and counsel the appointment of Somerset. The reasons for his first choice,

> York is meetest man
> To be Regent in the realm of France   (I. iii. 160–1)

recall Holinshed's 'a man most meet to supplie that roome', as does Suffolk's argument

---

[16] II. iii and iv. Holinshed 203, and Foxe 708, from *Polychronicon*. Not in Hall 202. *Mirror*, xxviii. 78–112, 139–48, 260, 239.

[17] This was Richard Beauchamp, father-in-law to the Warwick of the play. Hall 179, 187, 191, 206.

> To show some reason, of no little force,
> That York is most unmeet of any man . . .   (1. iii. 164–5)

whereas Hall never mentions any special understanding between Suffolk and Somerset. Finally, Holinshed observes 'the duke of Somerset still maligning the duke of Yorkes aduancement, as he had sought to hinder his dispatch at the first when he was sent ouer to be regent, as before yee haue heard', old grievances which, in the play, York recalls at the same point in the action.[18]

Concerning the fate of the armourer's servant, Holinshed is slightly clearer than Hall, but agrees that he was disloyal, while the libations vary from one text to the other: malmsey and aquavit in Hall, 'wine and strong drinke' for Holinshed, whereas Shakespeare mixes sack, charneco, and strong beer to bring down his traitor. Neither chronicler makes any allusion to the Duke of York, but the place of the anecdote in Holinshed's narrative is otherwise suggestive: it is the third instance of an issue settled by a court ruling, paralleled by the play's three demonstrations of the Protector's wisdom. Holinshed may also be responsible for Somerset's announcement at Act III that 'all is lost' in France. Historically it is only Normandy that is about to escape him, but a marginal note states that 'The English loose all in France'. This was but a phase in the war, as Holinshed must be aware, for he notes a little later 'All Normandie lost', then again, in 1451, 'All lost in France', and finally in 1453, 'Aquitaine lost'.[19]

Holinshed, we saw, is less insistent than Hall concerning York's determined underground work against the crown, a point on which Shakespeare seems rather to follow Hall. On the other hand, it may well be Holinshed who suggested the Duke's meeting with Cade in Ireland, for he writes twice that Cade was of Irish birth, one of them in the royal proclamation which he reproduces in full. Among other points, the proclamation refuted Cade's claim 'that the kings letters of pardon granted to him and them, be not auaileable, nor to none effect, without authoritie of parliament'. It possibly inspired Cade's harangue on stage to his wavering troops, 'And you, base peasants, do ye believe him? Will you needs be hanged with your pardons about your necks?'[20] Hall gives no date in the whole passage concerning Cade's end, but in Holinshed the royal proclamation is dated '10 die Iulij, anno regni 28', which concurs with Cade's allusion on stage to 'this hot weather' and his salad puns.[21] Holinshed's other details concerning Cade's flight and capture seem to have scarcely inspired Shakespeare, not even the tempting symbolism of the victor's name, 'a gentleman of Kent named Alexander Eden', which Hall writes 'Iden', the spelling used in F and Q. Cade's head is exhibited on London Bridge in Hall and Holinshed. As to his body, Hall says that it was transported to London,

---

[18] Holinshed 208. *2H6*, 1. iii. 166–73.
[19] Holinshed 215, 217, 229, 236. *2H6*, III. i. 83–5.
[20] Holinshed 220, 226. Cf. Hall 222: 'the lusty Kentishe Capitayne'. *2H6*, IV. viii. 21–3.
[21] This cooling salad deserves special treatment. In Molinet's *Chroniques*, I. 414, it is related to Edward IV's death: going on his customary pilgrimage to bless the rings, 'il fut alteré de chaleur, il se cuida rafreschir d'une salade et se refroida tellement qu'il termina le .IIIIe. jour aprèz Pasques.' Made thirsty by the heat, he sought refreshment from a salad and so cooled himself that he died on the fourth day after Easter. Cf. *2H6*, IV. x. 8–9.

but Holinshed reports it was cut up and the quarters sent for display to different places in Kent. In the play, the headless body is abandoned on a heap of manure to nourish the crows.

To complete the list of possible reminiscences, we find two details touching the Duke of York. In Act V the King recalls the allegiance sworn to him, to which Salisbury retorts:

> It is great sin to swear unto a sin,
> But greater sin to keep a sinful oath.   (v. i. 182–3)

According to Holinshed, 'The duke of Yorke hauing aforehand obtained an absolution of the pope, in discharge of his oath before taken, did now discouer his stomach against the duke of Somerset.' Finally York's declaration on stage, 'I am resolved for death or dignity', and that of Warwick evoking 'the tempest of the field' are close enough to York's exhortations to his men at St Albans in Holinshed's report: 'better it is for vs to die in the field, than cowardlie to be put to an vtter rebuke and shamefull death.'[22]

Apart from these isolated traces in the dialogue we find but two episodes for which Shakespeare drew extensively on other sources to eke out Hall's chronicle: Simpcox's false miracle, borrowed mainly from Foxe's 'Book of Martyrs', and the uprising in Kent, which draws on many accounts and will require closer attention. It is Holinshed who refers the readers 'vnto maister Foxes booke of Acts and Monuments' to complete his panegyric of Duke Humphrey. John Foxe relates how Gloucester exposed the deception of a man falsely posing as blind.[23] The incident, which took place 'in the young dayes of this king Henry VI, being yet under the governance of this duke Humprey, his protector', serves to illustrate the Duke's talents. The King is present but plays no part in Foxe's account. The scene is in substance faithful to the book: the fake blind man has come from Berwick with his wife, having been advised in a dream to go to the sanctuary of St Albans, and claims to have been cured by the saint.

The narrative, which takes the form of a dialogue here, supplies terms and matter to the exchange between the stage characters. Suspecting a trick, Gloucester questions the beggar about the colour of their clothing, concludes that he could no more name the colours than the persons present if he were truly blind from birth, and has the impostor put into the pillory. In the play, Simpcox further aggravates his case by knowing the colour of blood and jet. Shakespeare adds spice to the scene by making his sham blind man a true cripple: this infirmity arouses Gloucester's suspicions, which Foxe does not explain. The invalid leaps over a stool to escape whipping, and flees as fast as he can to the cries of 'A miracle!' The only allusion to his poverty is in his wife's defence: 'Alas! Sir, we did it for pure need.' And the episode comes to an end with an acid exchange between Gloucester and his enemies, each denouncing the 'miracles' of the other. It is then that Gloucester is informed of his wife's treason and arrest.

---

[22] Holinshed 218, 240. *2H6*, v. i. 194, 197.
[23] Holinshed 212. Foxe 712–13.

Concerning the accusation against the Duchess, Foxe asks himself 'whether it is to be judged true, or suspected rather to be false and forged', but does not connect the episode of the blind beggar with her disgrace, nor with the Protector's fall, though he reports it after the Duke's death to illustrate his qualities:

Furthermore, as the learning of this Prince was rare and memorable so was the discreete wisedom and singular prudence in him no less to be considered: as for the more manifest proof thereof, I thought here good amongst other his godly doings, to recite one example, reported as well by the pen of sir Thomas More ... (712)

In the play the scene illustrates Gloucester's talents and shows fortune's wheel tilting as he reaches the height of glory, a tragic theme summed up the image of the hawk's splendid ascent. After Talbot's, it is the second resounding fall on the way to the ruin of the kingdom.

Jack of all trades

The staging of Cade's rebellion involves complex procedures that need some light from its historical precedents and analogues. Shakespeare combines accounts of the episode of 1450, and those of the Peasants' Revolt under the reign of Richard II, in 1381. These two popular risings, reported by Richard Grafton and Holinshed, present various analogies.[24] On both occasions, starting from Kent, the rebels reached Blackheath, led by Jack Straw in 1381, by Jack Cade in 1450, put London to fire and the sword, opened the prisons, and freed the prisoners to increase their numbers. After various misdeeds and fights with royal troops, they surrendered against a promise of general pardon, then went home released by the King's grace while their leaders were executed.

Geoffrey Bullough signals two contemporary analogues of *2 Henry VI*, a play entitled *The Life and Death of Jack Straw*, and a spectacle celebrating the Lord Mayor through the merits of his predecessor, William Walworth, who killed the rebel leader: 'The Peasants' Revolt was topical in the year 1590/1 when the Lord Mayor was John Allot, a Fishmonger like the heroic Walworth who slew Wat Tyler'. Actually it was Jack Straw whom the Mayor killed. Holinshed sometimes treats the two men as one ('And the said Iohn Tiler tooke vpon him to be their cheefe capteine, naming himselfe Iacke Straw'), sometimes as two distinct people.[25] In *Jack Straw*, the rebel is 'tiler' by trade, which may explain the confusion.

Certain details figure in all three theatrical shows: the commands to kill the men of law, burn the Savoy and the Inns of Court, destroy the archives, and open the prisons. Holinshed reports that it was dangerous to know how to read and write, 'and more dangerous, if any man were found with a penner and inkhorne at his side; for such seldome escaped them with life', which inspires the hanging of the

---

[24] Grafton i. 417–27. Holinshed II. 736–52. Knowles, introd. 89–106, has informative pages on the rich complexity of Cade's literary background, but little on the historical sources. For those, see Hattaway 65–9.

[25] Bullough 91. Holinshed II. 736, 737, 740, 751. *The Life and Death of Jack Straw*, ed. Kenneth Muir and F. P. Wilson (Oxford, 1957).

clerk of Chartham 'with his pen and inkhorn about his neck'.[26] A line of *Jack Straw*, 'And wele not leave a man of law', coincides with Cade's menace: 'We will not leave one lord, one gentleman.' Holinshed's report on Wat Tyler, 'that within foure daies all the lawes of England should come foorth of his mouth', reappears in Dick the Butcher's suggestion to Cade, 'that the laws of England may come out of your mouth', and Cade's decision to burn the archives since, he haughtily decrees, 'my mouth shall be the parliament of England'.[27]

Cade's promises do not have equivalents in Hall's work, except his plan to abolish taxes. They all reflect the teachings of John Ball, a preacher of Kent denied a pulpit because of his unorthodox theses, who was one of the leaders of the revolt of 1381. In all our texts, Ball's egalitarian doctrines make due reference to the common origin of men. Holinshed and the author of *Jack Straw* use the same formula:

> But when Adam delued, and Eve span
> Who was then a Gentleman?

a medieval commonplace recognizable in Cade's retort, 'And Adam was a gardener.' Grafton's preacher, renamed John Wall, states that 'We be all come from one father and one mother, Adam and Eue', without specifying their humble labours. Men are born equal and free, claims John Ball, in the narratives of Grafton, 'What have we deserued, or why should we be thus kept in seruitude and bondage? ... We be called their bondmen, and without we doe them readie service, we must be beaten, punished or put out of our lyuings,' and Holinshed:

all men by nature were created alike, and that bondage or servitude came in by injust oppression of naughtie men. For if God would have had anie bondmen from the beginning, he would have appointed who should be bond & who free (II. 740)

as does the preacher Ball of *Jack Straw*:

> Brethren, brethren, it were better to haue this communitie,
> Than to haue this difference in degrees.   (ll. 84–5)

Shakespeare's Cade professes the same creed on two occasions: 'All the realm shall be in common,' 'And henceforward all things shall be in common.' In Holinshed, it is Wat Tyler who 'craved of the king that all warrens, waters, parks and woods should be common'. The question of enclosures, however topical under the Tudors, was a long-standing practice that had thrown a number of small farmers out of work. Neither the demands of Jack Straw nor those of Jack Cade were anachronisms.[28]

The facts dramatized are present in Holinshed, yet certain turns of the dialogue

---

[26] Holinshed II. 746. *2H6*, IV. ii. 103–4, IV. ii. 73.

[27] Holinshed II. 740. *Straw*, l. 519. *2H6*, IV. ii. 173, IV. vii. 5–6, 12–13. See Wilson, *Will Power*, 27–30, on Cade's hatred of literacy and law.

[28] Grafton i. 418. Holinshed II. 742. Robert Weimann, 'Das Bundschuh-Motiv ("clouted shoon") bei Shakespeare: Zu einer neuen Quelle der Jack-Cade-Szenen in *Heinrich VI*', *Aspecte* (1977), 21–33, associates the imagery with Kett's rebellion. Wilson, *Will Power*, 22–34, connects it with the clothiers' protests in 1592.

sound nearer to Grafton's terms. For instance, the people's complaint that their masters 'are clothed in Veluet and Chamlet furred richly, and we be clad with the poorest sorte of cloth' could have inspired 'The nobility think scorn to go in leather aprons', just as the words of Cade's follower, 'Well, I say, it was never merry world in England since gentlemen came up', echo John Wall's: 'A good people, matters go not wel to passe in England in these dayes, nor shall not do vntill every thing be common, and that there be no Villeynes nor gentlemen.' *Jack Straw* limits this theme to the exploitation of the poor by the rich.[29] But Cade's harangues when he upbraids the turncoats borrow from the preacher of the chronicles:

I thought ye would never have given o'er these arms till you had recovered your ancient freedom; but you are all recreants and dastards and delight to live in slavery to the nobility. (IV. viii. 25–8)

The Homily of 1547, 'An Exhortation Concerning good Order, and obedience to Rulers and Magistrates', uses these very terms to refute egalitarian principles. Should degree be upset, the homilist threatens, 'no man shall keepe his wife, children, and possession in quietnesse, all things shall bee common, and there must needes follow all mischiefe, and utter destruction both of soules, bodies, goodes, and common wealthes'.[30] In *The Book Named the Governor*, published in 1531, which Emrys Jones indicates as a probable source of 2 *Henry VI*, Thomas Elyot records a preference for the term 'public weal', rather than 'common weal' or 'common wealth' which has unpleasant connotations.[31] This may be where the homilist found the arguments for his anathema against egalitarian theories and their corollary, the putting of goods in common. Hierarchy is the reflection of divine order, he writes, 'for where there is no right order, there reigneth all abuse, carnall liberty, enormitie, sinne, and Babylonicall confusion', the very evils Jack Cade edicts as a new set of commandments:

The proudest peer in the realm shall not wear a head on his shoulders, unless he pay me tribute; there shall not a maid be married, but she shall pay to me her maidenhead ere they have it; men shall hold of me *in capite*, and we charge and command that their wives be as free as heart can wish or tongue can tell. (IV. vii. 112–17)

Grafton is the only one to voice his opinion explicitly about these theories: 'And of this imagination was a foolishe priest in the Countie of Kent called John Wall, for the which lyke foolishe words he had bene three times in the Bishop of Cauntorburies prison'. Holinshed contents himself with saying that the professed doctrine is not that which the bishops uphold, a euphemism if the bishops defend the homiletic principles. Yet no one could suspect him of revolutionary sympathies. Regarding Cade's revolt, his condemnation is unequivocal: 'in such cases there is no

---

[29] Grafton i. 417–18. *Straw*, ll. 79–103. *2H6*, IV. ii. 11.
[30] *Certaine Sermons*, 69–70.
[31] Thomas Elyot, *The Boke Named the Gouernour*, A Facsimile Reprint, ed. R. C. Alston (Menston, 1970), i, fo. 2. Jones, *Origins of Shakespeare*, 164–70, notes, however, that numerous other authors expressed similar ideas.

breeder of a broile but he shall find adherents enow no less forward to further his pernicious enterprise by their foolehardines.'[32]

The Life and Death of Jack Straw draws on accounts of several rebellions to represent the Peasants' Revolt of 1381, and shares with Shakespeare's play formal similarities nowhere to be found in the chronicles.[33] The uncertainties of dating make it impossible to assert which came first. Even if *Jack Straw* preceded *2 Henry VI*, there was little worth stealing in it. The analogies are more interesting for what they reveal of current views on rebellion. At the beginning of the play, Jack Straw kills a tax collector who has insulted his daughter. He is applauded by John Ball who encourages the people to revolt, with due reference to Adam the gardener:

> But merrily with the world it went,
> When men eat berries of the hauthorne tree ... (ll. 89–90)

It is 'this difference in degree' that Cade's men resent: 'Well, I say it was never merry world in England since gentlemen came up'. In that happy and carefree past, says Ball,

> There was no place for surgerie,
> And old men knew not vsurie: (ll. 92–3)

a nostalgia shared by Cade: 'before, our forefathers had no other books but the score and the tally.'

Just as Cade's men are 'Marked for the gallows', the shadow of the hangman hovers over *Jack Straw*: 'the fairest end of a Rebell is the gallowes'; 'Wele stuffe the Gallowes til it cracke'; 'Tyburn stand fast, I feare you will be loden ere it be long.'[34] In the two plays the rebels open the prisons, and march on London with numbers increased by all the rascals met on the way. The rebels of *Jack Straw* behave as cruelly and brutishly as in *2 Henry VI*, the ones killing those who mispronounce English, the others those who know how to read and write, all distrusting the written word.[35] After 'Burning vp Bookes and matters of records', Straw's men proclaim

> And wele not leaue a man of lawe,
> Nor a paper worth a hawe, (ll. 519–20)

Jack Cade orders his to 'burn all the records of the realm', and Lord Saye is charged with speaking French, 'therefore he is a traitor', besides his share in the use of print and paper-mills.

Both plays insert the theme of the foreign enemy and national union in the midst of rebellion, possibly inspired by Hall in both cases. Clifford upbraids Cade's men,

> Were't not a shame that whilst you live at jar
> The fearful French, whom you late vanquished,
> Should make a start o'er seas and vanquish you? (iv. viii. 41–3)

---

[32] Grafton i. 417. Holinshed III. 220.
[33] It was published in 1593, and may have been shown in 1590, Bullough thinks. On the dating of *2 Henry VI*, see Knowles's summary, introd. 11–21.
[34] *Straw*, ll. 56, 132, 162.
[35] Ibid., ll. 616–20. *2H6*, iv. ii. 159–61.

In *Jack Straw* it is Sir John Morton who is indignant:

> What means these wretched miscreants
> To make a spoile of their owne country:
> Vnnatural Rebels what so ere,
> By forraine foes may seeme no whit so strange,
> As Englishmen to trouble England thus
> Well may I tearme it insest to the Land.   (ll. 603–8)

As in Hall's lament for Matthew Gough, Sir John deplores the death of a hero, killed in his own land by his compatriots. Jack Straw's demands that the King come to meet him recall those that Hall reports of Cade, likewise encamped at Blackheath, who refuses to disperse his army 'except the kynge in person wolde come to him, and assent to all thynges, which he should requyre'. Shakespeare's Henry VI needs no prompting:

> And I myself,
> Rather than bloody war shall cut them short,
> Will parley with Jack Cade their general.   (IV. iv. 10–12)

Both kings wish to spare the blood of their subjects. Henry VI is pious and charitable,

> For God forbid so many simple souls
> Should perish by the sword!   (IV. iv. 9–10)

so is Richard II:

> Yet God forbid I should,
>   .   .   .   .
> Behold so many of my country men
> All done to death and strangled in one day . . .   (ll. 1003–6)

The two monarchs offer to pardon the rebels. Like Shakespeare's Henry VI, King Richard considers extending his pardon to all and, like Hall's Henry VI, has the principal leaders executed. In *Jack Straw*, the Lord Mayor receives his reward:

> Kneele downe William Walworth and receaue,
> By mine owne hand the order of Knighthood:
> Stand up Sir William first Knight of thy degree . . .   (ll. 1177–9)

Shakespeare follows the pattern by unhistorically knighting Iden for the same exploit.[36]

The similarities between the two plays do not end there. Both alternate the scenes in the rebel camp with scenes at court, disorder on the one side, formalism on the other, to confront rival views: the rebels', revolted by the injustice of their condition, the court's, shocked by the mob's misrule. In *Jack Straw* the preacher denounces a hierarchy which serves only to fatten the rich,

---

[36] v. i. 76–80. The Mayor is likewise knighted in Thomas Nelson's *Device for Lord Mayor's Pageant* (1590), in Bullough 137.

The landlord his rent, the lawyer his fees.
So quickly the poore mans substance is spent ...   (ll. 87–8)

The widow, with barely a roof over her head,

> Sometimes no penny to buy her bread,
> Must pay her Landlord many a groat,
> Or twil be puld out of her throat.   (ll. 97–9)

But his sermon is disqualified by one of the rebel leaders:

> You thinke ther's no knaverie hid under a black gowne,
> Find him in a pulpit but twise in the yeare,
> And Ile find him fortie times in the ale-house tasting strong beare.   (ll. 70–3)

Nobs, a member of the crew, establishes a critical distance within the rebel scenes, saluting each move with censorious comments. Having voiced concern for the poor man's lot, the play sides unambiguously with orthodoxy and the respect of 'degree'.

The term is also heard at the knighting of Alexander Iden, but in the form of a question by the King: 'what is thy degree?', precisely when hierarchy is seriously challenged. Here the two plays totally diverge. Far from celebrating order and the triumph of hierarchy, the denouement of *2 Henry VI* reflects the disintegration of these values. Shakespeare never tries to arouse sympathy for the demands of the rioters; this uprising, orchestrated by the nobility, does not exploit the legitimate grievances of an oppressed peasantry, but the anarchic tendencies of a manipulated urban mob. Cade's lieutenants play a critical role comparable to that of Nobs in *Jack Straw* with their witty cracks at his expense and deflating asides.[37] But where Nobs invites the audience to weigh the costs of rebellion, Cade's men are untroubled by moral issues, as devoid of scruples as their leader, and ready to enjoy the bloody feast ahead with brutal gaiety.

Cade's tirades, we saw, make implicit reference to the Homily of 1547. By a crafty reversal, he who licensed disorder now warns his troops against similar abuses from the royal party: 'Let them break your backs with burdens, take your houses over your heads, ravish your wives and daughters before your faces,' evils uncannily close to the Homily's vision of anarchy: 'no man shall sleepe in his own house or bedde unkilled, no man shall keepe his wife, children or possession in quieteness.' The character carries inversion to its extreme, as he announced in his guiding principle: 'But then are we in order when we are most out of order.' This inversion, or subversion, of all rules persists beyond his death, at the knighting of his conqueror, which Cade has proleptically parodied by dubbing himself to face Stafford: 'To equal him, I will make myself a knight presently. Rise up Sir John Mortimer,' another derisive crack at the chivalric code.

That Shakespeare drew inspiration from the revolt of 1381 is plain, but he was visibly not alone in drawing parallels between the two episodes. The treatment of popular unrest in the chronicles and homilies implies that all rebellions dress themselves up in the same motives, follow the same process, and come to the same end

---

[37] IV. ii. 30–58; IV. vii. 6–15.

after much waste: the defeat of the rebels and their just punishment. The Homily of 1547 still refutes the principles invoked by the rebels in 1381, while Holinshed notes that 'All rebels pretend reformation but indeed purpose destruction both of king and countrie.' It was an opinion widely shared by his contemporaries.[38]

3. COURT MASKS, STREET MASQUES

All the play's characters are present in the chronicles, some in anonymous fashion like the beggar of St Albans, the armourer and his servant, Suffolk's executioner, or the rebels of Kent. The chroniclers provide us with fairly detailed portraits of the most notorious figures, but seldom enquire into the motives or personalities of the minor ones. Cade's men are not only anonymous, they are totally undifferentiated. The theatre, of course, operates differently. The secondary roles who are just cogs in the historical mechanism appear in the flesh on stage and cannot dissolve into thin or hot air.

The royal pair

In Part 1, the characters predominantly serve to illustrate one aspect of the central theme, and are governed by one dominant motive, ambition, cupidity, honour. Their loves and lives are of no interest unless they play a political role in the design, like the feelings inspired by Margaret. The protagonists of Part 2 become more subtly varied, even if we learn little more about their intimate feelings. The mention of York's readiness to take offence brings in a more personal note, while preparing for his angry outbreak in the next scene.[39] Compared with the monoliths of *1 Henry VI*, the cast reveal multiple facets and suggest new areas of darkness.

This is due in part to the nature of the plot: secrecy and devious aims lead the characters to wear masks, and show different faces in turn to the public, as they unfold their hidden designs, or compose themselves to suit the occasion. Many characters remain emblematic, but a growing number of them exhibit both negative traits and positive traits. Gradations, half-tones, make their appearance at the same time as the uncertainties of moral judgements. The frontier separating good from evil, so clear and straightforward in Part 1, proves increasingly difficult to trace, as public duty and moral laws become arguable issues.

The King, who must grow from early childhood to maturity by quick steps, makes a late entrance in Part 1, but shares many features with the adult character he is to be: charitable, anxious to do right, and unable to master his unruly court. These traits are developed in the second Part, with large hints from Hall: King Henry 'gaped not for honor, nor thirsted for riches, but studied onely for the health of his soule' and won the people's affection, 'for his holines of life, and abundant clemencie, was of the simple sort, muche fauored, and highly esteemed'. All these

[38] Holinshed II. 738.
[39] Cf. the symmetry between the King's warning and York's invectives, IV. ix. 43–4; v. i. 91–2.

moral qualities appear in the stage character, whose first care in all occasions is to glorify the work of God. His forgiveness, we saw, is greater than that of the historical character: 'Forbear to judge, for we are sinners all.'[40]

But Hall's judgement on his abilities is severe: 'kyng Henry, whiche reigned at this tyme was a man of a meke spirite, and of a simple witte, preferryng peace before warre, reste before businesse, honestie before profite, and quietnesse before laboure'. Henry's virtues are not all blessings. Thus trouble brews in France 'while the Kyng, as thinges of the worlde, and of no great moment, did neglect and omit, as he which preferred & extolled godly thinges, aboue all worldly affaires and mortal cures'. On stage York considers himself as more regal than this Lancastrian 'Whose church-like humour fits not for a crown'. Like him, Margaret thinks Henry fitter to be Pope than King:

> His champions are the prophets and apostles,
> His weapons, holy saws of sacred writ;
> His study is his tilt-yard, and his loves
> Are brazen images of canonized saints.   (I. iii. 58–61)

The frustration of the Queen and the tartness of her reproaches are on a par with her model in the chronicle, who seized the power from Gloucester's hands, 'And although she ioyned her husbande with hir in name, for a countenaunce, yet she did all, she saied all, and she bare the whole swynge, as the strong oxe doth whē he is yoked in the plough with a pore silly asse.'[41] Be it from illness or from natural cowardice, Henry is guilty of various paltry actions, which Shakespeare emends to preserve his moral worth. The Tudors, as self-appointed heirs of the Lancastrians, did their best to sanctify their distant relative, but could not persuade the Pope to canonize an insane man.[42] Hall explains the failed attempt by the high cost of the operation, which led Henry VII to withdraw his request, and never discusses the King's 'sickness', though it was well known of his contemporaries, nor wonders how it affected his political rigour.[43] Neither does Shakespeare, who preserves the sanctity without treading such perilous ground.

Hall and Shakespeare broadly agree in ascribing to the King high moral qualities and feeble political talents, but they differ in their choice of examples. In spite of Hall's praises, the personality emerging from his narrative is far from admirable: Henry displays all the faults of the weak, and none of the charisma Shakespeare endows him with. On stage, Henry VI is still a disastrous ruler; the corrections brought to the chronicle are not meant to embellish his intellectual talents, but they give better consistency to Hall's encomium: charity, humility, love for his subjects prove active virtues when he faces Winchester's agony, or Cade's uprising. Once at least, they drive him to an energetic action, the banishment of Suffolk. In Hall, it is

---

[40] Hall 208, 223, 222. *2H6*, III. iii. 31; IV. iv. 8–13; IV. ix. 15–21.

[41] Hall 208, 212, 209.

[42] See Sydney Anglo, *Spectacle Pageantry and Early Tudor Policy* (Oxford, 1969), 37–43.

[43] According to Francis Bacon, *The History of the Reign of King Henry VII*, ed. Jerry Weinberger (Ithaca, NY, 1996), 198–9, Pope Julius II knew him for 'a simple man' and did not consider his 'famous prediction' concerning young Richmond to be miraculous.

out of fear that he consents to the favourite's disgrace, and he means to recall him when peace is restored. In the play, the blackness of the crime so revolts him that for once he shows the strength of a monarch. His inability to keep a straight course is that of a character open to every influence, not a sign of duplicity.[44] This pathetic interpretation of the Christian king allows an increasingly acute enquiry into the nature of political power. Henry's virtues as much as the vices of his entourage, friends and enemies together, mark him for sacrifice.[45]

Part 1 shows Margaret making a brief appearance in Joan's wake, like her a Frenchwoman and a dubious enchantress.[46] Suffolk, in arranging the marriage, is moved neither by the King's interest nor by that of the kingdom. Part 2 amply confirms these sombre omens. Margaret shows herself as noxious as one could fear, and her personality begins to wreak more havoc than the circumstances of her arrival. Among the historical data, 2 *Henry VI* retains the persistent discontent over the loss of the French provinces, Margaret's feelings for Suffolk, and her intrusion in state affairs. Of these three factors, it is the last that creates the most disturbance, as she takes sides with the enemies of the Protector. Dangerous at first as a foreigner and the source of division at court, she grows actively harmful by her behaviour. Like the rest of the cast, her symbolic role, action in the plot, and personality are now subtly fused.

According to Hall, many found the marriage 'vnprofitable to the realme of England, and that for many causes'. For some of these, Margaret is but indirectly responsible. When it comes to the plot against Gloucester, Hall gives her a large share in the misfortunes of the realm: 'while there was nothyng to vexe or trouble the myndes of men, within the realme, a sodain mischief, and a long discorde, sprang out sodainly, by the meanes of a woman.' In opposition to Henry's meekness,

the Quene his wife, was a woman of a greate witte, and yet of no greater witte, then of haute stomacke, desirous of glory, and couetous of honor, and of reason, pollicye counsaill, and other giftes and talentes of nature, belongyng to a man, full and flowyng ... (208)

here a list of abilities in which her husband is deficient, 'but yet she had one poynt of a very woman: for often tyme, when she was vehemēt and fully bente in a matter, she was sodainly like a wethercocke, mutable, and turnyng'. The inversion of masculine and feminine roles is but faintly suggested yet. As to the last point, Shakespeare's Margaret seems, on the contrary, remarkably constant in her hatreds as in the pursuit of her objectives.

Concerning the elimination of Gloucester, Hall reports that the project was executed by others but 'came first of her awne high mind, and ambicious corage', although she would have been wiser to abstain, for the death of this noble man

---

[44] Cf. Hall 208: 'yet he was gouerned of them whom he should haue ruled, and brideled of suche, whom he sharpely should haue spurred.'

[45] See Michael Manheim, *The Weak King Dilemma in the Shakespearean History Play* (New York, 1973), 77–82, 107–20.

[46] Rackin, *Stages of History*, 157, notes that they were associated in Margaret's own time, in the *Commentaries of Pius II*, i.e. Aeneas Silvius Piccolomini.

'brought to passe that thynge, which she woulde most fayne haue eschewed, and toke from her that iewel, whiche she moste desired'. The chronicle accuses her only of contriving Gloucester's disgrace. On stage Margaret joins the plotters to have him assassinated, and sees further than they:

> Beside the haught Protector have we Beaufort,
> The imperious churchman, Somerset, Buckingham
> And grumbling York; and not the least of these
> But can do more in England than the King.   (i. iii. 69–72)

Suffolk recommends patience, advises her to ally herself with one group to bring about the fall of the others, thus deserving the Lieutenant's accusation of Machiavellism better than his vainglorious model in the chronicle:

> So, one by one, we'll weed them all at last,
> And you yourself shall steer the happy helm   (i. iii. 100–1)

There begins, according to Hall, 'the first yere of the rule of the Quene', marked by the raising of Suffolk to dukedom. On stage, as in Hall, Suffolk is 'the Quenes chefe frēde & counsailer', but Shakespeare chooses a different rhythm and delays Margaret's usurpation of power. She plays no role during Cade's rebellion, contrary to the chronicle where 'The Quene, which bare the rule, beyng of his retrayte well aduertised, sent syr Humfrey Stafford knyght, and William his brother with many other gentelmen, to folow the chace of the Kentishmen.' She takes no interest in the Kentish rebels, except to diminish Henry by comparing him to Suffolk, who, were he alive, would soon have crushed the revolt. In the Q text, no sooner has she said this than Buckingham and Clifford enter, leading in the rebels 'with halters about their necks'. In F, she speaks this line much earlier, at the height of the insurrection, and it receives no ironical rebuff from facts.[47] Only after St Albans, at the end of the play, does she take the lead over her spouse, and the shrewish tone that will not leave her again:

> What are you made of? You'll not fight nor fly.
> Now is it manhood, wisdom and defence
> To give the enemy way and to secure us
> By what we can, which can no more but fly.   (v. ii. 74–7)

He wishes to stay; she decides to flee: 'We shall to London get, where you are loved . . .'

Ungracious persons

Hall, who depicts the Queen as a woman who 'excelled all other, aswell in beautie and fauor, as in wit and pollicie', never has a good word for her favourite. To the strictures of the Commons, he adds that Suffolk was generally held in low esteem,

---

[47] Hall 220. *2H6*, iv. iv. 40–1. Cf. Cade's 'Will you needs be hanged with your pardons about your necks?' iv. viii. 21–2.

and salutes the fall of 'this flagitious person', 'this froward person, and vngracious patron', with grim approval. Shakespeare's character has no redeeming trait either, but a catalogue of vices as full as that of his accomplice, who appears even worse than Hall's unfavourable portrait of the rich Cardinal. In the chronicles, Winchester is seen on several occasions to play a positive part in state affairs, even to collaborate with Gloucester when the Duke of Bedford needs supplies. Once he is called upon 'to appeace and represse certain diuisions and commocions, sprong vp, by mischeuous and pernicious persones, within the realme'. Having restored order, 'the Cardinall began to commen with the duke of Gloucester, concernyng the affaires and busines of Fraunce', and 'diuised, how to send more aide, and men to the Duke of Bedforde, and gathered vp more money, and treasure, for the further maintenaūce of the warres, and resistence of their enemies'. His demise is deemed a loss to the kingdom: 'After the death of this prelate, which was a great stay to the Kyng & the realme, the affayres in Fraunce, were neither well loked to, nor the gouernors of the countrey were well aduised.'[48] Here, again, Hall's syntax is slightly misleading, for it suggests a causal link with the situation in France, where Winchester had done nothing for a long time; only the first part of the sentence is undoubtedly eulogistic. The fact that he died so shortly after Gloucester, and the accusations of Foxe and the *Mirror*, conspired to make him the principal engineer of the murder, and to blacken him accordingly.

Winchester's services to the Crown disappear on stage, where he never shows the least concern for public affairs. The role of wise statesman, in Part 2, is entirely reserved for Good Duke Humphrey, which also explains why his declared enemy is denied any redeeming trait. And conversely Shakespeare suspends all criticism of the Protector, exercising total freedom towards the chronicle. In *1 Henry VI*, Gloucester belongs with the troublemakers who threaten division, not with the protective heroes, Bedford and Talbot. It is he who sets off the first quarrel during his brother's funeral, he who draws his sword within a royal enclosure, he who is scolded along with Winchester by the King:

> O, what a scandal is it to our crown
> That two such noble peers as ye should jar?
> Believe me, lords—my tender years can tell—
> Civil dissension is a viperous worm,
> That gnaws the bowels of the commonwealth.   (*1H6*, III. i. 69–73)

In the second Part his hostility to Winchester is no less strong, but he keeps a hold on his temper:

> Rancour will out: proud prelate, in thy face
> I see thy fury. If I longer stay
> We shall begin our ancient bickerings.—
> Lordings, farewell . . .   (I. i. 139–43)

The chroniclers unequivocally cast him as an exemplary ruler. Having been appointed Protector of England at the death of Henry V, the Duke 'called to hym

---

[48] Hall 166, 211.

wise and graue counsailers, by whose aduise he prouided and ordeined for all thynges whiche ether redounded to the honor of the realme, or semed profitable to the publique welth of the same'. And yet he is not always blameless in their eyes, but shares the Duke of Bedford's reproofs with Winchester, for 'sure it is that the whole realm was troubled with them and their partakers'. An arbitration by Parliament reconciles them without finding one more justified than the other. Some fifteen years later, another quarrel breaks out; but this time Hall lays the blame unequivocally on Winchester for acting without the consent of either the King or Parliament, 'wherwith the duke, (like a true harted prince) was neither contente nor pleased'.[49] Gloucester's new list of accusations remains without effect, and the ill will towards him soon manifests itself, with the disgrace of the Duchess. Thus the tragic sequence of Gloucester's fall is complete, from the beginning of his quarrel with Winchester up to the 'secret attempts' against him.

Gloucester's only grievous faults in the chronicle are his private life. He contracts two marriages, both disastrous. The first one arouses general indignation and the chronicler's disapproval: 'In this season Humphrey duke of Gloucester either blynded with ambicion or dotyng for loue, married the lady Iaquet'. Gloucester prepares for war, if need be, against her legitimate husband, the Duke of Brabant, but after a long polemic his marriage is finally annulled by Rome, 'Wherefore he, by wanton affeccion blinded, toke to his wife Elianor Cobham . . . whiche before (as the fame went) was his soueraigne lady and paramour, to his great slaunder and reproche'.[50] Gloucester's amorous adventures have no effect on the plot, only a faint trace at the end of *1 Henry VI*, when the young King begs his uncle's indulgence for his marriage plans:

> If you do censure me by what you were,
> Not what you are, I know it will excuse
> This sudden execution of my will.   (v. iv. 97–9)

It is the only reference, and a cryptic one, to his dubious past. The less erudite will infer that the Duke had a wild youth, which would not alienate their sympathies, if the *Famous Victories of Henry V* is a good index to the common feeling.

No trace of these excesses remains in Part 2, where the Protector's behaviour is a model of propriety. His excellence borrows much from Hall's encomia, eked out with Foxe's story of the blind beggar. Shakespeare's Gloucester shares with the character of Part 1 some angry starts, flashes of humour, and a sharp wit in repartee. To the derisive Suffolk, he flings back:

> But you have done more miracles than I—
> You made in a day, my lord, whole towns to fly.   (ii. i. 154–5)

Foxe's narrative is decidedly more hagiographic. Before exposing the impostor, the Duke gives us a sample of his piety: 'first showing himself joyous of God's glory so showed in the getting of his sight, and exhorting him to meekness, and to no ascribing of any part of the worship to himself, nor to be proud of the people's

---

[49] Hall 115, 130, 135–8, 197.   [50] Hall 116, 128–9.

praise'.[51] Shakespeare prefers to divide roles between the King and Gloucester, giving to the one pious prayers, to the other, an efficient cross-examination.

In his various roles, Gloucester observes a strict order of precedence: private feelings and blood ties must bow to public duty, while the ruler is ruled by divine law.[52] The impetuous man of Part 1 has learnt to dominate his humours:

> Now, lords, my choler being over-blown
> With walking once about the quadrangle,
> I come to talk of commonwealth affairs.   (i. iii. 153–5)

His choice of Regent is guided neither by personal feeling, nor by an exclusive care for efficiency: it is Somerset who will go, even if York would have made a better Regent. Historically the appointment of Somerset was a blunder, judging by the results, but as France is already lost on stage, the Protector's political prestige remains intact.

With the same integrity, Duke Humphrey reminds Eleanor of his double duty to Henry, as his relative, but first as his king. To the commons, he is the only recourse against the abuses of his peers. Most significantly, he is the last statesman to refuse the main rule of the political game: 'commodity'. It is he, at the end of *1 Henry VI*, who would hold the King to his word,

> How shall we then dispense with that contract,
> And not deface your honour with reproach?   (*1H6*, v. iv. 28–9)

against the casuistry of Suffolk's reply, 'As doth a ruler with unlawful oaths', the favourite argument of every oath breaker.

Gloucester's stance against realpolitik is doomed to failure. No more than the virtuous King can the wise governor contain the rise of violence. Other normative characters appear in the sequence, Lord Saye and Iden, to speak up for the threatened values, but they have even less power to make themselves heard. Gloucester is the last to reassert the hierarchy of obligations—God's law, common weal, king, liege, blood, and kin—before it breaks down in the clannish feuds. With the civil war, allegiance becomes loyalty to a party leader, and blood ties gain precedence before all other claims, until the new Gloucester, deaf to the voice of blood, wipes out the last traces of his homonym. Thanks to Richard, values are redefined as clearly as they had grown hazy and difficult to know, leaving his enemies in no doubt as to the nature of their duty.

The young Richard is allowed a long period of maturation, thanks to an early beginning in his military career: in the play his first exploit is the killing of Somerset, who did die at St Albans, but by a hand unknown—an unhistorical exploit which is not exactly necessary to the plot, but marks him for future feats. The suggestion may nevertheless come from the chronicle, where Richard did find himself 'face to face to the duke of Somersets battayl' whom he 'shamefully discomfited', but it was the

---

[51] Hall 209–10. *2H6*, I. i. 141; II. i. 37–51; II. i. 78. Foxe 713.

[52] See Jones, *Origins of Shakespeare*, 35–54, on the character's tragic itinerary and a parallel with the Passion scenes in the mystery cycles.

next Edmund Somerset, son of this one, on the battlefield of Tewkesbury.[53] Richard's entrance at Act V is saluted by gibes at his physical and moral deformity:

> Hence, heap of wrath, foul undigested lump,
> As crooked in thy manners as thy shape.   (v. i. 157–8)

He already has the pious speech, the virtuous poses that Richard III will artfully develop:

> Fie, charity for shame! speak not in spite,
> For you shall sup with Jesu Christ tonight.   (v. i. 213–14)

Of his father, the Duke of York, we have already seen that Hall painted him as a Machiavel, a long-distance schemer. In *1 Henry VI*, his unstated ambitions are a veiled threat for the future; the immediate danger for England lies in his rivalry with Somerset. Despite his share in the death of Talbot, York defends the national interests abroad, and is indignant at the prospect of losing the conquests that have cost so many English lives:

> Is all our travail turned to this effect?
> After the slaughter of so many peers,
> So many captains, gentlemen and soldiers,
> That in this quarrel have been overthrown
> And sold their bodies for their country's benefit . . .   (*1H6*, v. iii. 102–6)

Like Gloucester, he foresees 'with grief . . . The utter loss of all the realm of France . . . by treason, falsehood, and by treachery'. When this loss occurs in *2 Henry VI*, it does afflict him, but the reason subtly changes:

> Cold news for me; for I had hope of France
> As firmly as I hope for fertile England.   (iii. i. 87–8)

What he expresses now is resentment at seeing his patrimony wasted. Even though he claims to play a beneficial role by taking the lead:

> And force perforce I'll make him yield the crown,
> Whose bookish rule hath pulled fair England down . . .   (i. i. 255–6)

his desire to reign makes him the worst enemy of his countrymen:

> I will stir up in England some black storm
> Shall blow ten thousand souls to heaven or hell . . .   (iii. i. 348–9)

In the chronicle, Somerset's reverses in Normandy further increase York's animosity towards him. He gives up the town of Caen, which belonged to the Duke of York, to the French king, 'so that he and all his, might depart in sauegard with all their goodes and substaunce'. York is informed of this while he is in Ireland, 'whiche thyng kyndeled so so greate a rancore in his harte & stomacke that he neuer lefte persecutyng of the Duke of Somersette'. What Hall reports of Somerset's

---

[53] Hall 300. Richard, born in October 1452, was under 3 when the battle of St Albans took place, on 22 May 1455, and not quite 19 at Tewkesbury.

inglorious conduct in Normandy is hardly mentioned on stage except for York's bitter comments on his failure and cowardice, not just in the matter of Caen but all of France, which York looks on as his personal property.[54]

Hall shows us York, back from Ireland, who finds a crafty way to advance his rights: 'picke some querell, to the duke of Somerset, whiche ruled the kyng, ordred the realme, and moste might do with the quene: Whom, the commons, for the losse of Normandy, worse than a Tode or Scorpion, hated.' Somerset's influence at court and the popular hostility follow the course of Suffolk's, whose successor he is in the royal favour: 'ye duke of Somerset rose vp in high fauor w^t ye king & ye quene, and his worde only ruled, & his voyce was only hearde.'[55] Shakespeare does not re-employ these features for Somerset, whose dominant trait remains the venomous hostility he arouses in the Duke of York, thus causing his outburst before the appointed time:

> But I must make fair weather yet awhile
> Till Henry be more weak and I more strong.   (v. i. 30–1).

York keeps this resolution for exactly sixty lines before his fury gets the better of his Machiavellian plans.

Hall tells us little about the Nevilles, 'these twoo strong and robustious pillers' of York, 'his especiall frendes, the erles of Salisbury and Warwicke', but stresses the tenacity of their clandestine efforts:

their hartes were knitte and coupled in one, neuer forgetting, but dayly studyeng, bothe how to be reuenged of the olde dispites and malicious attēptes, against them committed and imagened, and also how to compasse their purposes, and to get the superioritie and ouerhand aboue their euilwillers, & apparant enemies. (236).

In the play, they become York's faithful partisans once he has explained his titles to them, but their role is not restricted to that aspect. In the first scene they are the only ones, with Gloucester, to express disinterested concerns:

> Pride went before; Ambition follows him.
> While these do labour for their own preferment,
> Behoves it us to labour for the realm.   (i. i. 177–9)

It is Salisbury who first proposes to York to unite their efforts 'for the public good',

> And, as we may, cherish Duke Humprey's deeds,
> While they do tend the profit of the land.   (i. i. 200–1)

A virtuous plan supported by his son:

> So God help Warwick, as he loves the land
> And common profit of his country!   (i. i. 202–3)

Both Nevilles deplore the loss of the French provinces, and express indignation at

---

[54] Hall 214–16. Holinshed's briefer account, III. 217, is more sensitive to the tears of Somerset's wife, which moved him to surrender. 2H6, III. i. 290–306.

[55] Hall 225, 227.

the selfish schemings of their peers, but their exemplariness goes no further. Having adopted the Yorkist positions, they become party men. If Salisbury's conscience really told him to defend the cause of York, it has led him into a deadlock, which Margaret promptly points out to him when he tries to excuse his breach of oath: 'A subtle traitor needs no sophister.' The Nevilles are not shaped into model characters, but being the only ones who do not seek their own interest, they perform the declining voice of *res publica* in the overture amid a chorus of wolves.

Hall seems to sympathize with Somerset's wish to eliminate York and his brood of traitors, yet his tone changes when the Queen attempts precisely this: the Yorkist trio answer her summons to a hunt at Coventry without misgivings,

but the serpent lurked vnder the grasse, & vnder sugered speache, was hide pestiferous poyson, so that if these noblemen admonished by their frendes, had not sodaynly departed, their lyfes threde had bene broken, and their mortall fate had them ensued, (236)

a device the chronicler condemns as 'sedicious and fraudulēt meanes'. There are dramatic tensions already perceptible in his narrative. He can be strongly opinionated, but he rarely likes to take sides in a conflict, and is able to invoke either moral or pragmatic principles, as the occasion demands, or in turn comment for himself, invent his characters' feelings, echo rumours and public opinion. Thus when Warwick recounts to his friends 'the assaute of the kynges seruauntes, and the pretensed purpose of the fraudulent Quene', they in answer 'somwhat exasperate and moued with this doble dealyng began to grudge and murmure: affirmyng that in the Quene rested nothyng, but fraude and feminine malice'. The expressions 'fraudulent Quene' and 'doble dealyng' must be ascribed to the three men rather than to the chronicler who does not necessarily share their views, and unambiguously disapproves of their every move in the next paragraphs.[56]

Hall can no more than Shakespeare be safely aligned with the Yorkist or the Lancastrian camp. Like a playwright, he may disappear behind his characters, allow them to express independent views, or supply them with remarks suited to the circumstance. Given this rhetorical mode, his own views on the dynastic wars and his famous providential pattern are easily confused with theirs. If his opinions seem to waver so, the fault often lies in his turns of phrase, not his turns of coat. Undoubtedly, his philosophy of history is shaky, neither consistently Machiavellian nor providentialist; like most chroniclers of the time, he resorts to the variety of doctrines available whenever facts defeat traditional beliefs. To write that 'Hall clearly seems to favor the providential view that "God by his divine prouidence, punished the offence of the grandfather in the sonnes sonne"', is to ignore his introductory clause,

Other there be that ascribe his infortunitie, onely to the stroke & punishment of God, afferming that the kyngdome, whiche Henry the .iiii. hys grandfather wrongfully gat, and vniustly possessed agaynst kyng Rychard the .ii. & his heyres could not by very diuyne iustice, longe continew in tha iniurious stocke:

[56] Ibid. 239.

among various samples of 'the vulgare opiniõ'. Holinshed suppresses the whole passage in favour of a reflection that 'neither part could securelie possesse the regalitie, when they obteined it; which highmindednesse was in the end the ouerthrow of both principals and accessaries'.[57] The one consistent exposé of the providential myth in their narratives comes between quotation marks, as it were: York's long oration in Parliament to present his claim runs from 'the fyrste vngodly vsurpacion of the forenamed Henry vntruely called kyng Henry the. iiij' to the conclusion that 'God of his ineffable goodnes' has sent the Duke 'to restore again this decayed kyngdõ, to his auncient fame & olde renoume'. Here Holinshed criticizes the recourse to prosopopoeia when reliable sources are missing, then proceeds to report the full speech, trimmed of a few rhetorical ornaments but identical in substance to that of 'Maister Edward Hall'.[58]

Shakespeare distributes the chroniclers' dialogues, reports, and opinions among the ad hoc characters. Hall's comments on the beauty of the Queen become the King's words of greeting.[59] The common views on their fated marriage and Suffolk's bill of expenses are given to Gloucester. Insults, maxims, and omens are attributed where they can be voiced with most strength and raise the dramatic conflict to the highest point of tension. The chronicler retains the privilege of speaking for himself whenever he wants to, unlike the dramatist who delegates all matters of faith and politics to his characters, and refers them to the public's judgement.

Classes in rhetoric

Gloucester, in refusing to let reason of state take precedence over moral law, recalls a hierarchy of duties which, ideally, sets the norm for both individual characters and social groups. In each group, the norm is both represented and transgressed at some point during the play. The Protector watches over the good of the people, who in return owe him obedience, but he seems alone in fulfilling his charge, as the petitioners' complaints show. Suffolk assures the Lieutenant that 'This hand of mine hath writ in thy behalf' but convinces no one. When Lord Saye claims, with more justice, to have watched for the people's good, as Gloucester did, he is killed on the spot. In this escalation of popular violence, Gloucester's murder is a crucial turning point, from the Commons' demands of justice, which still respect legal procedure, to ochlocracy.[60]

Under ordinary circumstances the people play no part in state affairs, though their potential for anarchy makes them a force to be reckoned with. In practice, *vox populi* can be a weighty argument in the claims of a pretender to the throne, even if their share in the designation of a sovereign is restricted to hailing the new king in recognition of his title.[61] All the usurpers in English history insist that they are

---

[57] Rackin, *Stages of History*, 8. Hall 286. Holinshed 301.
[58] Hall 245–8. Holinshed 262–4.
[59] Hall 205. 2H6, I. i. 21, 32–5.
[60] I. iii. 1–20; IV. i. 63; IV. vii. 78; III. i. 110–11; III. ii. 278.
[61] I. i. 191, 197; III. i. 240, 373–4. The claimant to the crown was submitted to the *consensus* of the

responding to the wish of the people.[62] The lower orders thus constitute a double threat: riot, and popular vote. In the play, Gloucester is accused of planning to seize the throne with the help of popular favour:

> By flattery hath he won the commons' hearts;
> And when he please to make commotion,
> 'Tis to be feared they all will follow him.   (III. i. 28–30)

Indeed, the Commons' anger at his death is only appeased by the banishment of Suffolk, as in the chronicles, where the King's council occasionally give in to their requests, just long enough to calm spirits. The chroniclers consider them to be a pressure group, though Holinshed uses slightly less offensive terms than Hall to define them. Where Hall reports in treating the case of Suffolk that 'this doynge incensed the furye of the mutable cōmons', Holinshed simply writes that 'This doing much displeased the people', but has no greater opinion of them: Hall's 'furious rage of yᵉ outragious people' is still to him 'the malice of the people'.[63]

The hierarchy of public duties is recalled by preterition in the chronicles, when placed under threat by wartime modes of behaviour, 'For while the one part studied to vanquishe and suppresse the other, all commō wealth was set aside, and iustice and equitie was clerely exiled'. The play illustrates this implicit moral rule with parallel pictures of observance and violation of the codes regulating each level of society, much after the fashion of the rhetorical exercises practised in Tudor schools. Emrys Jones points out a model comparison of Henry VI and Richard III, in Thomas Wilson's *Art of Rhetoric*, at the chapter 'Description of Persons'

Such a training in the writing of the *controversiae*, the devising of situations which could be broken down into a structure of division and opposition and then treated with the utmost emotional force of which the writer was capable, would undoubtedly make for the kind of drama we find in early Shakespeare.

Hall, whose writing abounds with such figures, was equally well trained in these exercises.[64] His comparative protocols may have contributed to place the characters on a scale of descending merits, but 2 *Henry VI* is more than a show of opposite pairs. The subtlety of the method grows in proportion with that of the characters, who are now spun of a mingled yarn. York, for instance, is successively measured against Gloucester, the Nevilles, Somerset, Cade, the King, and Iden. Characterization as well as plot confront each personality in turn with all the others, as every ambition runs up against opposite desires.

The scenes illustrating division in *1 Henry VI* are punctuated by the moral lessons

---

magnates, which the people endorsed by their acclamations, the *collaudatio*. See Percy E. Schramm, *A History of the English Coronation*, trans. L. C. Wickham Legg (Oxford, 1937), 143.

[62] See T. P. Taswell-Langmead, *English Constitutional History: From the Teutonic Conquest to the Present Time* (London, 1946); A. R. Myers (ed.), *English Constitutional Documents* (London, 1969), IV. 1327–485.

[63] Hall 218, 219, 220, 225, 231. Holinshed 220.

[64] Hall 231. Jones, *Origins of Shakespeare*, 14. See Riggs, *Shakespeare's Heroical Histories*, 34–61, on the generative function of *comparatio* and *controversiae*.

of exemplary figures. Similar adages can be heard in Part 2, but carried by speakers as dubious as York, who aim to convince interlocutors on stage, and no longer addressed directly to the audience. What the soliloquies impart now are the confidences of schemers revealing their plots. The chroniclers generally imply, and the events of *1 Henry VI* obliquely confirm, that union leads to victory; it is still possible at that stage to believe that virtuous behaviour will protect against misfortune. The second Part casts doubt, not on the notions of good and evil, which are defined unambiguously by the normative procedures we analysed, but on the efficacy of virtue, which seems a sure way to failure: the defeat of patient charity in the person of Henry VI is aggravated in the case of Gloucester, whose trust in justice is supported by an undeniable competence. The opening rift between ethics and politics dramatizes a major crisis of Christian monarchy which the chroniclers lack the mental equipment to detect, let alone discuss. Whatever denials are opposed by facts, their principles find compromises with Heaven. Hall's moral saws still provide the play with reminders of the norm, but these become part of a meditation riddled with uncertainty, and critically tested by the end of Gloucester's or Lord Saye's illusions.

According to Hall, the royal marriage initiates a concatenation of events, from Gloucester's fall to the destruction of the Lancastrian dynasty. But there are holes in his argument. After making Margaret's enmity with the Protector the main cause of England's misfortunes, Hall picks up a thread he had left hanging some years earlier: the dispute between Gloucester and the Cardinal was 'a smoke that rose in England, whiche after grewe to a greate fire, and a terrible flame, to the destruccion of many a noble man'. Its ultimate result will be the Protector's fall, Hall concludes, and embarks upon the disgrace of the Duchess. Thus he incriminates in turn Winchester, the Queen, and Suffolk, but does not succeed in bringing to light what the play represents, a complex conjunction of deep and fortuitous causes that are shown brewing up in Part 1.[65]

The death of Suffolk serves to introduce a new dramatic theme, by evincing Margaret's self-injunction, 'Think therefore on revenge, and cease to weep.' It is hard to see at this point of the plot what target she would aim at, unless it were her husband for having caused Suffolk's death. The Yorkists have as yet done nothing to deserve her hatred. The theme of revenge appears in Hall much later, at the battle of Wakefield, where Clifford refuses to spare young Rutland because 'by Gods blode, thy father slew myne, and so wil I do the and all thy kyn'. This is the first we hear of a duel, which Hall's report on St Albans did not mention, but which is shown at the end of Part 2: Clifford has killed York's horse; York immediately retaliates by striking down Clifford's. The two men still respect the chivalric codes: they fight a regular duel, each rendering homage to the valour of his opponent. Now Clifford's son opens the phase of family feuds:

---

[65] Hall 197, 208, 210, 219. Reporting Henry VI's deposition, 297–8, he again recalls Gloucester's death and Margaret's responsibility.

> York not our old men spares;
> No more will I their babes;   (v. ii. 51–2)

and swears to cut any infant of the enemy house into gobbets. When he insists that the King flee,

> But that my heart's on future mischief set,
> I would speak blasphemy ere bid you fly;   (v. ii. 84–5)

his personal rancour is about to supplant the service of the sovereign. The next step will be the murder of Rutland on the battlefield.

4

Unhappy Families

Seventy pages of Hall plus the overture of Thomas More's *History*, covering events spread over some fifteen years—1455 to 1471—provide the plot for *3 Henry VI*.[1] Here again, Shakespeare contracts time intervals, fuses characters or episodes, alters chronology, collects scattered data, detaches facts from their causes or equips them with new ones, reattributes actions or opinions according to his dramatic pattern. As in the earlier plays, whole sections of the narrative are omitted, others are amplified or consistently developed. Nevertheless the handling of sources presents new characteristics: the play is both more faithful and more indifferent to what the chronicle says. As in *2 Henry VI*, Shakespeare seldom departs from the relevant pages to seek material elsewhere, but he makes no attempt to renew their meaning, nor does he question the interpretations of the chronicler, as if the cause of the events, the political intricacies, the historical mechanisms were no longer his first concern. Whilst keeping close to the thread of the narrative, the dramatization simplifies it. The tribulations of the House of York up to its final triumph stretched over a quarter of a century, during which the Yorkists gained and lost ground several times; Shakespeare speeds up history whilst preserving the see-saw movement between York and Lancaster, which is heavily emphasized in the chronicle.

Part 2 ends with the death of Somerset, whose head re-enters, held by Richard, at the beginning of Part 3. Shakespeare has suppressed the interval between two Yorkist victories, St Albans in 1455 and Northampton in 1460, both followed by the designation of York as Protector of the Realm. In the play, York seats himself on the throne, as he did after his second victory. After a heated argument, Henry accepts York as heir, causing his disgusted partisans to leave and organize resistance around the Queen. The claims of the Yorkists draw on Hall's prosopopoeia unrolling the Duke's titles in 1460. Hall mentions no pressures from the rebel army, though the victorious Yorkists had the King in their power. The Queen was absent at the time and refused to come.

In the play, Margaret makes her daunting entrance, based on Hall's earlier mention of the terror she inspired, reproaches the King with dispossessing their son, and leaves to take arms, regardless of the truce concluded between York and

---

[1] Hall 233–303. More's *History of Richard III* occupies pp. 342–84 of Hall's chronicle, 360–405 of Holinshed's.

Lancaster.[2] In the chronicle it is she who initiates hostilities: having refused to answer the King's summons, she marched against Sandal Castle, where York was spending Christmas, with an army of 18,000 or 22,000 men, according to estimates, Shakespeare settling for an average 20,000. On stage the two camps arm simultaneously, and are equally responsible for the war. York's allies urge him to take the crown now, despite his oath to Henry, and fight without waiting for reinforcements, whereas in Hall, it was York who decided to attempt a sally, against the advice of his friends. The chronicle makes no allusion to his Mortimer uncles. Of his sons, only the eldest, Rutland, was present; Edward, who was expected with an army, arrived after the battle. The scene of York's death borrows elements from Holinshed, who records that he was mocked with a paper crown and a derisive show of allegiance. Shakespeare gives the initiative of this parody to Margaret, and goes one step further than the chroniclers with her presentation to York of a handkerchief dipped in Rutland's blood. The Duke's head, in conformity with both narratives, will be set over the gates of the city of York.[3]

Act II begins with the fortunes of York at their lowest ebb, and ends with their triumph. In Hall, they suffer several setbacks before Edward wins the throne. After the disaster of Wakefield, Edward saw three suns appearing to him in the sky and, encouraged by this prodigy, won the battle of Mortimer's Cross, just as his ally Warwick was beaten at St Albans. After a clash at Ferrybridge, where Clifford and Warwick's brother were killed, Edward gained a decisive victory at Towton. His younger brothers were in Utrecht, where they had been sent for safety, and stayed there until his accession. On stage, Richard witnesses the prodigy with Edward, while George returns from the continent just in time to join Warwick. The ensuing fight takes place on an unidentified battlefield near York, under the sad eyes of the King, who sees the Yorkists lose then regain ground, and discovers the price paid for their feud by humble families. This episode reflects the chroniclers' reports on many points: the three suns which become the emblem of the House of York, Warwick's movements, the knighting of the Prince of Wales, Warwick's vow to kill his horse rather than flee, the King's lonely wandering, the fratricidal nature of the war, Clifford's death. The Yorkist projects—Edward's coronation, Warwick's embassy to the court of Lewis XI, and the titles given to the new King's brothers— keep close to the source.[4]

The next scenes, halfway through the play, allow a brief respite where York and Lancaster exchange positions twice, before the war is resumed in the final act. During this pause, Henry returns secretly to England, where he is soon captured. Edward meanwhile pays court to the widow of Sir John Grey, ruining Warwick's efforts on his behalf in France. Hall gives two versions of this episode: one follows the report of Warwick's mission, the other is told retrospectively, at the time of Richard's usurpation, in Thomas More's *History*, which Hall inserts in his own

---

[2] I. i. 35, 50–188, 35. Hall 249–50, 241.
[3] I. iv. 179–80. Hall 251 (269).
[4] Hall 251, 252, 255, 244, 256, 257, 263, 258.

narrative. Shakespeare draws on both accounts for his wooing scene, and on Thomas More's portrait of the scheming monster for Richard's ensuing soliloquy.[5]

The historical Margaret and Warwick each made several trips to France before they met at the court of Lewis XI. On stage, they go once. Lewis pragmatically inclines at first to York, but the news of Edward's marriage to Elizabeth Woodville turns the tables in favour of Margaret. Clarence's grievances against the Woodville clan, those of his model in the chronicle, reflect the general feeling in England and abroad: surprise, scorn, displeasure.[6] Where Hall underlines the remote consequences of Edward's choice, on stage the effects are immediate. Clarence, Warwick, and Somerset, with troops of French soldiers, seize Edward, who escapes shortly after to Flanders with Richard and Hastings. Henry VI recovers his crown long enough to call a Parliament and hail a newcomer, young Richmond, as England's hope. Awareness of his persistent misfortune leads him to entrust his rule to Warwick who, as in the chronicle, is the principal agent of his liberation. Warwick's first commands,

> Forthwith that Edward be pronounced a traitor
> And all his lands and goods be confiscate.   (iv. vi. 54–5)

directly echo Hall's: 'kyng Edwarde was declared a traytor to his coūtrey, . . . & all his goodes were cōfiscate'. Hall's narrative treats in turn, as does the play, Henry VI's liberation, his persistent bad luck, the rulings of the Westminster Parliament, the Queen's vain attempts to return to England with her son, and the arrival in London of a young relative of Somerset named Richmond. It was Jasper, Earl of Pembroke, and not Somerset, who brought the young man to Henry VI. Hall specifies that Richmond was the grandson of the first Duke of Somerset, but Shakespeare avoids stressing his connection with the illegitimate Beauforts or the unattractive Somersets of Parts 1 and 2. Neither Hall nor Shakespeare discusses his hereditary rights at this point: it is God who designates him by the mouth of Henry VI. The throne will come in time to this Richmond, Hall insists, 'whom wee ought to beleue, to be sent from God, and of hym onely to be prouided a kyng, for to extinguish bothe the faccions and partes, of kyng Henry the. vi. and of kyng Edwarde the. iiii'. The turn of the phrase, 'ought to', seems uncannily apt. On stage, as in the source, Henry prophesies:

> If secret powers
> Suggest but truth to my divining thoughts,
> This pretty lad will prove our country's bliss.   (iv. vi. 68–70)

It is Hall who suggests the idea that Henry's saintliness enables him to see into the divine projects: 'So this holy man shewed before, the chaunce that should happen, that this erle Henry so ordeined by God, should in tyme to come (as he did in deede) haue and enioye the kingdome, and the whole rule of the realme.' Shakespeare sticks to the order of the narrative in giving here news of Edward, who has escaped,

---

[5] Hall 264–5. Hall/More 365–6. *3H6*, iii. ii. 124–95
[6] iv. i. 47–64. Hall 264–5, 271.

while Warwick complains, as in the chronicle, of the negligence of his brother, who was supposed to keep him. This news sends Richmond straight to Brittany for safety, though Hall reports his flight much later, after the defeat at Tewkesbury.[7]

The play abridges the trials of Edward on the continent: he disembarks without further ado at Ravenspurgh, and heads straight for his city of York. There, he soon lays the citizens' scruples to rest by assuring them that he wants only his duchy—Bolingbroke's argument on his return from exile in *Richard II*—and delays but the space of forty lines before he has himself proclaimed King again.[8] In the sources the discussions last all day; Edward is admitted into the city the next morning, then proceeds to Northampton, where Montgomery and other friends persuade him to declare himself, 'boldely sayng to hym, that they would serue no man but a kynge', echoed on stage by Montgomery's threat to leave: 'I came to serve a king and not a duke.' Hall unleashes providential thunders on Edward's progeny in punishment for his perjury, but immanent justice has no visible place in the play. Still, Fortune smiles on Edward in both versions.[9]

According to the chronicle, King Henry was led in great pomp by Warwick, Clarence, and other supporters from the Tower to the Bishop's palace. On stage, the Lancastrian party meet there to draw up a plan of action against Edward's troops.[10] It was the only time when the different characters taking part in this scene were actually brought together. When Warwick undertook to stop Edward's march, they were all away from London except Clarence. As to their relationships, they showed none of the affectionate friendship uniting them in the play: Warwick was dissatisfied with his brother Montague who had let Edward pass with his army without making a move, and with Clarence, who was meant to bring troops from London but was loitering on the way.[11] In narrative and play, they appoint to meet at Coventry. No sooner have they left the stage than Henry is retaken. Historically, his capture took place after the meeting at Coventry, when Edward entered London at the head of a powerful army. After some hesitations between the two kings, the Londoners opted for Edward. Somerset and his friends took flight, 'leuyng kyng Henry alone, as an host that should be sacrificed, in the Bishops palace of London, ... in which place he was by kynge Edward taken, and agayne committed to prison and captiuitie'.[12] This inversion deprives the combatants of any motive to choose Barnet as their battlefield, but saves them a trip to London for Henry's capture.

The sensational turn of events at Coventry had been prepared for in the chronicle:

It was no meruayll that the duke of Clarēce, with so small persuasion and lesse exhortynge, turned from the erle of Warwyckes parte, for as you haue hard before, thys marchandyse was

---

[7] Hall 287, 303.

[8] IV. vii. 17–24. Hall 291.

[9] Hall 276, 292. *3H6*, IV. vi. 19, 20, 28; IV. vii. 2.

[10] IV. viii. 2. The location, from Hall 285, 294, is given in the next scene: 'You left poor Henry at the bishop's palace' (v. i. 45).

[11] Hall 285, 291–3.

[12] Ibid. 294.

labored, conduyted and concluded by a damsell, when the duke was in the French court, to the erles vtter confusion. (293)

Edward IV had employed this 'damsell' as a double agent to make his peace with his brother. Shakespeare only retains from the narrative the 'small persuasion and less exhortynge' that sufficed to send Clarence back to the Yorkists. Clarence's provocative manner to Warwick is far from his apologetic tone in the chronicle, and though Warwick's retort is the same, 'perjured', there is no echo here of the divine punishment promised to him by Hall. The meeting itself conforms to the chronicle, save that in Hall it was Edward who challenged and Warwick who refused the fight, as he does at the end of the scene: Edward placed his camp in front of the city, 'hys men were set forwarde, and marshalled in array, & he valiãtly bad the erle battayle: which mistrustyng that he should be deceaued by the duke of Clarēce (as he was in dede) kept hym selfe close within the walles'.[13] Clarence arriving in the meantime, the two brothers were reconciled thanks to the mediation of Richard; then all three tried vainly to bring over Warwick, who distrusted his son-in-law well before Coventry. The play gives no advance warning of Clarence's defection. He and Montague perform a chassé-croisé, away from and back to the family camp.[14] Montague's change of sides is already known to the audience, who saw him earlier in the Lancastrian camp with his brother, but it is an unexpected blow for Edward: at their last interview, Montague had confirmed his loyalty to the Yorkist cause, despite Warwick's revolt. Somerset, another turncoat, enters next, though in fact he was not present at the meeting, any more than were Montague and Oxford. However, all fought at Barnet with Warwick's troops a month later.

King Henry being already taken, we go straight to Barnet. Having appointed to meet there, the two armies leave and re-enter straight away, transported to the battlefield where the struggle is nearly over, and Edward drags in the wounded Warwick. Hall does not say who killed the Earl; according to certain authors, he writes, 'this battaill was fought so nere hande, that kyng Edward was constrained to fight his awne persone, & fought as sore as any man of his partie', while Warwick 'was now aduised by the Marques his brother to relynquishe his horse, and trie the extremitie by hande strokes'—enough, perhaps, to suggest a duel between the two men. The dying Warwick advises Oxford and Somerset to flee, which in fact they did—'euery man fled whether his mynde serued him'—but certainly not to rejoin the Queen, of whose arrival they were still ignorant. Edward, Hall tells us, had brought Henry VI with him to Barnet, but the theme of the King as impotent spectator of the massacre has already served its turn, and Henry is sent back to the Tower in silence. The following scene speeds over the frenzied moves detailed in the chronicle. Everything is settled in three lines: hearing that his defeated enemies are leaving to join the Queen at Tewkesbury, Edward decides that he 'Will thither straight, for willingness rids way':[15] this golden rule governs movement in the

[13] Hall 293. Edward uses identical terms ('in good array', 'bid us battle') at v. i. 62–3.

[14] Clarence leaves, then returns to his brothers (IV. i. 118–23; v. i. 83–105), Montague swears to remain, then takes up arms with Warwick (IV. i. 133–42; v. i. 67–9).

[15] v. iii. 20–1. Hall 297–300 details the comings and goings on both sides.

theatrical space, as between Coventry and Barnet, anticipating the mode of travel advertised in *Henry V*.

Margaret landed in England with an army on the very evening of Barnet, 'a daie after the faire', and was so crushed by this latest of Fortune's blows that she was ready to give up the struggle. It was Somerset who 'merily required theim all, to bee of hardy harte and good chere', he who succeeded in comforting the Queen 'Although that she wer almost drouned in sorowe, and plunged in pein', a liquid note echoed in the dialogue by the image of the ship in the tempest.[16] Margaret declares that her tears prevent her from speaking, in a rhetorical mode entirely at odds with the resolute tone of her opening lines:

> Great lords, wise men ne'er sit and wail their loss
> But cheerly seek how to redress their harms.   (v. iv. 1–2)

In the more conventional sequence of her address, it is the chivalrous help for widow and orphan that Margaret asks for, composing a stylized figure of the weak woman, wholly unrelated to her indomitable personality. The Prince of Wales no less decorously gives the fearful ones leave to leave, a discourse saluted as one worthy of his heroic grandfather. Oxford's command, 'Here pitch our battle; hence we will not budge', corresponds to the decision taken by Somerset in Hall's narrative, against the advice of several captains who wanted to await Pembroke's reinforcements. The battle itself is restricted to one terse stage direction in the Folio: '*Alarum, Retreat, Excursions. Exeunt.*' Q is slightly more detailed, without saying much either about the feats of arms: '*Alarmes to the battell, Yorke flies, then the Chambers be discharged. Then enter the king, Cla. & Glo. & the rest, & make a great shout, and Crie, for Yorke, and then the Queene is taken, & the prince, & Ofd. & Sum.*'

The victorious Yorkists organize the fate of their enemies: Oxford will be held captive in the castle of Ham, but Somerset is to be executed on the spot, as he was in the chronicle. In fact, Oxford was not present at Tewkesbury; after Barnet he went to Cornwall and there continued to lead the resistance against Edward until his final surrender in 1474, when he was sent to Ham.[17] Edward offered a reward for the Prince of Wales, promising that his life would be spared. There are slight variations between the numerous accounts of the young Prince's end, but none show anything like his arrogance on stage, where he defies the York brothers, 'lascivious Edward', 'perjured George', 'misshapen Dick'. Margaret's presence emphasizes the retributive symmetry: her son is killed under her eyes by the three sons of the man who died cursing her.

From the chroniclers' reports, all Edward did was strike the Prince with his hand, then his brothers rushed in to stab him, as did Hastings and Dorset. The latter are not present on stage, though in *Richard III* Margaret accuses them of having stood by without interfering when her son was killed.[18] Despite the pledge given, the

---

[16] Hall 296–8.

[17] See Ramsay, *Lancaster and York*, ii. 398.

[18] An 'unconformity' which has not so far seemed ground enough to deny Shakespeare's authorship of *3 Henry VI* . . . or *Richard III*.

Prince was 'sodaynly murthered, & pitiously manquelled', Hall writes, 'The bitterness of which murder, some of the actors, after in their latter dayes tasted and
assayed by the very rod of Iustice and punishment of God.' The struggle is over; its
driving force was the defence of heritage, now the old Margaret has died with her
son, leaving a ghostly memory of her to descant malevolent litanies over her son's
assassins. Richard is ready to oblige when she begs to be killed—though she was
never threatened in the chronicle—but is prevented by Edward, and sets off to
dispatch Henry VI. It appears now that murder is Richard's vocation, which
he confirms on killing the King: 'For this amongst the rest was I ordained.' His
brothers observe his special talent with a benevolent eye, never imagining that he
will not stop at the enemies of his family.[19]

The assassination of Henry VI suffers no delay, although the chroniclers who
suspect Richard of this crime never say that he left the battlefield in haste to commit
it. Before dying, Henry has a prophetic vision of the countless woes in store for
England. The details of Richard's monstrous birth are drawn from Thomas More,
and embellished with extra nefarious signs—sinister birds, howling dogs, tempests.
It is likewise More who supplies the basis for Richard's soliloquy after the murder
and his cold-blooded plan to eliminate all those who separate him from the crown.
This soliloquy casts its ugly shadow over the final scene: the Yorks gloat over the list
of their vanquished adversaries, but the most dangerous foe is part of the family.
More's commentary on Richard's powers of dissimulation, 'outwardely familier
where he inwardly hated, not lettynge to kisse whom he thought to kill', inspires
the show of love to his nephew:

> To say the truth, so Judas kissed his master
> And cried, 'All hail!' when as he meant all harm.   (v. vii. 33–4)

The news that Margaret will be sent home against payment of a ransom by the
French King seems to close accounts and erase the cost of her dowry. Now that all
hostile clouds have been dispelled, the Yorkist feast can begin.

2. DRAMATIC TECHNIQUES

The fusion of episodes

By treating as one the two Yorkist victories of St Albans and Northampton,
Shakespeare smoothes over the break between Parts 2 and 3, and avoids the repetitiveness of a situation that scarcely evolved in the course of a five-year interval. The
first scene of 3 *Henry VI* adds up the casualties of the two battles: Edward claims he
has killed or at least seriously wounded Buckingham who, according to Hall, was
wounded at St Albans and killed at Northampton, though the chronicle does
not say by whom. Edward was present at Northampton but not at St Albans.
Northumberland, Clifford, and Stafford were killed at St Albans, as Somerset was,

---

[19]   Hall 301. *3H6*, v. vi. 58.

though certainly not by a 3-year-old Richard. The Earl of Wiltshire, wounded in line 14, had fled with Buckingham at St Albans. Other episodes provide details to the scene: thus the flight of the King is drawn from the battle of Hexham in 1464, where he fled at full gallop; shortly before, at Hedgeley Moor, the Lords of the North had fled in front of Montague's army without striking a blow. After St Albans the King was led back to London with proper respect, as Warwick's men are ordered to do in the play.[20]

Warwick's two missions to the King of France, and Edward's two escapes, each make but one on stage. Concerning the movements of the main protagonists, the narrative is at times incoherent, for the chronicler gets confused by the comings and goings of Margaret and Warwick, who made several trips to the continent. According to his report, Margaret crossed over after Towton to seek aid, and came back with 500 men who fought for her at Hexham. Henry fled to Scotland after their defeat but was soon recaptured, news of which sent Margaret, 'all desolate and comfortles', to her father's home where she stayed until her last fatal return to England. However, when Warwick came on his mission to the French court, Margaret was there again, soliciting the aid of Lewis XI, in vain, for Edward had Henry safe in the Tower, and seemed a more attractive ally than Lancaster. This anomaly arises from Hall's misplacing the rout of the Lancasters before Edward's marriage, on 1 May 1464: the battle of Hexham took place a fortnight later, 15 May, and Henry VI was not taken until July 1465. If Margaret was in France at the time of Warwick's mission, it was not 'all desolate' after the capture of her husband, but looking for support there. She went to seek troops and subsidies on the continent in April 1462 and again in August 1463; then after Hexham in May 1464, she stayed several years in France with her father, up to the time of her alliance with Warwick in 1470 and her last crossing to England, 'her infortunate iorney', in 1471.[21]

Warwick was so incensed by the news of Edward's marriage that he swore to depose the unworthy King, but he hid his rancour for several years, then allied himself with Clarence, who accompanied him to Calais. The following year, 1469, both men returned with troops, and managed to take hold of Edward. But their royal prisoner soon escaped, and dealt them a defeat which sent them fleeing to France for help. It was only then that Warwick met Margaret at the French court, struck an alliance with her, and went back leading an army supplied by Lewis XI.[22] Edward was forced in his turn to flee to Holland with Richard and Hastings, to seek help from the Duke of Burgundy. During his exile, in November 1470, Elizabeth gave birth to their son, the future Edward V, in sanctuary, while Henry VI was reinstated on the throne by Warwick. Edward returned to England the following spring, gained admittance in York, and from there went on to Nottingham where he was proclaimed king.

The events of those six years are so contracted in the play that the first three scenes of Act III are nearly simultaneous: Henry's capture is announced to Edward

[20] I. i. 33–4. Hall 233, 244, 259–60.
[21] See Ramsay, *Lancaster and York*, ii. 290–300.
[22] Hall 265–6, 275–8, 281.

while he is wooing Lady Grey; Margaret, at the court of France, does not know yet that Henry is a prisoner, but comes to beg help as in the chronicle. She mentions the aid supplied by Scotland, as in 1462, but she is accompanied by the Earl of Oxford, as in 1470. Warwick arrives, asking for the hand of Lady Bona for his master, but he is ignorant of both Henry's capture and Edward's marriage. Not only the time interval between the historical Warwick's two visits to the French court, but his long dissimulation on his return, disappear. Shakespeare treats as a continuous episode Margaret's prayers, the proposal to Lady Bona, Lewis XI's choice in favour of Edward, the letters from England, Warwick's anger—all incidents which correspond to the first period in Hall's narrative—and the events of the second period: the alliance between Margaret and Warwick, sealed by the marriage of their children, the hope of rallying Clarence to the cause of Lancaster, Lewis XI's military support, and plans of attack. Warwick and Oxford are to return first with 5,000 men, soon followed with fresh troops by Margaret and the Prince of Wales.[23] Rather than a pause, these three scenes form a turning point, the moment of dramatic reversal between two decisive phases of the Wars of the Roses.[24] The ten years of Edward's effective reign until the Lancaster restoration are reduced on stage to a brief moment of triumph, before his imprudent marriage precipitates a new fall of the House of York.

Act IV runs together several episodes: Warwick enters with Oxford at the head of the French troops, augmented with crowds of common people who welcome him on his return, as they did on his second landing in 1470, offers the hand of his daughter to Clarence as in 1467, and greets Somerset who has rallied to the Lancastrians, as in 1464.[25] Edward's ordeal likewise combines two sets of misfortunes: as in the first, the King being carelessly encamped, his guard is easily neutralized. Warwick's plan to free and reinstate Henry draws on Edward's second fall from power, as does the next scene, where the pregnant Queen runs to sanctuary: in the play, because Edward is a prisoner, and in the chronicle because he is in flight. The characters who took part in one or other of the episodes are brought together on stage: thus Richard, Hastings, and Sir William Stanley are confronted with Clarence, who was nearby with his army but is not mentioned in the account of the abduction, and Warwick, the only one to appear in both chronicle and play. Richard and Hastings were not there at all, but they did accompany Edward the following year to Holland. Warwick's fight with Pembroke and his men actually took place before Edward's capture; it was the battle of Banbury, which the Yorkist allies won against Pembroke, but neither Edward nor Warwick was present.[26]

Edward flies straight from prison to Holland, suppressing the interval when he regained the upper hand between his two captures. As in Hall's account of the first episode, Edward is the Archbishop's prisoner, enjoying a comfortable captivity, and seizes the occasion of a hunting party to escape without meeting any resistance,

[23] III. iii. 233–7. Hall 263, 282.
[24] These three scenes form Act III in Hattaway and Cox/Rasmussen.
[25] Hall 278, 282–3.
[26] IV. iii. 54. Hall 273–5.

which will greatly irritate Warwick. The action moves on smoothly to the second episode, the flight to Lynn and the embarking for Flanders, the restoration of Henry VI whom we find enthroned in the next scene. Henry's reinstatement historically followed Edward's precipitous departure for Flanders, but his allusions to hostile Fortune are inspired by the first episode, where Hall reads Edward's escape as a sure sign of Henry VI's persistent bad luck.

Finally, all the parliamentary activity of the period dramatized is dealt with in half a line: Edward reproaches Margaret with having excluded him from the succession in spite of Henry's oath, 'by new Act of Parliament'. This sums up a long series of measures:

- (July 1459) York is named Protector after the first battle of St Albans by the Parliament of Westminster, then divested of his functions by a Great Council summoned at Greenwich by the Queen, and, in September, accused of high treason by the Parliament of Coventry.
- (October 1460) The Parliament of Westminster names York presumptive heir, and declares the Parliament of Coventry illegal.
- (February 1461) After her victory at the second battle of St Albans, the Queen sets off for London to have the Act of Succession repealed, but is forced to beat a retreat.
- (March 1461) After the Yorkist victory at Mortimer's Cross, a Council of Lords spiritual and temporal confirms the Act of the Westminster Parliament; Edward is proclaimed king.
- (November 1470) During the Lancastrian restoration Edward is attainted, and his statutes rescinded. The crown is devolved to Henry and his male heirs or, in default, to Clarence and his male heirs.[27]

Of course Parliament plays no such role on stage, where the succession is decided on the battlefield.

The confluence of the sources

Thanks to the inclusion by Hall of More's *History* in his own, Shakespeare had at hand at least two versions of certain episodes, for instance Edward's ardent courting of Lady Grey. The two accounts differ on several points: according to Hall, Edward met the widow during a hunt; in More, she came to beg the restitution of her husband's lands. Here Shakespeare follows the second account, and uses the circumstances of the hunt metaphorically to illustrate the amorous chase. As in the chronicle, Lady Grey presents her petition to Edward, who is so struck by her beauty and wit that he takes her aside, makes advances, is repulsed, and resolves on marrying her, regardless of his family's hostility. According to More, 'she shewed him plain, that as she wist her self to simple to be his wife, so thought she her self to good to be his cōcubine'. Shakespeare's lady answers with the same modest wisdom:

[27] Cf. *3H6*, II. ii. 91. Hall, 233, 234, 245–9, 252–4, 286.

I know I am too mean to be your queen
And yet too good to be your concubine.   (III. ii. 97–8)

It is from More we hear that she had several children, and that Edward swept aside
the objections of his own mother in unambiguous terms: 'That she is a widdowe
and hath alredy children: By God his blessed lady, I am a bachelor and have some to,
& so eche of vs hath a proofe, that neither of vs is like to be barren.'[28] This reply,
barely rephrased, inspires Edward's wooing address:

Thou art a widow and thou hast some children,
And, by God's mother, I, being but a bachelor,
Have other some. Why, 'tis a happy thing
To be the father unto many sons.   (III. ii. 102–5)

Apart from these grace notes, the only scene drawing on several sources is the
ritualized murder of the Duke of York. Hall recounts that Clifford had the Duke's
corpse decapitated and that he offered the head, crowned with a paper crown, to
the Queen. Holinshed appends to Hall's version a second one, found in the
Whethamsted chronicle, according to which York's enemies forced him to climb a
molehill, crowned him with a garland of rushes and paid him a derisive homage:
before his execution, 'they knéeled downe afore him (as the Iewes did vnto Christ)
in scorne, saieng to him; "Haile king without rule, haile king without heritage,
haileduke and prince without people or possessions"'. A similar parody is performed on stage, but the tone of the mockeries strikes a different chord. Rather than
a parallel with Christ, the dialogue recalls the coronation ceremony, and the pledg-
ing of allegiance which included a ritual hand holding:[29]

A crown for York, and, lords, bow low to him.
Hold you his hands whilst I do set it on.   (I. iv. 94–5)

In the general opinion, Holinshed tells us, the Duke's sad end was a just punishment
for the breaking of his oath to his sovereign, but others assert that he had been
released from it by the Pope, which draws from Fleming this marginal note: 'A pur-
chase of Gods cursse with the popes blessing.' According to Thomas More, the
Duke had no intention of waiting for Henry VI's demise, and used the pretext that
the contract had been broken by the Queen to attempt to seize power. On stage,
York's mock coronation is derisively interpreted as a breach of his promise to let
Henry reign for life:

But how is it that great Plantagenet
Is crowned so soon and broke his solemn oath?   (I. iv. 99–100)

Ground enough, the mockeries imply, for the Queen of Hearts to command: 'Off
with the crown, and, with the crown, his head.' In the chroniclers' accounts, she was

---

[28] Hall 366–7. The beginning and end of More's *History* are signalled at pages 342 and 379, though it
actually goes on until 384.
[29] Holinshed 269. See Jacques Le Goff, 'The Symbolic Ritual of Vasselage', in *Time, Work, and Culture
in the Middle Ages*, 241; John Wickham Legg, 'The Sacring of the English Kings', *Archaeological Journal*,
51 (1894).

not present at the scene; it was Clifford who led this ceremony. Hall, for once, is briefer than Holinshed on this point. He, usually so concerned with immanent justice, mentions neither perjury nor divine punishment, but simply concludes, 'This ende had the valeant lord, Rychard Plantagenet, duke of Yorke, & this fyne ensued of his to much hardines.'

Holinshed does not connect the murder of Rutland with the death of Clifford's father, whose killer is never named, and if he is quite prolix on the subject of discord, there is no trace of the vengeful hatred that animates Hall's orphaned sons after St Albans. In a few instances, Holinshed supplies original details or striking anecdotes, most of which do not serve in the play. His longer account of the York brothers' reconciliation is very moving, and even provides excuses for Clarence's behaviour, whose alleged remorse will have more echo in *Richard III*. He also adds a few notes to Hall on Queen Elizabeth's flight to sanctuary, or the birth of her son, who entered this world like the son of a poor man. He gives alternative versions of Montague's death, of Warwick's, possibly killed whilst taking flight, and reports a tragic mistake at the battle of Barnet: Oxford's men were attacked by those of their ally Warwick, who, because of the fog, had confused their emblem—a shining star—with that of Edward, a shining sun. But Shakespeare did not see fit to use any of these points. We find at most, from time to time in the dialogue, a possible echo of the chronicler's remarks. The genealogical tree, so significant in chronicle and play, becomes in Holinshed the emblem of civil discord, 'that euill tree, which whilest some haue taken paine to plant, and some to proine and nourish, for others confusion (to whome they haue giuen a taste of those apples which it bare, far more bitter than coloquintida)'. This hybrid tree has multiple ramifications: it grew in the garden of Eden but is loaded with Apples of Discord, and may or may not be the one behind Warwick's seminal threat in the opening scene: 'I'll plant Plantagenet; root him up who dares.'[30]

All in all, the sum of Holinshed's influence on *3 Henry VI* seems quite modest. To the above list one might add two bloody tales, the first of which, in 1459, does not appear in Hall: 'In a little towne in Bedfordshire there fell a bloudie raine, whereof the red drops appeered in sheets, the which a woman had hanged out for to drie.' The other occurred at the battle of Towton, which caused an exceptionally high number of casualties: so many men perished while attempting to flee, Holinshed adds, that the water of the river turned red with their blood.[31] These images are especially striking by their brutal contrast with the familiar context in which they arise, the household wash, the little river, but they cannot be said to stand out in the metaphoric nexus. The imagery of blood plays an important role, especially in the laments of anonymous father and son, who mix blood and tears at the thought of their humble hearth, but without an echo of the river or the scarlet rain: on the contrary they shed tears to wash away the bloodstains.

Holinshed's main additions are three and a half pages enumerating the learned men of Edward's reign, and several lists of articles signed at various times between

---

[30] Hall 261. *3H6*, I. i. 48.
[31] Holinshed 278. Hall 256. *3H6*, II. v. 55–122.

opposite parties. On the other hand, he omits Hall's references to Clifford's blood feud with the Yorks, the fierce desire for revenge of both parties, the unnatural fight of father against son, acts of reprisal on the battlefield, as well as the consequences of Edward IV's marriage.[32] He makes no allusion here to the fate of Edward's children, but compensates later, when Edward breaks his word to the inhabitants of York, for which wilful perjury, 'as hath béene thought', his issue was deprived of goods and lives by their cruel uncle Richard. Here a long gloss by Fleming overrides any implicit scepticism: 'And it may well be. For it is not likelie that God, in whose hands is the bestowing of all souereigntie, will suffer such an indignatie to be doone to his sacred maiestie, and will suffer the same to passe with impunitie.' Holinshed suppresses Hall's disobliging comments on Henry VI's small wit, Edward's wanton living, Clarence's jealousy or complaints that his brother is 'vnkynd, and vnnatural', and moderates the violent despair of Margaret at the news of Warwick's death.[33] He draws a more attractive portrait of Henry, but apart from the truly Christian virtues of the King, supplies few original features to Shakespeare's protagonists.

That mighty sculptor, Time

As in the preceding plays, the characters' psychology requires no great insight. Some of the names carry more weight than the persons bearing them; several individuals can be fused under one patronym to share a powerful symbolic charge or endorse historical actions suited to their thematic roles. In this regard, the practice of the theatre teaches us to distinguish fusion from confusion. Most of the difficulties involved in identifying dramatic characters come from fastidious editors who have a hard time matching play-texts to history books, while an audience could remain happily unaware of the problems raised by a wealth of learning. Some editors note with surprise the 'disappearance' of Salisbury and Falconbridge, who are not in the list of characters nor in any stage direction of the Folio—but who should be there! Cairncross thought that they had been 'replaced' by Montague at the cost of a few minor inconsistencies, and even demonstrated that Shakespeare was mistaken over the identity of a character who never appears on stage.

The 'missing' Salisbury compels us again to mind our Qs and F. In Q, rechristened Octavo in Arden 3, Richard reports to Warwick the death of the old Salisbury, confusing him with his son, the bastard Salisbury. If Q/O is an early original as Arden 2 and 3 tend to believe, Shakespeare had vastly improved by the time he wrote the F version, judging on the respective merits of the two passages. Besides, the play does not use Hall's information that Salisbury's head was exposed at the gates of York along with the Duke's, which suggests that Salisbury had no place therein.[34] In F it is a brother of Warwick, anonymous, who dies; this still leaves

---

[32] Holinshed 247, 269, 277, 278, 292, 284. Cf. Hall 238, 251, 254, 256, 274, 265.

[33] Holinshed 305, 301, 295, 297, 290, 315. Cf. Hall 286, 284, 281, 271, 297.

[34] Cox/Rasmussen 164 are 'cautious about advancing this conclusion', and give a full facsimile of the Octavo in appendix 1, but do not signal the variant at II. iii. On O/Q, see introd. 149 n. 2. Cf. Cairncross, II. iii. 14–22 and appendix III, 180. Hall 251, 253, 255.

room for disagreement as to his identity, for Warwick had one brother killed at Wakefield and another at Towton.[35] Since Act II treats as a continuous series distinct battles that took place over more than a year, it is impossible to place the events staged unless by recourse to the chronicle. From the dialogue, Warwick situates York's death at Wakefield, his own defeat by the Queen at St Albans, while the armies meet in front of York where the Duke's head is on view. There is no other locating element in the whole act. How, then, can we determine which of Warwick's brothers is concerned? This nameless relative makes no other appearance in the play; what matters most is his family tie with Warwick, and his death at the hand of Clifford, a precision which neither Hall nor Q give, but which fuels the theme of tribal revenge.

Falconbridge's 'disappearance' is even more surprising, since he does not appear in any state of the text—proof enough, to some critics, that he was 'eliminated' from Q and F, to make room for Montague in the cast. Again, only a scholar could notice a void, and summon an ectoplasm to fill it: the only evidence for this missing character is the fact that Montague calls York 'brother', though he was York's nephew, and announces that he is going back to sea, but appears in the next scene on solid ground, at the Duke's house. According to Hattaway, Falconbridge 'may have been in an earlier version of the text of which this is a survival, to be later fused with Montague'.[36] Shakespeare may well have wished to save an extra character, but why posit an earlier state of the text with Falconbridge in the part, and conclude that the saving occurred after the text was written rather than before, the authors of the theory do not explain. The chronicle mentions Falconbridge several times, but in the play, he is referred to only once: 'Stern Falconbridge commands the narrow seas,' whereas Montague's part is necessary both to the plot and to the thematic structure.[37] The chronicle often served directly whoever composed the Q text, as we noticed in *The Contention*, but Shakespeare handles it so freely elsewhere that it cannot be a reliable check on the consistency of the dialogue, as the elusive Mortimers amply showed. At some stage in his composition, he concentrated the attributes and functions of several historical figures on the elusive Montague.

Somerset too is the product of a fusion, as was his father in the preceding play. Although the young Somerset was present at Towton, according to Hall, he makes a late entry on stage, in the fourth act, and then one mute appearance at Edward's court which he leaves in Clarence's wake to rejoin Warwick.[38] We next find him right at the end on the Lancastrian side, where he is taken and decapitated. This itinerary mixes the fates of two Somerset brothers. Henry, the third Duke, succeeded his father in the role of adviser to the Queen. It was he who commanded the

---

[35] Thomas Neville, and the Bastard of Salisbury. See Cairncross, II. iii n. 15.

[36] Cairncross, p. xxi, and I. i n. 14. Hattaway, I. i n. 241. The argument continues over the status of O (Q). To Laurie E. Maguire, *Shakespearean Suspect Texts: The 'Bad' Quartos and their Contexts* (Cambridge, 1996), 325, it lacks the features of a reconstruction.

[37] I. i. 239. In Hall 253, 255, Falconbridge asks the people's consent to the Proclamation of Edward, and commands the Yorkist vanguard at Ferrybridge, then at Towton.

[38] '*Exit Clarence, and Somerset followes*' (SD at IV. i. 123). Although Edward invites him to give his opinion about the marriage with Lady Grey (IV. i. 24–6), he says not a word in this scene.

royal army at Towton with Clifford and Northumberland. After their defeat he made his submission to Edward, but rejoined the Lancastrians as soon as they had assembled a new army, fought at Hexham with them, was taken and executed. His brother Edmund, always a faithful Lancastrian, commanded Margaret's army at Tewkesbury, where he was beaten and decapitated.[39] The brief appearance of Somerset at Edward's court is inspired by the double turn of the elder brother; the stage character pursues, after the defection of the first, the historical career of the second.

Exeter is listed in the chronicle among the Queen's friends, then scarcely mentioned again. On stage he appears twice, always at the side of Henry VI, in the non-historical role of conciliator. The Exeter of *1 Henry VI* was above all a choric figure, voicing the political conscience of the kingdom. In Part 3, Exeter—historically the heir of the preceding one, who died in 1426—keeps a position as arbitrator, but his moral stature is considerably reduced: when the Duke of York claims the crown, Exeter declares that on his soul and conscience the right is on the side of the House of York, and approves Henry's designation of them as heirs, but it appears to be more from a taste for compromise than from an acute sense of justice, for he does not stretch the courage of his convictions to the point of defending them before the Queen:

> *Exe.* Here comes the Queen, whose looks bewray her anger:
>   I'll steal away.
> *Hen.*   Exeter, so will I.   (I. i. 211–12)

Too late. Both have to endure Margaret's violent reproaches, but Exeter does not despair of restoring the calm: 'And I, I hope, shall reconcile them all.' From a normative character, he has fallen to the rank of a short-sighted pacifist. This Exeter, as we saw, could not be the same man who wears the title in Part 1.[40] But since his life is extended far beyond its natural time in *1 Henry VI*, he could as well be endowed with an unparalleled longevity and kept alive from one end of the cycle to the other. Here again, the continuity of the name and the tradition attached to it are more important than the particular identity of the individual who bore the name at a given time, father and son succeeding each other in the function without break. The narrowing of the moral vision expressed by the Exeter of Part 3 is symptomatic of a general decline in ethic standards.

The age of the protagonists is adapted to the plot: young Rutland was in fact the elder brother of Richard and Clarence, whereas Richard is made older to hold his part in the action. Because of the contractions operated on the chronicle's material, it is often meaningless to assert that the presence of a character at a given event is or is not historical. Impossible to decide whether Oxford could be at the court of

---

[39] Hall 250, 258–60, 298–301. Edmund called himself fourth Duke of Somerset, but never received official recognition of his title. He and Henry were the sons of Edmund, the second Duke, who was killed at St Albans.

[40] They did not belong to the same family. The Exeter of *1H6* was a Beaufort related to the King, that of *3H6* was a Holland, issued from a lineage at first hostile to the Lancastrians but who remained loyal to them. See *Handbook of British Chronology*, 307–8, 311–12.

Lewis XI, in a scene condensing two of Warwick's missions there and two visits by Margaret. Or which friends assisted in Edward's flight, those who helped him to escape from Middleham, or those with whom he left England a year later. Historically, the supporters of Lancaster were successive, not simultaneous, allies of Margaret: Henry Somerset, the defector, was dead before Warwick joined the cause, at a time when Clarence was veering back to the Yorkists. The Lancastrian faction never had in fact the power that the dramatic progression momentarily lends it, which explains why Margaret hesitated so long to risk her fortune and her son's with Warwick. She was not in England during Henry VI's restoration, but landed on the day of Warwick's death, nearly a year after their interview at the French court, by which time Henry had returned to his prison.[41]

A slower rhythm is impulsed through the references to past and future in the dialogue, by what develops in the intervals of the action. Time works in the hollows, between key moments that blow up to the fore from depths etched in on the distant background. In the chronicles, the events are all spread on a level plane, flattened out by the historian's will to say everything. On this flat canvas the dramatist designs perspective, in the way Michelangelo aimed to give his paintings the three-dimensional relief of sculpture through *chiaroscuro*, the clear delineation of his central figures, and a skilful ordering of his background into successive planes. As with crayons, Shakespeare creates clearings round the momentous events of the story to disengage them from the merely contingent. But these moments do not appear isolated from their context, nor developed solely for their spectacular qualities; the voids are equally pregnant, they carve volumes in the intermediary planes and the background right up to vanishing point. The secondary, the trivial are not eliminated in favour of the more dramatic episodes, but given a proper place in the perspective of the whole. For want of a clear cause to the mystery of things, the chronicler adds up all the motives he can summon for immediate accidents. In the theatre, the forces at work in the shadows of history are made perceptible; they bring dramatic climaxes to the front stage, and suggest the long shockwaves induced by the critical moments captured in performance. The cutting of space into perspective on Michelangelo's frescos finds an equivalent in the depth of dramatic time.

At the other end of Shakespeare's career, Time the storyteller is given leave to speak, as the first author of the play. It is in *Henry VI* that dramatic time learns to make sense of the chroniclers' linear tales by giving depth of field to the design. Time, in other words history itself, becomes the driving force of the plot, as the King recognizes in watching two of its minor tragedies. Thus in Henry VI's past, we perceive the dubious origin of the dynasty, and at close range his personal frailties. The weakness of his title is aggravated by his doubts on his own legitimacy, especially when faced with a determined opponent who feels certain of his right. The Yorkist claim, the Duke's undeniable *virtù*, are opposed to a rule established by three reigns, to a king indifferently royal but son and grandson of kings.[42] On stage, the King's

[41] Hall 281, 286–7, 293, 294, 297.
[42] See Manheim, *The Weak King Dilemma*, 77–115.

weakness is informed by all the planes designed in the perspective; the ancestral usurpation, his imprudent marriage, the loss of his Protector, and his own failure to command, form a disastrous conjunction of old and recent liabilities. Edward IV's rough courtship announces the children to come and Richard's murderous designs. But in the brief interlude of the Lancastrian restoration, the young Richmond receives Henry's blessing, which allows us a glimpse of a reconciled England beyond the present fratricide.

'The heroic and the infinite have been; the human and the finite are.'[43] The historical process brings to the stage that sensation of grandeur which the imagination demands, whether the grandiose resides in the individual will or in processes that exceed human understanding. History, then, plays the heroic role, compensating for the loss or impossibility of conventional heroism, in a form of reciprocal exchange, as Herbert Lindenberger shows:

History magnifies an action to create a properly 'tragic' effect, while it also provides the verisimilitude necessary for us to take a play seriously. Tragedy, in turn, gives history a way of making 'sense' out of what might otherwise be a chaos of events.[44]

In *3 Henry VI*, he points out, the contrasts between the pastoral and the historical world oppose the slow regular time of the shepherd to the unforeseen course of history, and the confrontation of the two worlds serves to define them both. Now, if one easily sees that the pastoral world is 'an imaginative construct', it is less patent but equally true that the historical world is one as well. The world of *Henry VI* is a literary and theatrical construction, designed to interpret historical tensions.

3. CRITICAL REWRITING

As with the other parts of the tetralogy, structural design and thematic pattern make *3 Henry VI* a consistent whole, while systems of echoes, memories, or prophecies ensure dramatic progression from one play to the next. How truly autonomous each one is remains arguable; I have yet to see *2 Henry VI* performed on its own, though the experiment was attempted successfully with Part 3.[45] It is impossible to assert when in the writing process the links between first and second Parts were wrought in, or whether *Richard III* was already in prospect when *1 Henry VI* was composed. Part 2 ends like a newspaper serial, 'To be continued', leaving its audience right in the middle of a war. That a fourth play was anticipated after *3 Henry VI*, the character of Richard would suffice to show. From his first entrance, he is clearly assigned for later developments, and only beginning to shape out towards the end of Part 3, when he reveals his plans for the next play. The whole point of Richmond's brief appearance is to prepare the ground for *Richard III*:

---

[43] Northrop Frye, *Fools of Time: Studies in Shakespearean Tragedy* (Toronto, 1973), 6.

[44] Herbert Lindenberger, *Historical Drama: The Relation of Literature and Reality* (Chicago, 1975), 73.

[45] By Kate Mitchell at The Other Place, Stratford's most audacious theatre, in 1994.

although it agrees with Hall's account, it would be superfluous to the dramatic construction of an independent *3 Henry VI*.

Marriage is destiny

The section of the chronicle corresponding to *3 Henry VI* again leaves one with a feeling of identical recurrence, as events mark time, and the chronicler draws similar morals from similar mishaps, not to mention the cases when historical parallels run contrary to moral or dramatic requirements, for instance the two protectorships of Gloucester and York induced by the King's state of infancy, youth in the first case, mental illness in the second. Hall's ethical system stretching no further than proverbial wisdom, facts and narrative vie in stuttering repetitions. Which explains why the poet makes increasingly selective choices as he goes: a good number of the chronicler's anthems are hackneyed by the time Richard enters.

Part 1 illustrates Hall's sermons on the benefits of union. In Part 2 where virtue fails miserably, even when supported by wisdom, Hall's straighforward ethics come under critical light, though he still provides many themes of inspiration. Part 3 takes even more critical distance. Edward's marriage enables Hall to harp on three favourite themes—perjury, providence, fortune: it causes offence all round, 'and al with one voyce sayde, that his vnaduised wowyng, hasty louyng, and to spedy mariage, were neither meete for him beyng a kyng, nor consonant to the honor of so high an estate'. On stage, it is Richard who embodies the *vox populi*: 'Yet hasty marriage seldom proveth well.' Early Modern moralists might be hostile to forced marriages, but they notoriously disapproved of princes marrying to satisfy their desire.[46] As could be expected, the consequences will be disastrous for all involved. How, Hall does not truly explain:

Yet who so will marke the sequele of this story, shall manifestly perceyue, what murther, what miserie, & what troble ensued by reason of this mariage; for it can not be denied, but for this mariage kyng Edward was expulsed the Realm, & durst not abide, And for this mariage was therle of Warwycke & his brother miserable slain. By this mariage were kyng Edwardes. ii. sonnes declared bastardes, & in cōclusion priued of their lifes. And finally by this mariage, the quenes bloud was confounded, and vtterly in manner destroyed. So yᵗ men did afterward diuyne, that either God was not contented, nor yet pleased with this matrimony, or els that he punished king Edward in his posteritie. (264–5)

Hall does not cite the precedent of Henry VI, but his lengthy conclusions on the subject do not vary. Henry's marriage alienated his best allies,

But moste of all it should seme, that God with this matrimony was not content. For after this spousage the kynges frendes fell from hym, bothe in Englande and in Fraunce, the Lordes of his realme, fell in diuision emongest themselfes, the commons rebelled against their souereigne Lorde, and naturall Prince, feldes wer foughten, many thousandes slain, and finally, the kyng deposed, and his sonne slain, and this Quene sent home again, with asmuche

---

[46] Hall 265. *3H6*, IV. i. 18. See 'The Book of Matrimony' in *The Workes of Thomas Becon* (London, 1564), i. 618 ff.

misery and sorowe, as she was reciued with pompe and triumphe, suche is wordly vnstablenes, and so waueryng is false flattering fortune. (205)

Hall could scarcely renew the inspiration of an author as innovative as Shakespeare. In the two passages quoted, most of the links between cause and effect are disputable; what matters first is the litany of misfortunes inflicted on the realm. Again, *post hoc, propter hoc,* Hall mixes evils following the King's marriage and evils resulting from it. All are sure signs of divine discontent. According to natural logic, Henry VI's match no more than Edward's caused the death of their sons, except in giving them birth. Thomas More, always a shrewder analyst than Hall, claims that Richard was able to accuse his nephews of bastardy by alleging a prior contract of marriage between Edward and Dame Elizabeth Lucy, where Hall never explains how their father could be held responsible for the death of the young princes.

Anyway, Shakespeare does not exploit the similitude between the two events. From the chronicle he keeps the political circumstances of the marriage and Edward's wantonness, but discards a number of irrelevant features. Sir John Grey, Elizabeth's first husband, was a Lancastrian in the chronicle; he becomes a Yorkist on stage. Hall is perfectly clear in his presentation of 'dame Elizabeth Greye, wydow of syr Ihon Grey knight, slayn at the last battell of saincte Albons, by the power of kyng Edward'. Thomas More, who specifies that she had been lady-in-waiting to Queen Margaret, is even clearer: Edward 'maried the lady Elizabeth Grey verie priuely, which was his enemies wife and had praied hartely for his losse, in which God loued her better then to graunt her her bone, for then had she not been his wife'. But Shakespeare's Edward means to grant the widow's petition,

> Because in the quarrel of the house of York
> The worthy gentleman did lose his life.   (III. ii. 6–7)

In *Richard III,* the 'mistake' is corrected, in a reminder that she and her husband were 'factious for the House of Lancaster'. If it is a mistake. The fact of taking a wife from the enemy camp is precisely a feature that would stress the resemblance with Henry's marriage. Now this theme has already been largely exploited in Parts 1 and 2, and here the role of enemy at the heart of the kingdom is reserved for Margaret, 'She-wolf of France', 'false French-woman', 'Iron of Naples hid with English gilt'. Ironically, it is Edward who attributes all of Henry's misfortunes to his disastrous marriage.[47]

The play makes no such charge about Elizabeth. To be sure, her clan threatens political stability by their rivalries with the royal family, but no Woodville is the infiltrated agent of an outside enemy. And above all, Elizabeth would be a poor copy of Margaret. She lacks epic dimension, and even the disorders which she attracts seem footling in comparison with her rival's capacity for harm; she wants her acre of land where Margaret cost England two provinces, a good index of their respective measure. Shakespeare does nothing either to compare or oppose them in this play. It is not Elizabeth who carries Margaret's symbolic succession, but Richard,

---

[47] Hall 367. *3H6,* I. iv. 111, 149; II. ii. 139; II. ii. 144–62.

through whom the theme of the near enemy, closest to the heart, will be developed, and it is Richard whom Elizabeth will oppose.

Though a more bourgeois affair than the first, this royal marriage has similar impact. Its acknowledged effects matter less, however, than the awakening of Richard's ambition. He first unveils his plans just after the wooing scene, and explicitly opposes amorous desire to the lust for power: for one who was weaned from love at birth, no pleasure remains but to devour the world. The direct consequences of the marriage, Warwick's defection and the pursuit of the war, will be settled before the end of the play. The wooing of Lady Grey occupies a central place in the composition, like a caesura between twice two acts of murderous violence, symmetrically rehearsing the 'Fall and Rise of the House of York'. Edward's amorous trifling, his cavalier courtship, the crude jokes of his brothers, mark a variation in tone with the more brutal scenes of war framing it. The frivolity of his whims appears outrageous against this background, especially as he does not bother to disguise the nature of his appetites. Edward's proposal is the last recourse of the seducer at bay: the adventure of the hunter hunted is replayed this time as comedy.

This business once settled, the whole network of affinities must be reorganized. Marriage, the great domestic matter, upsets all previous alliances and divides brothers. Failing to match Edward as he wished, Warwick pairs off his two daughters, while Edward arranges three lucrative marriages for the Woodvilles, which arouse Clarence's jealousy.[48] But these unnatural clusters are not stable; the enemy brothers are soon reconciled. Montague had refused to follow Warwick when Clarence left. He and Clarence cross paths again as each returns to his tribe. Warwick and Montague die shortly after, each with the name of his brother on their lips. As to the brides, they remain unseen and unheard. Anne, though born and bred a Yorkist, will appear in the next play definitely a Lancastrian.

According to Hall, the incensed Warwick hid his anger as long as he was not in a position of strength, all the while working in the background to rally the disaffected nobility. This long dissimulation disappears in the play, Warwick's anger bursts forth publicly and immediately. That Shakespeare was able to dramatize deferring and waiting if need be, Part 2 had amply proved: the slow maturing of the Yorkist threats to the Crown occupied half the length of the play. But the dramatic logic now demands a rapid evolution for the worst. The action gathers speed as the characters rush to their ends, carried away by their impulsive passions.

Family affairs

In Hall as in the play, disorder in the realm interacts with disorder in the family:

for as he is vnkind and vnnaturall, that will not cherishe hys natural parentes and procreators, much more vnnatural and wicked are they, which will suffer their natyue coūtry, beyng their common father and mother, by their contencion & stryfe to be brought to decay and vtter perdicion. (276)

[48] IV. i. 116–18, 47–64. Hall 281, 271.

This image derives from the *De Civitate Dei,* one of the major works printed in the reign of Henry VIII, which was itself based on Cicero's view of the family as the foundation of the state. The *De Officiis* distinguishes four levels in the hierarchy of social groups: the human species, the nation or the language, the city, and the family, which is the most natural and indissoluble of all communities.[49] *Henry VI* likewise stresses the perversity of wars fought between close relations over the devolution of patrimony. As the rivalries grow more passionate, kinship takes precedence over legal argument, while personal scores are settled at the expense of a weakened central power.

The chroniclers generally set a high price on loyalty to kin. In Hall's account, Henry Somerset had made his submission to Edward, but as soon as he learnt of Margaret's arrival, 'he without delaye refused kyng Edward, and rode in poste to his kynsman, kyng Henry the sixte: verefiyng the olde prouerbe: kynne wil crepe, where it may no go'.[50] Clarence may well attract divine wrath for his perjury to Warwick, yet Hall warmly approves the brotherly love that caused it, and extends his benevolence to Richard, who worked to bring him back into the family: 'in conclusion no vnnaturall warre, but a fraternall amitie was concluded and proclaymed.' And yet, 'it semeth that God dyd neither forgeue nor forget to punishe the duke with condigne punishment, for violating and brekyng hys othe . . . for God not many yeres after, suffered hym like a periured person to dye a cruell & a straūge death'. Holinshed is even more moved than Hall, and omits the divine punishment, when he reports extra details on the circumstances of this reunion, the feast that celebrated it, and the witnesses who thanked God for it: 'This was a goodlie and a gratious reconcilement, beneficiall to the princes, profitable to the péeres, and pleasurable to the people, whose part had beene déepest in dangers and losse, if discord had not beene discontinued.'[51] There is no such moment of grace nor retrieving love in the family struggles of *3 Henry VI.* The political debate gives way to a feud which wrecks all levels of the state organization from top to bottom of the social ladder.

The theme of the tribal feud was introduced at the end of *2 Henry VI,* when young Clifford swore to avenge his father by exterminating the Yorks to their last infant. Part 3 opens with the Yorkists' proud list of Lancastrian dead, followed by the entrance of their victims' sons. They instantly form two camps, each swearing to pursue the fight until the extinction of their opponents. It is plain that hatred of the hereditary enemy determines the choice of allegiance; the debate over York's claim soon slips from the legal ground to factional quarrels. Here the play significantly diverges from the chronicle. In Hall, York retraces at length the antecedents of the two families to demonstrate the superiority of his title, and Parliament takes time to

---

[49] Cicero's *Offices,* ed. John Warrington, trans. Thomas Cockman (London, 1966), i. xvii. 24–6. On these organic images, see Kantorowicz, *The King's Two Bodies,* 200–29. Juan Luis Vives dedicated his edition of the *De Civitate Dei* to Henry VIII.

[50] Hall 259. Holinshed 280 omits the reference to kinship and the proverb.

[51] Hall 293. Holinshed 308.

reflect before publishing its decision, four pages later.[52] Nothing so institutional on stage, where a crude light is shed on facts less glaring in the chronicle: the Yorkists have the upper hand and can dictate their conditions. It is Henry who is called upon to prove his rights, but he lacks assurance, and after twenty lines, it appears that justice is not truly the heart of the matter:

> King Henry, be thy title right or wrong,
> Lord Clifford vows to fight in thy defence:
> May that ground gape and swallow me alive
> Where I shall kneel to him that slew my father! (1. i. 159–62)

Warwick does not bother with periphrases, nor hesitate to bring his soldiers into Parliament, after two reminders of the respect due to the premises:

> Do right unto this princely Duke of York,
> Or I will fill the house with armed men,
> And over the chair of state where now he sits,
> Write up his title with usurping blood.
> *He stamps with his foot, and the Soldiers show themselves.* (1. i. 166–9)

This last argument carries the day. Henry himself suggests the solution which, in the chronicle, is the one reached by the Estates of the realm: he will keep the crown during his lifetime, and York will succeed him.[53] The presence of the soldiers on stage strongly contributes to the irony of the situation: the cavils of the Yorkists establish that Henry only owes his throne to his grandfather's usurpation. If a king can adopt an heir, Henry points out, then he is legitimate,

> For Richard, in the view of many lords,
> Resigned the crown to Henry the Fourth,
> Whose heir my father was, and I am his. (1. i. 138–40)

In York's view, the argument is not worth much:

> He rose against him, being his sovereign,
> And made him to resign his crown perforce. (1. i. 141–2)

But it is found to have some weight moments later, when the soldiers march in and York demands:

> Confirm the crown to me and to mine heirs,
> And thou shalt reign in quiet while thou liv'st. (1. i. 172–3)

Henry VI agrees to make York his successor exactly as Richard II 'consented' to designate Bolingbroke. If that is enough to make York a legitimate heir, then so is Henry, and the judicial argument ends in a deadlock. There is no trace of this paradox in the chronicle, which never says that Richard II designated a successor;

---

[52] 1. i. 64–5; 1. i. 70–1. Hall 245, 249. See Prior, *The Drama of Power*, 101–19. The Duke arrived in London on the Friday preceding the feast of Edward the Confessor, and the three Estates rendered their judgement on the eve of All Saints' Day.

[53] On the constitutional problems touching the succession, see George Keeton, *Shakespeare's Legal and Political Background* (London, 1967), 248–63.

on the contrary, the Yorkists assert that the whole procedure was a disguised usurpation. The dramatic dialogue keeps only a few details from Hall's long prosopopoeia, besides the fact that the Duke went to sit on the throne, and left the lords speechless 'as though their mouthes had been sowed vp'.[54] York is named heir by Henry, but the sons of his victims oppose the decision of the King in the name of the King's son. The royal party splits after a noisy domestic scene between the King and Queen:

> I here divorce myself
> Both from thy table, Henry, and thy bed,
> Until that act of Parliament be repealed
> Whereby my son is disinherited.   (1. i. 247–50)

Margaret rallies the angry lords, and the Prince of Wales follows her after a polite rebuke to his father:

> When I return with victory from the field
> I'll see your grace; till then, I'll follow her.   (1. i. 261–2)

York's sons likewise urge theirs to take arms and conquer 'The crown of England, father, which is yours'.

In Hall's narrative, as on stage, the cycle of murder and revenge originates at St Albans where Somerset, Clifford, and Northumberland were killed, though Hall first makes this point three years after the event, in March 1458, at the time of an official reconciliation between the two parties, by a note in the margin: 'The mortal hatered betwene y[e]. ii. lignages of Lācaster & Yorke.' On the Lancastrian side were 'the yong duke of Somerset, the erle of Northumberland, & the lord Clyfford, whose fathers were slayn at sainct Albōs'.[55] Hall does not say at that stage who killed Clifford's father, but two years later, at Wakefield, it is the motive invoked for the murder of young Rutland. Clifford is not held responsible for the killing of York in this account, only for the sacrilegious mockery that followed it:

this cruell Clifforde, & deadly bloudsupper not content with this homicyde, or chyldkillyng, came to y[e] place wher the dead corps of the duke of Yorke lay, and caused his head to be stryken of, and set on it a croune of paper, & so fixed it on a pole, & presented it to the Quene. (251)

There was much rejoicing, 'but many laughed then, that sore lamented after'. The heads of the Duke and his friends were displayed at the gates of York, 'in despite of them, and their lignage: whose chyldren, shortly reuenged their fathers quarell, both to the Quenes extreme perdicion and the vtter vndoynge of her husband and sonne'. Four months later, Somerset, Clifford, and Northumberland were put in charge of the royal army, 'as men desiring to reuenge ye death of their parentes slayn at the first battayle of Sainct Albons'. At first they had the advantage, but on hearing news of his brother's death, Warwick showed himself so determined to avenge it that, with Edward, he succeeded in reversing the situation. After an exceptionally

---

[54] Hall 248. For a detailed commentary on this oration, see Kelly 121–5.
[55] Hall, 233, 237.

bloody battle, the heads of their allies were replaced on the city gates with those of four Lancastrians.[56]

Hall continues to report reprisals, summary executions, and gratuitous acts of cruelty, without further comment, until the battle of Banbury, where a young cousin of Warwick gave himself up to Pembroke's Welshmen, who killed him regardless. Later, when Pembroke is captured with his younger brother, and pleads to have him spared,

syr Ihon Conyers and Clappam, remembryng the death of the yonge knyght syr Henri Neuel, Cosyn to the erle of Warwycke, could not here on that side, but caused the erle & hys brother with diuers other gentlemen, to the number of. X. to be there behedded. (274)

The sudden 'infirmity' of Sir Ihon possibly suggested that of Clifford, who in the play declares himself deaf to Rutland's prayers.

Act II dramatizes the above conflicts as successive phases of a single uninterrupted battle, for which Shakespeare selects the family misfortunes reported in the chronicle.[57] This exemplary sequence begins before the city of York: King Henry is shown the head of the decapitated Duke as a happy surprise, and told to dub his son knight under this grisly trophy, then go and take a walk while his wife goes to war. The next scenes bring the enemies face to face, trading insults before they come to blows. In the midst of the carnage, Henry meditates on a molehill, an echo of York's last stance in the preceding act, and witnesses two brief tragedies for which he confesses responsibility:

> *Son.* How will my mother for a father's death
>   Take on with me, and ne'er be satisfied!
> *Fath.* How will my wife for slaughter of my son
>   Shed seas of tears, and ne'er be satisfied!
> *K.Hen.* How will the country for these woeful chances
>   Misthink the King, and not be satisfied! (II. v. 103–8)

At Towton, Hall writes, more than 36,000, 'all Englishmen and of one naciō', were killed in three days: 'This conflict was in maner vnnnaturall, for in it the sonne fought against the father, the brother against the brother, the nephew against the vncle, and the tenaūt against his lord.' Civil war is equated with 'incest to the land', a common Elizabethan view expressed in the contemporary play *Jack Straw*,[58] and derived from Augustine's reflection on the cruel fate of the Sabine women, who

must either (in piety) bewail the death of their friends and kinsfolk, or (in cruelty) rejoice at the victories of their husbands. Besides (as war's choice is variable), some lost their husbands by their father's swords; some lost both, by the hand of each other. (III. xiii)[59]

---

[56] Hall 254–6 gives a figure of 36,776 victims in all, from both sides.

[57] Hall 250–5. *3H6*, II. iii. 14–32; II. v. 55–122; II. vi. 29–86.

[58] Hall 256. *Straw*, ll. 603–8. Plutarch writes that Caesar had an incestuous dream before he crossed the Rubicon to march on Rome, 'Life of Caesar', in *Lives of the Noble Grecians and Romans*, trans. Thomas North, ed. G. Wyndham (London, 1895–6), v. 35.

[59] *The City of God: John Healey's Translation of 1610*, ed. R. V. G. Tasker (London, 1967), 89. Healey's translation was based on Vives' 1522 Latin edition.

Pretty country folk

Both Hall and Holinshed note after the battle of Blore Heath how the aristocratic quarrels affected the humblest families: 'In this battail were slain. xxiiij. C. persõs, but the greatest plague lighted on the Chesshire men, because one halfe of the shire, was on the one part, and the other on the other part.'[60] The horrors of Blore Heath and Towton are fused in the continuous fighting scene, while the tableau of the anonymous father and son sums up the sinister toll of the press-gang in rural hearths:

> O heavy times, begetting such events!
> From London by the King was I pressed forth.
> My father, being the Earl of Warwick's man,
> Came on the part of York, pressed by his master;
> And I, who at his hands received my life,
> Have by my hands of life bereaved him.   (II. v. 63–8)

Augustine's model of fratricidal war stands not far behind this emblematic scene:

> But if two gladiators should come upon the stage, one being the father, and another the son, who could endure such a spectacle? How then can glory attend the arms of the daughter city against the mother? Do ye make a difference in that their field was larger than the gladiator's stage, and that they fought not in view of the theatre but the whole world, presenting a spectacle of eternal impiety both to the present times and to all posterity? But your great guardian gods bore all this unmoved, sitting as spectators of this tragedy. (III. xiv)

Had Shakespeare read the *De Civitate Dei* in Latin, one wonders, or did John Healey translate the Latin 'circus' and 'arena' of the original as 'theatre' and 'stage' after watching a production of *Henry VI*?

Hall provides so much matter for the central theme of the blood feud that Shakespeare does not use all the recorded cases of vengeance on the battlefield, though he adds a few domestic tragedies of his own making, to insist on the vengeful bond: two Mortimers absent from the chronicle enter only to get killed in coming to York's rescue. Clifford's death amid a ritual of insults and taunts is the symmetrical answer to the murder of the Duke of York. In the chronicles, his throat is pierced by an anonymous arrow. On stage, it is Richard who kills him. Here the Quarto's addition 'with an arrow in his neck', where F simply states 'Enter Clifford Wounded', is historically correct, but not necessarily welcome. It is hard to imagine Richard chasing his adversary with arrows, even though directors sometimes find the arrow attractive: Terry Hands used it to memorable effect in his 1977 RSC production. Whichever way Clifford dies on stage, Warwick has his head replace the Duke's over the city gates. In the chronicles, it is Edward who gives the order, but no specific head is mentioned.[61] Warwick and Montague end chased by the vengeful Edward, not by unknown hands through the hazards of war. With the murder of the Prince of Wales, the York brothers settle all vengeful scores with Lancaster. As

---

[60] Hall 240 *(251)*.
[61] II. vi. 52–5, 85–6. Hall 255–6 *(277–8)*.

Margaret had done for the Duke, Richard breaks the news of his son's death to Henry VI before stabbing him; they are the last two victims of the feud. Now the triumphant family rejoices as Richard embraces his nephew 'young Ned', who will soon follow in death 'Ned, sweet Ned', Margaret's son and heir.

Hall's tales of bloody retaliations, his references to the native land as one's natural parents, contribute much to the plot, but do not create a coherent obverse of the family theme as they do on stage. They are just gory incidents from which the chronicler draws independent moral or philosophical lessons. His theme of vengeance, blurred as it is by clichés on mutable fortune, ambitious princes, immanent justice, or God's mysterious ways, fails to provide a system of overall explanation. When Hall makes Heaven responsible for the death of the Prince of Wales, Clarence, or Edward's children, he forgets to mention family feuds as a more direct cause, and often imputes to Providence all too human acts of retribution. On stage, the fights over the crown increasingly obey private concerns in which both parties lose all notions of right and wrong.

The invasion of the public domain by the domestic is part of a larger regressive pattern. The protection of progeny takes its models in the animal kingdom. Warwick's words in the narrative, 'What worme is touched, and will not once turne again? What beast is striken, that will not rore or sound?' are transferred to Clifford: 'The smallest worm will turn, being trodden on.'[62] Many such echoes find their way in the play, to sketch a consistent decline towards animality. Nature is repeatedly invoked to justify savage acts of reprisal for, as in Hall, 'he is vnkynd and vnnaturall, that will not cherishe hys natural parentes'. Nature in its goodness gives the example of family attachment and the protection of the weakest, but by a significant shift, nature also provides models of defensive violence. It is the burden of Clifford's speech in the play: the beasts feed their young, and are pitiless for whatever threatens them. Even the most fearful will fight back to defend their progeny: 'For shame, my liege, make them your precedent!' Clifford is deemed by Hall fiercer than a lion, 'for the propertie of the Lyon, which is a furious and an vnreasonable beaste, is to be cruell to them that withstande hym, and gentle to such as prostrate or humiliate them selfes before him'. To call on savage nature for guidance, and still use animal names for insults, translates the confusion of standards prevailing since Gloucester's death.[63] The bestiary is more or less that of the preceding plays: wolves, bears, tigers, lions, dogs, serpents, toads serve as yardsticks to human ugliness, until men outdo them in brutality and place humanity at the antipodes of nature: 'Butchers and villains! Bloody cannibals!' are denounced as 'deathsmen' by the bereaved Margaret. After a detour via bestiality, the term 'human' takes on a surplus of meaning and is redefined as demoniac to concentrate on Richard, 'devil's butcher', at the end of the play.[64]

The dramatic bestiary draws heavily on the chronicler's images. The Duke of

[62] Hall 270. 3 *H6*, II. ii. 17.
[63] Hall 251, 276. 3*H6*, II. ii. 33.
[64] 3*H6*, v. v. 61, 67, 77. *R3*, I. ii. 71–2.

York is encircled by his enemies 'like a fish in a net, or a deere in a buckestall' in the narrative, on stage he struggles like a woodcock with the gin, a cony in the net; the enemy at bay are chased with greyhounds or falcons, and surrounded as in a battue.[65] The hunt, with its royal and ceremonial connotations, takes on new significance. As in the last battle of Part 1, it still serves as metaphor for war. Or it may be designed for entertainment, as in Part 2, and diverted against human quarry. In Hall's account, Edward, while a prisoner of the Archbishop of York, escaped during a hunting party. His stage meeting with Lady Grey takes place during a hunting party as well, but unlike other plays where 'heart' and 'hart' are fused in the amorous pursuit, here the images of venery are reserved for the martial and political theme. The deer hunt, a royal privilege, becomes both metaphor and metonymy of the struggle for power.[66] In the course of two successive hunting parties, a king is captured, another king regains his freedom. Two gamekeepers seize upon Henry VI:

> Ay, here's a deer whose skin's a keeper's fee!
> This is the quondam king; let's seize upon him.   (III. i. 22–3)

These changes of perspective, from predator to prey, clearly show Shakespeare's hand, for Hall reports only the second part of the hunt in Edward's case, the escape, and no hunt at all in the case of Henry VI's capture. The ambivalence of hunter–hunted is stressed as each inversion of these roles on stage accompanies the reversals of the political situation. Edward will be coming soon to this part of the park 'Under the colour of his usual game', Richard tells his accomplices, while the King, who is permitted to hunt during his captivity, twice reverses the words, and the roles, under the very nose of the hunter guarding him:

> *Hunt.* This way, my lord, for this way lies the game.
> *K. Edw.* Nay, this way, man. See where the huntsmen stand.
>   Now, brother of Gloucester, Hastings, and the rest,
>   Stand you thus close to steal the bishop's deer?   (IV. v. 14–17)

After which exchange, it is Edward who leads the hunter along in his recovery of the crown. In these parallel scenes, where the two pretenders to the throne switch places, the deer hunt upsets standard metaphorical practice by identifying the King with the game. For Henry, who notes how fortune has stripped him of all royal insignia, this metamorphosis ends the course of the monarch and initiates that of the sacrificial animal, while Edward regains his freedom, and his kingdom, by playing the part of the game. On this equivocal figure, all the ambiguities of the monarchic function meet, playing up all possible meanings of the word 'game'— play or sport, hunt or hunted—with the sovereign himself in each role.

---

[65] Hall 250. *3H6*, I. iv. 5, 41, 61–2; II. v. 129–33.
[66] See Richard Marienstras's brilliant analysis, *New Perspectives on the Shakespearean World*, trans. Janet Lloyd (Cambridge, 1985), chs. I and II. Edward I. Berry, *Shakespeare and the Hunt: A Cultural and Social Study* (Cambridge, 2001) adds little to the subject.

4. THE LITERARY TRADITION

The seeds of Fortune

Hall's divine justice is impartial, if not entirely consistent with partisan views. God punishes Edward for his imprudent marriage, his debauched life, and makes his descendants pay for those very faults, yet is no less severe on his enemies, who were caught or killed by numbers at Hexham: 'Thus euery man almoste that escaped, was after taken and scorged: so that it should seme that God had ordeined, all such persones as rebelled against kyng Edward, to haue in cōclusion, death for their reward and guardone.'[67] Hall repeatedly stresses the unequal treatment meted out by Fortune to the rival claimants of the throne:

> this good chaunce happed to kynge Edward, by the yll lucke of kynge Henry, for surely by this yll fortune a man may plainly cōiecture, that the extreme poynt of decay of hys house and estate was apparantly at hande, consideryng that neither by mannes pollicie, nor by worldly riches his vnhappy presdestinate chaunce coulde not by any pollicy be put by, nor by any instrumēt scraped away (well such was Goddes pleasure). (276)

All believe in Edward's luck, including his enemy Somerset who assures the Queen that

> notwithstandyng, that fortune shone on hym, in obteinyng the victory against therle of Warwicke, yet now she might turne her saile on the otherside, causyng him to tast eger vineger as she before had giuen hym to drynke dilicate Ypocrace. (298)

Leaving aside vinegar, the dramatic dialogue repeatedly draws on the same combination of metaphors, fortune's wheel and the wind's caprices, to illustrate the movements of history.

Hall's original mixture of Classical and Christian trends has very old precedents. Tyche, one of Ocean's daughters in Hesiod's *Theogony*, could, like the sea, either destroy or create wealth. A trace of her marine origin remains in the Roman representations, where Fortune is often shown holding a rudder. This is the first hint that there is a direction behind her apparent vagaries, while the ambivalence remains: Fortune, though blind, is life's pilot. In the Middle Ages, she is no longer, as in Antiquity, an unstable woman seated on a sphere, but a woman turning a wheel with deliberate malevolence, very like the hostile power behind the turmoils of *3 Henry VI*:

> Though Fortune's malice overthrow my state,
> My mind exceeds the compass of her wheel.   (IV. iii. 46–7)

Dame Fortune, a combination of God's will and Fate, draws her main features from Boethius, who is often represented in medieval iconography standing by the side of her wheel.[68] Saluted by Gibbon as 'the last of the Romans whom Cato or Tully could

---

[67] Hall 265, 284, 292, 301, 260.

[68] Pierre Courcelle, *La Consolation de Philosophie dans la tradition littéraire: Antécédents et postérité de Boèce* (Paris, 1967), 157, 135. As a victim of a barbarian tyrant, Boethius had earned himself a place in

have acknowledged for their countryman', Boethius translated an enormous body of works for readers who stood in danger of losing their Greek;[69] his definition of tragedy as the reverses of Fortune affecting heroic characters 'was passed on to the Middle Ages, long after any knowledge of the classical theatre had disappeared', Leo Salingar observes, through readers like Chaucer: 'What other thing doth the outcry of tragedies lament', asks Boethius, 'but that fortune, having no respect, over-turneth happy states?'[70] The seminal role of his *De Consolatione Philosophiae* extends much further than this formulaic recipe, as can be seen in the thematic variations of *3 Henry VI*.

Philosophy, who comes to comfort Boethius in his cell, begins by chasing out the poetic Muses, 'thise comune strumpetis of siche a place that men clepen the theatre', for they poison his reason with their sweet venom.[71] To Boethius' cries against inconstant Fortune, Philosophy objects that Fortune is deceitful only as an actor is, and constant in her fickleness, that her whims are in the nature of things. Fortune herself enters to answer the charges of injustice brought against her by the cupidity of men. Those whom she has wheeled to the top should not find it unjust to descend again when her wheel turns.

The philosophical Muses then evoke the happy age when men were content with the products of the earth. The warlike trumpet was silent, blood had not yet stained their armour. Now the rage to possess burns them more than the fires of Etna. But the gifts of Fortune only give the illusion of happiness, and end with life. If kings were stripped of their proud purple they would reveal the shackles that hold them enslaved: desires, sorrows, vain hopes—a tyrant has as many masters as he has passions; like all creatures, he is subject to time. No man can embrace the compass of his existence; having lost yesterday he does not possess tomorrow. God alone is the Sovereign Good, God is the helm and the rudder guiding the world. Only by the strength of divine love are the discordant elements held together, and restrained from each following its path towards disintegration. Behind her apparent whims, Fortune is part of this cosmic order, and ruled by universal Providence. As the revolution of the universe observes a strict regularity, so Fortune and destiny are tied by an inflexible causal chain, and appear fickle only in the limited human perception. Fortune is thus strongly linked to the seasonal cycle, the force of the elements, as well as to theatrical illusion and dramatic irony.

The characters of *3 Henry VI* are as immersed as Hall in Classical culture, and no less sensitive to the variations of Fortune.[72] Their world is perilously exposed to

Boccacio's *de casibus* tales, and was included in Lydgate's *Fall of Princes*. See Howard R. Patch, *The Tradition of Boethius: A Study of his Importance in Medieval Culture* (Oxford, 1935), 96.

[69] *The History of the Decline and Fall of the Roman Empire* (London, 1838), v. 35.

[70] Leo Salingar, *Shakespeare and the Traditions of Comedy* (Cambridge, 1974), 149. See Courcelle, *La Consolation de Philosophie*, 24–36, 341–3. It had many prestigious translators, from King Alfred to Queen Elizabeth I. Elizabeth's version, dated October 1593, is an elliptical rendering more than a translation of the text. *Queen Elizabeth's Englishings of Boethius, 'De Consolatione Philosophiae', Plutarch's 'De Curiositate', Horace's 'De Arte Poetica'*, ed. Caroline Pemberton (London, 1899).

[71] *Chaucer's Translation of Boethius' 'De Consolatione Philosophiae'*, ed. Richard Morris (London, 1868). It was printed by Caxton in 1479.

[72] IV. iii. 46–7; IV. vi. 19–25; IV. vi. 28–9; IV. vii. 2.

climatic change, as to all of nature's rhythms. Henry's pastoral dream shows him torn between the tumults of history and the Muses' nostalgia for the regular division of time, fresh water, and the restful shade of trees.[73] When York's supporters fly like ships before the wind, or swans swimming against the tide, the King fails to rejoice at the death of his enemy for he sees the rocks which threaten them all with shipwreck, and his subjects like feathers tossed about by contrary winds, obeying the strongest gust.[74] This war is like the eternally renewed struggle of the dawn against night, of the sea against the wind, to be endured as he endures the succession of each day and hour of his life until the promised tomb.

In Hall's account, the elements take sides in the struggle, but still operate under divine control, as when Warwick is threatened by the Duke of Burgundy's fleet: 'Se the worke of God, thesame night before the erle departed, ther rose such a sodain wynde and a terrible tempest, that the dukes shippes wer scatered one from another, some drouned, some wether driuen into Scotland.' They appear no more constant than Fortune, as Margaret experienced when she undertook her last voyage to England: 'yet once again (suche was her destinie) beyng letted for lacke of prosperous wynd and encombered with to muche rigorous tempeste, a daie after the faire, as the common prouerbe saieth, landed at the Port of Weymouth,' where she was greeted with the news of Warwick's death and the return of her husband to prison.[75]

On stage, not content with fighting the elements, the characters compete for mastery of them, unaware of the storm building up in Heaven. The King fears divine vengeance, but the Queen scorns his patience and drives his peaceful ship with imperious gusts. When beaten by Warwick, she is forced to strike sail, bow under the tempest, and make herself a humble suppliant before Lewis XI, as Warwick is now in command:[76]

Ay, now begins a second storm to rise,
For this is he that moves both wind and tide.   (III. iii. 47–8)

Edward likewise submits to the inevitable when he is made prisoner by Warwick—
'It boots not to resist both wind and tide'—but means to return in force:

my sea shall suck them dry
And swell so much the higher by their ebb.   (IV. viii. 55–6)

Warwick, who has not anticipated the change of wind, proudly refuses to strike his colours and is beaten, allowing Edward to mock the limits of his power over the elements: ' "Wind-changing Warwick now can change no more." ' His projected epitaph is drawn from Hall's funeral oration: 'death did one thyng, that life could not do, for by death, he had rest, peace, quietnes, and tranquillitie, whiche his life

---

[73] See Patch, *The Tradition of Boethius*, 122, on the most frequently quoted passages.
[74] II. ii. 5; III. i. 83–8.
[75] Hall 282, 297.
[76] I. iv. 145–9; II. ii. 5–8; II. vi. 33–6; III. iii. 4–5, 38.

euer abhorred.'[77] On stage, the incessant movement of the man of action refers more ironically still to the frequency of his changing sides.

Meanwhile, Margaret laboriously cheers her unfortunate sailors with the Platonic metaphor of the storm-tossed vessel: the ship of Lancaster has lost Warwick, its anchor, Montague, its main mast, and most of its rigging; it is threatened by Edward, 'a ruthless sea', Clarence, 'a quicksand of deceit', Richard, 'a ragged fatal rock', but they have spare ropes, masts, and anchors—Oxford, Somerset, and the French soldiers—and intrepid pilots, herself and the Prince of Wales; let them not hope to save their lives by abandoning the ship, only a fearless resolve will put them out of danger. 'We will not from the helm to sit and weep,' she promises. The most striking point of her formal rhetoric is her assumption of the pilot's role, one reserved since Antiquity to superior powers.[78]

Unaware that Richard has vowed to dry up the ocean separating him from the crown, Edward sees just one last cloud on his horizon—Margaret's landing. He chose his emblem one bright morning when he saw three suns join in the sky to make one.[79] Hall reports this prodigy as a good omen, preceding Edward's victory at Mortimer's Cross. On stage the vision occurs just before the news of the Duke's death. Having tumbled Phaethon from the sky, the Lancasters enjoy the fruits of their harvest, while the Yorkists vow to hack their usurping roots, and water the crops with their blood. Time is out of joint: day fights with night, spring is overtaken by winter, the drunken earth gives birth to monstrous plants.[80] In the ambient confusion, the farmers' tools become weapons. Conversely the axe serves to lop branches, uproot stocks, hew paths through brambles, deforest armies, or plant and cut down kings. Observing the scars of this savage agriculture, Henry VI vainly offers to let one rose wither if it will save a thousand lives. He is no exemplary gardener himself, as Clifford's dying speech reminds us: it is through the weakness of Phoebus that Phaethon set fire to the earth, just as the mildness of the air allows weeds to flourish.[81]

Again, we find at the source of the metaphoric web a rather worn-out cliché applied by Hall to York and his offspring Edward: 'out of the dead stocke, sprang a stronge & mightie braunche, which by no meanes could either be broken, or made sere.' Shakespeare grafts his images of blood and growth onto the branches of the old genealogical tree, and adds a variation to the theme of lineage by setting the foundation myth in the vegetal world. Thus Clifford, not content to lop off the young limb, Rutland, attacks the trunk. Richard means to blast any promising branch that might spring from Edward's loins. Warwick, having successfully planted the new Plantagenet, is furious to see his rhetorical bouquet to Lady Bona

---

[77] IV. iii. 59; v. i. 50–2, 57. Hall 296.

[78] v. iv. 21. In *The Republic*, 488a3, the state is like a ship whose pilot is the leader.

[79] II. i. 20. Hall 251. This phenomenon, known as a parhelion, is caused by the formation of ice crystals in the upper air. In Q[O], Edward's vision is confirmed by a SD: 'Three suns appear in the air.'

[80] II. v. 1–2; II. iii. 46–7; IV. viii. 60–1; III. ii. 156; II. vi. 46–51; II. ii. 163–9; III. ii. 174–81; v. iv. 67–71; I. i. 48; III. iii. 198; v. v. 48.

[81] I. iv. 33–4; II. vi. 11–13; II. ii. 163–9; II. iii. 7, 15–23, 45–7; II. v. 21–54, 101–2. Cf. *R2*, III. iv.

wasted by Edward's whims, and swears to 'replant Henry in his former state'. Yet in the end he, the cedar that sheltered the oak from winter, must fall before the axe.[82]

There remains to root up and burn Margaret's thorny wood of soldiers, fell the Prince of Wales like a young plant, and eradicate the stock.[83] In the Q text, Richard keeps up the rural good work: he rushes to the Tower to 'root them out', having earlier counted his corpses, 'ere I can plant myself'.[84] These bucolic images round up the long bloody sequence initiated by Warwick the Kingmaker's proud vow— 'I'll plant Plantagenet; root him up who dares.' The House of York can now enjoy a well-deserved rest:

> Once more we sit in England's royal throne,
> Repurchased with the blood of enemies.
> What valiant foemen like to autumn's corn
> Have we mowed down in tops of all their pride! (v. vii. 1–4)

Edward's request to kiss the newborn heir evinces from Richard a promise to 'blast his harvest, if your head were laid', topped by a show of vegetable love:

> And, that I love the tree from whence thou sprang'st,
> Witness the loving kiss I give the fruit.— (v. vii. 31–2)

The disturbance of seasonal cadences overspills in the following play:

> Now is the winter of our discontent
> Made glorious summer by this son of York ... (*R3*, I. i. 1–2)

Fortune runs through the cycle of vegetation and man's life with one turn of her wheel, converting prosperity into its opposite. This forward summer announces convulsed times, ushering in winter, decay, and tragic fall.

The ironies of fate

The image of Fortune as a deceitful actor, the turning wheel that masks and reveals the truth of man's condition, produce various ironic effects not only in the world of the plot but in the dramatic form itself, which links the irony of fate to the structure of the peripeteia. Man's ignorant bustle is a priceless source of amusement to the gods who watch the human comedy, an image even older than the theatre.[85] Like the gods, the audience are generally informed before the designated victims of what is in store, and able to savour their vanity. At best the characters have flashes of lucidity touching others, never themselves. Edward's mockery of 'Wind-changing Warwick' is double-edged—the weathercock imagines that it makes the wind turn.

---

[82] Hall 254. *3H6*, II. vi. 46–51; III. ii. 126; III. iii. 123–6; v. ii. 11–15; III. iii. 197–8; v. ii. 11–15.

[83] v. iv. 67–71; v. v. 60; v. v. 48.

[84] Q[O] at v. v. 50 and III. ii. 132. Cox/Rasmussen follow F, 'place myself', where Cairncross preferred the Q 'plant' finding it stronger, and 'an appropriate continuation of the "tree of Jesse" imagery'.

[85] Augustine's in *De Civitate Dei*, III. xiv, is derived from Plato's *Laws*, where man is said to be the puppet of the gods. On the detailed history of this pregnant metaphor, see Jean Jacquot, '"Le Théâtre du monde": De Shakespeare à Calderón', *Revue de littérature comparée*, 31 (1957), 43, 341–72.

The dramatic composition taps all the resources of macabre humour: the characters' blind spots, the denials opposed by facts to optimistic foresights, solemn vows, or pious speeches, Fortune's whims, deceiving oracles, and amateur prophets.

Hall amply contributes to the derisive vein that runs through the play, either by coincidences inviting tragic irony, or by his comments on the inanity of men's struggles against superior forces. The similarities between the royal marriages, or the simultaneous presence of two kings in one kingdom, supply a variety of ironic twists. In *1 Henry VI*, as in the chronicle, the death of the Talbots on the same day is treated with proper pathos. When York dies on the same day as his son, Hall does not stress the coincidence, although he records the parodic ceremony devised by his enemies, whereas Part 3 uses Rutland's death to ignite the Duke's wrath, and replays the motif in a different mode with the anonymous father and son.

Hall's comments on mutability, providential punishment, or the misfortunes of Henry VI are all adapted with nuances in the play. His remark on the ill-fated title of Gloucester is transferred to Richard, who tries to exchange it for his brother's:[86]

> Let me be Duke of Clarence, George of Gloucester,
> For Gloucester's dukedom is too ominous.   (II. vi. 106–7)

Hall reports that Clarence was sent to prison because his name was George, on grounds of a 'folysh' prophecy saying that Edward's line would be disinherited by 'G', and mocks those who deciphered it after the event, although he notes later in his account of Clarence's death that 'G' is also the initial of Gloucester.[87]

More often than not, the context or the dramatic construction creates irony in a situation where none originally existed. It is perceptible from the first scene, where the protagonists violate right with a clear conscience, and summon soldiers to prove the justice of their cause. Thus Warwick tells Edward he can be sure of a welcome in every town on their triumphant way to coronation,

> And he that throws not up his cap for joy
> Shall for the fault make forfeit of his head.   (II. i. 195–6)

Hall does write that the proclamation of Edward was greeted 'with many great showtes and clappyng of handes', but never implies that this joy might be forced: Edward's accession was well received, 'for he was so much estemed, bothe of the nobilitie and commonaltie' that 'aboue all other, he was extolled and praysed to the very heauen'. For a similar note of compulsive merriment, one must go to the proclamation of Richard III, told with More's sardonic humour, when Buckingham's henchmen 'threwe vp their cappes in token of joye' to the mute amazement of the crowd.

The characters are treated with ironical distance throughout the play, for instance when they denounce the breach of rules they have consistently ignored, like Margaret's righteous anger at the court of Lewis XI: 'Yet heavens are just, and

---

[86] Vergil 73, Hall 209, and Foxe 713 all record this remark, attributed to 'many men', at the time of Humphrey's death.

[87] Hall 326. *R3*, I. i. 54–129.

Time suppresseth wrongs.' In this connection, Hall points out that she bitterly complained of her misfortune but should blame herself first for having compounded the murder of Duke Humphrey: 'I would desire of God, that all men would in egall balance, ponder & indifferently consider the causes, of these misfortunes and euill chaunces,' he piously concludes. However, he does not recall the death of young Rutland when the York brothers stab the Prince of Wales, whereas the dramatic text stresses the symmetry of Margaret's despair with York's. The presence of two kings on the same territory does not tickle Hall's sense of humour either. He reports the hesitations of the Londoners before they decide for Edward who, all in all, seems a better proposition, and the scruples of the inhabitants of York. In the play, this historical fact creates a series of ludicrous dilemmas, emphasized by the sarcastic comments of hardened cynics. Even the saintly Henry VI betrays a touch of bitter irony in his exchange with the gamekeepers.[88]

The brevity of the restoration of the House of Lancaster, another historical fact, produces a comic double take: exit King, enter King, once, twice, like mechanic figures in a weather-house forecasting rain or sunshine. As in the Classical theatre, the main irony resides in the characters' lack of vision, which lures them into naive overconfident moves. The York brothers are not aware of their father's death when they interpret their vision of three suns as a happy omen. Likewise, when Margaret begs help of the French King for Henry, believing he is free in Scotland, he has just been captured. Warwick arrives to negotiate a marriage for Edward, whom the audience have just seen courting Lady Grey. According to Hall, Warwick was informed of Edward's marriage by letters which he received after his departure from France, having obtained Lewis XI's consent to the match. Shakespeare has the letters reach him in the middle of the negotiations at the French court, where they bring a stinging denial to his 'flowery' speeches on behalf of Edward.

For his part, Edward ignores all warning signs of a storm, but remains confident in his star when caught, and indeed soon escapes, taking his guard with him—another touch of comedy absent from the chronicle. The fusion of his two captures creates a situation which does not exist in Hall either: Henry VI rejoices in his newly recovered freedom when Edward has already fled. For once, the unhappy King has no fear for the future, confident as he is in the love of his subjects for his qualities of 'pity', 'mildness', 'mercy':

> these graces challenge grace,
> And when the lion fawns upon the lamb,
> The lamb will never cease to follow him.   (IV. viii. 48–50)

Immediately, a '*Shout within*' is heard, Edward enters, and sends him back to jail.

The two most hubristic characters meet at Coventry, where fate has surprises in store for them both. Warwick believes he sees friends come to give him support, but it is Edward approaching, who informs him of Henry's capture. Montague enters next, and goes to Warwick's side. This is a sad blow to Edward, who was not aware

---

[88] Hall 298, 294. *3H6*, IV. vii. 30–4; III. i. 72–88, 91–8.

of his defection, unlike the audience who saw him with the Lancastrians in the preceding act, but Clarence's reversal, a surprise for us all, gives Edward the upper hand
again. In the last scene, the House of York savour the eradication of their rivals,
alone and tranquil at last, O irony! alone with Richard. The fate promised by Hall to
Edward's children as a result of his ill-advised marriage only occurred twenty years
after the deed, whereas on stage Richard does not mean to wait: he is the precocious
winter preparing to nip Edward's spring in the bud.

Hall tends to read divine judgements in the misfortunes of the wicked. He
never jests with the decrees of Providence, reserving his sarcasms for those who
interpret God's mysterious ways retroactively. Each transgression—murder, perjury, betrayal—evinces a reminder that the culprits soon paid the price of their
heinous crimes, sometimes by a just and natural turn of affairs, more often through
a reversal of fortune. It is hard to disentangle natural from providential retaliation,
for immanent justice in the chronicle generally operates through human channels.
Hall's repeated assurances that criminals cannot long escape divine wrath find little
echo in 3 *Henry VI*. If the curses of the victims are addressed no less vehemently to
Heaven, they are but partially fulfilled: thus Rutland's curse on Clifford's progeny,
an echo of Hall's comments on the vicissitudes suffered by his son, has no effect in
the play where his children never appear.[89] Providence remains invisible in this
third Part. What parallelism there is between crimes and punishments results from
the play's structural symmetries.

With growing subtlety as the cycle progresses, irony plays in counterpoint to the
conventional discourses on honour, justice, and right, but not to deride these
notions, as it turns out. On the contrary, their decline reveals them to be authentic
values, of vital necessity to a human community. The mastery of irony plays a
crucial role in the shaping of the characters. A huge distance separates them from
the choric figures of Part 1. Clifford in his dying speech speaks only for himself and
cannot grasp the irony of his own words. As Edward I. Berry observes, 'A further
stage occurs in *Richard III*, when irony moves into the character's own psyche and
commentary becomes self-conscious.'[90] In developing Richard's scathing sense of
humour, Shakespeare will give him the control of the plot for three acts, before
submitting him to the irony of reversal.

---

[89]   I. iii. 40–2. Hall 255.
[90]   II. vi. 1–30. Edward I. Berry, *Patterns of Decay: Shakespeare's Early Histories* (Charlottesville, Va.,
1975), 67.

5

The Dawn of Tragedy

1. A TURN FOR THE WORST

The collapse of the institutions

Possession of the throne being reduced to a quarrel over inheritance, the King no longer embodies the collective interest against factions. With the weakening of the state, the advancement of the clan becomes a primary value, before the common weal. The only one who does not observe this rule of priority is Henry himself, who is unsure of his title, and infuriates his supporters by disinheriting his own son. Allegiance cannot brook this breach of lineal transmission:

> Farewell, faint-hearted and degenerate King,
> In whose cold blood no spark of honour bides.   (I. i. 183–4)

The royal party turn to a leader who shows more concern for the interests of his liegemen. That this new leader should be a woman, ready to destroy all family unity in order to recover her son's inheritance, makes the anarchy more blatant still. Margaret claims the superiority of the maternal blood in the line of descent. Had Henry suffered as she has for their child's sake,

> Thou wouldst have left thy dearest heart-blood there,
> Rather than have made that savage Duke thine heir
> And disinherited thine only son.   (I. i. 223–5)

   With the waning of ethical codes, the area of moral obligation shrinks gradually from *res publica* to self-defence and radical individualism: 'Chivalric community gives way to the narrower bonds of law, law to kinship, and kinship, as we shall see, to self-love.'[1] In Clifford's view, the Duke of York's ambitious attempt to advance his progeny was perfectly natural:

> He, but a duke, would have his son a king,
> And raise his issue like a loving sire . . .   (II. ii. 21–2)

Vengeance of the father, the logical counterpart to love of progeny, extends the blood obligation to include an archaic law of blood for blood. These two themes with their attendant motives—hatred, cupidity—supply the main dynamics of the action. York's issue dream of the crown. The anonymous father and son who emblematize the civil war both seek gold on the corpse of their victim before they

---

[1] Berry, *Patterns of Decay*, 59.

recognize the link. Passionate hatred, driven by a thirst for revenge, soon proves stronger even than covetousness. Those who betrayed their clan to serve their interest return to the fold like prodigal sons. Richard alone coldly counts the removal of his relations as so many steps to the throne.

The events show a progress towards horror, for each new crime further disrupts the communal institutions and allows new forms of disorder. Not so in Hall, who reports the battles as bloodier, the casualty figures and the level of violence as higher than ever before, but does not draw a diagnosis of virulent illness; even the cruellest acts of retaliation remain circumscribed in time, they do not signify a general decline nor an erosion of values. If Shakespeare refrains from exploiting all the sanguinary scenes narrated, those he chooses to represent, far from being gratuitous, are designed to explore the chronicler's vicious circle of crime and revenge, with a marked increase in cruelty as each reprisal sets back the borderlines of transgression.

Thus *3 Henry VI* selects the acute phases of an endemic conflict which, in the chronicles, alternate with long stretches of relative calm, or at least armed peace. Shakespeare darkens the picture, suppresses all the moments of respite, and drops twelve peaceful years in the interval between *3 Henry VI* and *Richard III*. Hall salutes 'The ende of the trobelous season of kynge Henry the. vj.', and begins the reign of Edward IV on a cheerful note, 'Prosperous fortune and glorious victory, happely succeding to this yōg Prince and couragious Capitain . . .' This anticipation of a smiling future passes, with heavy irony, in the closing lines of the play:

> Sound drums and trumpets! Farewell, sour annoy,
> For here I hope begins our lasting joy.   (v. vii. 46–7)

The Yorks are triumphant, but Richard's threats have warned the audience that there is no joy in prospect until the disease has run its full course to paroxysm and purifying bloodletting.

The suppression of Edward's reign constitutes the most decisive operation on the narrative. Others, less visible, contribute to the progress of moral decay. One of the early symptoms of an all-devouring evil was the loss of the great normative figures who stood as bulwarks to the kingdom—tragic deaths, all, leaving unbreachable gaps in the common weal. Part 3 shows the last vestiges of moral order falling apart; the absence of a great figure to thunder forth the voice of collective duty leads to the extinction of individual conscience.

From Hall's account, the inhabitants of York held long concertations before opening the city gates to Edward on his return from exile. He had to hear mass and take communion, then solemnly swear allegiance to King Henry before he was allowed in. In other words, the citizens did their best to solemnize the procedure, and guarantee that he would keep his word; that they failed does not discredit the method. It was this breach of oath—among other misdeeds—that attracted divine wrath on Edward's progeny.[2] In the dramatic version, the Mayor has but a slight

---

[2] In the chronicle, the cause of their tragic fate varies with the circumstances: Edward's debauched life, his marriage, or his perjury before York.

hesitation, which excites Richard's sarcasm—'A wise stout captain, and soon persuaded!'—and Hastings's condescending tolerance:

> The good old man would fain that all were well,
> So 'twere not long of him.   (IV. vii. 31–2)

Edward promises nothing as, indeed, nothing is asked of him. He is proclaimed King at the end of the scene without more ado.

Two other staged episodes raise similar cases of split loyalties. After the defeat, Hall tells us, Henry 'determined to make hys abode in Scotland, to se and espye, what way his frendes in Englande would studye or inuent for his restitucion and aduauncement'.[3] In the play, he is moved by an irresistible desire to see his country again. As he weighs the extent of his losses, reviewing the attributes of temporal and spiritual power conferred by the royal unction, it is the failure of his mission he deplores, more than the reversal of fortune. He is surprised, as Richard II will be, that the indelible marks of the divine will could be thus erased. The gamekeepers, who have recognized 'the quondam king', do not recognize his title: 'But if thou be a king where is thy crown?' It avails him not to remind them of intangible signs like unction, dynastic right, or allegiance:

> I was anointed king at nine months old.
> My father and my grandfather were kings,
> And you were sworn true subjects unto me:
> And tell me, then, have you not broke your oaths?   (III. i. 76–9)

Their reply, 'No, for we were subjects but while you were king', denies any contract between the person of the king and his quondam subjects. Their duty is to the King in power: 'We are true subjects to the King, King Edward.'

Kantorowicz notes an equally clear separation between man and office in documents of the Tudor period; the immortal body of the King had already lost most of its sacred connotations when Charles I's Puritan Parliament declared war on the monarch half a century later, had him judged, and executed, all in the name of the King.[4] The royal dignity is transmitted without break from one mortal body to another—the King is dead, long live the King. This fiction, whilst borrowing its terminology and images from theology, reveals a growing need to regulate the kingly office like any other human institution, to find a firm legal basis ensuring its permanence against human frailties, at safe distance from the religious and the sacred.[5] Shakespeare's gamekeepers embody the stability of the civil service in a changing world:

> We charge you, in God's name and the King's,
> To go with us unto the officers.   (III. i. 96–7)

Allegiance gives way to *alternance*, governing teams pass by, but the name of

---

[3] III. i. 13–14. Hall 257.
[4] *The King's Two Bodies*, 23.
[5] See Marc Bloch, *The Royal Touch: Sacred Monarchy and Scrofula in England and France*, trans. J. E. Anderson (London, 1973).

government remains, to which Henry submits: 'In God's name, lead; your King's name be obeyed.' In the gamekeepers' view, it behoves not the subject to identify the true king, only to obey the occupant of the throne, should he change ten times. Their attitude is close to that of the Mayor, who is not tied to Henry by personal allegiance either. He hesitates only because kings have changed so often lately; his brief pang of loyalty is directed towards the Crown, not to the man, and dictated by prudence:

> My lords, we were forwarned of your coming,
> And shut the gates for safety of ourselves,
> For now we owe allegiance unto Henry.   (IV. vii. 17–19)

All the subtlety of the reasoning resides in the 'now'. It is exactly what Henry predicted to his subjects who declared themselves loyal—to Edward:

> So would you be again to Henry,
> If he were seated as King Edward is.   (III. i. 94–5)

Hall explains these variations by the taste men have for change, but his comments on the crowds who rallied to Edward on his return from exile apply as well to the behaviour of the citizens of York, and to all the other loyal subjects in the canon —the citizens of Angers in *King John* who consult their interest, or the Roman crowd in *Julius Caesar* who acclaim the victor, every victor:

> what soeuer the occasion was, the moste parte thought it more for their securitie and auantage of theim selfs, to take parte and ioyne with kyng Edward, beyng at all poyntes furnisshed with men of warre, rather then to cleue to kyng Hēry, and to be alwayes in ieopardy, both of lyfe and lande. (292)

The role of the people in the monarch's investiture, as we noted earlier, is limited to a purely formal approval.[6] It is nevertheless understood that the King reigns by popular consent. In normal circumstances this tacit agreement raises no difficulty, whereas disputes over the royal title leave the loyal subjects without any clear rule of behaviour: cynical or opportunistic attitudes—like the fratricides of the popular scenes—are reactions to the demands of rival authorities no longer held in check by the central power.

In the other scene requiring a choice between two kings, it is a king who hesitates:

> Now, Warwick, tell me, even upon thy conscience,
> Is Edward your true king? For I were loath
> To link with him that were not lawful chosen.   (III. iii. 113–15)

Lewis XI invokes the same principles as the gamekeepers and, like them, adapts his oaths to the situation. Of course he vows to remain the friend of Henry and Margaret,

> But if your title to the crown be weak,
> As may appear by Edward's good success,

---

[6] See Schramm, *A History of the English Coronation,* 143, 166, 179–203.

> Then 'tis but reason that I be released
> From giving aid, which late I promised.   (III. iii. 145–8)

He sides again with them when interest requires, and sends an insulting message to 'false Edward, thy supposed king'. His reversals, however, are not a significant symptom of moral degradation; they simply reflect the usual image of the French in the histories as a race of versatile tricksters.

The Earl of Oxford, a minor character in the plot, is present at the court of Lewis XI to recall the other motive now dominant in the political choices: blood feud. When called upon to recognize Edward as king, he is indignant:

> Call him my king by whose injurious doom
> My elder brother, the Lord Aubrey Vere,
> Was done to death? . . .
> No, Warwick, no; while life upholds this arm,
> This arm upholds the house of Lancaster.   (III. iii. 101–7)

All those present end up by siding with Margaret: Lewis XI and his sister do it out of spite, Oxford to avenge his family, and Warwick to heal his wounded pride. They are soon joined by Clarence, who wants a rich spouse, and resents the fact that the new Queen's relatives have been served first. Concerns of legitimacy, monarchic titles, and duties drop out of the picture.

Evil in progress

The central doubt weighing on the legitimacy of the sovereign, or worse still, on his identity, produces in its wake a growing confusion in moral values. It is what the Prince of Wales emphasizes when the Yorkists maintain their cause is just:

> If that be right which Warwick says is right,
> There is no wrong, but every thing is right.   (II. ii. 131–2)

Is it right or wrong, after deserting one's camp, to return at the cost of a new perjury? The question is raised at each of the characters' change of heart, Clarence, Montague, et al. Clarence's arguments to justify his second volte-face may sound specious, but indeed, no extant code can help the characters judge if it is morally better to persist in treason or resume their initial loyalty by betraying the traitors. Just as there is no spirit of forgiveness in their tribal feuds, there can be no hope of a return to innocence, nor good cause to fight for.

Here again, with apparently minor alterations of Hall's material, Shakespeare calls a draw between the two camps when each claims to be in the right; justice has deserted the stage, though ironically both sides constantly appeal to it. This is not quite the case in the chronicle. Like Lewis XI, like the gamekeepers, Hall is a pragmatist: political stability comes first. The occupant of the throne is the rightful king; the pretender to the crown is an outlaw, whose ambitions, however legally founded, threaten the reigning order. Thus Hall impartially condemns those who rebel against Henry VI, or against Edward IV. He never decides unequivocally for

York or Lancaster. The Yorkists have a claim to legitimacy, but the Lancastrians have legality on their side—that is, until the legitimate pretender overthrows legality, and becomes in turn the legal occupant of the throne, against whom it would be damnable to rebel.

One could accuse Hall of turning his coat with each dynastic change, but this would be unfair, for there is after all a logic to his attitude. He may condemn the Duke of York's rebellion, but he does not deny the justice of his claims. Besides, as we saw above, it was the Queen who opened hostilities. When York had the King summon her, she 'not onely denied to come, but also assembled together a great army, intending to take the kyng by fine force, out of the lordes handes, and to set theim to a new skoole'.[7] Thus she caught him unawares. York was vanquished and killed at Wakefield before he could gather an army of equal force, whereas on stage, both sides break the truce at once. Urged on by his sons, the Duke decides to raise an army and seize power, in spite of his oath; he has no sooner spoken than the Queen approaches with 20,000 men to besiege him. Both parties are equally guilty of introducing foreign soldiers to English soil—an offence emphasized by the stage directions and the dialogue. With the help of French soldiers, Warwick places Henry back on the throne; then, a few scenes later, Edward returns with an invading army of 'hasty Germans and blunt Hollanders'—a scandal no doubt underlined by their costumes.

These various changes suggest a double purpose: to raise the level of transgression, and lay the blame for it on both camps equally. In the cruellest scene of the play, the Queen wipes York's tears with a handkerchief dipped in the blood of his son, a Shakespearian addition to the horror of the episode, possibly culled from *The Spanish Tragedy*.[8] Likewise, Warwick's last moments are further darkened by the account of his brother's death, and the Prince of Wales is killed under his mother's eyes, though the chroniclers say nothing of the sort. According to Hall, 'the Quene was foūde in her Chariot almost dead for sorowe, yᵉ prince was apprehended and kepte close', but she never appears on the scene of his murder. Holinshed does not even mention her presence at Tewkesbury but reports that she was found later, hiding for safety in a poor religious house.[9] In both chronicles, the Duke of York's death follows that of Rutland, Warwick does get killed soon after Montague, and the Queen is close to the battlefield, but these scattered pieces of information do not, as in the play, serve to enhance their misery.

On stage, York's sons are worse than the father, and Edward no better than his brothers; his list of misdeeds includes at least three crimes of which he is exempted in the chronicle. First, it is he who preaches perjury, swearing he himself would unhesitatingly break his oath to win a crown. He will indeed do so, but in this case, according to Hall's account of Wakefield, he was not present. Worse still, Shakespeare makes him share in the killing of the Prince, and condone the murder of Henry VI. Hall clearly absolves him of the first crime: irritated by the young

[7] Hall 249–50.

[8] Thomas Kyd, *The Spanish Tragedy*, ed. David Bevington (Manchester, 1996), III. xiii and IV. iv.

[9] Hall 300. Holinshed 321 diverges from Hall only on this point.

man's arrogance, he struck him with his hand, 'whom incontinent, they that stode about, whiche were George duke of Clarence, Rychard duke of Gloucester, Thomas Marques Dorset, and Williã lord Hastynges, sodaynly murthered, & pitiously manquelled'.[10] In the play, Edward is the first to stab him.

Touching Henry VI, Hall prudently hides behind the rumour according to which Richard killed him to relieve his brother of all disquiet, 'But whosoeuer was the manqueller of this holy man, it shall appere, that bothe the murtherer and the con-senter, had condigne and not vndeserued punishement, for their bloudy stroke, and butcherly act.' No names are given, the reader can draw his own conclusions, though the turn of phrase implies that Edward must have agreed to the murder. Yet Thomas More's account acquits him of any guilt: Richard killed Henry VI, 'without kyng Edward his assente, which woulde haue appointed that bocherly office too some other, rather then to his owne brother'.[11] Shakespeare opts for the worst. When told that Richard is gone

> To London all in post and, as I guess,
> To make a bloody supper in the Tower   (v. v. 84–5)

Edward is not otherwise moved: 'He's sudden if a thing comes in his head'. That is all the funeral oration of poor Henry.

2. THE NEW ETHICS

Corrections made to the narrative thus consistently darken a state of affairs which, in Hall, is not desperate. Evil occupies the stage unchecked; only vestiges of an earlier order remain to measure the extent of the damage. The codes of heroism and chivalry stand now detached from their moral, political, and religious foundations, but are still visited like monuments of the past.

The remnants

The York brothers seem to have an equal share of just about all the faults in the repertory, until Richard reaches new heights in crime that leave everyone else far behind. In 2 *Henry VI*, the Duke was the most Machiavellian and dangerous character of the cast, yet he kept some traces of a better age. His duel with Clifford was the last chivalrous combat of the War of the Roses—each man paying homage to the valour of his adversary before the fight. Against his sons he defends, be it only for a moment, the honouring of one's word; those after him no longer bow to that or any rule. He and Warwick are the last witnesses of a glorious age. Both men swear they prefer death to ignominious flight, as will Richard.[12] The funeral homages

---

[10] Hall 301.
[11] Hall 303, 343.
[12] 2H6, I. i. 115–30, 190–7, 210–37. 3H6, I. iv. 22–4; V. ii. 32–3.

identifying York with sun, oak, and eagle give him a place in the line of Worthies after Hector and Hercules:

> O Clifford, boist'rous Clifford, thou hast slain
> The flower of Europe for his chivalry ...   (II. i. 70–1)

But York's ambitions disqualify him as a worthy emblem of chivalry. Neither he nor Warwick are exemplary figures, just slightly tainted heirs to the heroic line, like gauge marks in the deteriorating process. Warwick the Kingmaker is decorated for the purpose with the martial exploits in France of his father-in-law Richard Beauchamp. He pronounces his own funeral oration, with similar images: cedar higher than oak, shelter of lion and eagle. Shakespeare spares him Holinshed's story that he was killed by one of Edward's men whilst fleeing on horseback, though with two flights from the battlefield, for which he is several times reproved during the play, he is a lesser hero than York. Their deaths evoke nostalgia for the bygone age of the warlike epic. The level of insults exchanged between camps is similar to *1 Henry VI*, where the honourable Bedford promises fire and massacres to the detested enemy, and Talbot swears to avenge Salisbury according to the rules:

> For every drop of blood was drawn from him
> There hath at least five Frenchmen died to-night.   (*1H6*, II. ii. 8–9)

These sanguinary threats are less exalting when exchanged by two armies of Englishmen. For want of foreign adversaries, heroism finds new releases in the war of the clans and personal hatreds. The valour revered as an absolute by causeless warriors is at best a dubious virtue in these troubled times, as York unwittingly suggests in the first scene when he congratulates Richard on his prowess. It is in dramatic order for Richard to usurp Henry V's memory against Richmond's 'over-weening rags of France',

>   whom our fathers
> Have in their own land beaten, bobbed, and thumped,
> And on recòrd left them the heirs of shame.   (*R3*, v. iii. 335–7)

Throughout the tetralogy, Henry V represents the standard of reference, a royal knight akin to the medieval ideal, and a victorious one at that, to the realistic 'modernists'. The lost leader and his age of legend are repeatedly summoned to set off the weaknesses of his heirs, and the mediocrity of present times. His glorious shadow is first conjured by Henry VI, who claims the heritage of England's pride:

> I am the son of Henry the Fifth,
> Who made the Dauphin and the French to stoop,
> And seized upon their towns and provinces.   (I. i. 107–9)

It is also the argument presented by Oxford to Lewis XI on behalf of Henry. In both cases, the retort is the same: he has lost all of his father's conquests. Edward too recalls the famous hero, to accuse Margaret of his offspring's decline. Even in the eyes of the Lancastrians, Henry VI is but a paltry successor to the great warrior. The true heir of Henry V is his grandson, the Prince of Wales:

O brave young Prince, thy famous grandfather
Doth live again in thee. Long mayst thou live
To bear his image and renew his glories!   (v. iv. 52–4)

The young man earns this tribute when he gives all fearful men 'leave to go away betimes', stealing the role of Hall's 'lusty kyng Edward' who at Towton 'made proclamacion that all men, whiche were afrayde to fighte, shoulde incontinent departe'.[13] Agincourt is also recorded, or heralded, in Somerset's answering speech:

And he that will not fight for such a hope,
Go home to bed and, like the owl by day,
If he arise, be mocked and wondered at   (v. iv. 55–7)

but his dream is cut short in the following scene. England must wait for another young man to grow, one not compromised in these bloody wars, who will lay Henry V to rest after his last flourishing by Richard.

The Prince of Wales was indecorously dubbed, at his mother's request, after the second battle of St Albans: 'Whē quene Margaret had thus wel sped, first she caused the kyng, to dubbe prince Edward his sonne, knyght, with. xxx. other persons, which in the morning fought on the quenes side, against his parte'.[14] For Hall, the only irony therein is that the King, that very morning, had created twelve knights for the other side, of whom he was then hostage. In the narrative, the dubbing follows the victory of the Queen who gives these rewards to her best warriors; on stage, it takes place, more significantly, before the fratricidal battle of Towton.

Besides the mockery of it in this context, the ceremony confronts two antagonistic notions of 'right'. The first is recalled in the ritual words of the ceremony:

Edward Plantagenet, arise a knight,
And learn this lesson: draw thy sword in right.

But the Prince interprets it restrictively as the defence of his 'right'—the recovery of the crown:

My gracious father, by your kingly leave,
I'll draw it as apparent to the crown,
And in that quarrel use it to the death.   (ii. ii. 61–5)

His firmness is approved by the clan: 'Why, that is spoken like a toward prince.' In their eyes, Henry VI's withdrawal is doubly reprehensible, for in abandoning the crown he also renounces the moral heritage of his father. The chivalric code has split into two conflicting forms of obligation: to defend the property of widow and orphan; to defend the right and justice.

In the new ethics, humane feelings are evidence of cowardice:

My gracious liege, this too much lenity
And harmful pity must be laid aside.   (ii. ii. 9–10)

---

[13] Hall 255, which to Cairncross is the source of both the Prince's speech and of Henry V's at Agincourt, *H5*, iv. iii. 35–7.

[14] Hall 252.

To show 'heart', the siege of courage rather than tender emotions, is to be bold, resolute, and hard as metal: 'Steel thy melting heart,' the King is advised. During the scene, the order to draw one's sword is given four times: to create a knight, defend justice, kill enemies, and perform the executioner's office. On the ruins of their crumbling ethics, the belligerents have built a new and no less rigid code of behaviour, retaining from the old one the veneration of courage, and pride in one's birth.

The Christian doctrine, endorsed by the reigning authority, was uncompromising: '"Vengeance is mine", saith the Lord.' Current opinion showed more nuances.[15] Elizabethan law courts and religious dicta might well condemn private justice; the code of honour still demanded it, and the duel was the fairest form of reparation. In the revenge tragedies so popular in the 1590s, religious morality was satisfied as well, by the inevitable death after the deed of the avenging hero, by suicide if need be. However, the tolerance did not extend to collective revenge, even if Seneca's tragedies admit the principle of clannish solidarity, on the grounds that all members of a family share the profit of the crime committed, hence the guilt, and are collectively accountable. The revenger should not depend on the audience's sympathy when he vents his spleen on the young and old of his enemy, Fredson Bowers reminds us.[16] Neither the scene of Rutland's death, which opens the cycle of retaliations, nor the tale of Priam's at the court of Denmark was devised to draw the audience's sympathy for the deed itself. Revenge is clearly shown as a deviant form of heroism, practised by reckless knights whose archaic notions of *jus sanguini* lead them to copy the animal world. Blood alternatively means birthright, nobility, valour, lineage, moral codes, family ties, or the voice of nature, which the self-appointed heroes invoke when challenged to prove their blood.

Retracing the Elizabethan background of vengeance, Bowers notes that the practice reached peaks during the War of the Roses, and quotes the murder of Rutland as the most terrible example of bloodthirsty revenge. However, he does not mention *Henry VI*, and passes quickly over the chronicle histories, which are 'an affair of armies', so that the theme of personal vengeance gets lost in the shuffle. Shakespeare solves this difficulty by giving the main antagonists a personal aim in the battles waged. Like Kyddian heroes, they feel in duty bound to exact vengeance, and 'ne'er satisfied', as they persistently remind the audience, until they have fulfilled their mission.[17]

Here as elsewhere, the casting of historical facts into an extant literary mould upsets all the conventions of the genre. Hamlet, when directed to endorse the role of avenger, will do so with extreme reluctance, and show pointedly enough that it is not such a 'natural' thing to do. In *3 Henry VI*, the pattern is fragmented into so many shards of a broken mirror. Each successive revenge tragedy convincingly voices the tortured soul of the avenger, both his hatred and his suffering, but the play differs from the model in one major aspect. No self-respecting Kyddian hero

---

[15] John Kerrigan, *Revenge Tragedy: Aeschylus to Armageddon* (Oxford, 1996), 170–216, shows the rich variety of Elizabethan revenge plays, from Kyd onwards.

[16] Fredson Bowers, *Elizabethan Revenge Tragedy, 1587–1642* (Princeton, 1971), 80–4.

[17] Ibid. 15, 102. 3H6, II. ii. 99; II. v. 104, 106, 108; II. vi. 84.

would dream of dodging his moral duty, or even pause to consider alternatives, whereas Shakespeare's characters are caught between rival ethics, and stand for a patent perversion of Christian or civic rules when they make vengeance a sacred duty. A newer, darker form of tragedy emerges from the addition of tragedies refracting the vengeance pattern to infinite nonentity.

Blood and tears

The opening scene fuses in the communion of blood the main themes of the play: family ties, tribal hatreds, thirst for revenge, royal descent, and inheritance.[18] The voice of blood drowns out all others, rendering one deaf to all other calls, as Clifford, 'bloody Clifford', explains to young Rutland:

> In vain thou speak'st, poor boy; my father's blood
> Hath stopped the passage where thy words should enter.   (I. iii. 21–2)

To all of Rutland's appeals—chivalry, honour, charity, justice, animal prudence—Clifford has but one reply: 'Thy father slew my father; therefore die.' Revenging hatred is exposed as an infirmity, a disease that contaminates all the murderer's kindred, and tortures the avenger. Even if Clifford dug up Rutland's ancestors, 'It could not slake mine ire nor ease my heart.' Until he has exterminated the hated race, he lives in hell, his heart turns to flint, his inflamed eyes shoot sparks or drop metal tears, the thought of revenge makes him 'mourn in steel'.[19]

The murderous cluster of blood, fire, and steel answers York's prediction in *1 Henry VI*, 'This quarrel will drink blood another day': the son of the victim proves his blood, both valour and lineage, by shedding it—or his enemy's—with his sword. He draws blood to quench the fire, and gets drunk on it without ever being slaked.[20] Like Clifford, Richard is consumed by his thirst for revenge after the death of his father:

> I cannot weep, for all my body's moisture
> Scarce serves to quench my furnace-burning heart;
> Nor can my tongue unload my heart's great burden;
> For selfsame wind that I should speak withal
> Is kindling coals that fires all my breast
> And burns me up with flames that tears would quench.   (II. i. 79–84)

Weeping mollifies the will to revenge and must be fought as a feminine weakness. Warwick resists it:

> Why stand we like soft-hearted women here,
> Wailing our losses, whiles the foe doth rage,   (II. iii. 25–6)

as does Richard:

---

[18] I. i. 13, 14, 39, 95–7, 170–4, 189–90, 227–30.
[19] I. iii. 32–3; II. v. 131–2; II. i. 201–3; I. i. 58.
[20] *1H6*, II. iv. 133. *3H6*, I. iii. 29; II. iii. 15, 23; II. iv. 79–84; II. vi. 82–4.

To weep is to make less the depth of grief:
Tears then for babes; blows and revenge for me.   (II. i. 85–6)

Tears of pity amount to a betrayal of the blood crying out for revenge, as the Queen reminds Northumberland when she sees him moved by the fierceness of York's pain:

What, weeping-ripe, my Lord Northumberland?
Think but upon the wrong he did us all,
And that will quickly dry thy melting tears.   (I. iv. 172–4)

If blood proves the man, Margaret with her 'tiger's heart' is denied the status of a woman by the Duke of York's invectives: how could she pour the life-blood of a child

And yet be seen to bear a woman's face?
Women are soft, mild, pitiful and flexible;
Thou stern, indurate, flinty, rough, remorseless.   (I. iv. 140–2)

The Queen only conforms to the canons of femininity in her character as suppliant, when asked the cause of her despair by Lewis XI:

From such a cause as fills mine eyes with tears
And stops my tongue, while heart is drowned in cares.   (III. iii. 13–14)

Indeed her tears have great persuasive power, as her husband knows:

Her sighs will make a batt'ry in his breast;
Her tears will pierce into a marble heart . . .   (III. i. 37–8)

She has just fired the flagging courage of her captains when she harangues the soldiers in a no less rhetorical weeping mode:

Lords, knights, and gentlemen, what I should say
My tears gainsay, for every word I speak
Ye see I drink the water of my eye.   (v. iv. 73–5)

Blood first mixes with tears on the cloth Margaret presents to the bereaved father:

Look, York, I stained this napkin with the blood
That valiant Clifford with his rapier's point
Made issue from the bosom of the boy;
And if thine eyes can water for his death,
I give thee this to dry thy cheeks withal.   (I. iv. 79–83)

York, failing to have the expected reaction, is further taunted:

What, hath thy fiery heart so parched thine entrails
That not a tear can fall for Rutland's death?   (I. iv. 87–8)

but he melts at this point. His flood of tears take on cosmic proportions,

Would'st have me weep? Why, now thou hast thy will.
For raging wind blows up incessant showers,
And when the rage allays, the rain begins: (I. iv. 144–6)

and by contagion, draws tears from his audience:

> See, ruthless Queen, a hapless father's tears.
> This cloth thou dipp'd'st in blood of my sweet boy,
> And I with tears do wash the blood away.   (i. iv. 156–8)

The choice between effusions of blood or tears is repeatedly made in the following act. The anonymous son who has killed his father prays for forgiveness and offers the same amends—'My tears shall wipe away these bloody marks'—assisted by the King's:

> Weep, wretched man; I'll aid thee tear for tear,
> And let our hearts and eyes, like civil war,
> Be blind with tears and break o'ercharged with grief.   (ii. v. 76–8)

There follows a litany of laments, where King, father, and son give up the struggle to immerse themselves in mourning and repentance. The King reads his guilt on the cheeks of the father, identifying the blood and tears with the roses of the rival houses, and offers to atone for the collective fault:

> Wither one rose, and let the other flourish;
> If you contend, a thousand lives must wither.   (ii. v. 101–2)

Again, it seems an echo of Richard Plantagenet's prophecy that the brawl in Temple Garden

> Shall send between the red rose and the white
> A thousand souls to death and deadly night.   (*1H6*, ii. iv. 126–7)

But the King's oblation is unacceptable to his vindictive friends and foes, who refuse even with their last breath to be softened.[21] The dying Warwick mixes tears and blood in his call for help, but without a trace of repentance:

> Thou lov'st me not, for, brother, if thou didst,
> Thy tears would wash this cold congealed blood
> That glues my lips and will not let me speak.   (v. ii. 36–9)

These characters do not renounce their revenge when defeated, but entrust its execution to higher powers. Rutland, a wretched schoolboy, sends Latin prayers to the gods: 'Di faciant laudis summa sit ista tuae!' York shakes the very Heavens with his curses:

> These tears are my sweet Rutland's obsequies,
> And every drop cries vengeance for his death
> 'Gainst thee, fell Clifford, and thee, false French-woman!   (i. iv. 147–9)

Soon it is Margaret's turn to call on Heaven for revenge, at the end of the play:

---

[21] Brownlow, *Two Shakespearean Sequences*, 49, notes a possible source to this passage in Lydgate's poem 'As a Midsummer Rose', in which the blood and water of Christ's wounds are the blazon of the Christian knight.

> But if you ever chance to have a child,
> Look in his youth to have him so cut off
> As, deathsmen, you have rid this sweet young Prince!   (v. v. 65–7)

She survives unhistorically to remember York's curse and take a leaf from it in *Richard III*. Her emergence as a choric figure of hatred begins here with the loss of her son. In Hall's chronicle, her sorrow broke forth earlier: she 'fell to the ground' when met on landing by the news of Warwick's defeat and death,[22]

> The calamitie and misery of her time, she detested and abhorred, her vnstable and contrariant fortune, she steadfastly blamed and accused, her peinfull labor, her care of mynde, turned into infelicitie she much lamented and bewailed the euill fate and destenie of her husband, whiche eminently before her iyes, she sawe to approche she accused, reproued, and reuiled, and in conclusion, her senses were so vexed, and she so afflicted, and caste into suche an agony, that she preferred death before life. (297)

It may be because of her desire to die, Hall further imagines,

> that her interior iye sawe priuily, and gaue to her a secret monicion of the greate calamities and adersities, which then did hang ouer her hed, and were likely incontinent to fall and succede whiche other persones, neither loked for nor regarded. (297)

At that point, Somerset revived her courage and organized the last battle. Shakespeare, while retaining her agony of grief, desire to die, and prescience, delays her breaking point to fit in the design of the familial pattern. In the play, she never relents until the struggle for the inheritance ends at last from lack of an heir, without a thought for the still living Henry VI. It takes a politic brain like Richard's, or Shakespeare's, to note that the weak King remains a threat to the victorious dynasty.

Richard is already on his way, to make a 'bloody supper' in the Tower. Henry VI's dying breath is to offer reparation for all the sufferings Richard will cause, 'many an old man's sigh, and many a widow's, | And many an orphan's water-standing eye'. But blood and steel have the last word: Richard's sword sheds purple tears for the death of the King.

3. THE ACTORS OF THE DRAMA

A visionary saint in the divine order, an inept governor in the eyes of men, Henry VI makes painfully visible the divorce operating between earth and Heaven; he is both the most innocent and the most guilty of all the protagonists, a *pharmakos*, and the first example, in the trilogy, of a character thus critically endowed with a double sign. So do, to a lesser degree, the characters who combine their role in the political events with the pursuit of a personal vendetta. It is the case for all the dramatis personae, with the exception of a few walk-on characters like Exeter or Pembroke, and Hastings who is called to a more important role later on. It appears from the

---

[22] Hall 297 resembles the picture of Elizabeth's violent sorrow at the murder of her children in Vergil 189.

chroniclers' accounts that revenge was a dominant motive, and that few families were uninvolved in the feuds that made the Wars of the Roses exceptionally vicious.

The historic roles

Some of the protagonists are wholly driven by a thirst for revenge, while others prove just as resolved to satisfy their passions, but constantly change their object: hence the precariousness of the alliances, and the numerous renewings of contracts between hardened perjurers who turn like weathercocks at each puff of wind. In a way, the cast of *3 Henry VI* was preselected by the requirement of theme. The only reason for Oxford's presence at the courting of Lady Bona is to remind us that Edward caused the deaths of his father and brother. Somerset—a fusion of two brothers, one who briefly allied himself with the Yorkists, the other a faithful Lancastrian—makes a silent entrance and exit at Edward's court, then re-enters to introduce young Richmond to Henry VI, in lieu of the historical Jasper Pembroke. The Somersets figure in the lists of victims framing the play at Acts I and V, but all that remains of the two brothers' military career is a patronym, a kinship with Richmond, and a double volte-face which no one bothers to explain.

That Montague should serve to illustrate the theme of defection is scarcely surprising: in the chronicle, one never knows whose side he is on. A Yorkist until secretly approached by his brother Warwick, he agrees to take the part of Lancaster, gives them lukewarm support, and eventually makes his submission to Edward, who forgives him. When the Lancasters are restored, Montague explains to Parliament that he surrendered to Edward only to save his life, and obtains his pardon. According to the chronicler, this pardon brought about his fall, for he was killed at Barnet in attempting to rescue his brother. And yet, says Hall, Edward had more grief at his death than joy at that of Warwick. Shakespeare does not linger to develop this interesting personality, despite his obvious charm and gift for persuasion: Montague is at first solidly attached to the Yorkist camp, and thus figures in several scenes where historically, as we saw above, he was not present. He assures Edward of his unwavering loyalty when Warwick passes over to the enemy—'So God help Montague, as he proves true'—and is next seen in the Lancastrian camp. During his transfers, on his way out and on his way back, he twice meets Clarence, the other notorious weathercock of the kingdom. But Edward is more vindictive than in the chronicle, and swears to have his skin; he will. Montague then brings his contribution to the familial theme in calling Warwick's name with his last breath, but the dialogue does not mention that he was trying to succour him. Montague qua Montague is scarcely an object of interest; the main point of his presence is his part in the ballet of renegades.

Even when dealing with characters more or less established by tradition, for instance the *Mirror for Magistrates*, where most of his cast appear, Shakespeare makes them fit several purposes without greatly diverging from their historic models. The roles are still emblematic, but the demands of theme no longer violate psychological verisimilitude. Though personality is not at the core of the action, the distance covered since Part 1 shows the process to be in train. Concerning the central motive, vengeful hatred, the chronicles offered an excess of riches. The dialogue pays greater attention to the tortures suffered by those in its grips than to its cause, which needs little explaining: the murder of a relative, wounded pride, jealousy, or frustrated ambition. The avengers brood on visions of themselves as creatures of blood, metal, flint, except the King, who melts like wax in the sun, and compares the ruin of his house with the fate of Daedalus and Icarus. The fluidity of the images makes them independent from any preset meaning. The animal king-dom provides foils, then models of behaviour, to humans who prove in the end more cruel than beasts. No system of comparison is immutable: hunter and hunted exchange roles, blood incarnadines tears.

If the characters are equipped with a few naturalistic touches, like Henry VI's prayer book, which is mentioned twice, or his touching attempt to read marks of love in his wife's abuse, these usually have some dramatic import beyond charac-terization. Edward's confession that he would break a thousand oaths to reign one year is obviously sincere, true to his historical model, and illustrative of ancestral teachings: 'Pride goeth before destruction, and a haughty mind before the fall.'[23] His notorious taste for women is repeatedly mentioned by Hall, who never fails to stress how he was punished for his debauched life. It is signalled early on in the play by Richard, and inspires frequent references to him as 'wanton', 'lascivious', even before it plays a decisive role in his political affairs: 'I ... must have my will', 'my will shall stand for law'.[24] It is also the cause of one of Warwick's complaints: at the court of Lewis XI, he suddenly remembers an assault on his niece, which is recorded in the chronicle among his grievances. In Hall, Edward's quarry was either a daughter or a niece of Warwick's, but Shakespeare wisely prefers the niece for a complaint that comes back to mind so fortuitously. Hall also mentions Edward's lack of foresight, which made him an easy catch when Warwick landed in England. He is equally imprudent in the play, and determined to crush his enemies rather than seek pacification, even when threatened on all sides, an arrogance bound to attract the irony of fate.

It is Hall who explains Clarence's defection by his jealousy of the Woodvilles, and who supplies the epithet designating him in the play, 'perjured Clarence', in prefer-ence to Holinshed's more lenient view of the character. His dramatic motives of desertion are the same, but the circumstances of his return are quite different, as we saw earlier. Where Hall had prepared the ground for his change, on stage it is a *coup de théâtre*. Like Edward in the preceding act, Warwick with Classical hubris declares himself invincible, and is doomed for a fall: just when he thought himself master of the situation, Clarence fails him, with the excuse that he cannot resist the voice of blood.

In the play as a whole, the reversals generally dispense with speeches or advance

---

[23] A passage in Proverbs (16: 18) quoted by St Augustine in *De Civitate Dei*, xiii. xiii, with reminis-cences of the Tarquinian rock.

[24] Hall, 264, 265, 282, 284, 341. *3H6*, ii. i. 41–2; iv. i. 16, 50. See also his brothers' sarcastic counterpoint to the seduction scene, iii. ii. 11–35.

warnings, unlike the hesitations, contradictory interests, and mixed motives recorded at great length by the chroniclers. Warwick took several years before openly declaring himself against Edward, while his brother Montague never quite managed to make up his mind. On stage, the process is so abrupt that the characters often turn up where least expected, on one side when we had left them on the other. In these cases, the effect of surprise matters more than their individual reasons, worst of all for the leader who thought himself near to victory. Unlike the plotters of *2 Henry VI*, whose alliances and betrayals occupy so many backstage conversations, here the characters act on unconsidered impulses and give way to their most recent feeling; even their calculations are short-term ones, except those of Richard, who never loses count of the steps to the throne. The others pass from one camp to the other, following the movements of their soul, with little concern for political or moral considerations.

Shakespeare gives his characters various traits authenticated by the narrative, but he does not use all the information available when it comes to explaining their conduct, most noticeably in the case of Clarence's double move. The features retained are usually those that govern the plot, like the cause of Clifford's relentlessness, Edward's imprudent marriage and capture, Clarence's betrayal, or Warwick's fury. The law of blood easily rules in the absence of any opponent other than the King, whose non-violent temper prevents him from performing any strong action. In this respect, both he and the Queen, without being strictly faithful to their models, behave as in the chronicle.

The heart of the matter

Shakespeare emends the portraits of the royal couple until they coincide with the rival options presented to the choice of the protagonists. With only minor adjustments, they are made to embody the ideological conflict at the core of the play. We saw above how the dramatization of Margaret's despair draws on Hall's report of her breakdown, but is delayed till after the death of her son. Thanks to this delay, she unambiguously belongs with the characters of blood and metal—'bloody-minded Queen', 'Iron of Naples'—an unfeminine antithesis to the King.[25] The inversion of roles in the dramatic couple owes much to Hall. In the years preceding the Yorkist rebellion, he had shown Margaret, 'of stomack and corage, more like to a man, then a woman', usurping the place of her weak but still lovable husband.[26] In 1459 when the King assembled an army, the royal convocation was answered by large numbers,

Many for the loue they bare to the king, but more for the feare y' thei had of the quene, whose countenaunce was so fearfull, and whose looke was so terrible, that to al men, against whom she toke a small displeasure, her frounyng was their vndoyng, & her indignacion, was their death. (241)

[25] Joan's masculine costume in *1H6* was a similar transgression. Cf. Lady Macbeth, who divests herself of her femininity to face the murder of Duncan (I. v. 45–55).

[26] Hall 205, 208, 209, 210.

Hall's comments on the Queen's victory at St Albans—'Happy was the quene in her two battayls, but vnfortunate was the kyng in all his enterprises, for where his person was presente, ther victory fled euer from him to the other parte, & he cōmōly was subdued & vanqueshed'[27]—likewise suggest what, in the play, Clifford says with rough frankness to the burdensome King:

> I wish your highness would depart the field.
> The Queen hath best success when you are absent.   (II. ii. 73–4)

The manly woman of the narrative is endowed with further atrocities of Shakespeare's own brew, just as in 2 *Henry VI* he made her directly responsible for the murder of Gloucester, which in the source she did no more than condone. To compose the cruellest scene of the play, York's mock coronation, Shakespeare borrows a molehill from Holinshed, a bloodied handkerchief from Kyd, and puts the whole blame on Margaret who, in the chronicle, was not present at the Duke's death. In the play her adversaries make her responsible for the war:

> Hadst thou been meek, our title still had slept,
> And we, in pity of the gentle King,
> Had slipped our claim until another age.   (II. ii. 160–2)

The audience heard from Edward's own mouth that he did not mean to wait indefinitely for the crown, but never mind: this charge accentuates the dialectical contrast between the King's weakness and the Queen's strength. When Henry gives in to York's demands, his spouse accuses him of putting their son's life in jeopardy by his surrender, though the chronicle makes no mention of her:

> Enforced thee! Art thou king, and wilt be forced?
> I shame to hear thee speak. Ah, timorous wretch,
> Thou hast undone thyself, thy son and me . . .   (I. i. 230–2)

In the final act, before Tewkesbury, instead of being so anxious to protect her son that she wanted to give up the fight, as in Hall, it is she who fires up the courage of her captains, and sends them all to the massacre. When all is done, the play imputes the destruction of their heir to her steeled force more than to the King's weakness.

Just as the portrait of the Queen is blackened for the needs of dramatic balance, Shakespeare subtly renews what the chronicle tells us concerning the character of Henry VI. Holinshed has a great deal to say in praise of Henry, and if Shakespeare needed suggestions to make up his character into a holy visionary, he is more likely to have found them here than in Hall's very harsh judgement on the 'poor sely' King. In reporting the Lancastrian restoration, Holinshed omits Hall's biting remarks on his feeble mind, cowardly stomach, or the suggestion that he might be paying for his grandfather's usurpation. After the interview with young Richmond, a lengthy insertion signed Abraham Fleming confirms Henry's holiness, hatred of bloodshed, and prophetic spirit. To a question why he had held the crown unjustly for so long, he answered with terms similar to those of his dialogue with the game-

---

[27] Hall 252.

keepers that he, like his father and grandfather, was anointed and sworn fealty to by all estates. The reason why his subjects rebelled is that the villainous people hate virtue. Holinshed also denies that he died from wrath at being dispossessed, a story put about by Yorkist writers, and completes Hall's short funeral portrait with anecdotes illustrating Henry's Christian virtues; thus having received a wound, he forgave the offender when restored to his throne, a nice touch that finds no direct use here but may have inspired the King's show of magnanimity in *Henry V*.[28]

Shakespeare does not use the chroniclers' story that the Lancastrian martyr would have been canonized, had the operation proved less costly, perhaps because he knew that the real cause was Henry's insanity. His King is as unlucky and incompetent as Hall's, but these signs are reversed into a positive stance against his partisans' bloodlust. Every feature of Hall's cowardly figure serves on stage to compose a living principle of *caritas*. The *rex inutilis* stands alone against the vendetta, exemplifying forgiveness and repentance.[29] The point of Edward's apostrophe to Margaret, that her husband's meekness would have triumphed where her strong will failed, opposes not only two armies but two ethics. At the gates of York, the King is invited to rejoice at the sight of his enemies' severed heads and, under these auspices, dub his son knight. We saw how the clannish spirit diverted the chivalrous code towards the defence of patrimony and progeny: Clifford, the clan's spokesman, presses the King to harden his heart and save his son's inheritance, to which the King's denial opposes the words of the Gospel—'for what is a man profited, if he shall gain the whole world, and lose his own soul?'[30]

The chroniclers often evoke the King's lack of interest in worldly affairs as a virtue that will elect him to a martyr's crown but brings little benefit to his subjects. On stage, it is by virtue of these deficiencies that he becomes a normative character, and redefines birthright, family pride, and patrimony, as a moral heritage:

> I'll leave my son my virtuous deeds behind,
> And would my father had left me no more.   (II. ii. 49–50)

But none will listen to words that are literally disarming, as in the chronicle:[31]

> My lord, cheer up your spirits: our foes are nigh,
> And this soft courage makes your followers faint.   (II. ii. 56–7)

He had the same cooling effect at Saint Albans on Warwick's men, whose weapons

> like the night-owl's lazy flight,
> Or like an idle thresher with a flail,
> Fell gently down as if they struck their friends.   (II. i. 129–31)

When Henry dubs his son with the ritual words, 'Draw thy sword in right', the freshly made knight interprets them as an incitement to fight:

[28] Holinshed 301–2, 324–8. Hall 285–7, 303–4. *3H6*, III. i. 76–9. *H5*, IV. viii. 58–61.

[29] On the theme of Christian forgiveness, see Jean Jacquot, 'Histoire et tragédie dans *Henry VI*', in Jacquot (ed.), *Le Théâtre tragique* (Paris, 1962), 161–78.

[30] Matthew 16: 26. *3H6*, II. ii. 45–50.

[31] Hall 262 (270).

My royal father, cheer these noble lords
And hearten those that fight in your defence.
Unsheathe your sword, good father, cry, 'Saint George!' (II. ii. 78–80)

To the King's expressed wish to stay on the battlefield, Northumberland retorts: 'Be it with resolution then to fight.' Twice more, in the same scene, he vainly tries to make himself heard, and is curtly told to keep quiet, first by Margaret: 'Defy them then, or else hold close thy lips,' then, of course by the irrepressible Clifford:

My liege, the wound that bred this meeting here
Cannot be cured by words; therefore be still. (II. ii. 121–2)

His enemy Edward ends the long exchange of abuse with a refusal to listen any longer to the Queen 'Since thou deniest the gentle King to speak', but he does not want to hear pacifist speeches either. When Henry is captured, Edward orders: 'Hence with him to the Tower: let him not speak.' There is no further risk, except for Richard who receives his last words, of being upset by the weak voice of Christian conscience. Though scarcely audible, it was intolerable to all.

Before they sacrifice to the conventions of funeral eulogy, the chroniclers never show the King's alleged virtues in action. If Henry surreptitiously returned from Scotland, it was not moved by love of his country, but to spy on the land.[32] There is no equivalent of his oblation, 'O that my death would stay these ruthful deeds!' Hall never credits him with a spark of the generous concerns he expresses on stage:

Was ever king so grieved for subjects' woe?
Much is your sorrow; mine, ten times so much. (II. v. 111–12)

If he wandered alone while his army fought, as in the play, it was because his partisans regularly lost sight of him on the field: at Northampton for instance, 'ye kyng hym self left alone disconsolate, was taken and apprehended, as a man borne, and predestinate to troble misery and calamitie'; or after Edward's return, 'euery man fled, and in hast shifted for hym selfe, leuyng kyng Henry alone, as an host that should be sacrificed'. This is how he was always caught: through bad luck, according to some; 'hys coward stommack', his enemies would have it. Once, he managed to escape, after the rout at Hexham, but not from Hall's sarcasms: 'Kyng Henry was this day, the beste horseman of his company: for he fled so faste that no man could ouertake hym.' Hall's funeral portrait of the martyr praises his mildness and devotion according to the rules of hagiography, with due regard but tepid admiration for these unheroic virtues.[33]

Henry's role as passive spectator makes him a visionary in the play, a superior witness of the action. After the frontal meeting between the two armies, the end of Act II represents successive phases of one long struggle: the Yorkists are forced to beat a retreat, then pull themselves together and carry off the victory. Historically, the rival houses lived through a similar succession of victories and defeats, even after Edward's accession, until the Yorkists were durably established. On stage, the

---

[32] III. i. 13–14. Hall 257.   [33] Hall 244, 294, 286, 260, 303.

King alone senses the vanity of a struggle where none can win, and mourns the lost cosmic harmony. Edward is proclaimed King at the end of the act after a clear victory, where Hall's account shows a more dubious one: the country was divided into two zones of influence, of nearly equal forces, North against South. Edward had beaten the Queen's allies, but the Queen had beaten Warwick; nevertheless he marched on London and called a Council of the Lords, who declared him King after consideration of his various titles: hereditary right, authority of Parliament, Henry VI's perjury, the people's consent. He then immediately resumed the fight to consolidate his crown, and had to wage two more battles, at Ferrybridge and Towton, to gain a few years of tranquillity.

On stage, the events mark scarcely a pause before the fortunes of war cause a new ebb and flow of victory. This wavelike motion, visualized by the King, impresses its shape on the dramatic work, within the limits traced by his double prophecy: the sufferings to come, and the hopeful conclusion promised to England. These visionary gifts do not erase the political failure of the Christian King, the mark of a deepening gap between spiritual and temporal reign. The hackneyed image of the saintly monarch proves irreconcilable with the modern imperatives of power.

Machiavelli's Prince evokes the centaur Chiron, to whom was entrusted the education of future rulers: 'Having a mentor who was half-beast and half-man signifies that a ruler needs to use both natures, and that one without the other is not effective.'[34] If he performs the task of a civilizing hero, Richard Marienstras observes, 'the king is only a mediator between civility and savagery because he participates in both' and fulfils his duty by exercising his savage nature; 'in short, the civilizing function of the monarch only begins after he has shown his "savagery" in order to master what is savage.'[35] By shirking the dark side of his function, the exercise of violence incumbent on the monarch, Henry VI lets it spread to the entire realm and produce his symmetrical opposite. Richard shows the other face of the *pharmakos*, as the religious harmonics of their final dialogue make clear. Margaret's accusation, 'murder is thy alms-deed', had pointed the parallel with her charitable husband. Richard the scapegoat is no less explicit than Henry about the role that must eventually absorb him: 'For this, among the rest, was I ordained.'[36]

In Louis Marin's analysis of absolute monarchy, power is established and maintained by violence, to which language lends the guise of justice: 'from then on the always possible, aleatory, and empirical continuity of war is transformed into institutional, obligatory, and legitimate succession.'[37] While the Tudor pageants represent Justice, Virtue, and Religion upholding good government, the *Henry VI* trilogy shows a growing awareness of the contrary, an open distrust of the Beatitudes: 'Blessed are the meek, for they shall inherit the earth.' Like the homilies invoking natural hierarchy to uphold secular powers, these civic allegories seek to establish

[34] Niccolo Macchiavelli, *The Prince*, trans. Russell Price (Cambridge, 1988), xviii. 61.
[35] Marienstras, *New Perspectives*, 23, 24, 25.
[36] v. v. 79. v. vi. 58.
[37] Louis Marin, *Portrait of the King*, trans. Martha M. Houle (Basingstoke, 1988), in a discussion of Blaise Pascal's text on justice and force, 35.

a political morality; far from expressing a common belief in a universal order miraculously embodied in the monarch, they pinpoint what the heresies suggest: that authority is not based on right but does violence to nature. Edward may well claim that the King's meekness would have disarmed his adversaries; there is no way of reconciling Jesus and Caesar.

We have reached the heart of the dilemma. Henry VI's patience cannot supply effective rules of political conduct. Humphrey of Gloucester, though neither weak nor naive, brought about his own fall and hastened the collective disaster by his moral rigour. There was no easy answer to this dilemma under the Tudors, other than Machiavelli's call to emancipate civil power from all moral obligation, but rulers and their subjects were still unresigned to the imperatives of realpolitik. Nothing short of a miracle could provide a way out of this painful alternative: to Shakespeare's reasonably conservative audience, God sends Richmond.

4. THE TRAGIC FRAME OF HISTORY

The irony of fate and the treacherous sea have since time immemorial united to thwart man's desires. In *3 Henry VI*, the King reviews them for the audience, who through his mediation watch the tragic struggles between fathers and sons as from above and, like St Augustine's gods, are informed before the protagonists of what is to come. This superior vision extends beyond the limits of the scene to embrace the plot of the following play, which Richard unfolds like a press release. He stands ready to govern the stage and the world, but the closure of his exploits has been traced as well by the visionary King.

Wave-motion theory

The action of wind and tide not only mocks the efforts of characters to control Destiny, it impresses its specific rhythm to the play. Neither camp succeeds in making decisive progress throughout this part of the chronicle, which stretches over a period of ten or even fifteen years.[38] Something of the kind occurred, over a longer period, during the wars with France. The dramatic answer to this stagnation in Part 1 was to stage in sequence the loss and recovery of some significant strongholds. In Part 3, this feeling of endless recurrence is translated into an abstract design imitating the rhythmic waves of history. The King notes the regular reversals of fortune, and compares the to-and-froing of victory with the struggle of morning against night, or sea against wind. A passive spectator, he stands at the right distance to foresee the ultimate combat of the morning light against the forces of darkness, and the inanity of a conflict where all play to lose.

The image of the sea is suggested by Hall's comment on the massacre of Towton: 'This deadly battayle and bloudy conflicte, continued. x. houres in doubtfull victo-

[38] Depending on whether the starting point is at the end of Part 2 (St Albans, 1455) or the beginning of Part 3 (Northampton, 1460).

rie. The one parte some time flowyng, and sometime ebbyng.'[39] It is transferred on stage to the helpless King, who measures the ineptitude of praying for victory:

> Sometime the flood prevails, and then the wind;
> Now one the better, then another best,
> Both tugging to be victors, breast to breast,
> Yet neither conqueror nor conquered:
> So is the equal poise of this fell war. (II. v. 9–13)

Beyond the specific event, what we are given to watch through his eyes is the drift of history, which structures the play into two symmetrical parts. Two sessions of continuous fighting follow one another in a wavelike motion, with a brief pause in the middle for matrimonial business:

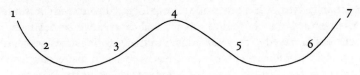

1. Victory of the House of York—
   Designation of the Duke as heir to the throne.
2. Defeat at Wakefield—
   Death of the Duke of York.
3. Edward's conquest of the crown—
   Capture of Henry VI.
4. Edward's marriage—
   Richard's plans
5. Lancaster coalition—
   Edward's capture
6. Edward's escape and reconquest of the crown—
   Capture of Henry VI
7. Final victory and triumph of the House of York—
   Richard's plans.

A symmetrical diagram, the negative of this one, would show the curve of Lancaster's rise and fall. The fluctuations of the houses' rival fortunes provide both the matter and the structure of the play: history like a mighty wave carries successive protagonists to the height of their hopes, and casts them down when they believe themselves immune to Fortune's blows. This historical drive impulses a new dynamics to the classical mix of violent elements, nature's cycles, mutable fortune, and tragic irony.

It is generally agreed among scholars that Shakespeare did not have access to the works cited in the *Poetics*, and may have known Aristotle's theories only in the corrupt forms inherited from the Middle Ages, via Chaucer's Boethius, for instance; that the nearest he could get to Greek theatre was probably Seneca, and post-

---

[39] Hall 256.

Classical romances.[40] He is nonetheless, in his generation of playwrights, the best interpreter of the Aristotelian lesson. In Aristotle's view, the reversal from happiness to misery 'must lie not in any depravity but in some great error [*hamartia*]'. Nothing arouses pity more than its occurrence 'within the family—when murder or the like is done or meditated by brother on brother, by son on father, by mother on son, or son on mother'. Better still 'for the deed to be done in ignorance, and the relationship discovered afterwards', for this creates surprise without making the agent odious. Such situations being rare, the poets must 'have recourse to the families in which such horrors have occurred'—only a few aristocratic families, in practice, whose social rank fits the nobility of the action and the elevation of feelings required by tragedy.[41]

From one man's many actions (*praxeis*), the poet selects the facts which compose the dramatic action (*praxis*).[42] Here Aristotle raises a logical difficulty unknown to the comic poets, who are only tied to the probable, and choose their heroes' names at random, whereas in tragedy, 'they still adhere to the historic names', because 'what convinces is the possible', and 'that which has happened is manifestly possible'. Like any other facts of history, these characters are data, transmitted by tradition. But there is no need for strict adherence to facts; the poet will prove himself a poet by his ability to convince and delight his audience. Here Aristotle extends the field of the possible—that which happened—to include the persuasive, and its ultimate test, suspension of disbelief: 'A likely impossibility is always preferable to an unconvincing possibility.' Dramatic probability, ensured by the faultless logic of the causal chain, excludes blind chance. 'Even matters of chance seem most marvellous if there is an appearance of design as it were in them,' for 'incidents like that we think to be not without meaning'. To be moved, we must feel a rationality behind the incident, the workings of Destiny or some mighty agent.[43] Along with the plot, the mark of the great poet is not his metrical expertise but the quality of his metaphors, 'since a good metaphor implies an intuitive perception of the similarity [*homoion*] in dissimilars'. Ricœur's concept of *métaphore vive* provides a helpful guideline to the theory: if metaphor stands supreme in *Poetics*, it is by virtue of its mimetic quality, which enlarges the range of language with eyesight. Like a good painter, the poet sees and makes visible with words.[44] At all levels of his composition, he is entitled to deviate from the rules, as long as the deviation is justified by an aesthetic success, generative of pleasure.

At this stage in the histories, Shakespeare systematically explores the inner workings of tragedy, and discovers or reinvents for himself the rules of the great Classical theatre. Some of these rules have been tried out in the other plays of the trilogy. Part 3 experiments further, and breaks new ground compared with Parts 1 and 2. The

---

[40] See C. and M. Martindale, *Shakespeare and the Uses of Antiquity: An Introductory Essay* (London, 1990).

[41] *Poetics*, 1453^{a}15, 53^{b}20, 54^{a}3, 13.

[42] 50^{a}15, 32, 51^{b}8–9, 51^{a}3–17.

[43] 51^{b}15–18, 60^{a}27, 52^{a}6–10.

[44] 59^{a}7. See *La Poétique*, text, trans., and vigorous exegesis by Roselyne Dupont-Roc and Jean Lallot (Paris, 1980), 367.

play wants a hero, but still lays claim to the status of a tragedy in the title of the Quarto edition, *The True Tragedie of Richard Duke of York*. The Duke cannot pretend to fill the role, though he does suffer a change from happiness to misery, for he disappears at the end of Act 1, by a reversal which is not the keystone of the dramatic construction. Besides, he is only part of the entertainment offered to the audience, who are also promised '*the death of good King Henrie the Sixt, with the whole contention betweene the two Houses Lancaster and Yorke*'.

Tragedy, however, can dispense with a hero if it satisfies the main essential: unity of design. In *1 Henry VI*, the concern for unity is patent, but predominantly thematic. The author has selected and disposed his material with the mastery required of the true poet, but the play is closer to 'the episodic plot', the lowest on Aristotle's scale, who stresses the difference between *tade dia tade* and *meta tade*, a thing happening because of or simply after another.[45] With *2 Henry VI*, the treatment of the historical material revealed a close attention to causality: the facts were represented as a concatenation driving the realm towards catastrophe; a rigorous causal chain, the symmetry between crimes and punishments, prophecies and their fulfilment, suggested the presence of some unnamed power, supporting Aristotle's observation that even in matters of chance, design is all.

That 'Characters come second' is clear at every step of the sequence. Indeed in Part 1 the protagonists are so accessory to the plot that character practically has no role. In *2 Henry VI*, they begin to develop beyond their thematic function. With Part 3 they grow in complexity, mixing positive and negative aspects, with some elements of introspective analysis. For the first time in the sequence, characters appear as the main springs of the action, all the while conforming to the known historical data, and to Aristotle's first rule, the primacy of the plot, which remains 'the first essential, the life and soul, so to speak, of Tragedy'.[46] The character who is to occupy centre stage, Richard, is dressed with the features that will make him the prime mover of the action in the next play, but these are far from exhausting the role.

Shakespeare had visibly grasped the essentials of dramatic engineering from the onset of the trilogy: the artificial order of the dramatic action, imposed by the poet, and distinct from the natural order of actions in real life—a principle developed in Horace's *De Arte Poetica*. Each play explores new ways and new forms of composition. Part 3 multiplies the tragedies of personal revenge, enhanced by scenes of Senecan horror. Tragedy in Seneca is often the result of an ancestral wrong repaid across several generations, but the hero's fall may also be due to the instability of Fortune, or to a fatal mistake, unlike most Elizabethan revenge plays where Seneca's aesthetic purpose is abandoned in favour of divine punishment for sin: 'When the bad bleeds, then is the tragedy good.'[47] Shakespeare never misinterprets the nature of *hamartia*, nor does he indulge in the monstrous or the spectacular unless

---

[45] *Poetics*, 51^{a}16–35, 52^{a}20: 'There is a great difference between a thing happening *propter hoc* and *post hoc*', in the 'English' translation.

[46] 50^{b}1, 50^{a}39.

[47] Cyril Tourneur, *The Revenger's Tragedy* (1606), III. v. 199.

they have a place in the design. The monstrosity of Richard acts out his harmful capability.

Discussing the Elizabethan notion of tragedy, Dietrich Rolle observes that Shakespeare hardly ever uses the term and its derivatives outside the histories.[48] This interesting point lends support to the theory that Shakespeare dialecticizes the relation of historical matter and tragic form. *Henry VI Part 3* offers an original answer to Aristotle's wish that the tragic deed be done 'within the family', by treating the dramatized period as a multiplication of tragedies affecting all the eminent families of the realm. England's tragedy is the breaking up of the commonweal into a plethora of individual tragedies. All go through the same movement of rise and fall, the classical *de casibus*. All are phases of an ampler sweep of the human tide, where dramatic irony plays a structuring role. If anagnorisis has no part in the key reversal of the play, it is neatly shown in effigy at the heart of the conflict: entering from both sides of the stage, two men rejoice in their victory over an unknown enemy, only to discover that they have done murder 'within the family'.[49] This playlet takes us nearer to the Greek fathers of tragedy than anything else written at the time: a change from happiness to misery with peripeteia and recognition, resulting from a grave mistake that inspires pity and fear, but not repulsion, for it is not due to vice or wickedness, but to an error or a blindness of the hero.

Aristotle, followed by Horace, insists that the dramatic poet needs to discern what should be told and what can be shown.[50] There is no doubt that, in both theorists' views, epic poetry has the advantage, though in practice tragedy can always borrow from the epic mode by incorporating the narrative into the dialogue. Certain episodes of *Henry VI* are reported, the capture of Talbot or the origins of the rivalry between the two houses, York's Irish adventures, the battle of St Albans, the deaths of Salisbury and of Montague.[51] Along with such reports by messenger or eyewitness, Shakespeare tries a new method in Part 2, both showing and narrating the Duchess's arrest, for instance. In Part 3, the audience first witnesses the death of the Duke of York and then hears the report of the messenger to his sons; likewise the alliance between Margaret and Warwick, and the threats made against Edward, are first shown at the French court, then repeated word for word in the following scene. Apart from the traditional 'revision' theories, there may be several reasons for these deliberate doublets: pathos, irony—and a fair probability that Shakespeare is testing the resonances proper to each mode, which he exploits with increasing virtuosity, as will appear in the report of Clarence's dream, the murder of Edward's children, or Richard II's degrading progress through the crowd.[52] For Horace and

---

[48] 'The Concept of Tragedy in Plays and Theoretical Treatises of the Elizabethan Era', in Ulrich Horstmann and Wolfgang Zach (eds.), *Kunstgriffe. Festschrift für Herbert Mainusch* (Frankfurt am Main, 1989), 336. The other occurrences almost all apply to plays within the play, *A Midsummer Night's Dream* or *Hamlet*.

[49] See Watson, *Shakespeare's Early History Plays*, 84, on the level of symbolic abstraction, 'unusual even for early Shakespeare', the degree of complexity, and 'the utter lucidity' of the scene.

[50] *Poetics*, 60^{a}12, 59^{a}23–8.

[51] *1H6*, I. i. 103–40; II. v. 61–92. *2H6*, II. ii. 10–52. *3H6*, II. i. 111–40; II. iii. 11–20; V. ii. 40–7.

[52] *R3*, I. iv. 2–63; IV. iii. 1–22. *R2*, V. ii. 1–40.

Aristotle, the procedure ensures against ridicule and dispenses with the representation of ugly or tedious scenes, which leads to an implicit hierarchy between what deserves to be shown and what is only worth reporting. Shakespeare's recourse to narrative is not imposed by decorum or convenience. He tries both manners on the same scene to establish which is more effective, and discovers the emotions released by a sad story well told. The quality of this emotion can be far superior to that of the scene represented: the enemies of the captured York watch his sufferings with no sign of compassion, until he imagines how the tale of his tortures will affect future audiences,[53]

> Keep thou this napkin and go boast of this,
> And if thou tell'st the heavy story right,
> Upon my soul the hearers will shed tears.
> Yea, even my foes will shed fast-falling tears (1. iv. 159–64)

A didactic experience, as indeed, one of the watchers immediately reacts to his words: 'What, weeping-ripe, my Lord Northumberland?' The raw event itself placed under our eyes fails to awake pity or fear unless it is shaped into a story by the poet.

THE PROPER USAGE OF RHETORIC

Aristotle's poet is allowed a fair degree of licence if he knows how to be persuasive. The connection between poetry and history raises the larger issue of the relations between art and truth. In the works of various Renaissance playwrights, the theatre is designated in turn as the art of deception and discovery; by calling attention to the wearing of masks, the metaphor of the theatre aims to extract the truth hidden beneath appearances. Metaphor and persuasion, the two elements common to *The Poetics* and *Rhetoric*, lead us to the founding ambiguity of the 'delight in discourse', its delicate balance between argument and emotion.[54] Both texts share a common definition of the probable, and a preference for a convincing falsehood over an unlikely truth. If the rhetoricians were suspect from the start to the likes of Plato, the right to defend rival opinions was generally recognized, and might even be the way to some elusive or impenetrable truth. Nature held the secret recipe of a perfect adequation between truth and beauty, the unreachable goal of the artist. 'Ut doceat, moveat, delectat' was Quintilian's prescription for rhetoric.

To teach, move, and delight: the first Renaissance historians advertised the same programme, even if they lacked Quintilian's keener sense of the rival demands made on history: 'it is written to narrate, not to prove, and the whole work is composed not to accomplish something or use in a present fight, but for the memory of

---

[53] Like York, Richard II initiates the pathetic narration of his trials in rehearsing the story that will send the hearers weeping to their beds, *R2*, v. i. 40–50.

[54] E. R. Curtius, *European Literature and the Latin Middle Ages*, trans. Willard R. Trask (London, 1953), 64.

posterity and the fame of talent.'[55] Thucydides was the first on record who required the historian to examine evidence, and never trust the poet's tales. His criticism of Herodotus, accused of sacrificing truth to his reader's pleasure, opened an argument that would continue throughout Antiquity in the historiographers' reflexive disputations.[56] Their topoi on history were relayed by Cicero and Quintilian no doubt, but more probably by Lucian, who was anything but a historian himself. His treaty on *How to Write History* played an important part in the transmission of Thucydides' portrait as a model historian, and of the commonplaces recognizable in the Tudor stocks of stereotypes on history.[57] As Fussner puts it, 'All prefaces praised TRUTH; but nearly all texts ignored the awkward consequences.'[58] The question of truth becomes central in Shakespeare's history plays, more urgently than in other genres. Part 3 of *Henry VI* tests the adequacy of shape to material, which requires special treatment because of its unique relation with truth, to confirm whether tragedy can not only make sense of, but do justice to history.

We saw earlier that even overworked sets of images like Fortune's wheel and the ship in the tempest, the irony of fate and theatrical illusion, are invested with fresh meanings when applied to a known historical reality, and serve as relays between the narrative structure and the thematic pattern of the work. These networks are a perfect illustration of the living metaphor—'the sign of a well-endowed nature'— pointed out by Paul Ricœur at the heart of the *Poetics*:

Drawing these three traits together—arrangement of the verses, interpretation by words, manifestation in language—we see the function of *lexis* taking shape as that which exteriorizes and makes explicit the internal *muthos*. We might even say that there is a relationship between the *muthos* of tragedy and the *lexis* like that between interior and exterior form. This, then, is how, within the tragic poem, *lexis* (of which metaphor is one part) is bonded to *muthos* and becomes in turn 'one part' of tragedy.[59]

To make metaphors well is to perceive similarity, Aristotle writes. In *Henry VI* the metaphoric process does 'put before the eyes', not only by representing reality through images, but by bringing to light an unseen truth. It is through metaphor that the poet resolves the tension between the wish to speak well and the will to speak true; his rhetoric exposes a hidden concordance between truth and beauty; art alone reveals the essential truth of the object represented. 'Such figures', as T. S. Eliot says of Dante's, 'are not merely antiquated rhetorical devices, but serious and practical means of making the spiritual visible.' An ideal adequation, indirectly confirmed by Ricœur: 'Now one might hypothetize that in poetry, the form or the

[55] Quintilian, *Institutio oratoria*, x. 31. See D. Goy-Blanquet, 'Elizabethan Historiography and Shakespeare's Sources', in M. Hattaway (ed.), *The Cambridge Companion to Shakespeare's History Plays* (Cambridge, 2002), ch. IV.

[56] See the bilingual edition of these documents in François Hartog (ed.), *L'Histoire d'Homère à Augustin: Préfaces des historiens et textes sur l'histoire* (Paris, 1999).

[57] *How to Write History*, trans. K. Kilburn, in *The Works of Lucian*, Greek and English, ed. A. M. Harmon (London, 1913), vi. 1–73, esp. 55–9 in praise of truth.

[58] Fussner, *Tudor History and the Historians*, 237.

[59] *The Rule of Metaphor: Multi-disciplinary Studies of the Creation of Meaning in Language*, trans. R. Czerny, K. McLaughlin, and J. Costello, SJ (London, 1986), 37.

"figure" and the meaning of a message are integrated to form a new unity similar to that of a sculpture.'[60] Nearer to Shakespeare's own time, a passionate reader of Dante, Michelangelo, whom André Chastel considers the only genuine Platonist among crowds of Renaissance artists, wanted the image represented to be 'a copy of divine perfection, a memory of God's own painting, a musical tune only perceptible to the spirit'. His whole work translates a desperate effort to bring his inner vision of beauty ever closer to this ideal form.[61]

In all three parts of *Henry VI*, the stylization of speech expresses a reality transcending the characters, and connects the particular with the timeless and universal. Thus 'relocated on the foundation provided by *mimêsis*, metaphor ceases to be arbitrary and trivial', to fulfil the role analysed by Paul Ricœur:

Considered formally, metaphor as a deviation represents nothing but a difference in meaning. Related to the imitation of our actions at their best, it takes part in the double tension that characterizes this imitation: submission to reality *and* fabulous invention, unaltering representation *and* ennobling elevation. This double tension constitutes the referential function of metaphor in poetry. (40)

The dramatic uses of rhetoric are many, Aristotle reminds us: 'to prove or disprove, to arouse emotion (pity, fear, anger, and the like), or to exaggerate or belittle things'. In *3 Henry VI*, insults, prayers, curses, lists of vices or virtues designed to praise or vilify, all observe a set protocol in reviewing a character's origin, education, physical and moral qualities, and the gifts of fortune. York's *vituperatio* formally develops Margaret's unsuitability to the role she usurps, as foreigner, woman, of shabby rank, with no beauty or virtues to speak of.[62] Rutland's prayer runs through a similar catalogue when he invokes in turn honour, charity, justice, and paternal instinct to remind Clifford of his quality as knight, Christian, citizen, and father. And Richard turns it upside down in his list of the 'qualities' that mark him for the throne, an exact counterportrait of the ideal sovereign.

By deviating from current usage, the rhetorical mode of address amplifies these violent feelings and lifts them above ordinary reality, thereby rejoining the poetic use of metaphor; for it is also 'by favour of this deviation the privileged instrument of the promotion of meaning which makes the mimesis'.[63] Political rhetoric seeks to convince, through arguments or through seduction, when the characters' passions drive them to eloquence:

Set between two limits exterior to it—logic and violence—rhetoric oscillates between its two constitutive poles—proof and persuasion. When persuasion frees itself from the concern of proof, it is carried away by the desire to seduce and to please; and style itself ceases to be

---

[60] *Selected Essays* (London, 1999), 267. Eliot's essay on 'Dante' is a sustained comparison between the Italian poet and Shakespeare. Ricœur 31–2.

[61] According to Francisco da Hollanda, who reports their conversation in his *Quatro dialogos da pintura antigua*, in *De la peinture: Dialogues avec Michel-Ange*, trans. S. Matarasso-Gervais (Aix-en-Provence, 1984). See André Chastel, *Michel-Ange: Lettres, poésies et témoignages* (Paris, 1958), and Pierre Leyris's introduction to his edition of Michelangelo's *Poèmes* (Paris, 1983).

[62] See Riggs, *Shakespeare's Heroical Histories*, 34–61.

[63] Ricœur, *The Rule of Metaphor*, 58.

the 'face' (figure) that expresses and reveals the body, and becomes an ornament, in the 'cosmetic' sense of the word.[64]

Two characters, Margaret and Warwick, employ this form of eloquence in *3 Henry VI*, each to win Lewis XI to their party, and Margaret again later, to reanimate her supporters. We have already noted the conventional aspect of these speeches: the Queen presents herself as defenceless and lachrymose, in a stereotyped posture that imperfectly masks her true nature, and before long she reassumes a more virile style, entirely at odds with Aristotle's sense of decorum: 'neither manliness nor cleverness is appropriate in a female character'—a breach strongly thematized in the play.

Warwick assures Lady Bona of his master's sincere love with a flowery style that does not fail to please:

> Myself have often heard him say and swear
> That this his love was an eternal plant
> Whereof the root was fixed in virtue's ground,
> The leaves and fruit maintained with beauty's sun.   (III. iii. 123–6)

When Warwick stands surety for Edward—'Thereupon I pawn my credit and mine honour'—Margaret is quick in accusing him of deceit, but her counter-rhetoric is ineffective against the material benefits of a union with the House of York. It takes the news that Edward is already married to discredit Warwick's discourse. Therein lies the whole ambiguity of rhetoric. Nothing distinguishes a lying from a sincere discourse unless raw facts help to establish the truth. The rhetorical discourse is not false *because* it is rhetorical; all vows of love whether sincere or not employ the same arts. In *King John*, the bastard Faulconbridge denounces the empty rhetoric of the Dauphin's speech to Blanche, probably because the hint was thought necessary to signal a seductive discourse. The events of the past century have taught us to distrust rhetoric as a mendacious and manipulative art, but the history plays' growing interest in its powers of persuasion suggest that what seems obvious now must have been less so in Shakespeare's time.[65]

The chief rhetorician is of course Richard, who first practises persuasiveness by 'demonstrating' how his father can legally break his oath, then confides in soliloquy that he masters all the rules of the art. He does not yet put his talents to work, but contents himself with telling us what he can do:

> To say the truth, so Judas kissed his master
> And cried 'All hail!' when as he meant all harm.   (v. vii. 33–4)

He is well aware of the many resources of eloquence, and fully armed for future plays with the signifier:

> Thus, like the formal Vice, Iniquity,
> I moralize two meanings in one word.   (*R3*, III. i. 82–3)

---

[64] *The Rule of Metaphor*, 32.
[65] See Roland Barthes, 'L'Ancienne Rhétorique', in *Communications*, xvi (Paris, 1970); and Pierre Bourdieu, *Language and Symbolic Power*, trans. G. Raymond and M. Adamson (Cambridge, 1991).

The duplicity of language is already perceptible in the ambiguity of the prophecies in 2 *Henry VI*. Their victims seem unable to decipher the plurality of meanings, but the discourse of the oracles is not designedly deceitful: it is the narrowness of men's vision, or their arrogance, that keeps them inscrutable. Villains do not lack in the two preceding parts: the French, Winchester, York, Margaret, Suffolk, all speak a double language, but by their own avowals, we always know precisely when they lie. They employ rhetoric to take a virtuous pose rather than to persuade or seduce by the discourse.[66] Richard has only one precursor, Jack Cade, who takes pleasure in making words say what he wishes, equivocates on the lying 'tongue' of foreigners, or reflects on the many uses of the word 'salad'.[67] Still, Cade addresses an ignorant and credulous crowd who readily accept the grossest fabrications and need no long argument to follow any leader. It is only in Part 3 that for the first time in the trilogy the art of eloquence is directly impeached as the art of lying; the seduction of language as opposed to the truth revealed in actions will be a dominant theme of the next play. The split is a dramatic one: it occurs somewhere between 3 *Henry VI* and *Richard III* through the hero's ironical distortion of eloquence, and leads to the tragic division of self in his final nightmare.

Choreographic figures

Rhetoric can expose the hidden meaning of events, or devise arguments to cover deceitful acts. Its third function, in synergy with the other elements of the mimesis, is to dispose these actions into a regular pattern, impose a coherent order on brute reality. As Ricœur observes,

The fundamental trait of *muthos* is its character of order, or organisation, of arranging or grouping. This characteristic of order, in turn, enters into all the other factors: the arrangement of the spectacle, coherence of character, sequence of thought, and finally the ordering of the verses. (36)

The function of the *lexis*, as we saw, is to make apparent the internal order of the *muthos*, for 'what this ordering *in* language still lacks is the coming *into* language, the fact of having been made manifest, of *appearing* in spoken words' (37).

The rhetorical manuals had a protocol for each mode of enunciation. Whether they revile, curse, or implore, Shakespeare's characters fall back on established procedures to voice their passions in style. Part 3 is an ordered representation of disorder. Insults follow the score, murders observe a ritual, battles are fought according to a strict choreography, figures of speech and ballet figures fill the dramatic space. The performers' hieratic attitudes mirror the rigid thematic construction: the symmetry between causes and consequences induces a symmetry between two camps, or two phases of the dramatic movement, between scenes of

---

[66] The nearest to a discourse of seduction in the earlier plays is Margaret's speech recounting how she braved the storm to rejoin an inconstant spouse (*2H6*, III. ii. 72–120).

[67] On Cade's subversive use of language, see D. Goy-Blanquet, 'Pauvres Jacques: Chroniques et spectacles en Angleterre au XVIe siècle', in Élie Konigson (ed.), *Figures théâtrales du peuple* (Paris, 1985), 68–70.

murder and scenes of revenge, captures and escapes, rival houses, rises and falls. The play begins and ends with the severed head of a Somerset. Between the two, York's and Clifford's take macabre turns above the gates of York.[68]

Symmetry, as a wishful expression of world order, is descanted by King Henry, stressed by a double sequence of anaphora, while the battle rages: 'How many hours brings about the day . . .', 'So many hours must I tend my flock . . .', but his vision of a homely swain's life is shattered by the intrusion of no less homely violence in the family of anonymous peasants. Witnessed by the King, the scene achieves a maximum tension between the formality of the design and the emotions released. Along with other rigidly stylized scenes, it provides a clue to the function of rhetoric in the histories. Under Henry's eyes, the killing fields become a stage, and on this stage a ballet of killers perform the cruellest murders with the coldest propriety.

The theme of revenge, with its talion demands of head for head and blood for blood, forms part of an overall pattern. When armies face each other in good old medieval fashion to exchange insults, both camps claim to fight for good against evil. Behind this pathetic fallacy, the King perceives a cosmic war of ethically blind forces, a sequence of tragedies as wave upon wave of inadequate heroes make up history. As in the earlier plays, the entrances and exits create confrontations between rival characters or principles. The bipolarity of the stage is constant in Part 1: French against English, blue coats to tawny, white versus red roses. The frontal opposition is less frequent in Part 2, where masked plots and intrigues take the stage, but returns in full force in *3 Henry VI* to make the whole kingdom a battlefield. The stage is either divided between two armies or occupied alternatively by each camp in exact proportions of time and space. Like the movements and the dialogue, the stage directions prescribe symmetry: at the beginning of the play, the entrance of the York faction 'with white roses in their hats' is soon followed by that of the Lancastrian side 'with red roses in their hats'.[69] During the battle: '*Enter a Sonne that hath kill'd his Father, at one doore: and a Father that hath kill'd his Sonne at another doore.*'[70] This tableau, made up of averred events borrowed from Hall, enacts St Augustine's epitome of civil war. The image, which recurs in many texts, from *Gorboduc* to the *Homily against Disobedience*, takes on added poignancy through a precise location, Shakespeare's own Warwickshire, where both men were pressed by the rival camps.

At court, after Edward's marriage, following the King and the new Queen '*foure stand on one side, and foure on the other*'. They are proleptic of a more sophisticated set of figures before Coventry in the final act. Four armies enter 'with drum and colours', declare themselves, and go into the city; 'Oxford, Oxford, for Lancaster' is followed with the same ritual by Montague, Somerset, and lastly 'Clarence, Clarence, for Lancaster'. But instead of completing the design, Clarence breaks up the dance. The symmetrical pattern is sketched, then destroyed. Clarence does an

---

[68] I. i. 16; I. iv. 179; II. vi. 52–4; V. v. 3.

[69] SD I. i. 1 and SD I. i. 49, a detail given by O (Q).

[70] SD II. v. 54. The Folio has them enter simultaneously by the two doors, and signals again '*Enter Father, bearing of his Sonne*' when he begins his account, SD II. v. 78.

about-turn and rejoins the enemy camp. In the Quarto, after he has declared himself, 'Clarence, Clarence, for Lancaster!', Edward shouts 'Et tu Brute!', and Richard brings him back. The Folio version is more abrupt:[71] there is no conferring among the brothers, Clarence enters with his troops, and answers Warwick's call with a brutal 'Look here, I throw my infamy at thee!', presumably taking the red rose from his hat as he does in Q. In both versions, the breaking of the symmetry speaks as loudly as the words exchanged.

The Duke of York evokes his heroic past when his sons urge him to fight, despite the inequality of their respective forces:

> Many a battle have I won in France,
> When as the enemy hath been ten to one.   (I. ii. 72–3)

The ratio of one to ten is reversed when his adversaries encircle him, but now his own compatriots declare:

> It is war's prize to take all vantages,
> And ten to one is no impeach of valour.   (I. iv. 59–60)

This used to be a French speciality, to the great glory of England.[72] In a more general way, the crimes find their exact counterparts in acts of retaliation, reprisals, or the turns of fortune. These symmetries, of structural rather than providential design, organize the tragic disorder into a dance of death. The avenging heroes strike their victims in high rhetorical style, chanting obsessive litanies. The pattern of York's death, stabbed by Clifford and Margaret, is taken up in successive ritual killings. When Richard has duly immolated Clifford, York's sons and Warwick bend over the corpse with antiphonal curses that foretell the incantations of *Richard III*:

> *Rich.* Clifford, ask mercy, and obtain no grace.
> *Edw.* Clifford, repent in bootless penitence.
> *War.* Clifford, devise excuses for thy faults.
> *Geo.* While we devise fell tortures for thy faults.
> *Rich.* Thou didst love York, and I am son to York
> *Edw.* Thou pitied'st Rutland; I will pity thee.   (II. vi. 69–74)

The Prince of Wales's turn comes next, performed with a similar ritual, launching Margaret into her interminable lament.

The heavy formalism of the construction is emphasized by a series of visual and auditive effects. The characters' attitudes, the rhetorical rigidity of the speeches, the ritualized murders, the incantatory litanies sharply contrast with the violent actions. The three parts of *Henry VI* represent, in various forms, the conflict between cultural values and the forces of anarchy: the elimination of the protective figures entails a rapid decline in the characters' behaviour and the values they stand for. When we come to Part 3, they fight like dogs over a bone. The *agon* now con-

---

[71] Cox/Rasmussen find it less dramatic than O (Q), Clarence having obviously made up his mind before he enters. Cairncross thought that this passage of Q (Q) must be authentic since Edward's 'Et tu Brute' is found in no source, and appears nowhere else except in *Julius Caesar*, III. i. 77.

[72] *1H6*, I. ii. 34; IV. i. 21.

trasts the history of a corrupted society and the representation of its disorders in a primitive Theatre of Cruelty. An increasingly rigid rhetorical form is set against the shapeless incarnation of an historical evil, a monster born by a perversion of the age. The Renaissance theorists generally interpreted Classical decorum as a restrictive principle of propriety which succeeded in banishing blood and violence from the stage. Here decorum holds its place in a dramatic confrontation with the living material of national history.

5. TO BE CONTINUED

From myth to muthos

Paradoxically, it is in departing from the Senecan model that Shakespeare comes closest to Greek tragedy. The House of Atreus or Labdacos did not belong to some extraneous legend for the Greeks, as it did in Seneca's time, but to their epic past. In portraying struggles still painfully alive in memory, Shakespeare was doing for his contemporaries what the Tragics had done in their own time, recreating a confrontation between past and present, 'a past sufficiently distant for the contrasts between the mythical traditions that it embodies and the new forms of legal and political thought to be clearly visible; yet a past still close enough for the clash of values still to be a painful one and for this clash still to be currently taking place'.[73] The coincidence of Shakespeare's emergent stage, the historical matter of his early plays, the enduring threat of civil and foreign war, the mixture of hope, fear, suspicion, doubt, lodged in the ageing monarch, the tense relations between city and theatre, re-create *mutatis mutandis* conditions repeating those of fifth-century Greece—a similarity sensed by Victor Hugo, who placed Shakespeare's Globe under its auguries: 'Athènes, sentant venir Eschyle, Sophocle et Euripide, s'est donné des théâtres de pierre. Pas de toit, le ciel pour plafond, le jour pour éclairage.'

It is now largely held among historians that tragedy was instituted long before democracy in Athens, possibly as far back as the Great Dionysia of 535 BC under Pisistratus, and may have been from the start 'un art de rupture', one that played an active role in the advent of the democratic regime.[74] The distinctive feature of tragedy is 'questionnement', the questioning of the heroic legends it dramatizes, though there are scholars who believe, with Di Benedetto, that no rational city would spend so much money just to quarrel with its own values.[75] But on this point, the Hellenists Vernant and Vidal-Naquet are unshaken: even if some consider it a

---

[73] J.-P. Vernant and P. Vidal-Naquet, *Myth and Tragedy in Ancient Greece*, trans. Janet Lloyd (New York, 1988), 9. See *Poetics*, 49ª15.

[74] See Pierre Judet de la Combe, 'La Tragédie grecque', in Dominique Buisset (ed.), *Poésie grecque et latine* (Marseille, 2002), 54–61.

[75] An echo of Plutarch, who observes in 'The Fame of the Athenians', 349a, *Plutarch's Moralia*, Greek and English, trans. Frank C. Babbitt (London, 1936) iv. 513, that Athens spent more on plays than on fighting for hegemony. V. di Benedetto, 'La tragedia greca di Jean-Pierre Vernant', *Belfagor*, 32/4 (1977), 'Il *Filottete* e l'efebia secondo Pierre Vidal-Naquet' (1981), and their answers in *Mythe et tragédie*, II (Paris, 1986). The argument is to continue in a forthcoming *Mythe et tragédie*, III.

waste of money, the fact remains that the city did question itself via the theatre, that this questioning sets tragedy apart from any naive version of the myth. There is no reviving of the Greek chorus, Vidal-Naquet argues, unless the *ecclesia*, the *boulè*, and indeed the whole Greek city, can also be revived.[76]

The Athenians throve on permanent competitive rivalries; democracy had not abated the ancient heroic emulation, but rather intensified it, Frédéric Picco observes, by guaranteeing the right of each party to an equal weight and value of speech in the law court: 'typically Greek' was the tension between the equality of viewpoints and the consequent exacerbated need for self-assertion, which made the essence of the tragic *agon*. Tragedy shows evil at work in the vital organs of the city; at the same time, it offers a remedy by way of an arbitrative third who urges reconciliation.[77] To Florence Dupont, the questions met by the poets were of aesthetic and ritual rather than of civic and historical nature, but she ends with the same focal point: the rulings of civic justice on crimes of blood.[78] If her severance of aesthetics from history is largely irrelevant for Shakespeare, her pages on the social system of revenge and the rhetoric of blood obliquely reflect on 'the sacred duty of blood-revenge' in *3 Henry VI*. The major difference is the place allotted to honour, vengeance, and homicide in, say, the *Oresteia*: having shown that citizens are not tied by consanguinity as were the legendary *oikoi* dramatized, and should not take vengeance into their own hands, the Areopagus reinserts the avenger in the city as a legitimate murderer. The place of violence cannot be thus circumscribed in the Christian realm of good King Henry.

Hall provided Shakespeare with both reality and its image—the facts of war, the ebb and flow of the waves—which, transfigured by the mimetic process, showed the ability of the tragic form to make truth visible, as if to check Aristotle's postulate, that tragedy had grown by phases to the full perfection of 'its natural form'. *Henry VI Part 3* explores techniques for ways of representing a properly tragic subject, England's recent past, and the divisive tensions at the heart of the commonweal, in a period answering the criteria of Vernant's 'historical moment of tragedy'—the brief lapse of time when man takes his independence from the divine, but still blames God for his sufferings. In the universe of *Henry VI*, the characters still believe that Heaven will punish crimes and preserve innocence, unlike those of *Henry IV* who have given up any such hope. But Heaven refrains from interfering. The protagonists are not the playthings of providence or blind fatality, even if some omniscient power looms in the background:

The true domain of tragedy lies in that border zone where human actions are hinged together with the divine powers, where—unknown to the agent—they derive their true meaning by becoming an integral part of an order which is beyond man and which eludes him. (22)

---

[76] Pierre Vidal-Naquet, 'Le Mythe à l'épreuve de la cité', in Bernard Mezzadri (ed.), *Les Tragiques grecs*, *Europe* (Jan.–Feb. 1999), 54.

[77] *La Tragédie grecque: la scène et le tribunal* (Paris, 1999), 15–16. He notes that the right to equal speech for adverse points of view was an obsessive topos of both judicial and dramatic rhetoric.

[78] *L'Insignifiance tragique* (Paris, 2001), chs. II and III.

Irony arises from 'the duality of the human condition which, just like a riddle, lends itself to two opposite interpretations. Human language is reversed when the gods express themselves through it.'[79]

Analysing the structure of *Oedipus Rex*, Vernant recalls the polarity inscribed in the social and religious practices of the Greeks:

If Sophocles chooses the pair *túrannos–pharmakós* to illustrate what we have called the theme of reversal, it is because the two figures appear symmetrical and in some respects inter-changeable in their oppositions. Both are presented as *individuals* responsible for the *collective* salvation of the group. (103)

Therefore, he concludes, 'when a divine scourge of God afflicts a people the normal solution is to sacrifice the king'. We noted above the interchangeable roles of hunter and hunted, of Henry and Edward, in the royal game. The symmetry is no less strik-ing at cycle level in the antithetical pair formed by Henry VI and Richard III. Tyrant and scapegoat show up an ambiguous complementarity as bearers of collective destinies in the course of England's tragedy.

In Shakespeare's dramatic treatment, killing the king is as inconceivable as it is inevitable. Here again, the convergence with Greek drama is revealing, as appears from Judet de la Combe's latest essay: 'tragedy (whose basic narrative schema is the necessary self-destruction of a king, whoever the agents are, divine or human, of his misfortune and the reasons that make this catastrophe necessary) concentrates the political disaster on an individual who is both reigning and deviant (guilty of and/or heir to a fault).'[80] Pending unarguable evidence that Shakespeare had more Greek than is usually believed,[81] the point confirms what modern anthropology has made increasingly clear, from Frazer's erratic but significant discoveries to Dumézil's ideology of the three functions—the recurrence across the globe of primitive rites surrounding the exercise of sovereignty, designed to ensure survival of the group.[82]

How far Shakespeare was acquainted with Greek drama is still a moot point; I agree with John Kerrigan that he knew more ancient tragedy than Seneca, though I would suggest a link with Euripides rather than Aeschylus.[83] 'In the background to Seneca are the tragedies of Euripides,' Jowett notes, though he doubts that Shakespeare knew them. Apart from Seneca's adaptations, the extant tragedies were all available in Latin versions, but 'if Shakespeare read them he gained little

[79] Vernant, 'Ambiguity and Reversal', *Myth and Tragedy*, 93, illustrates the joining of these two irreconcilable planes with Aristotle's famous riddle, 'I saw a man glue brass on another with fire', *Poetics*, 1458ᵃ26–9, and its solution in *Rhetoric* (iii. 1405ᵃ37): a brass cupping bowl.

[80] Judet de la Combe, '*La Tragédie grecque*', 56. See D. Goy-Blanquet, 'Sad Stories', in Maguin and Willems (eds.), *French Essays*, 142–4.

[81] In 'Le Recyclage de l'épopée dans *Philoctète* et *Iphigénie à Aulis*', in D. Goy-Blanquet (ed.), *Le Poète dans la cité* (Brussels, 2003), Picco shows that passages of *Coriolanus* are straight translations from Sophocles' *Ajax*, however they came there.

[82] James G. Frazer, 'The Magic Art and the Evolution of Kings', and 'The Dying God', in *The Golden Bough* (London, 1907–15), chs. I and III. Georges Dumézil, *The Destiny of a King*, trans. Alf Hiltebeil (Chicago, 1973). See also Luc de Heusch, *The Drunken King, or the Origin of the State*, trans. Roy Willis (Bloomington, Ind., 1982).

[83] Kerrigan, *Revenge Tragedy*, 173. See also his ch. II, 'Aeschylus and Dracula', on blood, pollution and sacrifice.

from the experience', according to the Martindales, who ignore *Henry VI*, and dismiss Euripides in favour of Seneca whom the Elizabethans much preferred.[84] Even if he was doomed to share the common taste, there is one tragedy at least that Shakespeare could have known. *Jocasta*, adapted by George Gascoigne and Francis Kinwelmersh from Lodovico Dolce's Italian translation of the *Phoenician Women*, was published in 1573.[85] Euripides' Italian translators did not greatly admire his works, which according to Giraldi Cinthio were marred by a natural diction unsuited to the dignity of tragedy:[86] he occasionally introduces comic elements into his tragedies, and gives an active part to low-born characters, features strongly disapproved of by the classic theoreticians. To a more recent translator, the *Phoenician Women* suffers from an excess of characters, and of dead bodies: too many people run around, too many things happen, while its inconclusive end makes it 'a mongrel play'.[87] But none of these 'faults' would have been deterrents to Shakespeare. The insistence on the virtues of mediation, a dominant theme in Euripides, exemplified by the theatre, would no doubt have struck a sympathetic chord.

The matter of *Jocasta* is that of Aeschylus' *Seven against Thebes*. In Euripides' version, the brothers' fatal struggle for power, a result of their father's curse, takes place under the eyes of their helpless mother Jocasta, who begs in vain for reconciliation and civic sense. The play is overcast by the shadow of Oedipus, who looms in the background, until he enters after the fight to hear the awful tale of their deaths, be sentenced to exile, and leave under the guidance of Antigone. Gascoigne's text, closely inspired by *Gorboduc*, was staged in 1566 at Gray's Inn; it must have been a spectacular show, if the translators' fabulous directions were followed.[88] The English play, which is approximately a thousand lines longer than the original, demands a much larger amount of visual effects than either Euripides or Dolce requires. Among other additions, a proleptic funeral precedes the first confrontation between Jocasta's sons: enter sixteen mourners, carrying two coffins which they proceed to bury and set fire to,

& after they had caried the coffins about the stage, there opened & appeared a Grave, wherein they buried ye coffins & put fire to them: but the flames did sever & parte in twaine, signifying discord by the history of two brethren, whose discord in their life was not onely to be wondred at, but being buried both in one Tombe (as some writers affirme) the flames of their funeralls did yet parte the one from the other in like maner, and would in no wise joyne into one flame. (261)

---

[84] Jowett 23. The Martindales, *Shakespeare and the Uses of Antiquity*, 41–4, disagree with Emrys Jones's conclusions in *The Origins of Shakespeare*, chs. III and IV.

[85] On Dolce's extensive and remarkable work with Aldus Manutius, see Ronnie H. Terpening, *Lodovico Dolce, Renaissance Man of Letters* (Toronto, 1997). Seneca's *Phoenician Women* and *Oedipus* both draw on *Phoenissae*.

[86] *Discorsi di M. Giovanbattista Giraldi Cinthio . . . intorno al comporre dei romanzi, delle comedie, e delle tragedie, e di altre maniere di poesie* (1554), BnF microfilm (Paris, 1995).

[87] *Les Tragiques grecs. Théâtre complet*, trans. and notes V.-H. Debidour (Paris, 1999), 1460–1.

[88] *Jocasta, a Tragedy*, trans. G. Gascoigne and F. Kinwelmersh, in *Complete Works of G. Gascoigne*, ed. J. W. Cunliffe (Cambridge, 1907), i. 247–326. See F. J. Child, *Jocasta*, in *Four Old Plays* (Cambridge, 1848), who detects traces of it in Pyramus' rantings, introd., p. xxxiii. For imprints of the dumb shows on the literary imagination, cf. 2 *Tamburlaine*, IV. iii SD.

A scene memorable enough to have lent notes not only for the anonymous fathers and sons, but for the duel of Hamlet and Laertes in Ophelia's open grave.

In the extended prologue, Jocasta provides a detailed account of Oedipus' former history, and when asked by her faithful servant how he could remain alive 'knowing he had done I So foule a blot', she neatly qualifies the notion of *hamartia*:[89]

> 'So deepely faulteth none, the which unwares
> Doth fall into the crime he can not shunne:' (I. i. 133–4)

Having small Italian and even less Greek than Shakespeare, I will venture no further here than to open a list of themes and structural devices he shares with Euripides' play: the fratricidal war, inspiring the symmetrical construction of the quarrel, the arguments over right, legitimacy, inheritance, often in the form of stichomythia, the clash between equally valid judicial notions, the breaking of solemn oaths, the curse on a tainted dynasty, the presence of foreign armies on the native soil, the violation of a cosmic order ruling the regular succession of day and night, the alternation of blood-drawing and tear-drawing scenes. In his analysis of the original Greek text, Picco draws a parallel with the account of the Peloponnesian wars, so vividly present at the back of Euripides' and his audience's memories: Thucydides recalls how the ordinary meaning of words touching political or moral notions was altered to justify what was until then judged blamable, giving many instances of such inversions by factious leaders. Eteocles' admission that 'if there is one thing worth violating right for, it is sovereignty, admirable iniquity', anticipates Edward's:[90]

> But for a kingdom any oath may be broken.
> I would break a thousand oaths to reign one year. (I. ii. 15–16)

One year—the exact length of time each of the Theban brothers was initially meant to reign. Their death brings destruction to their family, but does not end the fight, which continues among their supporters. Oedipus must hear the tale of his sons' murderous duel under Jocasta's eyes, her loud despair and suicide, and the 'bloudy fight' that left the ground 'coverde all with carcasses', before he leaves 'to everlasting banishment'. Fortune enters in the last dumb show, leading two kings and two slaves whose apparels she exchanges. A marginal reference to 'A mirrour for Magistrates' at the end of the play closes the circle.

---

[89] The opening scene is double the length of Euripides', which is a soliloquy.

[90] Picco, *La Tragédie grecque*, 41, renders thus lines 524–5, and quotes Thucydides, iii. 82. In Gascoigne, the lines become:

> If lawe of right may any way be broke,
> Desire of rule within a climbing brest
> To breake a vow may beare the buckler best. (272)

Nothing for Dionysos?

This brings us to the last piece of our tetralogy, which in a Greek *tragikè didaskalia* would be the *saturikon*. Very little is known about the genre, beyond the fact that it displayed a chorus of satyrs, who capered, sang, made unseemly jokes, and interacted with the public by repeatedly calling attention to their own performance. Only one has survived complete, Euripides' *Cyclops*, which opposes a one-eyed bloodthirsty ogre, Polyphemus, and a crafty liar, Ulysses. Again, the parallel should not be stressed too far, but its place and import in the sequence, like the possible meaning of its inscription in the *polis*, are worth investigating. Most Hellenists today consider there is no incompatibility between the Dionysiac and the civic dimension of the theatre, that, on the contrary, the Great Dionysia were designed to express the fundamental unity of the city. Patricia Easterling defines the satyr as a Dionysiac character, wearing many disguises, a creature of wild nature, with wild appetites and a strong link with wine, whose message, she claims, has nothing to do with representation, let alone celebration, but death.[91] I believe Richard has to do with all three, a perfect instance of Vidal-Naquet's 'logic of ambiguity'.

Is *Richard III* the sequel of *Henry VI*? On this point scholarship remains sharply divided, a sure sign that the question touches a sensitive point. If the answer is yes, and *Richard III* provides a happy end to the Wars of the Roses, the four-play monster comes unpleasantly close to the Tudor version of history. To those critics who shudder at the Wagnerian echoes of the word 'tetralogy', there can be only two ways of reconciling the final submission to the dominant ideology with the critical independence of *Henry VI*: detect the hidden ironies undermining the orthodox patterns of *Richard III*, or detach it from the series. Once relieved of this cumbersome appendix, the *Henry VI* plays are seen to exude a strong scepticism, bathed in a twilight universe where no trace remains of justice earthly or divine.

Concerning the subversiveness of *Richard III*, we shall see in the coming chapters what the confrontation of text and sources can tell us. Those who opt for its autonomy note a marked break between the episodic plots of the trilogy and the solitary adventure of Shakespeare's first memorable character—a historical, metaphysical, dramatic, stylistic break, confirmed by *Richard III*'s singular success in the theatre. In fact, what is true of the earlier plays is also true of *Richard III*: each play is dramatically valid, but significantly impoverished when isolated from its context. Renowned directors from Colley Cibber to Laurence Olivier or Al Pacino, usually less concerned than scholars to establish Shakespeare's political correctness, felt no qualms about using patches of *Henry VI* to fill in gaps of *Richard III*, and guide audiences through its complex cast. The qualitative leaps from one part of *Henry VI* to the next are no less remarkable than from the trilogy to *Richard III*, and the connecting links at least as strong as the discontinuities. The character of Richard is introduced in the plot of Part 2, against historical truth, for no urgent dramatic reason, while Margaret survives in the last play to embody a vindictive past by her impotent angry presence. The crimes inflicted on the House of Lancaster, the threat

---

[91] P. E. Easterling (ed.), *The Cambridge Companion to Greek Tragedy* (Cambridge, 1997), ch. II.

uttered against Edward's line, the prophecy concerning Richmond, the emergence of rival clans at the Yorkist court are all introduced in Part 3 but find their conclusion in *Richard III*. Not to mention the difficult position of Lady Anne, Warwick's daughter, wife of the Prince of Wales, daughter-in-law to Henry VI, all three of whom are killed in Part 3 by the York brothers.

Here again, the critics measure the race of history by the book, but if we keep to the dramatic facts, *Richard III* does follow on from *Henry VI*. Edward IV's ten years of reign before the Lancastrian restoration are reduced on stage to one scene which leaves him barely enough time to win the reluctant widow. No sooner has he recovered his throne than the play ends, and he is a dying man at the beginning of *Richard III*. The death of Henry VI masks the historic fault line: he is killed at the end of Part 3, and buried moments before Edward, who loses another twelve years of his prosperous reign. It was by a similar method that five years of relative quiet were erased between Parts 2 and 3. Now the presence of the royal corpse, Richard's threatening asides, the metaphoric round of the seasons—autumn harvest and winter sun—ease the transition between plays three and four.

The stylistic break already exists in the sources. Shakespeare found most of his material for the trilogy in Hall's ponderous chronicle, whereas *Richard III* is largely drawn from Thomas More's elegant biography, which Hall inserted whole after his account of Edward's reign, having up to then verbosely translated Polydore Vergil. Shakespeare makes use of Vergil's and More's conflicting interpretations of the character, but displaces the seam. Richard does not change course between *Henry VI* and *Richard III*; the break in his personality occurs during Part 3, and it is significantly connected with the death of his father. Although the chroniclers all note that Edward never lost a battle, we hear little of his military talents on stage; it is Richard who keeps up the family tradition with his feats of valour. One war ahead of his due time, he enters at St Albans, carrying the head of the Yorks' old enemy, and receives the praise of his father in the first scene of *3 Henry VI*: 'Richard hath best deserved of all my sons.' When the Duke is killed, Richard presents himself as branded to avenge him:

> Richard, I bear thy name, I'll venge thy death
> Or die renowned by attempting it.   (II. i. 87–8)

Like the other sons marked by a family tragedy in the play, he burns with hatred, claims the privilege of killing his murderer himself, and executes Clifford, who in the chronicle was struck down by an anonymous arrow. He spurs Edward on towards the throne with doubts about his brother's lineage:

> Nay, if thou be that princely eagle's bird,
> Show thy descent by gazing 'gainst the sun;
> For chair and dukedom, throne and kingdom 'ssay,[92]
> Either that is thine, or else thou wert not his.   (II. i. 91–4)

By this light, it seems unnecessary to tap hidden depths of psychoanalytic uncon-

---

[92] See Cox/Rasmussen, n. 93 on the emendation 'kingdom 'ssay' of F 'say'.

scious to find that Richard's own desire to seize the crown is doubtless a way of proclaiming his birth.[93] The text is perfectly clear and consistent in the development of his twisted ego, up to the rumour propagated in the next play that he is York's only legitimate son. It is only after Edward, 'lascivious Edward', forgets the interests of his family to satisfy his appetites, soon followed by Clarence, that Richard reveals his plans. He speaks for Clarence and himself when he complains to Edward that 'in your bride you bury brotherhood', just before Clarence leaves for a more rewarding alliance. Clarence's exit line, 'You that love me and Warwick, follow me', anticipates Richard's in the next play: 'The rest that love me, rise and follow me.'[94] Well taught by his brothers' disloyalty, Richard has climbed all the steps of radical individualism by the end of *3 Henry VI*:

> I have no brother; I am like no brother.
> And this word 'love', which greybeards call divine,
> Be resident in men like one another
> And not in me: I am myself alone.   (v. vi. 80–3)

The deviant offers his own psychological analysis of his ravenous hunger for power by casting himself as the sport of nature, kept apart from other men by his deformity:

> Then, since this earth affords no joy to me
> But to command, to check, to o'erbear such
> As are of better person than myself,
> I'll make my heaven to dream upon the crown ...   (iii. ii. 165–8)

It is left to the visionary Henry VI to decipher his monstrous features:

> Teeth hadst thou in thy head when thou wast born
> To signify thou cam'st to bite the world.   (v. vi. 53–4)

Richard's appetite is so devouring that, once crowned, he finds nothing left to eat but himself; his gnawed lip, culled from the chroniclers, brings to a climax the images of cannibalism and bestiality that run through *3 Henry VI*.[95] From his first entrance at the end of Part 2, he is greeted with gibes and repeatedly accused of being ugly as sin, though his behaviour so far does not noticeably mark him out from his adversaries. But he carries within himself the sum of human ugliness, and strikes them all with horror by exhibiting the countenance of their crimes.

Richard is the living metaphor of disorder, the offspring of civil war. As if in grim fulfilment of Clifford's ill-advised vow in the first scene—'May that ground gape and swallow me alive'—he burst forth from the bowels of the earth like a geological bomb:

---

[93] Ian Moulton's illuminating essay on 'Richard's unruly masculinity', *SQ* 47 (1996), has much more to say, not on the hypothetical unconscious of the character but on what the text reveals of his sexual drive.

[94] iv. i. 55, 123. *R3*, iii. iv. 78.

[95] *R3*, iv. ii. 27. Vergil 226, Hall/More 359, Holinshed 380. See Berry, *Patterns of Decay*, 81–95, on the auto-destruction of the self it suggests.

> Why, Love forswore me in my mother's womb,
> And, for I should not deal in her soft laws,
> She did corrupt frail Nature with some bribe
> To shrink mine arm up like a withered shrub;
> To make an envious mountain on my back,
> Where sits deformity to mock my body;
> To shape my legs of an unequal size;
> To disproportion me in every part,
> Like to a chaos or an unlicked bear whelp
> That carries no impression like the dam.   (III. ii. 153–62)

Here the Arden editors call attention to a parallel with Golding's translation of Ovid: 'The Bearwhelp . . . like an evill favored lump of flesh alyve dooth lye. | The dam by licking shapes out his members orderly.' Interestingly, the phrase 'euill fauored' had already served Hall about Richard, probably from a misreading of More, as we shall see below, to suffer one last poetic change in a notorious didascalia of *Richard III*.[96]

Whether Shakespeare started with a vague or a clear design for his first historical sequence, by the time he came to the end of Part 3, his central theme, the progress of evil, was fully sketched out. The phases of this dramatic project are so intimately tied to the maturing of his historical consciousness and to his artistic development that they are hardly dissociable. The increasing complexity of the subject goes hand in hand with the refining of his techniques of representation.

---

[96] Cox/Rasmussen, III. ii n. 162, from Arden 1. *Ovid's Metamorphoses: The Arthur Golding Translation of 1567*, ed. John F. Nims (Philadelphia, 2000), xv. 416–20. *R3*, SD III. v. 1. On his first entrance, *2H6*, v. i. 157, Richard is saluted as 'foul undigested lump'.

6

Unnatural Born Killer

Down with poets!

When we come to *Richard III*, the vexed question of folios and quartos returns with a vengeance. Analysing the sources of *Richard III* must always be a perilous exercise while doubts remain as to its nature and origin. Doubly perilous, when so much subtext is perceptible beneath the academic arguments, as in all the fierce battles touching the Shakespeare canon. The positions adopted today betray more often than not a continuity with the more explicit fights of the 1960s.

The textual history of *Richard III* being fully reported in the recent editions of the play, I will try to keep it short. Basically there are two texts, Q1 dated 1597, and F. Five more quartos were published before 1623, all dependent on Q1. The two versions differ in many ways which no hypothesis so far has satisfactorily explained. Q has fewer characters than F and no act divisions; it is some 200 lines shorter but has twenty-seven passages, about forty lines in all, which are not in F, including one important piece, the Rougemont prophecy. The arrangement of scenes, order of entrances, and speech-headings vary, but the narrative lines are identical, and there are approximately 2,000 verbal differences between the two versions, roughly 10 per cent of the play. Despite these differences, Peter Davison concludes in his edition of the first Quarto, they are far more closely akin than are *The Contention* and *The True Tragedy of Richard Duke of York* to the Folio texts of *1* and *2 Henry VI*.[1]

Until recently, D. L. Patrick's theory in 1936 that Q1 was based upon a memorial reconstruction of the play, designed for provincial touring, was largely accepted. Greg, reviewing Patrick's work, suggested that the company reconstructed the text themselves to replace a missing prompt-book, and assumed the company were Chamberlain's Men, as the title page of Q indicates. Apparently most of the company were involved, at least the main actors, including Shakespeare. Cairncross made the suggestion the company was Pembroke's, who had the bad quartos of *2* and *3 Henry VI*, but Antony Hammond argued against it and gave Q *Richard III* back to Chamberlain's. In John Jowett's view, the play was originally written for Lord Strange's Men, but given finishing touches around 1592 for performance by the newly formed Pembroke company, and reappeared later with other early plays

---

[1] *The First Quarto of King Richard III*, ed. P. Davison (Cambridge, 1996), 5.

of Shakespeare in the hands of the Chamberlain's Men.[2] Kristian Smidt was the first in 1964 to question the memorial reconstruction theory, with arguments based mostly on his feeling that some of the Q variants were much better than F, and should not be read as corruptions but revisions of the original, though he eventually revised his position and admitted a degree of memorial work in Q1. Stephen Urkowitz quarrelled with the theory, suggesting we should look on *Richard III* as 'a work in progress, an early state in the Quarto, a later state in the Folio', while Jowett defends the opposite order.[3]

Admittedly, a large number of changes in Q had been made to suit performance conditions, though what those conditions were remained uncertain. To Davison, the change in the ghosts' entrances, which does not observe the chronological order of their deaths, arose not as Hammond thinks 'through some confusion in the reporting process' but as a result of doubling, suggestive of 'a very tight recasting of *Richard III* for a small number of players'.[4] For the cast is a large one even by Elizabethan standards: fifty-two speaking and three mute roles in F. It had long been an accepted fact that, good or bad, the Quarto was designed for a reduced company, but this is no longer the case. The numbers required vary between scholarly estimations: twenty-six for either Q or F in T. J. King's computation, twenty for one and fifteen for the other in David Bradley's, and still a minimum of ten men and two boys for Q in Davison's lowest figures. For Jowett, Q reduces the number of persons represented but still requires the same number of actors. Its advantage is to make the play dramatically more intelligible, if historically less accurate. This specific point recently started a campaign to end discrimination between the capital and provincial backdrops. According to David Bradley, there is no evidence 'that the provinces were regularly treated to maimed or truncated performances'.[5] Stuart Hampton-Reeves from Lancashire goes one step further: touring was the Tudor norm, and playing in London the exception. Once we move to the idea that these plays were actually written with an eye on the provinces, 'then a new space opens up, a new context for the study of early Shakespearean drama, and in particular those history plays in which regional histories are dramatised alongside national histories, in which the relationship between regional identity and national identity is in conflict—the social condition, if you like, of civil war'.[6]

Once agreed that the Q variants were very likely of theatrical origin, the fight continued as to which text had priority, what kind of manuscripts were used by the printers, how to account for the variants, whether imposed by touring circum-

[2] D. L. Patrick, *The Textual History of Richard III* (Stanford, Calif. 1936). W. W. Greg, *Library*, 19 (1938), 118–20. Cairncross, 'Pembroke's Men and Some Shakespearian Piracies', *SQ* 11 (1960), 335–49. Hammond 10. Jowett 5–8, 122–3.

[3] Smidt, *Iniurious Impostors and 'Richard III'* (Oslo, 1964). *Memorial Transmission and Quarto Copy in 'Richard III': A Reassessment* (Oslo, 1970). Urkowitz, 'Reconsidering the Relationship of Quarto and Folio Texts of *Richard III*', *ELR* 16 (1986), 442–66. Jowett 120–7.

[4] *First Quarto*, ed. Davison, 50. Jowett notes that the arrangement of ghosts in Q1 enables one of the children to re-enter as the ghost of Anne.

[5] *From Text to Performance in the Elizabethan Theatre: Preparing the Play for the Stage* (Cambridge, 1992), 74.

[6] 'Alarums and Defeats: *Henry VI* on Tour', *Early Modern Literary Studies*, 5 (Sept. 1999).

stances or meant for a normal London production, whether Q was an abridged version, revision, or reconstruction of F or F a revision of Q, and, above all, which should be selected for a modern edition. If Q and F were two equally legitimate versions, a hybrid of both, which had been so far the common editorial practice, was no longer acceptable, though Honigmann recently argued that it is difficult to rule out conflation in the case of related Q and F texts of a play.[7]

Antony Hammond's 1981 edition for Arden was based on F, with additions of passages special to Q. Janis Lull's New Cambridge text published in 1999 'is based on F throughout', rejecting all the usual emendations based on 'superior' readings in Q. In her view, the Folio *Richard III* 'is both a reading text and a playable one', but readers who do not find it dramatic enough can consult the New Cambridge Quarto edition, published separately. Her one concession is an appendix giving the Q-only 'clock' passage.[8]

No one questions the authority of the longer Folio text, nor its greater proximity to the sources; according to Gary Taylor,

In general, F in its verbal variants is closer than Q to the play's acknowledged sources.... F seems a text closer to the author's original composition than Q, which by contrast shows clear signs of theatrical provenance.[9]

The play is more likely to have moved away from the source material than closer to it, as Jowett notes—unless, of course, some austere transcriber brought the text into conformity with Hall. Jowett's edition of *Richard III* is based on Q and gives the omitted F passages in an appendix, though he occasionally bends his rule to include pieces of F, on the grounds that 'compositorial omission of two lines is possible', like Buckingham's allusion to Richard's prayer book, or their 'rotten armour'.[10] In his view, F is so long as it is that he cannot imagine anyone wanting to expand it with an extra 200 lines. Despite their respective dates of publication, the manuscript for F must be an earlier version of the play, one probably that had not yet reached the theatre. Q was elected not because it is the later one, and presumably Shakespeare's last word on the subject, but because it is of high theatrical authority. A complete reversal of earlier policies, initiated by Gary Taylor's diagnosis for the *Textual Companion*: 'Q offers a more "experienced" text, one which has both suffered and benefited from direct contact with the theatre.'[11]

How to weigh the benefits against the suffering, that is the question. Both critical positions have sound arguments to invoke. There are notorious examples of playwrights who learnt their trade in the theatre, like Giraudoux with actor-director

---

[7] 'Minding your Fs and Qs', *TLS*, 22 Feb. 2002, 8.

[8] Lull, 'Note on the Text', 42–3, appendix 1, 220–1, and 'Textual Analysis', 217. Unless otherwise stated, all the references here will be to her uncompromising F-based text and her 'policy of restrained emendation', and to Davison's for the Q variants. See also *The Tragedy of King Richard the Third: Parallel Texts of the First Quarto and the First Folio with Variants of the Early Quartos*, ed. Kristian Smidt (Oslo, 1969).

[9] Wells and Taylor (eds.), *Textual Companion*, 230. It is also Bullough's opinion, 221, and Jowett's, 121.

[10] III. vii. 93–4 and SD III. v. 1, for instance, are both in F, not in Q.

[11] Wells and Taylor (eds.), *Textual Companion*, 228.

Louis Jouvet, or creative teams like David Hare and Richard Eyre, and no less notorious lines like Victor Hugo's 'lion superbe' killed by actors. Recalling the eventful creation of *Hernani*, Alexandre Dumas notes that the censorious Mademoiselle Mars was not up to performing Hugo's impetuous verse: 'she was inadequate in poetry as in anger.'[12] Davison's comment on Richard's paid murderers, in his section entitled 'Actors' "Improvements" ', should likewise give us pause: 'There can be little doubt that what Shakespeare drafted appears in F and that Q prints what was performed by the two actors—the two clowns, Kemp and Cowley.'[13] This may well explain Hamlet's hostility to clowns.

Editorial politics obviously involve more than a preference for the collaborative over the isolated work of art. The Quarto offers 'a subtly different reading of the play . . . towards a more secular, free-standing, and psycho-political drama', claims Jowett: 'Quarto *Richard III* is breaking free from the *Henry VI* trilogy. By 1597 the play had already achieved on the stage a resilient independence that would endure'.[14] This should be great news to scholars of the 1960s who tried so hard to liberate *Henry VI* from *Richard III*, which they found too Providence-ridden as a conclusion to the more 'secular' trilogy. The millennial *Richard III* suits the book to the stage, and adopts the Q cuts, although they are not imposed by consideration of theatre audience or time limits, but destined to readers. Now the question remains whether they were 'intelligent' (Oxford) or 'unfortunate', 'misguided' cuts (Arden). Antony Hammond accurately sums up the dilemma facing an editor:

to distinguish between 'Shakespeare' the solitary artist, scribbling in his garret (as it were), and 'Shakespeare' as the complex of author/book-keeper/actor/prompter and others who actually created the play in the sense of a living performance on the stage is to find oneself on one side or other of a philosophical issue concerning the nature of artistic creativity. (49–50)

To Jowett, 'Q1 is a theatrically cleaner and more intelligible text', yet he is aware of the difficulty:

A persistent theme running through the deleted passages is the begetting, presence, or killing of children. These passages are significant to a reading of the play that stresses its moments of pathos, as are the deleted lines in which the speaker utters prophecy or prays for a merciful outcome (Passages B, C, F, K). From another point of view these passages clog the play with sentiment and slow its action. (131)

On these and other minor losses—the extended dialogue between Richard and Elizabeth, the rhetorical *gradatio* of Anne's curses, Clarence's last prayer for his wife, the Queen's apostrophe to the Tower, 'Pity, you ancient stones . . .'[15]—Gary Taylor is even more outspoken: 'most of the material present only in F consists of static poetic elaboration which slows up the dramatic pace.'[16] Down with poets!

---

[12] *Alexandre Dumas Père et la Comédie française*, ed. Fernande Bassan (Paris, 1972).

[13] Davison's 'Introduction shows how the actors' involvement helped to produce the text we have', the front blurb announces.

[14] Jowett 132.

[15] For a full list of the variants, see Jowett, appendices A–D, 359–85.

[16] Wells and Taylor (eds.), *Textual Companion*, 228.

Down with playwrights who make you sit upon the ground and tell stories instead of carrying on with their plots.

Europe's nightmare

'Now': the first word of *Richard III* sounds like a whiplash, a command to translate the past into the present, and interpret Shakespeare as a living author.[17] Yet there are things in his play that will never please, as Al Pacino discovers while looking for him in the streets of New York: medieval history, obsolete language, hermetic metaphors, insular pentameters. World news may give the play special relevance, too much of it sometimes, or the illusion that its horrors are things of the past. Post-war *Richard IIIs* were often circular replays of *Arturo Ui*, until in 1981 *Ui* seemed obsolete to its editors, inspiring them with these famous last words:

whatever we may think of the reactionary regimes still to be found in the civilised world today no great technologically and administratively advanced country is now open to the unchecked rules of demagogues propelled by expansionist ambition . . .[18]

Jan Kott's *Shakespeare our Contemporary* was a milestone in the interpretation of the history plays, at least as decisive as the Brechtian *V-Effekt*.[19] Kott's Polish nationality was guarantee enough for his belief that Shakespeare speaks to us now, very now, when to be awoken by violent knocks at one's door before dawn is a common experience. Kott attaches himself primarily to this aspect of the histories: tyranny on one's doorstep. All kings are alike to him, there is no dividing good from evil ones. Henry, Edward, Richard, the same recurrent names, are only distinguished by the level of the step on which they stand when Shakespeare frames them. In Kott's view, Richard is not even cruel: 'No psychology could account for him. He is just history itself. One of its chapters endlessly repeated. He has no face.'[20] Yet the actor must give him one: for Kott, Richard took on the face of Jacek Woszczerowicz, a clown with the most terrifying laughter, who saw the world as a gigantic buffoonery.

The century of Richard III begins in Germany, in the general lurch following world peace negotiations and the deposition of the Kaiser. Leopold Jessner put on the play in 1920 at the Staatstheater, Berlin, in a great show of expressionistic lights and shades.[21] After the interval, the curtain revealed the key image of the production: a massive red staircase, outlined on each step by courtiers bowing low to Richard who stood at the top, dressed in a long scarlet cloak, beneath a flaming sky;

[17] For a performance history of *Richard III* from the seventeenth century to now, see Scott Colley, *Richard's Himself Again: A Stage History of Richard III* (London, 1992); on the history of RSC productions, Gillian Day, *King Richard III* (London, 2002). See list of productions quoted on pp. 242–3.

[18] Bertolt Brecht, *The Resistible Rise of Arturo Ui*, ed. John Willet and Ralph Manheim (London, 1981), introduction, p. xix.

[19] The 'Verfremdungseffekt', or alienation effect.

[20] Jan Kott, *Shakespeare our Contemporary*, trans. Boleslaw Taborski, (London, 1964), 50–3.

[21] See Dennis Kennedy, *Looking at Shakespeare: A Visual History of Twentieth-Century Performance* (Cambridge, 1993), 83–90. Kott, *Shakespeare*, 38.

he was killed on the bottom step by four men dressed in white who made up Richmond's army. Jessner did not hesitate to reshape and simplify the text to bring out his 'Regiegedanke', a notion that would henceforth dominate German dramaturgy. As for the *Jessner Treppe*, the image imprinted itself on the European imagination, producing Kott's grand staircase of history. The actor Fritz Korner interpreted Richard in the expressionistic style of Murnau's films, a strident hybrid of hell-hound and human creature, and left indelible marks on the role as 'the spectre of the new age, the dictator, the man of the masses, the great temptation to suicide'.[22]

The next memorable production of *Richard III* was in 1937. Jürgen Fehling, 'a passionate anti-nazi', 'took a devilish pleasure in turning the last scion of the house of York into a likeness of the club-footed Minister of Propaganda [Goebbels] with all his lies, treacheries and womanizing', and dressed Richard's bodyguards up in uniforms evocative of the SS storm troopers.[23] The author of these reminiscences is a Jewish musician, Hans Neumark as he was then named, whom Fehling had recklessly recruited to accompany the march of the armies in the last act, though it is not quite clear whether the idea of having Aryan soldiers marching to the tunes of a Jewish pianist was a deliberate or an unconscious offence. The famous Gustaf Gründgens, who was in charge of the Staatstheater then, suppressed it as soon as he noticed the point. Actually, there was no need to spell things out for an audience finely attuned to any political innuendoes. They sat breathless, by all accounts, through a five-hour-long performance, and found the actor's interpretation grandiose for its satanic humour, ruthlessness, and dangerous charm. This was Werner Kraus, who had played Shylock for Max Reinhardt and would do so again under the Nazi regime, along with the infamous *Jew Süss*. Meanwhile in 1942, the Londoners could see Donald Wolfit booming around the stage of the Strand Theatre and crossing every T with a vengeance:[24] the more he studied the part, we are told, the more he was struck by the likeness with Hitler, which he stressed further still by wearing a wig with a strand of hair across the forehead—the ogre of Laurence Olivier's nightmares, who would take it out on his followers, and visit Antony Sher every night during rehearsals, just as he had been haunted by the ghost he aimed to unseat.[25]

In France, after various ersatz of the kind long favoured on both sides of the Channel, the first truly Shakespearian version of *Richard III* was Charles Dullin's at the Atelier in 1933, which was to impress future French interpreters as durably as Olivier's would in Britain. The extreme sobriety of the production was more of a necessity than a choice, imposed by the minute size of the stage.[26] Dullin explored

[22] Walter Kiaulehn, *Berlin, Schicksal einer Weldstadt*, in Wilhelm Hortmann, *Shakespeare on the German Stage: The Twentieth Century* (Cambridge, 1998), 61.

[23] John Newmark, *Frankfurter Rundschau* (31 Oct. 1987), in Hortmann, *Shakespeare on the German Stage*, 137.

[24] See Wolfit's autobiography, *First Interval* (London, 1954).

[25] See Julie Hankey's dossier in Cahiers Renaud Barrault, *Interpréter Richard III* (Paris, 1987). Antony Sher, *Year of the King: An Actor's Diary and Sketchbook* (London, 1985).

[26] See Fortunato Israel, '*Richard III* sur la scène française' in D. Goy-Blanquet and R. Marienstras

the human aspect of the character, focusing on Richard's cold, brilliant brain, which on his own admission he could never entirely catch in performance. In 1967, Roger Planchon's production concentrated on Richard's seductive powers, because 'if evil showed a hideous face, every one would know it for what it is. The shocking thing is that it resembles good so much.'[27] French interpreters of the part generally work the nuances, Richard's shades of humour and the many facets of his comedian's gifts. Like Dullin, they often feel that they cannot give a faultless performance, that there is always one or another facet that escapes them. The fascinating Ariel Garcia-Valdes, who played him in 1984 as a fallen angel amid a court of Velázquez grotesques, confessed that he always missed at least one scene, though not the same one every night.

Most of the century's European productions thus wavered between the evolutive image of tyranny, and the scrutiny of its protean vehicle, stressing historical process or timeless myth. During the twenty years dominated by Brecht and Kott, political readings multiplied, bringing *Henry VI* into unprecedented popularity. In 1963, under the powerful influence of the Berliner Ensemble, John Barton and Peter Hall opened the era of complete cycles at Stratford. Their *Wars of the Roses* broke away from the current illusionist dramaturgy, favouring ensemble work, and contemporary uniforms designed primarily to tell the rival camps apart. The stage was empty, save for a few functional props and accessories charged with symbolic value—cannons, throne, crown, clouds of mist. To make their own analysis of violent power clear, Barton and Hall cut savagely into the tetralogy, and added 1,400 lines of their own writing—hardly distinguishable from Shakespeare's, they declared with enviable confidence.[28] The following year, Giorgio Strehler's version of *Henry VI* for Piccolo Teatro staged the end of the feudal system as a conflict within the leading aristocracy, whose selfish pursuits proved unable to extract any form of order from the general chaos. Entitled *Il gioco dei potenti*, Strehler's vision deeply impressed Peter Palitzsch, who had directed the world premiere of *Ui* in 1958. His *Der Krieg der Rosen* was performed below a gallery of skeletons: 'The nobles and peers hang on to the wheel of power as long as it carries them upward, and they try to cut off the heads, or at least the fingers, of anyone they feel to be a competitor.'[29] Shakespeare, like a true realist, does not allow them any philosophical depth until they have lost the game, Palitzsch concludes, and then what they have learnt is of no use to them or anyone else.

Jean-Louis Barrault put on a shortened version of *Henry VI* at the Odéon at around the same time as Palitzsch, and kept a bitter memory of the attempt: 'All we got for it were insults. The critique tore us to shreds. The public, prejudiced,

---

(eds.), *Le Tyran: Shakespeare contre Richard III* (Amiens, 1990), 151–67. Its most prominent feature, a Tower of London drawn from a miniature by Charles d'Orléans, probably suggested the use of *Les Très Riches Heures du Duc de Berry* in the film sets of Olivier's *Henry V*.

[27] Planchon's interview for *L'Humanité*, 13 Mar. 1967, in Goy-Blanquet and Marienstras (eds.), *Le Tyran*, 157.

[28] *The Wars of the Roses, Adapted for the Royal Shakespeare Company from William Shakespeare's 'Henry VI, Parts I, II, III and Richard III'*, BBC (London, 1970), introd., p. xi.

[29] Peter Palitzsch, in Hortmann, *Shakespeare on the German Stage*, 227.

expressed indifference. I was deeply hurt.' Barrault, an old friend of Olivier, and of Peter Brook whom he had just put in charge of a creative workshop in Paris, was a pioneering admirer of Shakespeare. With these juvenile plays which he thought typical of the Renaissance, he hoped to show in one evening the passage from primitive medieval witchcraft to a theatre of cruelty and the birth of the monster Richard, 'the complete renewal of a human cycle'.[30] But his public, who hardly knew these plays existed, could not follow. France would not properly begin to respond to the epic style for another ten years, when Denis Llorca's magnificent *Kings* in 1978 created a real enthusiasm with a nine-hour version of the first tetralogy. Fifteen years would elapse before the next *Henry VI*: Stuart Seide opened the new Centre Dramatique in Poitiers with an energetic, youthful performance of the trilogy by twenty actors, which allowed none a star turn, but displayed an inventive variety of killing methods.

These large frescos conferred a new dimension on the tragedy of power. Emerging from the wounds of the Second World War, Henry VI's Christlike figure took a prominence that critical analysis had not yet measured, while Richard often failed to shock after the ravages of civil strife. In most cycle productions, the monster is but lightly misshapen: he cannot be too crippled if he is to play his busy part on the battlefields of *Henry VI*, nor allowed to upset the whole balance by showing off. In Barton/Hall's version, he seemed quite the most attractive of Mrs York's unruly sons, 'a reasonable, winning, personable boy, despite the withered hand, the buckled back and club foot, whose acrid humour is expressed in deadpan politeness rather than sardonic snarls'.[31] Childish, and content with playing second fiddle to Buckingham, he was also a disappointment to many who found him rather light on the evil side. In Adrian Noble's *Plantagenets*, he was an impertinent imp, amicably whispering into Anne's ear his plans for remarriage once she is gone, and so terribly alone that his first reaction on seeing Clarence's ghost was a smile of pleasure. The 2000 RSC production amply confirmed these tendencies with a charismatic Henry and a reasonably cruel Richard, rather less blood-curdling than the fiercest Margaret ever.

Most producers of the cycle were resolutely opposed to museographic recreations of the past: 'history does not worry me when I am doing a play', Jane Howell explained, and owned herself more interested by similarities with current politics, for instance the fact that York returns from Ireland at the head of an army: 'Where do the English armies train? They train in Ireland. It is still the same.'[32] To Michael Bogdanov, equally determined to treat Shakespeare as his contemporary, Richard's reign was the last stage before nuclear holocaust.[33] Most directors refuse anything so simplistic as the victory of good over evil, and see the conclusion as the replacement of one political monster by another. Richard is seldom allowed his last

---

[30] J.-L. Barrault, 'Henri VI', in *Souvenirs pour demain* (Paris, 1972), 335–6.

[31] Alan Brien, *Sunday Telegraph*, 21 July 1963.

[32] 'Représentations télévisuelles de la guerre', in M.-T. Jones-Davies (ed.), *Shakespeare et la guerre* (Paris, 1990), 165–6.

[33] 'Mises en scène de Shakespeare en Angleterre', panel chaired by Russell Jackson, Société Française Shakespeare, 20 Jan. 1989.

bravura piece. The duel with Richmond is often replaced by a ritual sacrifice or a collective execution. Adrian Noble had him nailed to the ground like a beetle by a team of entomologists. In Ian McKellen's film, he is shot and falls straight into Hell.

In Germany, where theatre ethics were long dominated by an even stronger revulsion than the British against war and dictatorship, Robert Weimann's works had opened other routes to explore towards the end of the 1960s: 'No topical effects are wanted, but a sense of history which can discover permanence in change but also change in seeming permanence; the past in the present but also the present in the past.'[34] He stressed Richard's link with the character of Vice, his manipulations of discourse through speeches aimed directly at the audience. In Manfred Wekwerth's Berlin production, the actor came down and walked through the aisles to harangue the spectators at close range, opposing a plebeian, wholly human view of history to the medieval belief that it is made by the powerful of this world and the Almighty above.[35] That same year, 1972, the public of the Comédie-Française were treated to a farcical bloodbath by Terry Hands, who sat the Mayor and his aldermen with their backs to the audience like children watching a Punch and Judy show. A decade later, in Georges Lavaudant's production, Clarence's murderers added spice to the election scene by putting on bishops' mitres and standing with Richard on a balcony framed by red velvet curtains.

Back in Britain, the same Terry Hands opened the era of 'pyscho-social' Richards, in Gillian Day's classification, with the first integral, and apolitical, version of *Henry VI*, discarding Brechtian uniforms in favour of sober period costumes.[36] This was a great relief to the critics, who owned themselves very tired of having moral lessons hurled at them. The conflict between York and Lancaster was one of country against court, in which the Yorks appeared a bunch of social misfits. In 1980, while Alan Howard played *Richard III* in Stratford, interpreting the part as a cripple turned paranoid, London was visited by the Georgian Rustaveli Theatre, whose Richard ran through the gamut of past tyrants by changing costumes, from Napoleon's to a Wehrmacht officer's greatcoat. In the audience was Antony Sher, who thus recorded their stunning production: 'Ramaz Chkikvadze plays Richard like a giant poisonous toad. And he touches people as if removing handfuls of flesh.'[37] His own Richard, performed over tombs drawn from the Westminster crypt, marked the triumphal return to character, in the grand Olivier tradition.

Ian McKellen got but a tepid response in comparison, despite his original interpretation of Richard as a stiff-backed veteran. Eyre's production was thought a step back towards Ui-tyrants, and discarded as old hat. Actually those images cut much nearer than most critics realized: the evocation of Oswald Mosley's right-wing party under Edward VIII was meant as a reminder that Fascism had not stopped at the

[34] Robert Weimann, 'Shakespeare on the Modern Stage: Past Significance and Present Meaning', *ShS* 20 (1967), 117. *Shakespeare and the Popular Tradition in the Theater* (Baltimore, 1978).

[35] Hortmann, *Shakespeare on the German Stage*, 231–2.

[36] Her categories, political, psycho-social, metatheatrical, are useful but less immune to periodization than her structuralist approach suggests, and more often than not, as she is aware, 'a production challenges a single definition' (175).

[37] *Year of the King*, 28.

Channel, and that no democracy is ever safe from its re-emergence. To Richard Eyre, the audiences who identified the emblems as Nazi imagery were too literal-minded: 'The language of demagoguery in this century is identical everywhere. Stalin, Mao Ze Dung used the same kind of iconography as Hitler.'[38] Like all the coronations of twentieth-century dictators, this one was a synthetic display of medieval robes and rites, duly recorded by TV for the evening news. When the young Prince was expected to arrive 'with some little train', a toy electric train crossed the stage, bathed in *Nacht und Nebel* lighting. In the film version, the full-size train was even more directly evocative of the newsreels showing transport to concentration camps.[39] The queens' wailing scene had more recent sources: the women's protest against nuclear energy on Greenham Common, and the Romanian mothers who lit candles on the spots where their sons had been killed.

Along with the probings of moral conscience, integral versions raised the level of concern about textual integrity in the academic and theatrical consciousness. We have come a long way since the days when Laurence Olivier could perform Shakespeare's play 'with some interpolations by David Garrick and Colley Cibber' without raising any objections.[40] Cibber's version aimed at giving Richard the maximum lines, but deprived him of any antagonist. Olivier simply got rid of Margaret, a precedent all directors invoke when they want to dispatch this heavy mother of rhetoric, even though, like him, they often reinsert fragments of *Henry VI* to fill her part. She long suffered from a treble handicap: her litanies were difficult to naturalize, hardly compatible with a sceptical reading of the play, and not strictly necessary to the plot. Even the entrancing Peggy Ashcroft was made a powerless Margaret by Barton/Hall's editing of her part. The feeling was so common that Antony Sher's partner, Pat Routledge, volunteered cuts herself: 'I can imagine someone in the front row saying "Dear oh dear, I thought she'd never go." '[41] It took Rustaveli's visit to Britain to show up her virtual potency: Robert Sturua kept her on stage throughout, speaking the stage directions as if she conducted the executions of her enemies. Sam Mendes had her appear at each death to savour her vengeance; her ghostly figure emerged from the shadow as each new victim recalled her curse, while her last appearance at Bosworth made Richard lose his aim. His production won much praise, but stood alone of its kind for some time. Ian McKellen put on gloves to explain that Margaret is absolutely necessary to the play and yet had to be cut out of his film, for 'her powerful presence would not compensate for the time spent in explaining clearly who she is and has been'.[42] Too much time spent explaining, learning, understanding—and time, especially in the movies, is money.

By then, the militant urge to make Shakespeare accessible to popular audiences had got reinforcements from other no less powerful motives: the BBC 'Complete

---

[38] 'On Directing *Richard III*', in Goy-Blanquet and Marienstras (eds.), *Le Tyran*, 135.

[39] See Peter Holland's review of the film for the *TLS*, 10 May 1996.

[40] See Anthony Davies's fine analysis of the actor's manipulative camera, in *Filming Shakespeare's Plays* (Cambridge, 1988), 68–82.

[41] *Year of the King*, 206.

[42] *William Shakespeare's 'Richard III'* (London, 1996), 17.

Dramatic Works', an expensive Anglo-American production primarily designed for schools and universities, sold to over forty countries around the world.[43] Now the main question of the late 1960s—how far could one interfere with the text in order to clarify its ideological import—has come down to how much of the text one can keep and still be understood. In Al Pacino's film, highly educative if not wholly devoid of demagogy, the actor humbly asks around for what he already knows, reads those Cliff notes abhorred by any self-respecting academic, and throws ridicule equitably on pedantic actors and professors. 'You know more about Shakespeare than any fucking Don from Columbia or Harvard,' his partner screams, and is rewarded by a promotion to knighthood: 'Arise, Sir Frederic, Ph.D!'

Shakespeare is no longer our contemporary, and no one understands what he's talking about, Pacino claims, but instead of masking the problem, he turns it into a heuristic quest. The actor's Studio method of approach, the way he turns around the character, to watch, question, sniff, try to know everything of his life and forebears, becomes the very mode of access to a work which keeps escaping him. It is also a convenient way to provide the minimum of knowledge required to follow the story. His Cliff notes pass unobtrusively between the lines rehearsed, which amount to one-third of the play. Pacino allows himself to be confused by the crowd of characters, and deftly answers every crux as it arises, for our benefit. In *Gloucester Time*, Matthias Langhoff solved the problem with a voice-off lesson in medieval history, while pictures of the Gulf war rolled on a screen, like a classroom lecture with slides.

The latest Richards have deserted the political stand altogether. Patrice Chéreau's *Fragments* in homage to Strehler concentrated on the women's sorrowful chorus. At the 1999 Avignon Festival, Geneviève de Kermabon cast a legless actor in the title part, and explained that the tyrant's inhuman behaviour reflected the inhuman look that his intimates, beginning with his mother, had always focused on him.[44] But her freakish attempt to capture truth by using disability instead of performing it caused great unease among the critics, who justifiably objected to this post-modern confusion between mental and physical deformities, not to mention what it implied about theatrical art—a regression from the forum to circus arenas of live entertainment.[45] In France, the year 2000 pursued the unique domination, and political decline, of *Richard III*, displacing the battle for the crown to the world of corrupt finance. The film star Richard Bohringer, who played the lead in Hans-Peter Cloos's production, compared it to Brando's Godfather, arguing that 'Today, power *is* money.'[46] Milianti's version, *Le Tombeau de Richard G.*, closed on Richard's selling the maison d'York, or is it Dior, to Richmond for a caseful of

---

[43] See Michael Mullin, 'Shakespeare USA: The BBC Plays and American Education', *SQ* 35 (1985), 582–9.

[44] Press dossier, Festival d'Avignon, July 1999.

[45] Originally the part was to be played by Pierre Grenier, who died of his illness, glass bones, before the opening. Henri Paillet took up the challenge and played the part, showing only from the waist up above the stage.

[46] In a personal interview. He was even more right than he thought: owing to shady business dealers, the tour scheduled for fifty performances was cancelled after only six.

banknotes: 'Reality in Shakespeare's time meant politics. Now it's economics.'[47]
The subtitle, *Une furieuse foire d'empoigne*, confirmed the desecration of the play-
ground by multinational firms fighting for supremacy, and, indirectly, Al Pacino's
view that we should now go looking for Richard in New York. Now the question is,
will he make it to Silicon Valley?

Michael Boyd's RSC cycle opened at Stratford-upon-Avon in November 2000.
Highly physical and inventive, it was drawn between the 'Heavens' and 'Hell' of
both real and stage worlds, laying emphasis on witchcraft, superstitious rituals, raw
hatred, and unhappy families. The theatrical and political worlds of make believe
were brought together with masterly strokes. The sight of dead Henry's bleeding
wounds so startled Richard that he dipped his fingers in and smelt them as if
suspecting a trick. Margaret's laying of her dead son's bones on stage to quicken her
curses petrified all around her, and is sure to live long in her audience's recollections. The ghosts literally haunted the stage as constant visitors. Richard was
severely shaken by the return of the Talbots in the roles of Richmond and Stanley,
and finally crushed when his beloved father disowned him: his last call for rescue
was met by the silent apparition of York standing between his other son's sons,
Edward's children.

Boyd's production, the last of the century, showed a regression within the family
circle as a shield against primitive fears, in a world where the power of myths and
religious rituals once again makes sense. Post-Second World War scholars and
directors were intent on showing the impact of historical agents, stressing the 'want
of men and money' above adverse planets or witchcraft. The evolution of the
stage mirrors the violent backlash of this scepticism in the convergence of various
cultural trends: the return of superstitious practices at all levels of society, from
witching teenagers to government leaders who consult astrologers; the re-
emergence of archaic values preserved in clannish structures; the deadly fascination
of death. Once the first victims of directorial rationalism, women, children, and
ghosts are now vindicated as the strongest force, mightier even than armed troops.

This new balance of stage power seems the symptom of a major shift in our reception of the play. Until recently, with the possible exception of Jessner's grand staircase, the images printed on the collective consciousness were those of Richard's
great interpreters, and more especially those who stole the show. Antony Sher's
diary records the genesis of a monstrous body, almost independent from his own,
for which he sought models in psychopaths' clinics: a six-legged spider leaping
across the stage on crutches, creeping up to the throne for the triumphant coronation of misrule.[48] Discussing film versions, the *Sunday Times* reviewer of *Looking for
Richard* set the range of acting possibilities between the two poles established by
Laurence Olivier and Ian McKellen, the vitality of evil or the banality of evil: 'But
Pacino's black, basilisk stare bores through into something we'd all but forgotten:
how about the plain old evilness of evil?'[49] Psychology's diagnosis of his singularity

---

[47] In the press dossier of the Athénée theatre (Apr. 2000).
[48] See Marienstras, 'Of a Monstrous Body', in Maguin and Willems (eds.), *French Essays*, 153.
[49] 'In Search of Shakespeare's Worst Villain', Tom Shone, *Sunday Times* (2 Feb. 1997).

as the growing pains of a loveless ugly devil falls far short of the enduring fascination he exercises in the theatre. 'Do we love him now?' asks the *TLS* reviewer of the latest Richard, who finds Kenneth Branagh less demonic than his great predecessors but praises his ability, not universal among actors, to do almost nothing: 'Evil is, after all, the name we give to a kind of silence, a gap in motive.'[50]

We have yet to see Richard turn up on stage in the guise of Osama bin Laden, but Shakespeare was soon mobilized by the international press and TV commentators, as he had been during the Falklands war, to voice the unspeakable horror of 11 September. Along with exploding the concept of 'the end of history', the philosopher André Glucksmann claims, the fall of the Twin Towers showed Western civilization to be still entertaining the fallacy that evil is but the herald of some future good, instead of recognizing it for what it is: nihilism. In chapters headed by quotations from *Richard III* and *Macbeth*, he argues that the 'cogito' of nihilism is the awareness that evildoing, sheer destructiveness, is at least as pleasurable as good-doing, a permanent fact of human kind that Thucydides could already detect in the figure of Alcibiades.[51] 'Motiveless malignity', unabated and unfathomed still 500 years after Richard's death.

2. POSITIONS OF THE TEXTS

Thanks to Shakespeare, Richard III's short reign remains the most famous and infamous one in all English history. Few characters have inspired such radically opposed views, and such enduring conflicts among historians. Richard's true personality, and his part in the many crimes he was accused of, are still hotly debated, even now when all agree that Shakespeare's monster had little basis in reality. The most reliable account of the reign, the Croyland *Continuation*, written in the year following Bosworth, has none of the fantastic tales that decorate the later narratives. Still, the idea of a Tudor plot designed to blacken the character of the last Plantagenet no longer stands in the light of modern research: the late unearthing of a contemporary account by an Italian visitor to England shows that most of the hostile rumours began circulating in Richard's lifetime.[52] Dominic Mancini's report on his usurpation, written shortly after the event, more or less tallies with the official records of those momentous days when town and council were preparing the coronation of young Edward V.

The bulk of Shakespeare's historical matter comes from the Tudor chronicles which H. A. Kelly regroups under the label 'Vergil–Hall–Holinshed report', augmented with More's *History of Richard III*.[53] Actually there is no such thing as

---

[50] Stephen Brown, *TLS* (5 Apr. 2002).

[51] *Dostoïevski à Manhattan* (Paris, 2002), 121, 128, 157, 232, and 'Ma part de vérité', *Figaro Magazine* (2 Mar. 2002).

[52] *A Third Continuation of the History of Croyland*, in *Ingulph's Chronicle*, trans. H. T. Riley (London, 1854), 453–533. Mancini, *The Usurpation of Richard III*, ed. C. A. J. Armstrong (Oxford, 1936). See Rosemary Horrox, *Richard III: A Study in Service* (Cambridge, 1989), 90–3.

[53] Kelly 251.

undifferentiated Vergil–Hall–Holinshed material: the three versions differ in a host of minor details, while broadly agreeing on the main facts. The question that still exercises modern historians—the fate of the Princes in the Tower—is raised by none of Shakespeare's sources, since none entertains any doubt of Richard's guilt. As to which narrative served him most, and how far it shaped his reading of national history, the question is even trickier than usual. That More played a major part in the shaping of the play and its eponymous hero is unarguable. The filiation between the two characters is striking; there is no certainty, however, that it is a direct one.[54] Both Hall and Holinshed insert More's *History* in theirs, which have but few original specific details. Last crux, and most crucial for today's reader, why did Shakespeare, who had grown so independent from any ready-made political theory with *Henry VI*, endorse the narrators' orthodox conclusions to the Plantagenet saga?

It is worth noting that no 'Yorkist' version of Richard's reign was extant when the play was written. Both Vergil and More were linked in some way with the victor's camp. Vergil was introduced to Henry VII by friends who had known the King when he was still Earl of Richmond, while Thomas More grew up in the household of Cardinal Morton, who had some share in the Earl's victory. The Latin *Continuations* of the *History of Croyland Monastery*, possibly written by John Russell, Bishop of Lincoln, who was briefly Chancellor during Richard's reign, furnished the basic script, which was soon buried under successive layers of hostile tales. Of these, the first and most influential was John Rous's *Historia Regum Angliae*. An admirer of Richard in his lifetime, Rous turned his coat after Bosworth and tried to destroy all records of his earlier praise, but failed to recover the English version.[55] He was the first to report monstrous details about Richard's birth and physical appearance, to which his followers brought new features. Vergil is thought to have used an analogue of the original Croyland, though he probably read it after completing the first draft of his manuscript.[56] More used the same sources, plus Vergil. Grafton in his 1543 *Continuation of Hardyng's Chronicle* absorbed More's *History*, and was likewise absorbed by Hall, whose variants Grafton later adopted in his compilation, *A Chronicle at Large and Meere History of the affayres of England* (1568). Beside Hall and More, Holinshed used a Yorkist *Historie of the Arrivall of Edward IV, in England and the Finall Recouerye of his Kingdomes*, which ends with the battle of Tewkesbury. John Stow, who consulted all the material extant, was the first to question Rous's authority in his *Annales*, published in 1580 and 1592.[57]

According to Bullough, Shakespeare probably had no access to the primary

---

[54] See Bullough's list of the versions available in the sixteenth century, 222–8, drawn from G. B. Churchill's *Richard the Third up to Shakespeare*, Palaestra X (Berlin, 1900). Alison Hanham, *Richard III and his Early Historians, 1483–1535* (Oxford, 1975).

[55] See Charles Ross, introd. to *The Rous Roll* (Gloucester, 1980).

[56] See Kelly 90 n. 16 for a discussion of this point, and 55–69 on the identification of the third Croyland Chronicler as Russell.

[57] John Stow, *The Chronicles of England from Brute unto this present yeare of Christ 1580* (London, 1580), whose account of Edward V and Richard III 'was written by Sir Thomas More', 751–835, and 'abridged out of Edward Hall' for the end.

sources, but he knew at least Hall, Grafton, Holinshed, and Stow, who all derive from Vergil and More.[58] It is not so much the matter of the play but the genesis of its shape which needs exploring. Most of the material used is common to all accounts, while the rumours circulating about Richard before and after his death were numberless. Though the play has the same sequence of events as the Croyland chronicle, the dramatist probably had to cut his way through wordy narratives to achieve something of comparable clarity. Only More's *History* offers an equally clear script, but an unfinished one. For the end of the story, all our authors depend on Vergil.[59] Hall and Holinshed's much longer accounts had little outside information to add to theirs, and hardly any on the episodes staged. That Shakespeare read both, we know. Whether he contented himself with these two versions or was tempted by their differences to consult an original More remains open. This kind of curiosity would be natural to a scholar, not necessarily to a dramatist looking for material. He could have found ready-made scripts elsewhere, in various handier versions of the story, then gone to historical sources for more matter instead of the reverse. All the relevant episodes of the play are aligned in Foxe's sharp summary of the facts, for instance, where the old adage, 'Wo to the kingdom, the king wherof is a child', is quoted with ominous misgivings after Edward's death as in the play, not later as in More, when Buckingham uses it to manipulate the crowd.[60] The whole tale is brief, since Foxe sees no need 'to make a longer discourse of this matter which is sufficiently set forth by sir Thomas More, and so ornately', with a special note of 'the history of Polydore Vergil, whom sir Thomas More doth follow word for word'.

Bullough does not mention Foxe, but completes his list of chroniclers with literary works derived from the common sources: *The Mirror for Magistrates*, Thomas Legge's *Richardus Tertius*, and *The True Tragedy of Richard III*. None of the three seems guided by More's well-trimmed tale, indeed they use far less of the recorded material than Shakespeare, each choosing different episodes, as we shall see. Lily Campbell's opinion that 'the *Mirror for Magistrates* isolated the chief events exhibited in Shakespeare's play' must be qualified. Baldwin, in his preface to the tragedy of Hastings, acknowledges his debt to More, Fabyan, and especially Hall, whose authority he will follow in case of variance, while deploring 'the disagreynge of wryters' which is 'a great hinderaunce of the truthe'.[61] However, the Tragedies do not make a complete sequence of events; only nine are centred on characters who appear in the play, and even with the episodes narrated by Richard's ghost, this still leaves a large portion of Shakespeare's plot unprovided.

As to the dramatic parallels, either Richard was a popular theme, or he was made fashionable by Shakespeare. The promising young man who announces his plans for future mischief in *3 Henry VI* may well have inspired competition. Legge's

---

[58] *The Chronicle of Iohn Hardyng . . . together with the Continuation of Richard Grafton*, ed. Sir Henry Ellis (London, 1812).

[59] *The Anglica Historia of Polydor Vergil, A.D. 1485–1537*, ed. Denis Hay, (London, 1950).

[60] Foxe 787, 788, 782.

[61] *Mirror*, xx. 4–26. Campbell, *Shakespeare's 'Histories'*, 319.

Richardus Tertius, written in 1579, certainly enjoyed popularity before Shakespeare: it survived in nine manuscripts, was quoted by writers like Harington or Nashe, and still recalled years later in Meres's *Palladis Tamia*.[62] The anonymous *True Tragedy of Richard III* was performed by the Queen's Men at some date very close to Shakespeare's own play. Both *Richardus Tertius* and the *True Tragedy* observe chronology, while giving a more prominent part to politics, and to feminine characters, than the *Mirror*. The critics generally point out their differences from *Richard III*, on the grounds that Shakespeare, who had just been accused of plagiarism by Robert Greene, was probably eager to show he did not need to copy anyone. His *Richard III* towers so far above the other two that this is really not an issue. Granted that they do differ significantly in many ways beside quality, they signal important evolutionary stages, however crude, in the shaping and pruning of the historical material, and they left their imprint on the story, however little help Shakespeare may have gained from it.

Vergil had finished a draft of his *Anglica Historia* around 1513, but his complete work—twenty-six volumes of impeccable Latin—was published only in 1534, after a labour of twenty-eight years. A manuscript translation in elegant English of his chapters on Henry VI, Edward IV, and Richard III, precisely the section corresponding to Shakespeare's first cycle of histories, was written at a time close to Hall's composition of his own chronicle. It has been impossible so far to establish whether any of our writers had read it. Very little is known of this anonymous work, except that it is based on the 1546 edition of Vergil. The signature 'Lumley' on the first page of the manuscript may be a clue, though, pointing towards one of Vergil's fiercest detractors, the Welsh antiquary Humphrey Llwyd, who served the Earl of Arundel for fifteen years, and eventually married Lumley's sister. One may imagine that Llwyd, who wrote and translated many volumes while living in the Arundel household, may well have translated this piece himself, or at least used it to write the chronicle with which he meant to stop Vergil's 'venomous tongue'.[63] Thomas More's longer account of Richard was written, like Vergil's first draft, 'about the yeare of our Lorde .1513', simultaneously in two fairly different Latin and English versions, and left unfinished. It first appeared in print in 1543, appended to the *Continuation of Hardyng's Chronicle* by Grafton, who 'garbled it at will'.[64] Hall took it over from Grafton, considerably lengthened it with elaborations of his own, and completed the account of Richard's end with Vergil. When Hall's Protestant chronicle was banned, in the reign of Mary, More's nephew, William Rastell, took the opportunity to restore the text to its original condition, and published the

---

[62] *The True Tragedy of Richard the Third, to which is appended the Latin play of Richardus Tertius by Dr. Thomas Legge*, ed. Barron Field (London, 1844), 'Old Plays', IV. xxi. 1–74, 75–166. Sir John Harington, *Apologie for Poetrie* (1591), Thomas Nashe, *Have With You to Saffron Walden* (1596), Francis Meres, *Palladis Tamia* (1598).

[63] Llwyd's *Cronica Walliae*, ed. Ieuan M. Williams and J. Beverley Smith (Aberystwyth, 2003) was completed in 1559, and never published until now. Praised by his contemporaries for his universal learning and great eloquence, Humphrey Llwyd or Lhuyd bought the books that formed the basis of Lord Lumley's library. After Lumley's death his library was purchased together with that of his father-in-law the Earl of Arundel by King James 1 for the Prince of Wales.

[64] *Richard III*, ed. John Dover Wilson (Cambridge, 1954), introd., p. xiii.

English *History* in 1557.[65] It is this emended text which Holinshed inserted in his own account.

The authorship of More was first advertised in Hall's chronicle, when there was no further risk of alienating the despot who had sent him to the block.[66] Even before Rastell's publication, the *History* had become an object of national pride, as appears from Roger Ascham's comment in 1553 that 'if the rest of our story of England were so done, we might well compare with *Fraunce, Italy,* or *Germany* in that behalfe'.[67] By the time Shakespeare composed his *Richard III,* there were over half a dozen editions of More's work extant.[68] Though all these versions are largely copies of each other, they are never identical. The chroniclers cultivate variants, and collect matter from various origins, regardless of the resulting contradictions. The insertion of More's stylish, concise *History* between portions drawn from other sources created more than the average lot of anomalies. His successive editors divide between those who correct his numerous slips, fill in the gaps he left, or emend his 'uncouth orthography', and those who prefer his original text complete with its mistakes.[69] Rastell, who rejects both Grafton's and Hall's texts as 'very much corrupt in many places', will have none of their emendations, even when appropriate.[70] Holinshed adopts the same policy, following Rastell's More in patent errors. All give different figures for Edward's age at the time of his death: about 50 years old in Vergil, in his fiftieth year according to Hall, 53 in More and Holinshed.[71] Actually he was 41.

To complicate matters further, some of More's zealous editors alter his narrative sequence. Both Grafton and Hall rearrange the opening pages of the English version into proper chronological order. Rastell innovates by restoring More's narrative structure, but then proceeds to reupset it by adding to the English text three passages translated from his Latin version.[72] Holinshed follows Hall step by step through the Vergil-based account of Richard, then, reaching the point where Hall inserts More's *History,* he goes to Rastell's version instead and copies it integrally, marking with asterisks the passages translated from the Latin, and adding original

[65] Rastell's 1557 edition of *The history of king richard the thirde,* a facsimile, ed. W. E. Campbell, in *The English Works of Sir Thomas More* (London, 1931), vol. 1.

[66] See R. W. Chambers, introd. to the facsimile of Rastell's 1557 edition, *English Works,* i. 27.

[67] Roger Ascham, *Report of the Affaires and State of Germany,* written in answer to John Astely, 1553, in *English Works,* ed. W. A. Wright (Cambridge, 1904), 126.

[68] Grafton's *Continuation of Hardyng* (1543), Hall's *Union* (1548), Rastell's *Workes of Sir Thomas More* (1557), Grafton's *Chronicle at Large* (1568), the first and second Holinshed (1578, 1587), John Stow's *Chronicle* (1580)—the most faithful copy of the lot—plus the Latin version published in the 1566 edition of More's *Works.*

[69] J. S. Phillimore's phrase, 'Thomas More and the Arrest of Humanism', *Dublin Review* (July 1913). See preface to the Campbell facsimile, *English Works,* i, p. x. All references to More's *History,* as distinct from Hall's More (Hall 342–84), are drawn from the Yale *Complete Works,* vol. ii, which prints the text of Rastell's 1557 English edition and the Latin text of 1565 on facing pages.

[70] Thus he maintains 'the kinges daughter of Spain' against Hall's 'Bona sister to the French kyng' as Edward IV's prospective bride. Actually Bona was sister to the French Queen, but 'sister' often stands for 'sister-in-law'.

[71] Vergil 171, Hall 341, More 3, Holinshed 360. Edward was born at Rouen in 1442 while his father was lieutenant-general in France.

[72] Pages 39, 41–4, and 81–2.

material from Hall. He makes no attempt either to merge his sources, and simply returns to the Vergil-by-Hall continuation at the end of More's tale. The only reason why Holinshed is rather more readable than Hall is his more regular use of paragraphs and less variable spelling. By rule of thumb, their sections on Richard are about three times as long as Vergil's or More's.[73]

This tangled web of *translatio* creates an unusual amount of doublets. Rastell's interference causes More to repeat himself in ways unpremeditated. The three additions from the Latin bring very little matter that does not appear elsewhere. The second and longest one, inserted after the young princes' entrance to the Tower, reports the alliance sealed between Gloucester and Buckingham to secure the crown. As a result, their secret dealings are reported twice, first after the capture of the children, as in the Latin *Historia*, and again retrospectively at the time of Buckingham's conspiracy. Rastell's version mentions the Hereford inheritance in both places, but only the first one specifies that Richard had promised it as part of their deal. Hall's and Holinshed's conflations cause larger redundancies. Both tell the story of King Edward's marriage twice, and allow him two very different dying speeches.[74] Both report two versions of Clarence's murder, one with the 'G' prophecy but no suggestion of Richard's guilt, the other blaming him for the deed but without mention of a prophecy.[75] Whatever the chroniclers gain from the addition of memorable scenes is usually at the expense of inner consistency, most visibly when it touches Richard's behaviour. In Vergil's account, Richard's usurpation of power was unpremeditated and broke a long pattern of loyalty to his brother, where More asserts he had long nursed a hidden desire for the crown. Their interpretations of his every act vary accordingly. As they shift from one to the other source, Hall and Holinshed find themselves alternately supporting their incompatible views.

How far these well-meaning mediators could create confusion, two details among many will illustrate. Shakespeare's large cast of characters is made larger still by his division of one individual into two, a mistake probably traceable to Hall. Where More writes that the young Prince was entrusted to 'sir Antony Woduile Lord Riuers and brother unto the Quene, a right honourable man', Hall tries to improve matters with one extra title for this gentleman, 'lord Antony Wooduile erle Ryuers and lorde Scales, brother to the quene, a wise, hardy and honourable personage', thus producing a split character.[76] Here Holinshed, who copies More correctly, is not responsible for Shakespeare's mistake, but he certainly is for another small slip: on stage, Richard in his final oration refers to Richmond as a 'milksop', a term used by both chroniclers, 'long kept in Bretagne at our mother's cost'. Whether it is just a *lapsus calami*, 'the final sign of Richard's own matriarchal perversion' in Barbara Hodgdon's reading, or simpler and better 'our mother

---

[73] Events of the play correspond to Hall 326–421, Holinshed 346–447, Vergil's much shorter pages, 167–227, and More's, 3–93.

[74] Hall 339–41, 344–5. Holinshed 355–8, 363–5.

[75] Hall 326, 343. Holinshed 346, 362.

[76] Hall 347. More 14. Holinshed 365.

country' as in Lull's, does not alter the issue.[77] Deliberate or not, the intrusion of the mother results from a misprint in the 1587 edition, 'moothers', where the earlier Holinshed correctly copied Hall's 'brought vp by my brothers meanes'. Evidence again, if need be, that Shakespeare did consult the two chroniclers.

As to the relations between More's *Historia* and his *History*, the main question has long been which came first, and whether one was a translation of the other. It was still a matter for heated argument in the early twentieth century when Churchill wrote that beyond doubt the English version was 'a translation from the Latin, contrary to Ellis' opinion'.[78] It is largely agreed now that neither is derived from the other, but both were written independently and simultaneously. The Latin version stops earlier, at Richard's coronation, and differs in many turns of phrase. Less concise at times, it is slightly more explicit. Thus the murder of Clarence was a softening of the original sentence: he had been condemned by Parliament 'acerbissimo supplicio' but the King suspended it ('sustulit'), and he was drowned 'in vini Cretensis'—actually grown some distance from Malmsey, on the opposite side of the Cytherean Strait. Many imaginative efforts have been applied to Richard's request for strawberries, involving for instance an allergy to the fruit, which perhaps he used to bring on a rash and support his accusations of witchcraft.[79] Modern scholars who rack their brains to explain this point, entirely More's invention, might have found a clue in his Latin version of the scene: 'Pater, inquit, fragra tibi in hortis audio insignia mitescere, non grauatim scio ferculum unum tot nobilibus in prandium, velut simbolum tuum conferes.'[80] The gesture is entirely politic: Richard is so kindly disposed that he wishes to offer these strawberries for breakfast to the lords of the council, 'quantam haud temere ante in illo viderant, simulque humanitatem benignitatemque animi laudantibus'—they have seldom seen him so cheerful before, and applaud his benevolent mood. One wonders if More devised variant versions just to trick his learned commentators into betraying their want of Latin ... or curiosity.

3. HISTORIES OF RICHARD

The Prologue

Knowing Hall's rigid political opinions, one wonders what led him to insert whole a piece of impertinent writing, authored by a limb of the detested Roman Catholic faith, one whose martyred death had damned his master Henry VIII as a

[77] Hall 415. Holinshed 440. *R3*, v. iii. 326–7. Hammond emends to Q's 'brother'. Hodgdon, *The End Crowns All: Closure and Contradiction in Shakespeare's History* (Princeton, 1991), 115. Lull, n. 203.

[78] Churchill, *Richard the Third up to Shakespeare*, 77. See Daniel Kinney, 'Textual History', *A New Text and Translation of Historia Richardi Tertii*, in *Complete Works*, xv, pp. cxxxiii–cliv.

[79] For a record of other far-fetched explanations, see Hammond, appendix II, 339. Jowett 254 notes 'Richard's seeming genial indifference to matters of state'. To Chambers, 32, this being Friday, a meatless day, Richard wants a tasty dish for dinner after the beheading of Hastings.

[80] *Historia*, Yale, xv. 47, from MS fr. 4996 (*P*), 406, which according to Kinney is the least garbled transcript of More's Latin history, and a fuller version than either of the two in Yale, ii.

bloodthirsty tyrant in the eyes of half Europe. Why, if he was irresistibly attracted by a wit foreign to his, did he rewrite it out of all recognizable shape? And why, granted that borrowing was common usage, did he so pointedly mark out the part written by More, when he rarely bothers to identify his sources? Perhaps Hall, who never missed the chance to turn out a good long speech on any occasion, however inadequate, was not immune to the charms of a well-told tale. The reception of Vergil's *Anglica Historia* was a notorious precedent: it had been welcomed by a stream of anti-foreign abuse, but the abusers all rushed to copy it extensively.

Churchill notes that Hall's most important additions to More were largely adopted by his followers, Rastell excepted, and that all found their way into Shakespeare's play; he also reminds us that a major part of what is known as 'Hall's Chronicle' is in fact Richard Grafton's work.[81] Modern commentators on the sources have generally given up telling them apart, loosely ascribing to 'Hall' many additions he took over from the *Continuation of Hardyng*. Then, after the publication of *The union*, 'Grafton copied Hall where possible, using his text with some verbal alterations, and adding incidents from Vergil and Fabyan, with some passages translated from More's Latin Life' to compile *A Chronicle at Large*, a work that 'Shakespeare may well have known', Bullough thinks, 'but it is so near to Hall that to distinguish between his use of the two books is hardly worth attempting'. On the strength of this he will just 'give excerpts from Hall, which has more authority'.[82] Actually the *Chronicle at Large* is much briefer than any of the other narratives, which Grafton aims to reconcile on specific details. He duly quotes 'Polidore' as one of his authorities, notes the insertion of More's *History* at the right points in his own account, and suppresses a few of Hall's additions to More, like the extra title of Lord Rivers, or Richard's crabbed face, as well as Hall's redundant dying speech for Edward.[83]

Hall becomes properly original only with the Tudor reigns. His personal contribution on Richard consists mostly in various embellishments, set speeches and heightened pathos, of his material, plus a few additions which eventually found their way to the stage, like the rescue of Lord Strange. But Vaughan's dying speech, the two bishops exhibited at Baynard's Castle, the burial of the children, the appellations Raffe Shaa, Pynkie, Thomas Cooke, the correct Christian names of Buckingham and Hastings, were already in Grafton's *Continuation of Hardyng*. It is also in the *Continuation*, followed by Hall, that Richard declares on the morning of the divided councils he has 'been a sleper' as he does in the play, instead of merely 'a slepe' (asleep) as in More's original.[84] Holinshed, who adopts none of the above additions, here makes him a 'sleeper' like Hall.

Where Hall's section corresponding to *Richard III* begins depends on when the

---

[81] For a detailed survey of what is due to each, Churchill's essay remains unparalleled.

[82] Bullough 226–7.

[83] For instance, on the native country of the princess promised to Edward IV, Grafton writes that Warwick went to Spain before he visited the French court, so both More and Hall were right. Grafton, ii. 6, 31, 79–123, 78, 83

[84] More 47. Hall 359. Holinshed 380. *R3*, III. iv. 23. The Folio and Quartos 1 to 5 all have 'a sleeper', which Q6 emends to 'a sleepe', as in More's original.

play is supposed to start: just after Tewkesbury, as the corpse of Henry VI indicates, or just before Edward's death, as in More. We saw earlier how Shakespeare advanced Richard's entrance by several years in Part 2, to show him actively sharing in the family struggle of Part 3, up to the crowning of Edward. At this point, Hall reports an interesting little scene, which Shakespeare uses later. After his victory at Mortimer's Cross, Edward called a great council of lords spiritual and temporal who elected him to the crown. When they came to Baynard's Castle with the news, he alleged his insufficiency for so great a burden, 'yet in conclusion he beynge perswaded by the Archebishop of Cāterbury, the bishop of Excester, and other lordes, thē beyng present, graunted to their peticion, and toke vpō him the charge', probably the model aped by the stage Richard, whereas Edward's accession in *3 Henry VI* is a soldiers' affair devoid of such niceties.[85]

In the play, Richard complains after the overthrow of Lancaster that he is idle and bored by peace. Not so in the sources, where he is kept busy for years with Scottish wars, while his brother the King spends all his time in diplomatic affairs and ineffective traps to catch Richmond, who has taken refuge at the court of Duke Francis in Brittany. Hall proves especially prolix on the subject of relations with France and Burgundy, an area where he can eke out Vergil with Philippe de Commynes, historiographer of the Burgundian court, 'whiche wrote al these doynges in a Chronicle'. Not to be outdone, Holinshed adds two more pages on the solemn transfer of Edward's sister Margaret to the continent for her wedding with Charles the Bold.[86] The triangular diplomatic game leads to a nine-year truce with France, and a corresponding coldness between Edward and his Burgundian brother-in-law. Like his father and his namesake Humphrey of Gloucester before, Richard with a few others thirsty for French blood cried out against the signing of this truce, but Shakespeare saw no need to harp still on that old tune.[87]

The death of Charles the Bold drew many suitors around his heir, the young Mary of Burgundy, including the recently widowed Clarence, whose overreaching ambition may have caused his downfall by making him suspect in his brother Edward's eyes. The true reason for their renewed quarrel remained a conjecture— 'the certayntie therof was hyd, and coulde not truely be disclosed': among the causes rumoured, Hall mentions the hostility of the Queen's Woodville relatives, and 'a folysh Prophesye' saying the name of Edward's successor would begin with a G, which some later thought confirmed, 'when after kyng Edward, Glocester vsurped his kyngdome', but no blame goes to Richard at this point. Why Clarence was 'taken and adiudged for a Traytor', then 'priuely drouned in a butt of Malusey', is left unexplained. He was cast into jail after loud complaints that a servant of his had been unjustly executed, which may have fuelled Stanley's plea for his condemned servant at II. i. Clarence's bid for Burgundy disappears on stage along with

---

[85] Hall 253–4. Holinshed 272. *R3*, III. vii. 94–236. *3H6*, II. vi. 87–99.

[86] Hall 266–9, 278–85, 287–90, 305–17, 322, 324–8, from *Memoirs of Philippe de Commynes*, v. xx. 365–70; vi. viii. 411–13; vi. xii. 428–9. Holinshed 287–8. Commynes's Memoirs, written between 1488 and 1504, were first printed in 1504, and published in an English version by Thomas Danett in 1596.

[87] Hall 314. Holinshed 335. Burgundy is seldom mentioned on stage after the breach of alliance in *1 Henry VI*, apart from scant allusions in Part 3.

his widowhood, but Edward's bitter reaction at his death reflects his words in the chronicle: 'O infortunate brother, for whose lyfe not one creature would make intercession.'[88] His guilty avowal that 'The order was reversed' and Richard's neat retort—'But he (poor man) by your first order died'—echo Hall's opinion that 'although kyng Edward were consentyng to his death and destruccion, yet he much dyd bothe lamente his unfortunate chaunce, and repent hys sodayne execucion'.[89] Clarence left two young children, both of whom were attainted for treason and beheaded under the Tudors. Hall firmly reproves the 'abhominable and detestable treason' of the daughter, Margaret, whom Henry VIII had made Countess of Salisbury, but forgets to say she was 68 when her magnanimous grand-nephew sent her to the block. As for her brother, he had spent fourteen years locked in the Tower before his execution.

After several pages of diplomatic fencing with France, we move to Scotland where Hall sheds a tear on yet another sad tale of treachery between brothers. As Edward with Clarence, so King James of Scotland with Albany: 'what a pernicious serpent, what a venemous toad, & what a pestiferous Scorpion is that deuelishe whelp, priuye enuye', a feeling duly echoed by Holinshed.[90] Appointed Lieutenant General, the young Duke of Gloucester marches on Edinburgh, destroying a few towns on the way, negotiates 'wisely and circumspectly', and regains Berwick. The recovery of this strategic place greatly pleased Edward, 'whiche much cōmended bothe his valiaunt manhode, and also his prudent pollicie', praises neither Vergil nor Holinshed thought fit to report. The Croyland Chronicler dismissed it as a very expensive victory, a view supported by modern historians, who consider the campaign showed no outstanding military talents and brought little profit. The only allusion to this country on stage is in one line where Buckingham records for Richard 'all your victories in Scotland'.[91]

In England, Edward who has had enough of Lewis XI's duplicity decides to fight, a plan warmly approved by his idle nobility, when he suddenly falls grievously ill. He summons the court, delivers a long moral speech on the vanities of this world, without a word suggesting that he is worried about the divisions in his family, and recommends his kingdom to their cares. Edward is not credited with a dying speech in Vergil, but he leaves a will committing the tuition of his children to his brother Richard. In Hall he stresses the need to bring them up in godly knowledge, but entrusts their education, and the governance of the realm during their minority, to no one in particular.

---

[88] Hall 326. At I. iv. 72, Clarence prays God to 'spare my guiltless wife and my poor children', the last of his four lines of repentance in F, absent from Q. Again 'a misguided cut' in Hammond's opinion, 333, but according to Patrick, they were a late addition to the F text.

[89] *R3*, II. i. 88–9, 128–36. Hall 326.

[90] Hall 338. Holinshed 355.

[91] According to Croyland, 481, 'King Edward was vexed at this frivolous outlay of so much money, although the recovery of Berwick above-mentioned in some degree alleviated his sorrow.' Vergil 170. Hall 335–7. Holinshed 350–1. *R3*, III. vii. 15. See Charles Ross, *Richard III* (London, 1981) 47.

More on Richard

After twenty-two years of reign 'more in trouble then perfecte quietnes', Hall writes, Edward 'left his realme, of all thynges riche and abundaunt' although he had found it almost empty both of men and money. Now begins '*The Pitifull Life of Kyng Edward The. V.*' with a marginal note stating that what follows was written by Sir Thomas More.[92] A valuable document on how chroniclers understood quotation, for it is indeed all More and yet nothing like More. Rastell had good reason to complain at the opening of his own version that More's work as printed in Hardyng's and Hall's chronicles was 'very muche corrupte in many places, sometyme hauyng lesse, and sometime hauing more, and altered in wordes and whole sentences: muche varying fro the copie of his own hand'.[93]

Hall could be said to handle his source fairly, in so far as he never tries to subvert More's meaning or adapt it to his earlier report on Richard. He does not seem to mind going through the same episodes again, and makes no attempt to smooth out the discordances.[94] As to the form and style, he cannot leave well alone, but makes many pinpoint changes, substituting more banal terms for More's learned or rare ones, spelling out his ironical innuendoes, repeating, expanding, or stressing for better clarity. Extra sentences are added to recall past events, or the identities of characters casually referred to by More as 'all', 'the fore remembred lordes', 'a knight', 'another lorde'. Where More evokes Richard's unattractive face 'suche as is in states called warlye, in other menne otherwise', Hall obligingly translates 'such as in estates is called a warlike visage, and emonge commen persones a crabbed face'.[95] Here as in the rest of his narrative, his commonest trick is to double words, often without noticeable gain. Thus malice cannot be just 'repressed', it has to be 'repressed and put vnder'; goods simply 'pilled' become 'plucked and pilled', 'procure' is expanded to 'procure and sette furthe', 'his abominable dede' to 'his abhominable murther and execrable tyrannye', 'escape his handes' to 'auoyd his handes or escape his power'.[96] Some of these alterations are deliberate, others are probably unintentional, like 'enuious scorne' for 'enemious', 'end his cause' instead of 'amend' it, while Richard 'thought to be greued' where 'he ought' to be, or 'his body priuely feinted' instead of being 'priuily fenced', and Buckingham 'a litle rounded' where in More he simply 'rouned'.[97]

One at least of these emendations found its way into the play, and takes us as close as we can come, perhaps, to its linguistic alchemy. A rare 'authorial' stage direction signals Richard and Buckingham's entrance 'in rotten Armour, maruellous ill-fauoured'. More had dressed them in 'old il faring briginders', which Hall,

[92] Hall 341, 342.

[93] More 2. Just how corrupt, modern editors seem unaware when they read More in Hall's 'garbled' text, and impute to him phrases he never wrote. Jowett's notes and appendix are a mixture of Hall/More and Holinshed/More. Lull refers Hall's historical material to Holinshed, which is also confusing.

[94] One paragraph on the results of Warwick's anger, from More 66, is omitted by Hall 367 and reinserted by Holinshed 388–9.

[95] More 65, 57, 51, 36, 7. Hall 367, 364, 361, 356, 343.

[96] More 79, 69, 80, 87, 90. Hall 373, 369, 374, 379, 382.

[97] Hall 361, 377, 373, 379, 373. More 50, 83, 78, 87, 79

following Grafton, rewrites as 'olde euill fauored brigranders'. We saw above that the phrase 'euill fauored' occurs also in Golding's Ovid, one of Shakespeare's favourite books, a coincidence which suggested the image of Richard as an 'undigested lump' or 'unlicked bear whelp'. Close reading here brings its own rare reward, as it enables us to retrace the genetics of a poet's creation: an unpredictable variety of fragments that hit his fancy find themselves absorbed, crystallized, and reset into an original portmanteau word. The salt of More's phrase comes from the fact that it is applied not to a veteran soldier but to his tired equipment, where 'ill' carries the hint of a double or treble meaning, in poor condition, ill-tempered, with evil intent. Of these, Hall's misreading stresses the third, and accentuates the anthropomorphic flavour of the image.[98] Shakespeare conflates the two expressions, dismisses the unfamiliar brigander, which has disappeared from usage since, divides contents from containers, coins a new phrase and redirects it towards the men, then gathers the dregs to qualify their armours, whose 'rotten' attribute reverberates on them and adds pungency to their ugly looks. Marvellous indeed, thus to costume his characters afresh 'With odd old ends stol'n forth of holy writ'.

To his credit, Hall also corrects a few minor slips, overdoing it as we saw in the case of Anthony Woodville, but restoring Buckingham and Hastings to their proper names, Henry and William, where More mistakenly calls them 'Edward' and 'Richard'. Holinshed who keeps close to More manages a fifty-fifty settlement here with 'Edward duke of Buckingham, and William lord Hastings.[99] Nor is Hall responsible for the intrusion of 'Sir Richard Grey' in the dialogue, for he gives the correct name of Lady Grey's first husband, John. The two doctors in divinity, 'Iohn Shaa clerke brother to the Maier, & freer Penker' in More, come to some harm: Hall correctly emends John into Ralph Shaa but mars his record with Pynkie or Pynkye, Holinshed copies More with the unemended Iohn Shaw and Penker, Shakespeare's Folio has Doctor Shaw and Friar Peuker, on a rough estimate closest to Holin-shed—an emblem of their special brand of intertextuality.[100]

Apart from his minute rewriting, Hall interferes with the narrative sequence at several points. He skips More's opening pages on Edward's reign and the York family, goes straight to his main theme, the destruction of his heirs by their un-natural uncle, draws in the memorable portrait of Richard, up to the suggestion that he had long hoped for the crown and may have helped Clarence to his death, then launches into More's version of Edward's dying speech, with the added comment that his last sickness 'continued longer then false and fantasticall tales haue vntruely and falsely surmised'. This speech, much shorter than Hall's first version, is wholly spent on healing the breach between the Queen's and the King's relatives, all in vain, as in the play.[101] Hall now inserts the various fragments he had omitted,

---

[98] Hall 362. More 52. *R3*, SD III. v. 1, from F. Q simply has 'in armour'.

[99] More 10, 15. Hall 344, 348 corrects both names. Holinshed 366 gets one name right and one wrong. On the titles of Anthony Woodville, Holinshed 365 follows More 14, not Hall 347.

[100] More 58. Hall 365. Holinshed 386. *R3*, III. v. 103–5. Q escapes the dilemma by omitting these three lines.

[101] Hall 343–5. More 11–3. *R3*, II. i.

More's opening pages on the York family, the fate of the young princes, an earlier anecdote testifying to Richard's hidden designs, plus a retrospective passage moved up from More's last pages on his pact with Buckingham, and returns to More's sequence to meet the young King at Ludlow. This he follows straightforwardly, word for word or with only minor variants and a few interpolations, up to Richard's acceptance of the crown.[102] It is here that Rastell inserts his longest extract from the Latin *Historia*, on Richard's deal with Buckingham, where More's English version reports their complicity later, when it comes to an end with Buckingham's rebellion. It seems Hall was not satisfied either with this sequence, for he introduces Buckingham early as Richard's accomplice, before their coup at Ludlow, by moving up More's paragraph, where Rastell used the Latin extract, presumably for the same reason. Shakespeare's Richard promises the earldom of Hereford to Buckingham while preparing the trap for Hastings, as in Rastell's rearrangement, perhaps via Holinshed.[103]

The chroniclers differ on the location of the separate councils set up by Richard. In Hall, the loyalists meet at Baynard's Castle—the York residence in London—while Richard's friends conspire at Crosby Place. The separate councils are mentioned several times in the play, Hastings means to be 'at the one' while his friend Catesby will sit 'at the other', then he is summoned 'to the Tower | To sit about the coronation', while Catesby must report 'ere we sleep' to Richard and Buckingham at Crosby House.[104] The first mention of Baynard's Castle comes later, when Buckingham is told to bring the Lord Mayor there. The Mayor and his aldermen dutifully offer the crown to the Protector, who treats them to a comedy of denial along the lines rehearsed by Edward. After much entreaty, 'At the last he came out of his chambre, and yet not doune to theim, but in a galary ouer them' as in More. Here Hall adds a detail, 'with a bishop on euery hand of him', found in Grafton, which inspires the tableau on stage: '*Enter Richard aloft, between two Bishops.*' Shakespeare's contribution is the prayer book in his hand, signalled by Buckingham in F, which puts the final touch on the pose, a parodic parallel to the saintly Henry VI.[105]

The execution of the Queen's friends at Pomfret is devised to take place at the same time as Hastings'. Where More simply calls them 'the fore remembered lordes and knightes', Hall gives the full list, 'the earle Ryuers and the lorde Richarde the quenes sonne, syr Thomas Vaughan and sir Richard Haute', of which only the first three appear on stage.[106] They were not allowed to speak, More writes, but hastily beheaded, for fear they would move men to pity them and hate the Protector. Sir

---

[102] Hall's pages 342–7 are taken from More's 6–13, 3–6, fragments of 9, 10, 88; Hall 347–74, from More 14–81.

[103] More 41–4 and 81–2. Holinshed 378, 403. Hall 347, 381–2. Vergil 193 mentions the promise only when Buckingham's reminder of it infuriates Richard, who thought the matter forgotten. *R3*, III. i. 198–200.

[104] III. ii. 21–2,III. i. 174–5, 190–2, at Crosby House in F, Crosby Place in Q.

[105] Hall 372. *R3*, III. vii. 93, 97–8. Jowett keeps the prayer book, which is not in Q, with a note asserting that the bishops come 'from More (in Hall but not Holinshed)', 272.

[106] More 57. Hall 364. *R3*, III. iii.

Thomas Vaughan is nevertheless allowed by Hall a dying speech, where he suddenly understands that the prophecy about G means Gloucester, not George Clarence,
and appeals to the high tribunal of God. His last words 'I dye in right, beware you
dye not in wrong' inspire his one line on stage in the F text: 'You live that shall cry
woe for this hereafter', while a Ratcliffe less rough than his source model allows
them all to speak before he orders them to 'Make haste', the leitmotiv of Richard's
clique in both chronicle and play.[107] The prophecy which plays an important part in
the *Mirror's* 'Tragedie of Clarence' is reported at the time of his death by Vergil,
Hall, and Holinshed, Hall being the only one to recall it at Pomfret.

The rest of Hall's additions do not noticeably affect the play. One at least would
please mystery lovers: in Buckingham's speech to the Mayor, the list of Edward's
faults includes the summary beheading of one Burdet, on which Hall sheds some
little light: Edward was thrown in a rage because this merchant said his son would
inherit the Crown, meaning his own alehouse. In fact this Burdet was no other than
Clarence's unnamed servant, who, being considered responsible for treasonable
rhymes about the G prophecy, was charged with sorcery, and executed. This was the
prelude to Clarence's no less mysterious arrest and murder, but Hall does not
connect the two cases.[108] He has a few other additional details like the fact that
Hastings had lain all night with Shore's wife on the eve of his death, or the list of
those arrested with him. The anonymous knight who escorted Hastings to the
council, and 'the other lord' present at the sanctuary episode in More's text, are
properly identified: one is Thomas Howard, whose ironical 'you haue no nede of a
prist yet' is transferred on stage to Buckingham;[109] the other, Lord Howard, who
argues with Queen Elizabeth in sanctuary, has no voice on stage where the debate is
not represented.[110]

Crown...

Hall begins 'The Tragical Doynges of Kyng Richard the Thirde' with an original
preamble explaining how he abhors to write this miserable story, but feels in duty
bound to do it as a warning to expel all sin and mischief.[111] Here Rastell places his
third extract from the Latin: the Protector devised solemnities to place his reign
under the sign of the law, and win the approval of his subjects with a show of
clemency, 'Whiche thyng the common people reioysed at and praised, but wise
men tooke it for a vanitye.' After his mock election, Richard is crowned on 6 July
'with the selfe same prouision that was appointed for the Coronacion of his
nephew'. More's Latin history ends there.[112] Hall does not have the Latin passage,

---

[107] *R3*, III. iii. 6. In Q, Vaughan is present but mute. Vergil 167. Hall 326. Holinshed 346. Jowett, n. 151,
again mistakes Hall for More, who never mentions the prophecy or Vaughan's dying words.

[108] Hall 326, 369. *Third Continuation of the History of Croyland*, 478–9 tells the full story of Burdet, in
which Richard is clearly not involved. The historians set on rehabilitating him make Clarence's plotting
a strong point of their defence.

[109] 'Your honour hath no shriving work in hand', III. ii. 115. More 51. Hall 361.

[110] More 36. Hall 356.

[111] Hall 374.

[112] More 82.

but he amply makes up for it by a detailed account of the coronation. Vergil simply reports that having summoned 5,000 men from the North, Richard was 'adornyd with the regall diademe, togethyr with Anne his wyfe, the people rather not repyning for feare than allowing therof', with this laconic and consistent comment: 'Thus Richerd, without assent of the commonaltie, by might and will of certane noblemen of his faction, enjoyed the realm, contrary to the law of God and man.'[113]

Instead of paying heed to this or More's drier tales, Hall follows Grafton's *Continuation*, which gives the first published account of the ceremonies. Richard's 5,000 ride in all dirty from the North. At the beginning of the feast, the monks sing Te Deum 'with a faint courage', but soon everyone gets into the spirit of the occasion. The full array of prelates and peers, all splendidly dressed, take their place in the procession, from Stanley to the Countess of Richmond who bears the Queen's train. After the holy rites, the banquet proceeds without any false note until dark night, including the moment when the King's champion makes the traditional proclamation, offering to fight whoever shall claim Richard is not lawfully king, 'and threwe downe his gauntlet: and then al the hal cried kynge Richarde'.[114] The feast continued late into the summer night by the light of wax torches, 'probably the best argument that the affair was a success', as modern historians observe.[115] Apparently no one defied the champion and a good time was had by all, in contrast with Hall's earlier claims, on the faith of More, that the people could not hide their grief at Richard's election and had 'to turne their face to the wall, while the doloure of their heart braste oute at theyr eyen'.[116]

The newly crowned Richard sent an embassy to France, hoping to obtain the tribute that was paid to Edward, 'but the Frenche kyng so abhorred hym and his crueltie, that he would neither se nor heare his Ambassadors'. Having picked this plum from the gossipy Commynes, Hall now returns to More, for Richard's murder of the young Princes.[117] To his source he adds the tale that their coffin was immersed in the Black Deeps at the mouth of the Thames, by a priest who died shortly after without disclosing the place; Dighton, one of the murderers, who was still alive when More wrote, died since at Calais in great misery.[118] Here, a marginal note signals the end of the *History*, although More has another six pages on Buckingham's conspiracy that Hall will silently use in due time.

Hall repeats More's view of Richard's motive, 'that his nephewes liuynge, men woulde not recon that he coulde haue righte to the realme', but he must have sensed a discrepancy with More's earlier statement that 'some remain yet in doubt whether

[113] Vergil 187.

[114] Hall 376. Holinshed 400. Unlike his usual practice, Fabyan makes but a brief note of the ceremony in *The Great Chronicle of London*, ed. A. H. Thomas and I. D. Thornley (London, 1938), 232. The only extant account of Richard's coronation is from a roll in handwriting nearly contemporary with the events, with which Grafton's and Hall's narratives agree in substance, in Samuel Bentley (ed.), *Excerpta historica or Illustrations of English History* (London, 1831), 379–84.

[115] A. F. Sutton and P. W. Hammond (eds.), *The Coronation of Richard III: The Extant Documents* (Gloucester, 1983), 288.

[116] More 77. Hall 372.

[117] Hall 377. Commynes, VI. viii. 413–15.

[118] Hall 379, from More 87, with minor additions from Vergil 226.

they were in his days destroyed or not': there was no great point in keeping the children's death secret if it was done to prevent any claim to the crown on their behalf. So he adopts Vergil's version, that the King spread a rumour of their sudden death, only to fall into another difficulty. Having portrayed—from More—a restless Richard, haunted by fearful dreams, Hall writes that he thought himself 'well releuyd bothe of feare and thought' by this crime. The next three pages, borrowed from Vergil, report the loud indignation of the whole realm at the murder of these innocent creatures, followed by Richard's attempt to appease riots in the North with a solemn procession through the city of York. All this is jumbled so in Hall's narrative that the rioting seems part of a nationwide protest, but it is clear from Vergil, who does not mention any riots, that the procession was part of the coronation feasts and had nothing to do with the children's murder. Several of Hall's points serve in the play, like the chorus of laments for the 'innocent babes', the Queen's kneeling down, 'when she sawe no hope of reuengynge otherwyse', to call on God as her only avenger as Elizabeth and Margaret do on stage, while traces of her violent grief—'her fayre here she tare and pulled in peces & being ouercome with sorowe and pensiuenes rather desyred death then life'—are transferred to her black despair at Edward's demise.[119]

Once rid of his nephews, Richard determines to remove the note of infamy from his name. Trusting to obtain God's forgiveness, 'he shewed hymselfe more iuste, more meker, more familiar, more liberall (especially amongest the poore people) then before he had accustomed to do'. But the many public and private good works he undertook were cut short by his death. Besides, they were motivated by fear more than justice, and soon waxed cold in the face of trouble. This, a close paraphrase of Vergil, is completely at odds with what Hall had written earlier, following More, that 'throughe all the tyme of his vsurped reigne, neuer ceased there cruell murther, death and slaughter, till his awne destruccion ended it'.[120] The ways of Vergil and More meet again when trouble begins, with Buckingham's disaffection, at which point Hall discreetly returns to More and follows him through the last pages of the *History*. This leads him to repeat how the accomplices met at Northampton when Edward died, and how they continued together till Richard was crowned King.[121] The enrolment of Buckingham in Morton's plans for England occupies the rest of More's *History*, which ends abruptly on Morton's politic wish that the King had some of the virtues needed to rule the realm 'as our lorde hath planted in the parsone of youre grace'.

Hall develops Morton's overture into five solid pages of cautious conversation between the two conspirators—a fascinating exercise. As in those games where an appropriate conclusion must be found to the opening paragraphs of a tale, the challenge here is to supply logical steps from the inception, suggesting that Buckingham himself deserves the crown, to its actual conclusion—he will support

---

[119] Cf. *R3*, IV. iv. 9–34; I. iii. 180–212; II. ii. 34–46. Vergil 188–91. Hall 379–81. More and Holinshed are silent on these counts.

[120] Hall 377, an exact copy of More 82, with the addition of two words, 'vsurped' and 'murther'.

[121] Hall 347, 381–2. Vergil 174, 192–3. More 87–8.

Richmond's claim. More gave up, but Hall struggles bravely through the logical deadlocks. Under Morton's crafty guidance, the Duke draws up the list of Richard's faults, his own dynastic titles, the scruples which led him to renounce them, and the happy notion to end all civil wars by matching Richmond and Elizabeth, if their mothers agree, 'by the whiche mariage bothe the houses of Yorke and Lancaster maye be obteyned and vnite in one, to the clere stablyshement of the title to the crowne of this noble realme'.[122] Incidentally, the story that Richard went back on his gift of the Hereford lands is untrue: Buckingham did obtain the coveted Bohun inheritance, and no one quite knows why he rebelled.[123] Hall's attempt to elucidate Buckingham's motives leaves this and many other cruces unsolved, for instance how Richmond could bypass the princes' rights while marrying their sister, unless their deaths were officially confirmed. Nor does it make clear how the intrigues that flare up all at once in various parts of Europe are connected with the oath taken at Rennes by the Earl to marry Elizabeth. And least of all why Buckingham renounced his own dynastic rights to support Richmond's.

Vergil, from whom Hall borrows the matter of this programme, explains Buckingham's titles to the Hereford inheritance via his ancestor Thomas of Woodstock, without entering into the rival claims of their houses; his employment, like More's, in the Tudors' service may well account for his reticences. Hall meets the challenge head on, but tackles the question of Buckingham's title via other branches of his family tree, namely Edmund Somerset, which place him respectfully below Richmond and avoid all mention of Woodstock. As a result of this manipulation, Buckingham presents his own claim by right of his mother Margaret Beaufort, not a very convincing one, where he stands in fact as in Vergil's genealogy much closer than Richmond to the common ancestor Edward III, as the direct issue of Woodstock. Hall's guiding theme, the union of the two houses, helps him to cover up this delicate matter, and provides the main point of Richmond's speech at the end of the play, while Morton's share in the scheme has disappeared entirely.

The end of Richard's reign is mostly taken up by Scottish affairs and the hunt for Richmond. Shakespeare's dramatic plot makes a strict selection in what Hall needs another thirty pages to unfold, three times as much as Vergil, his main source here. Richard appears increasingly sombre as the play rushes headlong towards his doom and the forces gathering against him gain strength. In the chronicles, his mood shifts from groundless fears to groundless security, depending on the news brought from France by his spies: after doubting even his own people, 'continually vexed, tossed and vnquyeted with feare of the retourne of the erle of Richemond', he rejoiced to hear of Richmond's poor success at the French court, Hall tells us, as he 'thought hymselfe neuer so surely delyuered of all feare and dreadfull ymaginacions, so that he neded nowe no more once for that cause eyther to wake or breake his golden slepe'. His relief was such that he called his ships home. Vergil more

---

[122] Hall 389.

[123] Horrox, *Richard III*, 164 rejects as unfounded Vergil's explanation, that Richard saw him as a 'Lancastrian' rival to the throne.

soberly paints him as 'soomwhat easyd of his griefe' and growing careless, though not to the point of recovering his golden sleep.[124]

The chroniclers report at varying lengths the plots and uprisings in favour of Henry Tudor, all of which are glanced at or ignored in the play. The marriage negotiations between Queen Elizabeth and the Countess of Richmond leave no other trace on stage than the brief appearance of their go-between, Sir Christopher Urswick. Richard's treaty with Scotland, Richmond's waverings, the execution of his confederates in London, the betrayal of Buckingham by an old retainer, Humphrey Banister, Collingbourne's offensive rhyme and his beheading, disappear completely. Buckingham confessed willingly, Vergil reports, hoping that he would be allowed to speak with Richard, but he was beheaded after his confession. Hall adds the unwarranted hypothesis that he hoped to gain admittance either to sue for grace or to stick Richard with a dagger, but again the play stresses the speedy dispatch without using Hall's ornaments.[125]

... and punishment

Morton's escape and his activities abroad, the armed rebellion in various parts of England, Buckingham's failed attempt, the scattering of Richmond's navy, and his later invasion are summed up in a few lines of dialogue. The longest exchanges in the play at this point are moved by more intimate feelings. One, Margaret's cursing lessons to the sorrowful women, has no direct basis in history. Margaret had left England, Elizabeth was still locked up in sanctuary, and the Duchess of York is only heard once in the chronicles, very loudly so, at the time of her eldest son's marriage to a low-born bride. The other scene, Richard's seduction of Queen Elizabeth, is documented in the sources. To thwart Richmond's marriage plans, Richard imagined that 'yf it shoulde happen quene Anne his wife to departe oute of this presente worlde', then he could marry his niece himself, but first he must be reconciled to her mother. Like all the narrative episodes untouched by More, what Hall offers here is taken straight from Vergil, down to his opening comment, 'Let him take the bul that stale away yᵉ calfe.'[126] Richard does not court the Queen himself as in the play, he sends messengers who ply her with so many large promises that she agrees to deliver her daughters into his hands and advise her son to forsake Richmond. In Vergil, the messengers are just 'grave men' who soon mollify her. Hall's messengers, 'beynge men bothe of wit and grauitie', are rather more wordy in arguing the case, and cause a more emotional response from the Queen, as well as louder exclamations from the narrator, with little more matter to convey all round. Hall's view that she was 'blynded by auaricious affeccion and seduced by flatterynge wordes' when she sent her five daughters as lambs to the ravenous wolf contribute to Richard's appeals to her vanity and greed; the injuries she had suffered, the promises she now forgets, lend fuel to her fire of rebukes on stage.

---

[124] Hall 402, 408, from Vergil 205, 213–14.
[125] Vergil 201. Hall 295.
[126] Hall 406. Cf. Vergil 209, 'He will lyft up an oxe that hath caryed a calfe.'

Richard's scornful judgement, 'Relenting fool and shallow, changing woman!' directly echoes Hall's notion that she had been led 'into a fooles paradise', and the certainty of both chroniclers that she was indeed reconciled to his plan. Her easy surrender confirms their opinion of women, from Vergil's one-liner, 'so mutable is that sex', to Hall's inflated three, 'Surely the inconstancie of this woman were muche to be merueled at, yf all women had bene founde constante, but let men speake, yet wemen of the verie bonde of nature will folowe their awne kynde,' which Holinshed copies to the last word, substituting 'sex' for 'kynde'. At least, Shakespeare's Richard does not cast aspersions on the whole gender.[127]

There remains to dispose of Anne. Hall's Richard, who has been posing as a righteous man, fears that by her sudden death 'he should lese the good and credible opinion which the people had of him', or rather, as Vergil more finely puts it, 'the good opynyon which he belevyd the people had conceavyd uppon him'.[128] He complains of his wife's sterility, in the hopes that hearing of this grudge she will not live long, then spreads rumours of her death. When she comes to him in tears asking why he wants her dead, he comforts her with many kind, deceitful words, but she dies a few days later, of sorrow, or more likely of poison according to Hall (not Vergil). There is no such confrontation in the play, where speed is of the essence. Richard does not waste time inventing devious means to be rid of her. He has it rumoured that she is sick, before not after planning his next nuptials, and by the next scene she has left this world noiselessly.[129] As to his complaints over her sterility, the play having suppressed the existence of their only child, they appear obliquely in her own curse on Richard's issue, and her belated realization it was a self-curse.

In the narrative, Richard is now free to court his niece, but he soon abandons his wedding plans as everyone, beginning with the maiden, is revolted by the prospect, and he has other more pressing worries. Many of his nobles sail to Richmond, causing him to distrust all around him, especially some 600 of them, the Stanley brothers in particular, and worst of all Thomas, who is married to Richmond's mother. This is when he decides to keep Lord Stanley's son George as hostage. In fact, Richmond's affairs were not as prosperous as they sound in the play. Richard, who was informed of his setbacks, 'beganne to be somewhat more merier & toke lesse thought & care for outwarde enemies then he was woont to do', else he might have avoided his destiny. Such is the force of divine justice, Hall after Vergil exclaims, that a man grows more improvident when he is nearest punishment.[130] On stage, events move too fast to allow him any respite, but in the sources Richmond is nowhere near the end of his struggles. He is kept waiting endlessly at the French court, while many of his friends begin to lose heart. Dorset, who secretly escapes to England, enticed by his mother and Richard's promises, is caught and persuasively brought back, but Richmond fears he may lose all by procrastination.

---

[127] Hall 406. Vergil 210. Holinshed 430. *R3*, IV. iv. 436.
[128] Hall 407. Vergil 211.
[129] IV. ii. 51–8; IV. iii. 39.
[130] Hall 409. Vergil 214.

Queen Elizabeth had promised him her eldest daughter's hand or, in case of her death, her younger one's. Now that they are both in Richard's hands, Richmond believes that 'by no possibilite he might attayne the mariage of any of kynge Edwardes daughters, which was the strongest foūdacion of his buyldyng', and promises to marry Herbert's sister in return for help from his Welshmen. The thought that the York marriage is his strongest asset is Hall's, not Vergil's, just as it is Hall who stresses the union of the two houses in Buckingham's speech to Morton. In the play, the only trace of Herbert's effective role is his one line at Bosworth.[131]

After a devout prayer for prosperous wind, Richmond took the plunge at last, and all texts meet with news of his safe landing at Milford Haven.[132] On stage, Catesby delivers the news in one breath with that of Buckingham's arrest, which actually occurred nearly two years earlier, at the time of Richmond's first failed attempt to cross. In the next scene the Earl is somewhere in Wales, 'at Pembroke, or at Ha'rfordwest', and when we first see him, just after Buckingham's execution, he has reached 'the bowels of the land' unimpeded, with 'Oxford, Blunt, Herbert and others'. All are fully confident of success, since Richard 'hath no friends, but what are friends for fear', a point repeatedly stressed in the sources.[133] His march is not quite so smooth in the chronicles, for after a joyful welcome on landing, he is kept some time in 'timerous doubt' by a succession of news, alarms, and alarming rumours of enemy troops on their way to fight him. Support comes to him piece-meal, far from the overwhelming tidal wave evoked in the play. He is joined by diverse noblemen 'whiche inwardely hated kynge Richard worsse then a toade or a serpent', but avoided by Stanley, who fears for his son. The news that he has reached Shrewsbury without hindrance sends Richard into a foul rage. Still, Richmond drags pensively behind his own army, even loses it in the dark one night, and pre-tends the next day it was done on purpose to meet secret allies. The fact that Stanley is keeping a safe distance worries him much more than his stage equivalent, as he is not at all sure which side his stepfather will take. When he does at last meet the Stanleys, he regains heart but is still far from confident. Richard's troops more than double his. Treble, Richard declares on stage, but if both men include Stanley's 3,000 in their reckoning, their figures more or less tally with the chroniclers'.[134]

However, Henry has nothing to fear, for all is ordained: Richard 'was appoynted nowe to finyshe his last laboure by the very deuyne iustice and prouidence of God, which called him to condigne punyshemente for his scelerate merites and myscheueous desertes'.[135] Fame reports that the King had a terrible dream on the

---

[131] Hall 410. *R3*, v. ii. 19. In Q, he is never present on stage. Both F and Q inform us that 'Sir Walter Herbert, a renowned soldier' has joined Richmond. For his possible connection with Pembroke's Men, see Jowett 5–6.

[132] Vergil 216. Hall 410. Holinshed 434. *R3*, IV. iv. 541–2.

[133] IV. v. 10; v. ii. 3–4, 20. Richmond's allies are named in the Folio, but in the Q SD they are just '*lords*'; all but Oxford are identified in the next scene. Vergil 220, 223, 224. Hall 416, 417, 419. Holinshed 441, 442, 445.

[134] Hall 411–14. Vergil 223. Holinshed 439. *R3*, v. iii. 10–11.

[135] Hall 413–14. There is no equivalent here in Vergil, who expresses a constant belief in providential justice at other points.

night before the battle, 'ymages lyke terrible deuelles whiche pulled and haled hym', making him lose his customary 'alacrite and myrth of mynde and of countenance' to such an extent that he began to doubt the outcome of the battle. This was no dream, the chroniclers assert, but his guilty conscience, which is wont to show us all our sins on the last day of our life so that we may leave it penitently. On stage, these sins 'Throng all to th'bar', in the tribunal of Richard's tortured mind.[136] In Hall's version, the two armies were lying close to each other: Richmond 'pitchid his feld iuste by yᵉ cāp of his enemies, & there he lodged yᵗ night', but the sources do not tell us how he slept. It remained for Shakespeare to put a human name on these 'terrible deuelles' and have them visit both leaders' tents.

It is Hall, followed by Holinshed, who outlines the symmetries so pointedly stressed in the play, first with parallel phrases to depict Richard and Richmond planting their camps near to each other in 'a place mete for twoo battayles to encountre', and after the fateful night, with symmetrical speeches identified in marginal notes as 'The oraciō of kyng Richard the. iii.' and 'The oraciō of Kyng Henry the. vii.' In Vergil's account, Richard arrived first at Bosworth, and 'ther, pightching his tentes, refresshyd his soldiers that night from ther travale, and with many woords exhortyd them to the fyght to coome', then retired for a night of horrible dreams, and the next morning disposed his troops in order of battle. Only then does Vergil mention Richmond, who 'encampyd himself nighe his enemyes, wher he restyd all night' after which he commands the soldiers to arm themselves, but harangues them no further. His first concern is with Lord Stanley, who answers the Earl's summons with a promise he will come in his own good time, and waits with his band midway between the two armies. 'No lyttle vexyd', but compelled by necessity, Richmond disposes his vanguard under the command of Oxford, leaving a marsh to be used as a fortress on his right hand, in order to have the sun behind his back—'and in the face of his enemies', Hall adds, though in the play it refuses to shine for Richard. The precise ordering on stage of the King's battle, behind a very long vanguard, horse and foot, led by Norfolk and Surrey, conforms exactly to Hall, where Vergil mentions only Norfolk.[137]

The orations devised by Hall contribute several items apart from their formal symmetry, though they are delivered in reverse order on stage. First Hall craftily makes Richard confess his own guilt, thus strengthening his rival's case. The King begs his army to forget a long list of all his past crimes, pleading he has lived in good amity with his subjects ever since. The crown that he got by chance, he has kept by wit and policy, and will defend by force, with their help. For the devil has entered the heart of an unknown Welshman, son of an unknown father, who comes with an army of beggarly Britons and faint-hearted Frenchmen to destroy them, their wives and children. There is no call for fear, however, Richmond is but a milksop, his soldiers are all 'effeminate & lasciuious people' like those their ancestors used to beat. The renegades will return to their anointed King when they see his banner unfurled. He will this day 'triūphe by glorious victorie, or suffer death for immortal

---

[136] Hall 414, from Vergil 222. Holinshed 438. *R3*, v. iii. 202.
[137] Hall 414–18. Holinshed 439–43. Vergil 221–3. *R3*, v. iii. 278–89, 295–302.

fame'.[138] Onward, by St George. Shakespeare wisely ignores Richard's ill-timed confession, to play up the nationalistic strains and nostalgia of chivalrous feats against the paltry Welshman and his imported scum of Bretons.

This speech did not greatly advance Richard's cause, according to Hall, for those present 'kissed thē openly, whome they inwardly hated', and betrayed him as he had betrayed his nephews. Here Holinshed further insists that the King could not stand long without the love of his subjects, 'whose harts fell from him as isicles from a penthouse in a sunnie daie'. Meanwhile Richmond mounts on a hill for all to see him, not very tall but so well formed by nature 'that he semed more an angelical creature then a terrestriall personage', hair like burning gold, eyes grey and shining, yet of such sobriety 'that it could neuer be iudged whyther he were more dull then quicke in speakynge'—Hall's unique blend of hagiography and realism.

The Earl's oration stresses the justice of his cause against the usurper of his right-ful inheritance and theirs. God will not let them be vanquished by those who do not fear his laws, 'for what can be a more honest, goodly or Godly quarell then to fight agaynste a Capitayne, beynge an homicide and murderer of hys awne bloude and progenye?' The good are appointed to suppress tyrants, and what worse tyrant was there ever than this one? Richmond goes on to rehearse all Richard's crimes, equat-ing him with both Tarquin and Nero, only worse. Another powerful argument is that if they win, 'yᵉ hole riche realme of England with the lordes and rulers of the same shall be oures, the profit shall be oures and the honour shall be oures. Therfore labour for your gayne and swet for your right.' He makes a similar promise in the dialogue, 'Your country's fat shall pay your pains the hire.' Shakespeare retains from this harangue the assurance they are God's soldiers fighting God's enemy, and the word 'homicide', as he kept Richard's insult, 'milksop'.[139]

The phases of the action are fairly similar in all the narratives, Hall's being as usual more verbose than Vergil's, and Holinshed closely holding to Hall. In the field, the whole affair lasted approximately two hours. On stage it takes up thirteen lines, ending with the second most famous one of the entire canon, and a dumb show. In both cases, the war is over as soon as Richard falls. Our three accounts agree that he could have saved himself by flight, but he answered that he would this day make an end of all battles or of his life. Shakespeare does not enter into details of the fighting beyond the usual alarums and excursions, calls for rescue, and report of Richard's 'wonders', which lead up to the decisive duel: 'Seeking for Richmond in the throat of death', he has already killed five men looking like him when they come face to face.

In Hall, when Richmond saw Richard running towards him 'like a hungery lion', he 'gladly proferred to encountre with him body to body and man to man', where Vergil more soberly writes that Henry 'perceavyd king Richerd coome upon him', and 'receavyd him with great corage'. However the final confrontation, in all three chronicles, is not exactly a duel: both leaders fight among their troops, Richmond keeps Richard at sword's point longer than anyone expected, but his companions

---

[138] Hall 414–16. Holinshed 439–41. *R3*, v. iii. 316–43.
[139] Hall 416–18. Holinshed 441–3. *R3*, v. iii. 259, 247, 327.

are losing hope, when William Stanley comes to their rescue with 3,000 soldiers who drive back Richard's men, 'and he him selfe manfully fyghtynge in the mydell of his enemies was slayne'.[140]

In this last episode, as often before, Hall is carried away by his taste for rhetorical embellishments. Among other anomalies, Richard's soldiers who would rather have him lose than win, 'fought very faintlye or stode stil', but a little further 'the two forwardes thus mortallye fought, eche entendyng to vanquishe and conuince ye other', where in Vergil many 'fowght faintly', although the battle continued 'hote on both sydes betwixt the vanwardes'. Nearer to the play, Hall quotes the rhyme warning 'Iack of Norffolke' his master is 'bought and solde'. Lord Stanley's part is amplified, at the price of a few discrepancies. After repeatedly saying Stanley dare not move on account of his son, Hall improves on Vergil by having him join in when the vanguards come to handstrokes, and lend effective aid to Oxford; when the battle is over, it is he who takes Richard's crown from among the spoils and puts it upon the Earl's head. Shakespeare's Stanley claims he plucked it off from Richard's dead temples.[141]

It is Hall who adds the story of how George, Lord Strange, escaped death. On arrival at Bosworth, Richard ordered Stanley to come with his company, swearing to have his son beheaded before dinner if he refused. Stanley sent an answer that 'yf the kynge dyd so, he had more sonnes a lyue, and as to come to hym, he was not then so determined', which Shakespeare mends to a simple denial, while the rest of his scene follows the chronicle. Richard immediately gave command to execute his son, but as the two armies were in sight of each other, the King's counsellors persuaded him to delay the execution. In the play, as in the narrative, the good news is deferred till after the fight, but it is Richmond himself who thoughtfully enquires after young George.[142] He also asks for a list of those slain, which is drawn from Hall's enumeration. His order to give them a decent burial glosses over the indignities inflicted on Richard's corpse, and signals a return to proper decorum: the desecration of dead bodies had been an important fact of war since Wakefield, when Margaret had the heads of her Yorkist enemies planted on pikes overlooking York town.

The main features of Richard's funeral portrait, the way he used to bite his lower lip, or half unsheathe a dagger he always wore, common to all three chroniclers, have already served in the course of the dialogue. They also double in part those given earlier, from More's opening pages. The conclusion of the play erases all memory of the boar to concentrate on Richmond's decorous but much abridged thanks to God and friends and his offer of pardon, which are culled from the end of Hall's section on Richard; his promise to unite the two roses by his marriage, end fratricide, and hopefully produce heirs who will give England enduring peace over-steps into the account of the next reign.

---

[140] Hall 419, from Vergil 224. Holinshed 444. Cf *R3*, v. v. In both F and Q, '*Enter King Richard and Richmond. They fight. Richard is slain.*'

[141] Vergil 223–4. Hall 418, 419, 420–1. *R3*, v. v. 4–6.

[142] Hall 420. *R3*, v. iii. 344–8; v. v. 9–10.

4. HALL OR HOLINSHED?

The bottom of Hall's stock

The union of the rival families, the keystone of Hall's politics, is proclaimed in full strength at the end of the play through the official Tudor voice, as if to bring the whole sequence into conformity with the authorized version of history. In a way, *Richard III* finally acts out Hall's obsessive image of the civil war, brother against brother, inflicting mortal wounds on their native country, the common father and mother of all true Englishmen. 'Wherefore, let euery indifferent persone, serche Histories, rede Chronicles, looke on aucthores, aswell holy as prophane,' they shall find no worse enemy 'as is roted malice, inwarde grudge, and dissimuled hatred'. The similes with pernicious serpent, toad, scorpion, and other animals apply alternately to privy envy, civil strife, or to Richard himself. Crafty dissemblers like Stanley or Peter Landoys are just wily old foxes.[143] After a hundred pages or so, these similes become so predictable that one understands why Shakespeare would have wanted to avoid them. More's image of the children delivered like lambs into the claws of a wolf serves Hall for both Edward's sons and his five daughters, but also for Richmond, who tends to fall out of jeopardy into a maze or labyrinth, like Buckingham and like so many before them. Shakespeare reserves the wolf to the young princes and keeps away from the labyrinth, where the Talbots had ended their lives.[144] Other recurrent images, of Fortune turning her wheel, or her sail, and collaborating with divine justice to punish wrongdoers, are worn out by the time we get to Richard's reign.

Hall's stock of *loci* being limited, he tends to use the same ones for antagonistic purposes. Thus Edward's reign is both a failure and a success, depending on whether he is favoured by Fortune or made to suffer for his fateful marriage, breach of oath, and wanton living. The Lancastrian rebellion is God's scourge for his many faults, yet his enemies are taken and scourged as if by God's will, Hall remarks, an opinion omitted by Holinshed.[145] Hall's venomous attacks on the wily French, Gloucester's heated opposition to the peace treaty, repeat feelings voiced earlier. Being aware of historical process in a way Hall is not, Shakespeare cuts the repetitive coils that blur its impetus, with an urgency mimetic of his character's. There is no calling back yesterday, no time for diverting anecdotes, no indulging in parasitic themes. The war against France was well lost in Part 1, and has not returned on stage since, except in the form of bitter memories or vain hopes of reconquest. That young Edward V should make it his first concern places him in line with England's heroic warriors and increases the sense of public loss at his death, but foreign affairs have no room in this intimate family plot. Hence the disappearance not only of France, but of Scotland and Burgundy.

The concentration of the plot around Richard leaves out a number of episodes,

---

[143] Hall 338, 355, 413, 412, 404.

[144] More 24. Hall 351, 406, 323, 388, 404. *R3*, IV. iv. 22–3. More could have found the simile in Rous's Latin *Historia* and many places elsewhere. See Churchill, *Richard the Third up to Shakespeare*, 47.

[145] Hall 260. Holinshed 281.

even those thematically related to it, like the rewards of perjury: Humphrey Banister's betrayal of his master, which brings down God's double-edged justice on both Buckingham and Banister's children, the ignominy of Peter Landoys, the Duke of Brittany's treasurer, who sells Richmond to Richard, or the King of Scotland's betrayal of his brother mirror the central action in Hall's narrative, explicitly so in the last case, for Hall compares it to Edward's treatment of Clarence.[146] In a passage omitted by Holinshed, the same Clarence complained that Edward was unkind and unnatural to advance his wife's kin before his own brothers:

> But by swete saincte George I sweare, if my brother of Gloucester would ioyne with me, we would make hym knowe, that we were all three one mannes sonnes, of one mother and one lignage discended, whiche should be more preferred and promoted, then straungers of his wifes bloud. (271)

At this point in Hall's chronicle, Richard proves his loyalty to both his brothers in reconciling them, and remains Edward's strongest supporter up till the King's death, when he suddenly disappears behind More's evil creature.

Hall denounces each attack against the family ties which are for him the bedrock of order, but he cannot spin them together into a meaningful pattern, any more than he is able to construe a coherent design out of the individual acts of retaliation that make up the core of *3 Henry VI*. He retains from Vergil the idea that the York family began to shed their own blood once they had destroyed all outside enemies, but he cannot make a consistent monster out of the last Plantagenet king. His Richard kills off half his family, accuses the rest of bastardy, or threatens them with incest, without clearly emerging as the wilful destroyer of all social bonds; he entirely lacks the founding ambiguity of Shakespeare's character, who is at once 'like no brother' and very like them all, only worse. On stage, his mother sends him to his death with her most grievous curse, moments after he has reminded her that he has a touch of her own condition.

Why Shakespeare still goes to Hall for material when he has obviously ceased to trust his critical judgement can only be answered by guesswork. Hall's intellectual talents come far behind More's and Vergil's, yet he has a taste for the sensational, even at times for the dramatic potential of an episode, which leads him to play up the emotions of his characters for all they are worth, sometimes even to set the stage for them: 'Now let vs speake of the erle of Warwickes doynges, whiche muste nedes play a pagiaunt in this enterlude, or els the plai wer at apoynt.' Whenever he drops his decorous tone for spontaneous similes, he instantly sounds less trite. Some of his comments seem to have caught the dramatist's imagination and ignited chains of images or thought patterns, with meanings sometimes far removed from the original. It is the common fate of children, in his and other chronicles, to suffer for their parents' faults. Clarence's offspring, 'folowynge the steppes of theyr auncetours, succeded them in lyke misfortune, and semblable yll chaūce'. In the play, all the children are thus enrolled at an early age in their parents' feuds. Clarence's young boy and girl refuse their 'kindred tears' to their aunt in retaliation for the

---

[146] Hall 395, 412, 338.

unmourned death of their father.[147] It is the most significant point of their presence on stage, that they mark the long way before Richard's victims learn to unite in mourning.

Set speeches occupy a good many pages in Hall's narrative. His struggles with rhetoric are not just for the pleasure of the exercise, even if there may be an element of competition with the likes of More. They are his main instrument to treat causation, as we have already noted, and unfailing pointers to the weaknesses in his own argument when he uses the device to defend his case. On the eve of the Tudor reigns, the speeches offer opportunities to plead for his—or rather Henry's, both Henrys'—cause, a motive less blatant when he dealt with the Yorkist claim. Hall adds to those devised by More his own deathbed speech for Edward, Buckingham and Morton's private talks, Richard and Richmond's orations to their armies. Only three of these are actually performed on stage. For Edward's dying speech, Shakespeare unerringly chooses More's version, whose urgency results from the political situation at court, where Hall's could fit any dying father of young children. The rest provide some dramatic matter, an occasional phrase, a posture, but no line of argument. Paradoxically, Hall's flamboyant style contributes more to the characters' portraits than his own pieces of eloquence to their tirades, most of which are devoid of historical basis.

Thus Margaret comes out a far stronger character in Hall's narrative than in Holinshed's or Vergil's, both in her determination to win and in the violence of her despair. Where Vergil recounts how 'the myserable woman swownyd for feare' on learning Warwick's defeat at Barnet, which left her 'distrawght, dismayd, and tormentyd with sorow', Hall dedicates a full paragraph to her loud expressions of grief, how she detested and abhored her fortune, blamed, accused, reproved, and reviled fate, which Holinshed cuts down to a sparse image of her as 'right sorrowfull'. He also cuts Vergil's and Hall's view that she ought to blame herself for the death of Duke Humphrey who would have protected her. In all three accounts, Margaret's first concern is for her son, and she is prepared to give up rather than expose him. In Hall, 'this prudent and politique Quene' is persuaded by Somerset to take the role of captain against their enemies, as she had often done before. Her fears overcome, she regains hope of good fortune and decides to fight, whereas in Vergil and Holinshed she must bow to the Lancastrian leaders. She is absent from the battlefield in Holinshed, who reports she was found hiding three days later, and sends her back to her father without further comment. Here Hall draws a haunting picture of her remaining days in France, 'more lyke a death then a lyfe, languishyng and mornyng in continuall sorowe', consumed by the thought that she and her husband were 'both ouerlyuer of their progeny, and also of their kyngdome'.[148]

Hall's system of anticipation in this section of the chronicle does not differ much from what we saw before—neutral or sceptical reports of prophecies, a dose of irony about naive believers in omens, plain scorn for fablemongers and talecarriers, rather like a pinch of salt on a plateful of superstitions. Hall may sneer at the crude-

---

[147] Hall 279, 327. *R3*, II. ii. 62–5.
[148] Vergil 147–8, 152–3. Hall 297, 301. Holinshed 315, 321.

ness of Richard's pretending to be a victim of witchcraft when all know he was born with his deformities, but sorcery itself is no laughing matter. Nor does the chronicler seriously question the signs of God's judgements on sinners, even if he distances himself from common opinion with cautious 'many think', 'perhaps', and other such 'it seems'. In the case of Richard, he unreservedly adopts More's view, as will Holinshed, that 'god neuer gaue this world a more notable example ... what wretched end ensueth such dispiteous crueltie': after the murder of Edward's children, Richard lived tortured by fear and horrible dreams until his own death on the battlefield.[149] Here More goes on straight to the rewards of sin, in other words Buckingham's conspiracy, but Hall loses the pattern and digresses with Richard's triumphant progress through Yorkshire, drawn from Vergil, before he returns to the subject of divine anger. Its first sign is the death at the age of 11 of Richard's only son, whose existence More never mentions, for fear perhaps of arousing some touch of pity in his readers.

Where Holinshed agrees to differ

Holinshed's credit has gone up in the past decades among anti-Tillyardian scholars, as reputedly more 'secular' than Hall. This may be the impression derived from the samples appended to Shakespeare's texts in today's editions, but a more extensive reading shows him to be the loudest herald of providential justice, second only to Vergil for signs of immanence, especially in the 1587 version. Holinshed's version of the last Plantagenet reign is not 'largely copied from Hall's' and augmented with 'new details' taken from Rastell's edition of More, as John Jowett writes, it is Rastell's More integrally, punctuated with new details from Hall and moral tags mostly of Abraham Fleming's coinage. Thanks to these pious comments, instead of following Hall's alternation of good and bad days, Holinshed emphasizes More's links between the rise and fall of the tyrant. If he does suppress some of Hall's vaticinations on the displeasure of God at Edward's marriage, he compensates with marginal notes stressing 'The iust iudgment of God seuerelie reuenging the murther of the innocent princes vpon the malefactors'. When Hall writes that the children paid the price of his perjury at York, not only does Holinshed endorse this view, he adds a gloss to the effect that God, bestower of all sovereignty, is unlikely to let such an indignity pass unpunished. If he cuts Hall's comment on young Richmond 'whom wee ought to beleue, to be sent from God, and of hym onely to be prouided a kyng', in the next sentence he stresses 'the coherence of holie Henries predictions' and the fact that 'suerlie the epithet or title of holie is not for naught attributed vnto him'.[150] He may omit a passage suggesting that Oxford was set free by heavenly inspiration to help Richmond, but amply makes up for it by repeated warnings that none can escape divine vengeance. Touching Richard's end, it is Holinshed who insists over Hall that 'such is Gods iustice, to leaue no vnrepentant wickednesse vnpunished, as especiallie in this caitife Richard the third, not

---

[149] More 86–7. Hall 379. Holinshed 402–3.
[150] Holinshed 284, 402, 305, 302. Cf. Hall 265, 379, 292, 287.

deseruing so much as the name of man, much lesse of a king, most manifestlie appeareth'.[151]

On the whole, there is not much to choose between the two chroniclers' themes of retribution. They may differ on specific points, but both are equally unimpeachable on matters of political and religious orthodoxy. On the other hand, it is not obvious which is Shakespeare's most regular source; I agree with Jowett that 'there are aspects of plot and vocabulary that have specific links with both chronicles, and there is no immediately clear pattern to their distribution'.[152] Let us try to sort them out. Up to the end of Edward's reign, Holinshed follows Hall with variants, the most significant of which we noted above. Then he refers his readers to More's *History*, reproduced here 'word for word', and indeed drops Hall to take up Rastell's text, complete with the passages translated from *Historia*, but augments it further with extraneous pieces. A variety of sources provide him with brief news of everyday life at court and in London, new buildings, climatology, economics, public health, judicial decisions, and so on, which have no noticeable echo in the play. Apart from these insertions, he seldom alters the text itself, and ignores most of Hall's updating or minor corrections. At the end of More's *History*, he returns to Hall and, except in spelling, punctuation, marginal notes, and paragraph divisions, follows him closely until Richard's death. Apart from minimal changes, an odd word here and there, their narratives for that portion of the reign are near to identical. This section of Hall's, as we have seen, is mostly derived from Vergil, but Holinshed does not trouble to check his copy against the original as he did for More's *History*. He simply suppresses some of Hall's redundancies, and occasionally tones down his acrimony, especially against the French nation.

As a result of this patchwork, Holinshed, like Hall, gives two accounts of the main events, one inspired by Vergil, the other by More, and lands himself in similar incoherences. These do not worry him any more than they did Hall, apparently, since he does not mind creating a few more with his insertions. His prejudices, though less strongly voiced, still run ahead of his historical sense, most noticeably when he writes that in memory of the English alliance with Burgundy, Queen Elizabeth I came 'to the defense of the people afflicted & oppressed in the low countries by the Spaniards', forgetting that the descendants of Burgundy were those hateful Spaniards, not the oppressed people. Touching the circumstances of Edward's marriage and the alleged bastardy of his children, Holinshed reports as More does that Warwick's embassy was to 'conclude a mariage betwéene K. Edward & the kings daughter of Spaine', with a marginal note inviting the reader to 'Sée before *pag.* 283', where he states, correctly, that the bride to be was Lady Bona, sister to the Queen of France. Hall, who follows Vergil, names Lady Bona in both cases.[153]

Some of Holinshed's original comments come close to feelings or meditations voiced in the play, but they are also close to similar comments made at other points

---

[151] Holinshed 428, 478. Hall 405, from Vergil 209. On divine vengeance, Holinshed 390, 424, 432, 438, to quote but a few.

[152] Jowett 13.

[153] Holinshed 287, 283, 386. Hall 264, 365. More 60. Vergil 116.

by Hall. For instance the Lancastrian restoration inspires a gloss to the effect that 'Thus was the principalitie posted ouer somtimes to Henrie, sometimes to Edward; according to the swaie of the partie preuailing', a passage Hall does not have, which seems echoed not only in *3 Henry VI* but also in the Duchess of York's reminiscence that 'often up and down my sons were tossed | For me to joy and weep their gain and loss'.[154] However there are so many other such reflections in Hall that there can be no certainty Shakespeare used this particular one in *Richard III*. Indeed, the end of the Duchess's speech echoes Hall's phrase, 'brother against brother', and brings us back to Hall's theme:

> being seated, and domestic broils
> Clean over-blown, themselves the conquerors
> Make war upon themselves, brother to brother,
> Blood to blood, self against self. (II. iv. 63–6)

Having no more enemies to destroy, Hall writes but Holinshed omits, the York brothers 'exercised their crueltie against their awne selfes' and 'with their proper bloud'.[155]

Shakespeare no longer exploits the disagreements between the two chronicles to fuel conflicting views. The main interest of Holinshed's variants is that they give a different face to the characters, of the kind we noted above about Margaret, even at the cost of further discrepancies. Although Holinshed disapproves of Edward's perjury as strongly as Hall, he presents a more attractive portrait of the King, does not tax him with wanton living or negligence when he is deposed by Warwick, and completes Hall's account of Tewkesbury with the free pardon granted to his enemies: 'O the patience and clemencie of this good king, who (besides the putting vp of wrongs doone to him by violence of foes without vengeance) fréelie forgaue the offendors, and did so honorablie temper his affections!' Coming just after his part in the death of Margaret's son, this is praise indeed. It is also in flat contradiction with the report that Somerset and a few others were beheaded three days later, and with Vergil who presents Edward as set on destroying the remnants of his enemies after his victory.[156]

The murder of Henry VI, which rounds off the eradication of the Lancasters, is reported twice, as in Hall, but owing to Holinshed's more lenient view of Edward, with better concordance. Hall's second version, from More, that Gloucester slew Henry VI 'without kyng Edward his assente', clashes with his first, from Vergil, that murderer and consenter alike soon suffered for their offence. Holinshed reproduces both versions at the same places, but suppresses the allusion to the consenter and to the Yorks' self-punishing cruelty. He has other information to convey instead: Henry's body bled 'in presence of the beholders' on two successive days while exposed at St Paul's and Blackfriars, then it was conveyed to Chertsey 'without priest or clerke, torch or taper, singing or saieng', rather like the poor ceremonial

---

[154] Holinshed 301. *R3*, II. iv. 61–2.
[155] Hall 256, 303, from Vergil 156. Holinshed 324.
[156] Holinshed 320. Vergil 156, 164.

procession shown on stage. Of course it is Shakespeare, not the chronicler, who has the prodigy take place in front of the murderer and make the seduction of Lady Anne more wondrous still.[157]

Clarence too comes out improved by Holinshed, who suppresses all allusions to his envious nature. His breach with his family is imputed to the wiles of Warwick, an excuse not found in Hall, whose account of the brothers' reunion is far less moving. In Holinshed's version, Clarence feels remorse, his mother and sisters work to reconcile him with the King, the clergy act as mediators—but not Richard, who was the main go-between in Hall—and Hastings does his best to join them in true friendship. Richard stands with Edward but plays no active part in the episode. When the brothers lovingly meet, all rejoice and thank God, for 'this was a goodlie and a gratious reconcilement'. Clarence then does his best to make peace with Warwick, with noble motives at heart, but to no avail despite the generous conditions offered. There is no mention of a damsel. Hall's anticipation of God's punishment for perjury is omitted, though Shakespeare's Clarence will remember it in his nightmare and beg forgiveness.[158]

The circumstances of Clarence's death reproduce Hall's narrative exactly, with just a change in the order of the motives, and as in Hall, the story is told twice. Only in the second telling, from More, is Richard judged responsible for his murder; in the first, from Vergil, the guilty ones are the Queen's party who poured oil on their quarrel, and the King who consented to his death. The case of Burdet is reported at a different place from Hall's, and tells a different story, but does not identify him as Clarence's servant nor connect the two events either.[159] Holinshed remains neutral about the ulterior fate of Clarence's daughter, omitting Hall's comment on her 'abhominable and detestable treason'. One anecdote finds no use in the first group of histories, but may well have inspired the pragmatism of the Angiers citizens in *King John*: after his wedding, Clarence sent his wife for safety at Exeter, where the Duchess's escort required the city gates to be closed, while Sir William Courtney, on behalf of King Edward, wanted the gates open. Faced with their conflicting demands for the keys, the Mayor and citizens

did so order and handle the matter, as that by good spéeches and courteous vsages, euerie partie was stopped and staied, vntill by means and mediations of certeine good and godlie men, an intreatie was made, the matter was compounded and the siege raised, and euerie man set at libertie. (298)

Holinshed's next addition, a pestilence which occurred soon after Clarence's death and killed more people in four months than fifteen years of war, has no specific echo on stage. The theme of contamination, by which 'whole climats maie be poisoned' and 'euerie part of the aire maie be pestilentlie corrupted' undoubtedly hangs over the whole series of plays, but it is so recurrent in the chronicles that nothing shows

---

[157] Vergil 156. More 8. Hall 303, 343. Holinshed 362, 324. *R3*, I. ii. 1–32.

[158] Hall 293. Holinshed 308–9 got those details from the Yorkist *Historie of the Arrivall of Edward IV in England*, ed. John Bruce (London, 1938), pt. ii. *R3*, I. iv. 48–52, 69–71.

[159] Holinshed 345–6, 362. Hall 326, 343. More 9. In Hall, it is Buckingham who tells the story years later, in his speech to the Lord Mayor, 369.

if this particular passage served more than others in shaping it.[160] The end of Edward's reign, including his first dying speech, presents no significant variant from Hall, except an added list of its prominent writers.

Holinshed now goes on to More's history, 'according to a copie of his owne hand, printed among his other Works', actually Rastell's 1557 edition, complete with the passages translated from the Latin. Rastell's text is reproduced verbatim, but punctuated with a number of inserts, Latin quotations from psalmists, poets, and other wise men, aphorisms on the power of eloquence, brotherly concord, bloody tyrants, flattery, worldly pleasures, princely lust, God's judgement, and marginal notes stressing the main point of a paragraph, or the chronicler's righteous expletives—'O singular dissimulation of king Richard'! Thus a guiding note confirms the identification of Anthony Woodville as 'Lord Riuers'—and just one man.[161] Another sums up the matter at hand, Richard's opposition to the treaty signed with France, in a vignette that could stand for the opening theme of the play: 'The duke of Glocester an enimie to peace.'[162]

Contrary to his brothers, Richard emerges rather worse from Holinshed's additions, mostly in the shape of Abraham Fleming's gushes of horror. In these inserts signed *Ab. Fl.*, the words 'blood', 'blodthirsty' recur insistently, from the death of Hastings, by which Richard began 'to establish his kingdom in blood', to the moment when he 'came to a bloudie death, as he had lead a bloudie life'—the very fate promised him on stage by his mother: 'Bloody thou art, bloody will be thy end.'[163] Most chroniclers pile up evidence, plus an increasing number of physical deformities, to prove Richard was evil from the start. He cannot do right either in Holinshed's eye, nor be credited with a respectable motive. His action in Scotland, which earned him praise in Hall's narrative, goes without laudative comments and is cut short of his brother's encomium. The one virtue no one denies him, his valour on the battlefield, is qualified in a note as 'K. Richards vaine confidence and bootlesse courage'.[164] These added slights do not seem motivated by a will to make the character more consistent, for as in Hall, he alternately strikes terror or deceives the people with shows of virtue, wins love with largesses, and reduces all to abject silence amid a constant rumble of rumours. Such variations might correspond to different phases of the reign, but neither chronicler manages to put them into historical perspective as Shakespeare does, by linking them to a break in Richard's own experience. Such as they are, they add fuel to Holinshed's view that the Yorks were guiltier than Lancaster, and consequently more severely punished in this King, the last of their line.

In a few cases where More slips, over surnames mostly, Holinshed sometimes gives the corrected name in the margin, with a note like '*Persiuall, saith *Ed. Hall*' or 'The lord Howard, saith *Edw. Hall*' to implement More's 'quoth another lord',

---

[160] Holinshed 347.
[161] Ibid. 393, 374, 381, 384, 388, 390, 395, 365. Cf. More 14, Hall 347.
[162] Holinshed 335. *R3*, I. i. 24–31.
[163] Holinshed 381, 444. *R3*, IV. iv. 195.
[164] Holinshed 440.

instead of altering the phrase in his own tale. Once he emends 'Richard Lord Hastings' to the proper 'William', though he lets 'Edward Buckingham' be, but does not otherwise retouch the text itself. He prefers to write about Mistress Shore that 'yet she liueth', with a marginal note to specify '*Meaning when this storie was written', rather than follow Hall who puts this passage in the past tense and adds that she died in the reign of Henry VIII.[165] When Richard usurps the crown, Holinshed strays from More, tempted no doubt by the glamour of the coronation festivities.[166] The next pages are borrowed from 'maister Edward Hall and Richard Grafton', augmented with a full list of the peers present at the ceremony. But he omits Hall's other digressions, on Richard's progress in York, or the reactions after his nephews' death, the rumours leaked, Richard's remorse and attempts to mend his conduct. He carries on with Buckingham's conspiracy, and recalls his secret dealings with Gloucester after the death of Edward, following Rastell's More.

The end of the *History* is signalled by a marginal note stating that what follows now is taken from Hall. From here to the end of Richard's reign, Holinshed does indeed copy Hall very closely, with just a few emendations in favour of common English, 'disquieting' for 'iniquietacion', 'floud' for 'inundacion', 'lingering' for 'procrastination', 'fearfull' and 'fixed' rather than 'timerous' and 'perplanted', but still with his usual aphorisms, Latin tags, and marginal comments.[167] One of his rare corrections is a mistake, when he sends Richmond to Rheims, instead of Rennes, for his solemn oath to marry Princess Elizabeth. Hammond's assertion that the episode took place 'in Rheims cathedral, as Hall reports' is unfair to Hall, who gives the right name, and doubly misleading; the choice of a place attached to the coronation of French kings might have increased the solemnity of the occasion but scarcely pleased Charles VIII, whose help Richmond badly needed at the time. They had just met at the King's court in Normandy, closer to Brittany than Champagne.[168]

Holinshed's next innovation is more rewarding. He has it from John Hooker, alias Vowel, that coming to Exeter after Richmond's failed attempt to land, Richard went to view the castle,

and when he vnderstood that it was called Rugemont, suddenlie he fell into a dumpe, and (as one astonied) said; Well, I sée my daies be not long. He spake this of a prophesie told him, that when he came once to Richmond he should not long liue after: which fell out in the end to be true, not in respect of this castle, but in respect of Henrie earle of Richmond. (421)

This passage appears only in the 1587 edition. Shakespeare's use of it, one of the rare notes which visibly served in the play, is true to type. First, it is removed both in time and space from its original circumstances. The scene is set in the palace where the newly crowned Richard is enthroned, planning his nephews' death and resenting Buckingham's lack of response. In the chronicle it takes place at Exeter where various supporters, come to meet Richmond on his landing, were executed after

<hr />

[165] Holinshed 384. Hall 363. There is no such note in Holinshed 402 concerning Dighton, who is said to be still alive, though Hall 379 reports his death at Calais.

[166] Holinshed 397–400.

[167] Ibid., 408, 417, 437, 433–5. Hall 386, 394, 412, 409–10.

[168] Hammond, n. 330. Holinshed 420. Hall 397 got the correct place, Rennes, from Vergil 203.

Buckingham's capture. The terms of the prophecy are the same; it is a reminiscence in both versions, of unspecified origin in the narrative. The Q text attributes it to an Irish bard, ties it up to the larger scheme of anticipation, and has the characters react with mixed feelings. The reminiscence, kindled by the memory of Henry VI's prophecy to young Richmond, is at the same time a trick to evade Buckingham's requests, just the hint he needed to turn rebel. Richard pours irony on the prophet who could not see what was coming to him, but the sarcasm thinly veils his anxiety and points to his own lack of vision. In F, he only remembers Henry VI's words.[169]

The next variants have no such visible impact on the play. Holinshed allows larger space than Hall to the Earl of Oxford's past history, Charles VIII's flourishing realm, and the fate of the poet Collingbourne, author of an offensive couplet on Richard's friends, while the long articles of peace with Scotland are cut, the readers being advised to consult his History of Scotland. One insert aims to excuse the inconstancy of Queen Elizabeth: women are proud, the best way to win them is by promise of preferment. Against this wily and dangerous man, she, a weak woman of timorous spirit, stood not a chance. Other additions accentuate Richard's cruelty as doom draws near. Not content with Hall's 'truculente aspect', Holinshed gives him a 'cruell visage', full of 'malice, which vttered it selfe from the inward hart by the mouth, out of which flowed speaches of horrible heate, tempered with cruell threatnings'. Even as he grows careless, Richard remains prudent in this account: victory is not always for great multitudes, the commentary goes, 'the small viper is the huge buls deadlie bane, and a little curre dooth catch a bore boisterous and big'.[170] Alliteration with a vengeance but no audible trace in the verse.

Where Hall abandons Richard's maimed body to its fate, Holinshed continues with the funeral and tomb generously allowed him 'although he deserued no buriall place either in church or churchyard, chappell or chancell', just as Richard did for Henry VI, but of course in his case 'mooued of an hypocriticall shew of counterfeit pitie'.[171] Holinshed's last significant addition is his concluding judgement on both houses. In punishing the tyrant, God's Providence very properly extinguished the whole dynasty. For although the right might seem to be with Richard, Duke of York, he was wrong to seek the crown before the time appointed by Parliament, and rightly suffered for it. Edward, despite his qualities, deserved punishment as well for, not content to cut off all his armed enemies, 'he also of a gealous feare, made awaie his brother the duke of Clarence', thus destroying the only one who could have stayed Richard's cruelty:

And as it thus well appeared, that the house of Yorke shewed it selfe more bloudie in séeking to obteine the kingdome, than that of Lancaster in vsurping it: so it came to passe, that the Lords vengeance appeared more heauie towards the same than toward the other, not ceassing till the whole issue male of the said Richard duke of Yorke was extinguished. (478)

So much for the 'secular' views of Holinshed, as opposed to Hall's 'providential'

---

[169] Holinshed 421. *R3*, appendix 1, 220. IV. ii. 98–116.
[170] Holinshed 430, 437, 436. Hall 407, 412.
[171] Hall 420. Holinshed 446–7.

ones. In conclusion, Holinshed recalls his earlier remark—and Hall's—that the title 'duke of Gloucester' was joined with misfortune and ill luck, a feeling expressed on stage by the recipient himself at his creation.[172] Richard would have fared better, had he been content with the title of Protector, 'than to haue cast vp his snout, or lifted vp his hornes of ambition so high'—wild pig, devil that he was—'as to hacke and hew downe by violent blowes all likelie impediments betwixt him and home'. These images, so vividly deployed over the whole cycle, could easily have been found elsewhere, but their context is no less stimulating. Holinshed, alias *Ab. Flem.*, inserts here a reference *ex Guic.*, in other words Fleming draws from Giucciardini some parallels with 'Lodowike Sforce duke of Milan by vsurpation', and with 'Ione, a name vnhappie and much accursed for the kingdome of Naples'. Excellent plots, worth storing for future use.

LIST OF PRODUCTIONS QUOTED

Leopold Jessner, Fritz Kortner, *Richard III*, Staatstheater, Berlin, 1920.

Charles Dullin, *Richard III*, Théâtre de l'Atelier, Paris, 1933.

Jürgen Fehling, Werner Krauss, *Richard III*, Staatstheater, Berlin, 1937.

Laurence Olivier, *Richard III*, London Films, 1956.

[The text of *Richard III* with additions by Colley Cibber, and extracts from 3 *Henry VI*.]

Peter Hall and John Barton, *The Wars of the Roses*, Royal Shakespeare Theatre, Stratford, 1963–4.

[The three parts of *Henry VI* and *Richard III*, plus approximately 1,400 lines by Hall and Barton, cut down to three plays entitled *Henry VI, Edward IV, Richard III*.]

Giorgio Strehler, *Henry VI: Il gioco dei potenti*, Piccolo Teatro, Milan, 1965.

Roger Planchon, Michel Auclair, *Richard III*, Festival d'Avignon, 1966.

Peter Palitzsch, *Der Krieg der Rosen*, Stuttgart, 1967.

[*Henry VI* adapted as an eight-hour production in two parts, *Henry VI* and *Edward IV*.]

Jean-Louis Barrault, *Henry VI*, Théâtre de l'Odéon, Paris, 1967.

[The three parts of *Henry VI* contracted into a four-hour production.]

Manfred Wekwerth, Hilmar Tate, *The Life and Death of King Richard the Third*, Deutsche Theater, Berlin, 1972.

Terry Hands, Robert Hirsch, *Richard III*, Comédie-Française, Paris, 1972.

Terry Hands, Anton Lesser, *Henry VI, Parts I, II, and III*, RST, Stratford, 1977.

Denis Llorca, *Kings, ou les adieux à Shakespeare*, Festival de Carcassonne, 1978.

[A prologue, 'Le Printemps', narrating the deposition of Richard II; *Henry VI* and *Richard III* treated in three parts entitled 'L'Été', 'L'Automne', 'L'Hiver'.]

Robert Sturua, Ramaz Chkhikvadze, *Richard III*, Rustaveli Theatre, Tbilisi, and Edinburgh, 1979, Roundhouse, London, 1980.

Terry Hands, Alan Howard, *Richard III*, RST, Stratford, 1980.

Jane Howell, *Henry VI Parts I, II and III, Richard III*, BBC Television, 1983.

Jane Howell, *Richard III*, Delacorte Theater, New York, 1983.

Bill Alexander, Antony Sher, *Richard III*, RST, Stratford, 1984.

---

[172] Hall 209. Holinshed 211, 478; the pagination here jumps from 447 to 478. 3*H6*, II. vi. 106–7.

Georges Lavaudant, Ariel Garcia-Valdes, *Richard III*, Avignon, 1984.

[→ film by Raoul Ruiz, unreleased.]

Michael Bogdanov, Andrew Jarvis, *Wars of the Roses*, English Shakespeare Company, London, 1986.

[The two tetralogies, performed in chronological order.]

Adrian Noble, Anton Lesser, *The Plantagenets*, RST, Stratford, 1988.

[The three parts of *Henry VI* and *Richard III*, condensed into three episodes.]

Richard Eyre, Ian McKellen, *Richard III*, National Theatre, London, 1990.

Sam Mendes, Simon Russell Beale, *Richard III*, The Other Place, RSC, Stratford, 1992.

Stuart Seide, Richard Sammut, *Henry VI*, Centre Beaulieu, Poitiers, 1993.

[Two parts entitled 'Le Cercle dans l'eau' and 'L'Orage des fous'.]

Matthias Langhoff, Marcial di Fonzo Bo, *Gloucester Time–Matériau Shakespeare–Richard III*, Avignon, July 1995.

Ian McKellen and Richard Loncraine, *Richard III*, United Artists, MGM, 1996.

Al Pacino, *Looking for Richard*, Fox Searchlight Pictures, 1996.

Patrice Chéreau, Jérôme Huguet, *Henry VI 3e partie; Richard III, fragments*, Manufacture des œillets, Ivry-sur-Seine, 1998.

Geneviève de Kermabon, Hervé Paillet, *Richard III*, Parc de la Villette, 1999.

Hans Peter Cloos, Richard Bohringer, *Richard III*, Massy, 2000.

Alain Milianti, adapt. Bernard Chartreux, Serge Valletti, *Le Tombeau de Richard G.*, Théâtre de l'Athénée, 2000.

Michael Boyd, Aidan McArdle, *Henry VI 1, 2, 3, Richard III*, Swan, RSC Stratford, 2000.

Michael Grandage, Kenneth Branagh, *Richard III*, Crucible Theatre, Sheffield, 2002.

7

Certain Dregs of Conscience

1. SHADES OF VERGIL

Guilty Richard

The chroniclers, who are quite open about their adoption of More's *History*, generally fail to advertise their equally important debt to Vergil, who was also More's main source.[1] Both these famed humanists wrote monuments of similar lengths on Richard, having consulted the same documents, possibly the same witnesses, and there the likeness ends. More is passionately involved in his country's politics, where Vergil the outsider keeps a critical distance even though he writes at the request of the Tudor monarch. More's *History* is a tribute to the great classic models, probably the last of its kind, while the *Anglica Historia* initiates a new mode of writing history. All the Tudor historians do but repeat one or the other, or some strange mixture of both, regardless of their radical differences.

The combination of Vergil and More inspires Shakespeare's first masterpiece in very tragical mirth. Their conflicting views of Richard provide material for successive phases of the character's development in the play, as the gleeful schemer of the first half gives way to the nervous, irate, lonely figure riding straight into Hell. More's bantering tone pre-empts any deep sense of horror. He treats the tyrant with scathing irony and wastes few tears on his victims, as the emphasis bears less on the bloody acts of tyranny than on its moral destructiveness. Only with the horribly detailed stifling of the children, a few pages before the end, is emotion allowed to creep in, affecting even Richard, whose growing fear of all around him is his one human trait. His punishment begins here, and will end with the execution of God's wrath in the field. It is the only explicit reference to divine justice, which More anticipates with a vision of Richard's body 'hacked and hewed of his enemies handes, haryed on horsebacke dead, his here in despite torn and togged lyke a cur dogge'.[2]

Vergil's Richard is grave and sombre, kept under close watch by a relentless divinity, and subject to change as More's is not; he goes through alternate phases of hope and despair, tries to mend matters with his subjects and his own conscience, and sinks into deeper gloom as he recognizes the form of 'no future' awaiting him,

---

[1] Hall names 'Polidorus' among sixteen 'Latin aucthors' in a prefatory list of sources, but never otherwise indicates what he owes Vergil.

[2] More 87. Hall 379 adds it was naked, from Vergil 226.

a fate which excites no spark of humour from the narrator. Vergil is far more prolix than More on the subject of Richard's tormented soul: as soon as he is crowned, 'the haynous guilt of wicked conscyence dyd so freat him every moment as that he lyvyd in contynuall feare', a feeling of insecurity that drives him to order his nephews' death. In Churchill's opinion, 'even Shakespeare's picture of the torment in Richard's soul is not greatly superior in vivid power to that description of More which forms its basis'.[3] Actually there is nothing in More's jumpy creature to compare with the stage character's divided self and the image of his sins, thronging at the bar, 'crying all, "Guilty, guilty!" ' Churchill comes nearer the mark when he allows Vergil's hero-villain greater psychological subtlety but less dramatic force.[4]

The parallels between Shakespeare's and More's Richard have often been stressed. It is equally interesting to find out what makes them both so memorable and so unlike, some part of which may be traced to Vergil's portrait. Unlike the stage Richard, who loves to share the excitement of his tricks with us, More's never takes off his mask, and leaves to his author the task of explaining what goes on behind appearances. Even the brief sight of his troubled nights depicts him from outside, eyes rolling, hand on dagger, leaping out of bed and running about the chamber, but gives no access to his inner soul, whereas Vergil does not hesitate to draw the reader into the tyrant's anguished mind.

Vergil's Richard seems doomed from the start. Six years before he was even born, the death of Duke Humphrey elicits a comment on the title Gloucester, which proved fatal to Humphrey, Spencer, Woodstock, and 'also, after them, king Richard the Thirde, duke of Glocester'. He first enters in the narrative to receive this ominous prize when Edward wins the crown, then is not heard of again until he flies to Flanders for the length of the Lancastrian restoration. His active part begins shortly after the landing of Edward, when he plays the mediator between his brothers 'as thowghe he had bene apoyntyd arbyter of all controversy'. He is out of sight again until Tewkesbury, where he takes part in the murder of Prince Edward. Rumour has it that it was he who killed King Henry, to free his brother from further trouble, but he is not charged with Clarence's death.[5] In the first edition of *Anglica Historia*, Clarence suffers God's punishment for the violation of his oath to Warwick, the first crime he confesses to on stage.[6] Vergil 'cannot tell what cause' turned the King against him, nor the true motive of his death, but apparently not the jealousy of the Woodvilles, who are not accused of any part in his fall.[7] The only allusion to Richard is the ominous reference to G, and the only record of him till the end of Edward's reign is at the head of his army fighting the Scots. He is in Yorkshire when the King dies after committing the tuition of his children to him, a point omitted by More but confirmed by Mancini's narrative, which gives some justification to Richard's pre-emptive attack on the Woodvilles.

[3] *Richard the Third up to Shakespeare*, 124.
[4] Vergil 187. More 87. *R3*, v. iii. 180–209. Churchill, *Richard the Third up to Shakespeare*, 164.
[5] Vergil 73, 113, 133, 139, 141, 151, 152, 156.
[6] See Kelly 99. *R3*, i. iv. 48–51.
[7] Vergil 120. Hall 271.

Richard, it appears, had no prior plan to seize the crown, nor any open conflict with the Woodvilles. On receiving news of the King's death, 'he began to be kyndlyd with an ardent desyre of soveraigntie', yet his behaviour at first seems beyond reproach. He sends 'most looving letters to Elyzabeth the quene', then summons to York all the honourable men of the country and has them swear an oath of obedience to his nephew. The first allusion to latent discords comes later, after the Woodvilles' arrest at Stony Stratford: it is 'the lord Hastinges who bare pryvy hatryd to the marquis and others of the quenes syde, who for that cause had exhortyd Richerd to take upon him the government of the prince'. Hastings soon repents, however, when they are arrested, understanding that Gloucester means no good, and confers with loyalist friends on how best to stop him in his wicked plans. Despite their misgivings, all agree to wait and give him a chance to explain his motives. Richard delivers himself of a long speech to his gathered nobility, pleading that the Woodvilles tried to frustrate his brother's last will. They have poisoned the mind of the Queen, who has carried 'the kings children as wicked, wretched, and desperate nawghtie parsons into saynctuary', to the great dishonour of the whole realm. Allowances have to be made for her sex, 'from the which suche rages readyly procede', yet one must 'provyde remedy betimes for this womanishe disease creping into owr commonwelthe'. After which manly speech Buckingham, Howard, and the Archbishop of Canterbury have no qualms about demanding that the Queen release her son once their 'many fayre wordes and perswations' have failed to convince her he will be safe. 'And so was thinnocent chyld pullyd owt of his mothers armes.' Richard's sophistry, that sanctuary is for wrongdoers, returns on stage in Buckingham's pithy argument against sanctuary children.[8]

At this point, Richard, 'whose mynde partly was enflamyd with desire of usurping the kyngdom, partly was trubblyd by guyltynes of intent to commyt so haynous wickednes', still hesitates to make the decisive move, 'according as a guyltie conscyence ys wont to be of many myndes'. No such ditherings appear in More's account. Hastings being determined to see young Edward crowned, Richard decides to remove him and lays his trap by calling two separate councils, one in the Tower, one at Westminster Hall.[9] This is the occasion of another long address to the assembled lords. Richard accuses the Queen of witchcraft, then Hastings himself, as a signal to the men waiting outside for the purpose, who arrest him along with Stanley and the bishops of York and Ely. Hastings is executed without even time for a confession. His death is a just punishment for his share in the like murder of King Henry's son. It marks the beginning of open tyranny, as all understand that Richard will spare no one to climb the throne.

There remains but to find an honest pretence for Gloucester's claim to the crown. This, Dr Shaa's sermon and Buckingham's speech soon achieve with audiences who fear for themselves. Richard does not hesitate to defame his own mother by claiming to be the only legitimate son of Duke Richard, with whom, allegedly, the late

---

[8] Vergil 175, 177–8. *R3*, III. i. 44–56. It is debated at length in More 25–7.

[9] Vergil 178–9. More 45. Vergil follows the locations of the Croyland Chronicler who, if he was indeed Bishop Russell, was among those present at the Tower.

King Edward shared not one feature, 'for he was highe of stature, thother very little; he of large face, thother short and rownd'. Richard himself is present at the sermon with a large guard of armed men, while the people stand aghast and terrified. The preacher was severely rebuked by his friends, and suffered worthy punishment for his infamy by dying shortly after his infamous speech. There is, Vergil notes, 'a common report that king Edwards chyldren wer in that sermon caulyd basterdes, and not king Edward, which is voyd of all truthe'. His caution is easy to understand, as the report would also implicate their sister, Richmond's future Queen. However, none of our authors follows him on this point. All include tales of bastardy about both Edward and his children in Shaw's sermon, with reminders that the Duchess's adultery was to be handled tactfully.[10]

The Yorkists are horrified, while the surviving Lancastrians rejoice, at the presumptuous boldness of Duke Richard, thinking that the revolted nobility will yield their allegiance to Richmond. This makes the Earl a likely candidate much earlier than in other narratives, where this transfer occurs only after the death of Edward's children, and exonerates him from owing the crown to his Yorkist connection. Meanwhile Richard confidently executes his plan and is crowned with his wife Anne, 'the people rather not repyning for feare than allowing therof'. However he does not seem to enjoy his success much, for fear and conscience so torture him that he decides to dispatch his nephews. It is during his triumphant trip to the North that he sends Brakenbury a warrant to procure their death 'with all diligence, by some meane convenyent'. As the Lieutenant tarries, the charge is given to Tyrrell, though how the children were killed is not known. Richard allows the rumour of their death to be spread, in the hope people will bear his rule better now that there is no other surviving heir, but the grief is so great that it subdues all fears. Their mother swoons at the news, giving all the signs of violent sorrow that the stage Elizabeth gives at the death of Edward: 'after cooming to hir self, she wepeth, she cryeth owt alowd, and with lamentable shrykes made all the house ring, she stryk hir brest, teare and cut hir heire, and, overcommyd in fyne with dolor, prayeth also hir owne death', as Margaret does in Hall's narrative.[11] In Vergil, Elizabeth does learn to curse like another Margaret: 'after long lamentation, whan otherwise she cowld not be revengyd, she besowght help of God (the revenger of falshed and treason) as assuryd that he wold once revenge the same.' In the play, God is often called upon by the victims to strike down their enemies, Anne first, whose hatred leads her to curse Richard's issue, and breed violence in endless repetition. The chroniclers in general, Vergil especially, have provided ample material for these vengeful cries but, unlike the playwright, never seem to doubt God's will to oblige. Theirs is a fierce God, who punishes 'these two innocent impes because Edward ther fathyr commytted thoffence of perjury'.[12]

[10] Vergil 183–4. More 60–2. Hall 365. Holinshed 386. *R3*, III. v. 74–94.

[11] Vergil 189. Cf. Hall 297. *R3*, II. ii. 34–46.

[12] Vergil 189–90.

Political Providence

After this horrendous crime, the people lay the blame on Richard at the least sign of storm, 'exclaming that God did revenge the kinges wickednes uppon the powr Englishe people; whom therfor they accusyd, detestyd, and fynally besowght God to take extreame vengeance uppon'. Since he cannot reform the past, Richard determines to abolish the note of infamy staining his honour by good government, 'and so first might meryte pardon for his offences at Gods hand; than after appease partly thenvy of man', but being counterfeit, and motivated by fear, this show of virtue cannot last long. Apparently it does not appease God's anger, for within three months Richard loses his only son, while his former ally Buckingham rebels.[13]

The origin of their quarrel, Buckingham's claim to the Hereford lands, causes Richard's anger because it involves the succession to the House of Lancaster. Disgusted with Richard's behaviour and his own complicity in it, Buckingham evolves a plan to restore the rights of both royal houses by uniting their progeny in marriage. In More's account, Morton is the initiator of this plan. In Vergil's, he immediately agrees to it, and supplies a go-between, Reginald Bray, to act as messenger between the Duke and Richmond's mother, Margaret Stanley. This, Vergil asserts, is the true cause of Buckingham's alienation from the King, although it was commonly believed that he wanted the crown for himself, as direct heir to Thomas of Woodstock. Buckingham is executed on All Souls' Day without being allowed to see Richard. Such is the price for helping an evil man.

Providence seems to take a rest after this, for Richmond's affairs suffer many drawbacks. Richard's movements, his plans to remove Anne and wed his niece, and his reconciliation with the Queen are those reported with a few ornaments by Hall, in the sequel to More's *History*. Despite Vergil's poor opinion of that 'mutable sex', his women do not only weep and rage, they work with a complete lack of scruple for the advancement of their children, and play an active part in bringing down the tyrant. Elizabeth is won over by Richard's promises, but being a practical woman she carries on plotting with the other camp. As time passes without noticeable improvement for Richmond, Richard grows careless and leaves the guarding of the coast to the inhabitants: 'for suche is the force of the divine justice, that a man lesse seathe, lesse provydeth, and lesse hede taketh when he ys nighe the yealding of punishement for his haynous offences.'[14] Again natural and supernatural forces unite on Richmond's behalf. After so many mishaps, he lands at Milford Haven.

The most significant features of Vergil's concluding episode serve their turn in the final act of the play. Richmond advances unchecked via Tamworth and Leicester, his army growing on the way as the troops sent against him take his part. Stanley 'dyd enclyne as yeat to nether partie', held back by fear for his son, quite unlike his insolent answer to the King's summons in Hall, but as plainly anxious not to take sides before he is sure of the winner. Richard's forces are far superior in number to his enemy's, though many in their ranks would rather see him lose than win. Having pitched his tents at Bosworth, and exhorted his soldiers 'with many

---

[13] Vergil 191–2.   [14] Ibid. 214.

woords' to the coming fight, he is visited in his sleep by horrible images that revive his fears. The next day, filled with foreboding, he suffers an unusual loss of heart and tells his dream to many—no dream, says Vergil, but a guilty conscience, which 'in the last day of owr lyfe ys woont to represent to us the memory of our sinnes commyttyd, and withall to shew unto us the paynes immynent for the same'. In the play he confesses before, not after, the night's fateful visions, that he no longer has his wonted 'alacrity of spirit I Nor cheer of mind'.[15]

Richmond, who 'encampyd himself nighe his enemyes, wher he restyd all night', has received no visitors from beyond. He rises early next morning, commands his soldiers to arm, and chooses his ground so as to have the sun at his back. Whether Richard sees the sun or not, Vergil does not say, but as soon as he spots his rival he rushes upon him. Richmond resists the assault but would no doubt have lost if William Stanley's men had not come to the rescue. Those around the King, suspecting treason, bring him swift horses and exhort him to fly, but he, 'owt of hope to have any better hap afterward, ys sayd to have awnsweryd, that that very day he wold make end ether of warre or lyfe, suche great fearcenesse and suche huge force of mynd he had'. He defies augury to the very end, which 'he rather yealded to take with the swoord, than by fowle flyght to prolong his lyfe'. But God does not play dice. Richard meets the fate of those who scorn the law.

The Yorks have only themselves to blame for the extinction of their lineage. Vergil's position concerning the Yorkist claim varies slightly from one version to the next, but he does not find fault with them for claiming the crown, to which they had a better title than their rivals. However they had no need to commit crimes to seize what was theirs by natural right, God would have assisted them to it. In wise men's views, the misfortunes of the Lancasters must be ascribed to the righteousness of God, 'because the soveraignty extortyd forceably by Henry the Fourth, grandfather to king Henry the Sixt, cowld not therby be long enjoyed of that famyly, and so the grandfathers offence redowndyd unto the nephews'.[16] Henry VI's virtue is not in cause, although he himself explains his sufferings by 'his ancestors manyfold offences', in addition to his own; indeed Vergil praises him far more than Hall does, and considers that the Lancasters' failure is more Margaret's fault than his. Once rid of their rivals, the Yorks begin to destroy themselves:

whan as afterward they had none enemyes uppon whom to satisfy and satyate ther crueltie, exercysyd the same uppon themselves, as hereafter in place convenyent shalbe declaryd, and embrewyd ther hands in ther own bloode. (156)

The rewards for the three brothers' sins will be the destruction of their offspring. As for those who supported Richard against their conscience, they won more peril than power in return, for whoever helps a wicked man 'both receaveth of him for the most part an evell dede for a good, and of God alway in the ende condigne punishment'.[17] Conversely, Fortune, gentle winds, men's goodwill, and God's hand

---

[15] Ibid. 222. *R3*, v. iii. 75–6.
[16] Vergil 154. For a precise account of the variations between manuscript, first, and second editions, see Kelly, 95–107.
[17] Vergil 201.

are on the side of Richmond, whose lucky chance is confirmed by his repeated escapes.

After due thanks to heaven for his victory, Richmond is acclaimed as King by his joyful soldiers, and has the crown set upon his head by Lord Stanley, 'as thoughe he had bene already by commandment of the people proclamyd king after the maner of his auncestors, and that was the first signe of prosperytie'. It is a warrior's election to the throne. A no less archaic ritual sees the body of his defeated adversary slung naked across a horse's back, to be buried without pomp or solemnity. The narrative closes with a funeral portrait of Richard: deformed body, sour face, hand on his dagger, continually biting his nether lip 'as thowgh that crewell nature of his did so rage agaynst yt self in that lyttle carkase'. The anonymous English translation ends here, but not the *Anglica Historia*. In the next chapter, the newly crowned Henry VII marries the Princess Elizabeth, an alliance accomplished with the aid of God. Their union is blessed by a true royal heir, Henry VIII, who has inherited from his Yorkist mother an unchallengeable right to the crown, so England can now enjoy a long awaited peace.

2. MORE'S DRAMATIC *HISTORY*

The *History of Richard III* is inspired by the great Latin historians, Sallust's comments on the moral decline of Rome, and more particularly Tacitus, on whose Tiberius More modelled his villain. The metaphor of the theatre gives tragic urgency to the conditions of living under tyranny: those who watch Richard's pious attitudes know that they are counterfeits, as in a play, but that anyone intrepid enough to interfere with the production would have his head broken. 'And thei y^t wise be, will medle no farther.'

Eloquence is action

More's methods of investigation remain medieval, although—Tacitus be praised— he avoids the chroniclers' day-by-day report of events. His interest for this particular reign is not that of an antiquarian, hardly that of a biographer. When his sources vary, he relies on verisimilitude and common sense, rather than waste energy in counterchecks. Nor does he bother much with exact details like proper names or dates. Deliberately or not, he makes Elizabeth Lucy the partner of Edward's alleged pre-contract, though the Croyland Chronicler could have told him that it was Eleanor Butler. Defenders of Richard consider this a deliberate distortion, designed to suppress a plausible case in support of Richard's claim.[18] More accentuates the Classical symmetries and ironies of his plot, sometimes at the expense of historical truth, for instance when he multiplies the warning signs on Hastings's last ride, and makes him die on the same day as his enemies at Pomfret. If Divine Providence

---

[18] See Charles Ross's update on this theory, *Richard III*, 88–92.

undoubtedly executes God's punishment on Richard, it sacrifices first and foremost to dramatic justice.

With humour at its driest, More sums up the action in a brisk metaphor: 'these matters bee Kynges games, as it were stage playes, and for the more part plaied vpon scafoldes. In which pore men be but ye lokers on.'[19] The story opens *in medias res*, at the onset of crisis: good King Edward is dead, leaving the realm prosperous and at peace, but his children are young, and their relations divided by petty rivalries. These will prove fatal to his heirs, as their cruel uncle Gloucester will take advantage of the situation to deprive them of both dignity and life. The portrait of Richard here drawn, in parallel to the opening eulogy of Edward, inverts the set rhetorical pattern for the portrayal of great men: betrayal of parentage, murder of kin, moral and physical deformities, deviant birth, criminal record, evil designs. There may be doubts as to whether he helped remove Clarence, while pretending to speak for him, but sure it is that he contrived the destruction of his nephews, which he achieved by fostering the quarrel between the Queen's and the King's parties. And yet Edward with his last breath had tried to reconcile them: as in a tableau, we see the royal family gathered around his deathbed to hear his last will, which is to love each other and protect his innocent children from harm. To no avail, since 'ech forgaue other, & ioyned their hands together, when (as it after appeared by their dedes) their herts, wer far a sonder'.[20]

The cast of characters once introduced, Richard starts work, first setting afire all those hostile to the Woodvilles. Nothing in his brother's will entitles him to a position of authority. He is only appointed as Protector by the council, thanks to Hastings's mediation, after the arrest of the Woodvilles. More does not specify, but must have known from Vergil, that Richard was in Yorkshire at the time of his brother's death, noticeably absent from court, and expecting to join his nephew on the way to London. The ensuing events selected by More form ten sequences, linked by retrospectives:

Prologue. Past history of the York family
1. Death of Edward
2. Arrival of the young Prince and arrest of his maternal uncles
3. Argument in sanctuary over custody of his younger brother
4. Plot against Hastings, omens and premonitions
5. Story of Hastings's mistress Jane Shore
6. Plots referring to the story of Edward's marriage
7. Sermon alleging the bastardy of the princes
8. Buckingham's speech at Guildhall
9. Richard's comedy of denial
10. Murder of the children

---

[19] More 81. The 'dramatic' qualities of the *History* have often been stressed. See A. N. Kincaid, 'The Dramatic Structure of Sir Thomas More's *History of King Richard III*', *Studies in English Literature*, 12 (1972), 223–42.

[20] More 13.

The eleventh episode, which would be Buckingham's rebellion, is cut in the middle of Morton's speech, but Richard's doom is already forecast.

The corresponding part of Shakespeare's plot seems to take its shape from un-diluted More. The play like the *History* begins with Richard's hidden ambition, the King's last illness, and his vain attempt to reconcile his family, but gives much greater space to the fate of Clarence, whom the stage Richard wants to dispatch before Edward dies. The core of what follows, from II. ii to IV. iv, dramatizes nine of the ten sequences, with few or none of Hall's additions. Most of More's speeches are cut short, some are reallotted. The debate on sanctuary takes up one-fifth of More's narrative where in turn Richard, the Archbishop, Buckingham, the Queen, the Cardinal, and various lords develop their points. On stage the argument is con-tracted to twenty lines of dialogue opposing Buckingham to the Cardinal, and we do not hear the Queen's side of the dispute. The main divergence is the role of Margaret, who forces her way into the play, while Bishop Morton fades out, and Jane Shore disappears completely. As to Richard, he is largely endowed with More's grim humour and eloquence.

The *History* concentrates on a few spectacular events, in which oratory plays a major part; here, we should note that although Richard prompts most of these speeches, he seldom speaks for himself. In the Latin version, he makes the Queen agree to a small escort for her son not 'by diuers meanes' but 'per viros idoneos', through suitable intermediaries. Having set the plot into motion, he lets his accom-plices speak for him, while in the play he humbly gives the lead to Buckingham—'I, as a child, will go by thy direction'—and plays his part as told for a short while.[21] Strangely enough, these pieces of eloquence usually fail to persuade anyone; More's well-built speeches show both his own mastery of rhetoric and their vanity. One is reported posthumously: Edward took pains to gain his mother's agreement to his marriage, which he had no intention of giving up, 'toke she it wel or otherwise', and plainly failed to reconcile her to his views. The Duchess, though 'with these wordes nothyng appeased', could not oppose his will, however equally matched their disputation. In a similar way it is force, not eloquence, that enables Buckingham to win the argument on sanctuary against the Queen. Indeed her performance is as good as his, but Richard's men are everywhere. Looking out of the window, her friend the Archbishop could 'see all the Temmes full of bootes of the Duke of Gloucesters seruantes, watchinge that no manne shoulde go to Sainctuary, nor none coulde pass vnsearched'.[22] On stage she does not even get a hearing, but the point is made no less clearly, that the plotters will use the letter of the law to violate moral right. The Scrivener echoes More's statement that the proclamation of Hastings's death was 'so fair writen in parchment in so wel a set hande, & therwith of it self so long a processe, yᵗ eueri child might wel perceiue, that it was prepared before'.[23] In Richard Eyre's production for the National Theatre, the beam of a torchlight caught him as he ended his speech, and he was led away by two strong arms.

---

[21] II. ii. 153; III. vii. 50.   [22] More 22.   [23] More 54. *R3*, III. vi.

In both narrative and dramatic versions, the presentation of Richard's claim to the Londoners is met with plain disbelief. At the end of Buckingham's tirade in More—seven pages long—'all was husht and mute, and not one word aunswered therunto'. The Duke repeats his arguments more loudly, using different words, with such appropriate gestures that all thought 'they neuer had in their liues heard so euill a tale so well tolde', but again 'not one woorde was there aunswered of all the people that stode before, but al was as styl as yᵉ midnight'. So the crowd is treated to a third helping of the same, this time by the recorder, who carefully stresses that they are the Duke's words, not his. Still no reaction. Amazed by this 'maruelouse obstinate silence', the Duke demands an answer from the crowd: will they or not have Richard for king? His straight question raises a stir of murmurs, 'neyther loude nor distincke, but as it were the sounde of a swarme of bees'. A fake show of enthusiasm is contrived, which no one dares contradict, then all depart either pretending joy or turning their faces away to hide their sorrow. This eloquent silence permeates the texture of More's narrative: lofty speeches, met by heavy mutism, and a soft but constant ripple of whisperings, rumours, secret talks, thematize the difficulty of living under tyranny, and its corroding power. On stage the episode is efficiently summed up in forty lines by Buckingham himself, before the entrance of the Lord Mayor and Richard's star turn 'aloft'.

In an earlier scene, a trio of anxious citizens have voiced exactly More's 'muttering amonge the people, as though al should not long be wel', which is heard in the background of the separate councils: 'before such great thinges, mens hartes of a secret instinct of nature misgiueth them. As yᵉ sea wᵗout wind swelleth of himself sometime before a tempest.' Hall slightly missed the point here, leaving the sea out of the picture, 'as the southwynde sometyme swelleth of hym selfe before a tempeste', but Shakespeare restores More's image:[24]

> Before the days of change still is it so.
> By a divine instinct, men's minds mistrust
> Ensuing danger, as by proof, we see
> The water swell before a boisterous storm.   (II. iii. 43–6)

With his acute sense of the power of rumours, the dramatist is the only one to note that they are as reliable as old wives' tales, and imply that those circulating about Richard may be just plain gossip. The young Duke of York asserts that Richard's nurse told him his uncle was born with teeth, but his sharp grandmother is not easily fooled:

> *Duch.* His nurse? Why, she was dead ere thou wast born.
> *York.* If 'twere not she, I cannot tell who told me.   (II. iv. 33–4)

This, allied with his elder brother's concern about the truthfulness of historical records, suggests that Shakespeare did not entirely believe all that he had read of Richard's monstrosity, even though he did not choose to quarrel with the tradition.

---

[24] More 44. Hall 358. Holinshed 379 has More correctly.

More's last orator is Morton, who must have succeeded in winning over Buckingham to his side, judging by what followed, but leaves us forever wondering how he achieved this. A page earlier, he has treated us to one false stop, 'saying that he had alredy medled to muche with the world, and would fro that day medle with his boke and his beedes and no farther'. His reticence works wonders with Buckingham: 'Then longed the duke sore to here what he would haue sayd, because he ended with ye king & there so sodeinly stopped.' After much begging, Morton continues his tale with a fable borrowed from Aesop to show there is no arguing with tyrants, and just as he seemed about to offer the crown to the Duke, stops again for good. A tantalizing little scene, if one thinks Chancellor Morton may have told it to a young page who would eventually give up his book and beads to serve the Tudors in the same post, against his own better judgement not to meddle with kings' games.

Characters in excess

Why More left his work unfinished has not yet been satisfactorily explained, nor why he stopped at that particular point. Perhaps because the direction taken by Morton's speech must inevitably lead him into tricky areas: 'Titulus Regius', the official statement of Richard's claim to the crown, based on the illegitimacy of Edward's children, was repealed on Henry VII's accession.[25] The newly crowned Tudor did not encourage speculations on the subject and had all copies of the Act destroyed. Even Vergil, who enjoyed a moderate degree of independence, asserts it is untrue that the bastardy of the young princes was claimed: it was Richard's mother who was falsely accused of adultery.[26] Hall like More reports that both Edward and his children were taxed with illegitimacy, but both stories are dismissed as equally ludicrous, the second one being made more ludicrous still by the exchange of Elizabeth Lucy for Eleanor Butler.

Vergil never suggests that Buckingham might be a pretender to the crown, except when Richard accuses him of pressing his title through a claim to the Hereford lands. Hall evades the issue by avoiding all reference to Buckingham's direct line of descent. But More may have felt there were too many improbabilities in having the rebel renounce his claim, as he does in Hall, and too many risks in discussing any claim that involved the Tudors' dynastic rights. His lapsus in misnaming Buckingham 'Edward' is revealing, for Edward was the name of the then living Duke his son, Henry VIII's presumptive heir, whose arrogance and high birth eventually led to his execution in 1521.[27] By a strange coincidence, Wolsey found out that the Duke had paid several visits to a Carthusian monk who prophesied he would one day be King, somewhere around the time when the *History* was written, and

---

[25] *Rotuli Parliamentorum*, ed. J. Strachey et al., (London, 1767–77), vi. 240–2.

[26] Vergil 184.

[27] Edward Buckingham was heir presumptive to Henry VIII until the birth of Mary in 1516, and even after that date, many witnesses including Vergil thought he would probably succeed in displacing her, should Henry die without an heir male.

straightaway charged him with high treason.[28] Unless Wolsey manufactured these charges himself, it is possible that he had had evidence of these visits for some time and kept it close for later use, and that his collaborator More knew about it and dropped the subject of rebellious dukes like hot cakes. To round off the irony, after the trial it was More who defended the manner of the Duke's attainder in the Court of Aldermen, and was rewarded by the King with a gift of Buckingham's manor in Kent.

More is often taxed with having done wonders for the Tudors' propaganda by vilifying the last of the vanquished dynasty. He does indeed exonerate all the other protagonists from ugly designs, as Shakespeare does not, to lay the blame on the Protector alone, but in fact there is not a shred of evidence that he meant to build up the Tudor claim with his prejudiced treatment of Richard. On the contrary, he seems to have refrained from offering such support to Henry VIII, possibly choosing to leave the work unfinished rather than inspire him with fresh ideas. When advising his Grace, he once said to Thomas Cromwell, 'ever tell him what he owght to doe, but never what he is able to doe. For if a Lion knewe his owne strength, harde were it for any man to rule him.'[29] He certainly made no effort in his lifetime to advertise or circulate the *History*. Only after his death, and that of his tyrannical master, did it become famous.

If More is quite clear as to Morton's role in the story, he is less so about other churchmen, for instance when he credits the Archbishop of York with the deeds of two different prelates. Thomas Rotheram, Archbishop of York and Chancellor of England, did give the Great Seal to the Queen, but it was Cardinal Thomas Bourchier, Archbishop of Canterbury, who fetched young York from sanctuary, as Hall correctly reports. This is probably just a slip of More's pen, since the mistake occurs only in the English *History*, not in the Latin one.[30] Shakespeare, like Hall, has two distinct characters in F, but Q has only one, identified in both scenes as 'Cardinall', who exits after giving the seal to the Queen and re-enters immediately in the next scene with the Dukes' train. In the play, this is the last we hear of the seal, but in More, the Archbishop soon fears he has made a mistake, secretly retrieves the seal, is nonetheless severely blamed, dismissed from his office, and replaced by Dr Russell, Bishop of Lincoln, the probable author of the Croyland *Continuation*.[31] Russell is arrested with Stanley and Morton at the fated council, and released a few days later.[32]

---

[28] The visits took place in 1514 or 1518, according to Bernard Cottret, *Henry VIII: Le Pouvoir par la force* (Paris, 1999), 92–5.

[29] William Roper, *The Lyfe of Sir Thomas Moore, Knight*, ed. Elsie V. Hitchcock (London, 1935), 56–7.

[30] More 21, 22, 25, 27, 28. Hall 350, 351, 352. Holinshed 371, 378. Rastell has a passage from the Latin at More 44, where both prelates take their proper place at the Tower council, but does not emend the earlier error. Neither does Holinshed, who adopts both Rastell's insert and More's mistake, rather than Hall's correction.

[31] See Kelly 59. Russell was dismissed from the chancellorship three weeks before Bosworth, and replaced by Dr Thomas Barowe (Ross 135).

[32] Hall 407. Vergil 211. More 25 reports his replacement by Russell, but not the bishops' arrest at the Tower council (48). Hall 351 omits the dismissal but reports the arrest and the release, 360, 375. Holinshed 369, 381 follows More.

Despite his lapsus, More certainly makes a difference between the churchman who took the Queen's part, if only briefly, and the one who agreed to serve Richard. The fact that we hear no more about the seal suggests that Shakespeare did not attach great importance to it, and did not need two separate fearful priests to show the Church bowing to the Prince. The critics' opinion is that he fused the two characters in Q for the sake of economy. How much of an economy this actually was is not clear, though, since he still has two bishops in both Q and F play the props to Richard's show at Baynard's Castle, in concordance with Hall's narrative. As for Morton, this was no weak priest but a most resilient politician, who survived through several Lancastrian and Yorkist regimes. He would succeed Bourchier as Archbishop of Canterbury, and eventually become Cardinal, as More tells us before reporting his conversation with Buckingham at Brecon.[33] Yet he leaves the stage after providing strawberries for Richard's party, while his active plotting is cut down to three lines. The only tribute to his abilities is grudgingly paid him by Richard:

> Ely with Richmond troubles me more near
> Than Buckingham and his rash-levied strength.   (IV. iii. 49–50)

Shakespeare may have wished to avoid meddling with Tudor politics when he chose to ignore Morton's significant part in the action, just as he omitted the Stanleys' share in the victory of Bosworth. From Vergil's account, William, not Thomas, was the last-minute rescuer of Richmond; Thomas is not mentioned again after his evasive answer to the Earl's summons. Still, there is little support in the texts for the view that 'Shakespeare alters More's account of events to present Stanley in a favourable light', or apply 'a favourable gloss' to Stanley's wait-and-see policy.[34] More never mentions him again after the Tower episode. Stanley refuses to join Richard, that is all we know on stage of his movements on the battlefield. If we were meant to understand that he actually saved Richmond from death, then Richmond's lack of proper thanks would be conspicuous. The point is that he owes the victory to no one but himself, with God's blessing. The Barton/Hall adaptation had to draw on the chronicles to make Stanley and Morton leaders in a political counterplot to unseat Richard. If they were such favourites with anti-Tillyardians, it was essentially as secular substitutes for Providence.[35]

The motives for erasing Jane Shore from the play must have been quite different. She is the third strong feminine figure of the *History*, with Queen Elizabeth and the Duchess of York, and by far the most graceful of the three, which may be the very reason of her exclusion. Shakespeare's plot has no room for earthly grace; what little there is comes from beyond and is grimly unforgiving. But there is nothing

---

[33] More 91.

[34] Nor for 'his role in crushing Buckingham's uprising', since More's narrative does not get that far. Jowett 4–5.

[35] See for instance A. L. French, 'The World of Richard III', *ShSt* 4 (1968); Pierre Sahel, 'Les Voies des hommes dans *Richard III*', *EA* 4 (1972); Andrew Gurr, 'Richard III and the Democratic Process', *Essays in Criticism*, 24 (1974). On the padding of these characters in the Hall/Barton text, see Day, *King Richard III*, 54–8.

ghostly about More's attractive Jane Shore, she is flesh of the tenderest kind, and harmless, supporting his view that private pleasures seldom do great public harm. Her part in the accusation of witchcraft is More's invention; in Vergil, who never mentions Jane Shore, the accusation only concerns the Queen. From a man famous for his monastic habits, this unexpected tolerance has a purpose. As a survivor of Edward's merry England, Mistress Shore stands in vivid contrast with Richard's austere virtue, and unmasks its hypocrisy. More is at his ironical best when Richard puts her to open penance 'as a goodly continent prince clene & fautles of himself, sent oute of heauen into this vicious world for the amendement of mens maners'. When her shame turns to open triumph, More visibly delights in making this notoriously light woman serve a variety of moral lessons. Fame, beauty, princely favour, material riches do not last, friends will desert you when fortune does, a kind heart is worth more than a golden name, evil deeds are written in marble but good deeds in dust. Of these adages, only the last finds an echo in the play, when young Edward expresses concern for the recording of truth by future ages.[36] Shakespeare's ethical designs are more ambitious, and his feminine characters far more passionate than this amiable Magdalen. Besides, there is no need to point out Richard's assumed virtue as he takes immense pleasure, comparable to More's, in telling us so himself:

> And thus I clothe my naked villainy
> With odd old ends stol'n forth of holy writ,
> And seem a saint when most I play the devil. (i. iii. 336–8)

Inductions dangerous

In pure Classical style, More makes Hastings's hubris the butt of a superior dramatic irony: 'O good god, the blindnes of our mortall nature, when he most feared, he was in good suerty: when he rekened him self surest, he lost his life, & that w'in two howres after.'[37] Thus Hastings disregarded all the warning signs he received, Stanley's ominous dream, his own horse's near falls on the way to the Tower, the successive meetings with a priest, a knight, and 'one Hastinges, a purseuant of his own name', happily secure in the Protector's friendship and its first benefits, the beheading of his Woodville enemies on that very day at Pomfret. In the play, the anonymous knight is replaced by a gleeful Buckingham who further stresses the parallel with the Woodvilles' fate. Most of the omens take place before, not after the event, while Richard has already informed us of his plan for the loyal Chamberlain: 'Chop off his head.' In both texts, the Londoners note the palpable device of a proclamation executed in less time than it took to pen it, exciting sarcastic rumours in More that it was 'written by profecy', and the Scrivener's dark premonitions on stage.[38] But prophecy is a serious matter in the play, whereas More does not lend much credibility to omens. There is no trace in the *History* of the various prophecies reported in the other chronicles, about G, Rougemont, or Henry VI's promise of a return to grace, which infer a supernatural design to the human drama.

[36] More 55–7. *R3*, III. i. 72–8. [37] More 52. [38] Ibid. 54. *R3*, III. vi.

Where his fellow playwrights, Marlowe especially, will confront a rival theory squarely, state its argument, discuss, and eventually reject it in proper academic mode, Shakespeare feels no need to define his own position, but integrates a *disputatio* verbatim without expressing agreement or disagreement with its thesis, which allows the dynamics of dialogue to expand and raise it to a much higher level of philosophical questioning. We saw how soon in his career he chose to ignore Hall's pedestrian interpretations. When he comes to More, he turns large sections of the *History* into dramatic episodes without rewriting them in any way implying criticism, yet most of the transplants develop new meanings and associations as if driven by a life of their own.

If Shakespeare visibly found much to feed his imagination in this narrative, he nowhere displays how far he valued More's intellectual talents or theories about Richard. The Catholic humanist is never honoured with a personal tribute, nor any sign acknowledging him as a familiar author, even on the two occasions when he is allowed a stage appearance. In *Henry VIII*, More is just a passing shadow. In the hagiographic *Sir Thomas More*, he delivers a vibrant plea against rebellion on Ill May Day and persuades the rebels to surrender, but if Shakespeare did write this fine speech, as is now largely accepted, then it is the only one of its kind in the whole canon. The discourse of the dominant orthodoxy is usually left to sycophants, and undercut by subversive ironies, but this is a truly moving plea for order, peace, and hospitality to foreigners. Erasmus wrote a little wistfully that his friend More had become 'totus . . . aulicus', wholly a courtier, on entering the King's service, while he himself thought it wiser to preserve his independence. That the eponymous hero of the play sincerely believes in the value of authority is obvious; that he might be naive in his trust has to be inferred from what follows, a testimony to his moral rather than to his historical judgement. The irony of penning this unique speech in support of a regime that would prove so ungrateful to the orator cannot have escaped Shakespeare.

Among the most memorable insults hurled at Richard in the play, Margaret's 'cacodemon' occurs but once in the canon. Strangely enough, this unusual word, meaning ugly spirit, is used at least once by More, not in the *History* but in a pamphlet vilifying Luther.[39] The most likely places where More could have found this rare Greek word were Euripides' *Hippolyta*, or Lucian's *Lexiphanes*.[40] To Alison Hanham, More's narrative is 'a Lucianic, and so irreverent, comment on the whole craft of history'. His account of Richard's birth should be read as a tongue-in-the-cheek charge against the chroniclers' exaggerations, she argues: if their tales are to be believed, then nature changed her habits.[41] But More was certainly not immune

[39] 'Cacadaemonem se fore comminatur', he threatens to be a cacodaemon, *Responsio ad Lutherum*, written in Feb. 1523, Yale, v/1. 36–7. One of the rare occurrences quoted by *OED* is in Nashe's *Terrors of the Night*.

[40] See J.-C. Saladin, *La Bataille du grec à la Renaissance* (Paris, 2000), 316. Lucian, *Lexiphanes*, trans. A. M. Harmon, in *The Works of Lucian*, v. 314.

[41] Hanham, *Richard III*, 155–9. To Hammond, 77, she 'badly overstates the comic and what she calls the theatrical content of More's *History*'.

to his contemporaries' current beliefs, even if he had no illusions about the nature of power games, or the fact that it is all make-believe. Perhaps his affinity with the Greek satirist should be sought elsewhere: Lucian begins his *True History*, a parody of Homer's *Odyssey*, by stating that he tells the truth only when he says all is pretence. In a stage play, More reminds us, everyone knows that the man playing the sultan is a shoemaker, that an ignoble butcher can call himself king: the theatre reflects political reality by stressing its own powers of delusion, and contributes to the service of truth by unmasking all villainous hypocrites. Those who joined hands in feigned amity around Edward's deathbed are soon outdone in deceit by Richard's manipulations. World and stage thus hold mirrors up to each other as they have done from time immemorial. Even before the Globe was built, the Elizabethan arena insistently called itself a *theatrum mundi*, an ambivalent reminder that all the world's a stage. In More's *History*, it is a puppet show.

The characters in *Richard III* constantly borrow from a theatrical vocabulary that reduces all endeavours to a futile comedy: *act, scene, cue, part, plot, pageant, induction, show, shadow, paint, tragedy*. For a complete list of relevant allusions to the stage, one would need to quote the entire play. Elizabeth's 'act of tragic violence', her dismissal as 'a queen in jest, only to fill the scene', Margaret's voyeuristic enjoyment of her enemies' woes, Tyrrel's 'bloody act', the incantatory ritual of grievances, all illustrate Margaret's lessons in curses. A degree of overacting is required to make them true to life:

Think that thy babes were sweeter than they were
And he that slew them fouler than he is.
Bett'ring thy loss makes the bad causer worse;
Revolving this will teach thee how to curse.   (IV. iv. 120–3)

These associations were brilliantly knit together in one powerful scene of Michael Boyd's RSC production: the bleeding of dead Henry's wounds caused an obvious shock to Richard, who put his fingers in the wound like an unbelieving Thomas and smelt them, plainly wondering if this could be paint or red jelly, which it was, of course. From actor's body to corpse and back again to live body playing dead, a reminder that transfiguration, on and off stage, needs an act of faith.

Richard outlines the script of his show on his first entrance: 'Plots have I laid, inductions dangerous.' Only after three acts, when his power begins to fray, does he realize he is performing a part in someone else's play. The reconciliation organized by Edward makes clear the extent and the limits of kingly power: the King can press all into a show of goodwill but he cannot change hearts. His courtiers compete in hyperbolic declarations of love and forgiveness, and swear loyalty to his offspring. Richard swears and forgives harder than anyone else, then shatters the fake harmony with news of Clarence's death, which causes the King unwittingly to confess: 'Is Clarence dead? The order was reversed.' No one else is going to order shows after this but Richard. The protean actor treats us to a series of talented impersonations, devoted brother, knight errant, veteran soldier, saint, penitent, shy maid, offering each protagonist the face he wants to see, except his mother who recognizes

Vice under his visor. Hastings, who thinks he can read Richard's heart, does not pay
heed to Buckingham's warning:

> We know each other's faces. For our hearts,
> He knows no more of mine than I of yours,
> Or I of his, my lord, than you of mine.   (III. iv. 10–12)

Only the audience have this privilege. Unlike More's character, Richard lets us in on
every trick, explains all innuendoes we might have missed, and invites us to share
what Thomas Van Laan calls 'a highly favourable review of his own performance'.[42]
In the show devised for the Lord Mayor, it is he who instructs Buckingham into the
art of make-believe:

> Come, cousin, canst thou quake and change thy colour,
> Murder thy breath in middle of a word,
> And then again begin, and stop again,
> As if thou were distraught and mad with terror?   (III. v. 1–4)

Despite Buckingham's boast that he 'can counterfeit the deep tragedian' to grace his
stratagems, he does not win much applause. On their next meeting, he exchanges
roles, rehearsing Richard for his next scene, prayer book in hand between 'two
props of virtue',

> And be not easily won to our requests;
> Play the maid's part: still answer nay and take it.   (III. vii. 49–50)

Richard's awareness of role-playing shows up the whole court as a bunch of
amateur actors, and the world of politics as a game of appearances. If More's
metaphors have faded into clichés on today's stage, in his own time they offered an
original viewpoint on the way governors divert sacred rituals to parade in front of
the vulgar—intuitions to be fully exposed in *Henry V*'s wooden O by his ambiguous Muse, when the King understands the people's hunger for heroic legends, and
finds it wisest to write them himself. As the political arena shrinks to the size of a
bear-baiting ring, the theatre emerges as the only place to show the truth, when it
mimicks the theatricality of real life. The Elizabethan playwrights who fought to
establish its rights in an ideal City could not guess, even if they feared some such
murderous showdown, that the closure of playhouses would transform the whole
state into a theatre of operations. For the last time in England, people would then
watch kings' games with the King himself upon a scaffold.

Smiling villain

For all its acclaimed 'theatricality', More's *History* provides no proper antagonist to
Richard. Buckingham who makes a late entrance in his tale has no time to develop.
Margaret is gone, Anne non-existent, and the Queen keeps to her sanctuary.

---

[42] *Role-Playing in Shakespeare* (Toronto, 1978), 141. On the link between theatricality and
Machiavellianism, see Rackin, *Stages of History*, 72–82.

Richard's only worthwhile opponent, Morton, never confronts him, with the result that he alone emerges from the narrative. Deceit, cruelty, cunning, ugly shape, pious looks, theatrical skill, restlessness, nightmares, a gnawed lip, and a taste for strawberries . . . Many of Richard's trappings can be traced to More. Not all are entirely his creation. The literary legend of the tyrant acquired new features with each telling, all of which eventually merged in the stage character. For instance the Croyland chronicle mentions Richard's dream, as an omen of disaster rather than the sign of his guilty conscience. John Rous compares Richard explicitly with Antichrist, and reports monstrous details of his birth, with teeth and long hair, after a gestation of two years.[43] To these, More puts the finishing touch with a note that he entered life as men enter death, feet forward. In the grimmer Latin version— 'Quippe quem fama est haud aliter aluo materna eximi, quam obstetricante ferro potuisse. Quin Agrippam etiam natum eum pedibusque prelatis exijsse ferunt'— fame has it that a knife acted as midwife to extract him, an Agrippa, from his mother's womb.[44]

In *3 Henry VI*, we saw Richard interpret these signs of a devious nature himself— legs forward to make haste, teeth to bite the world. Shakespeare gives them further depth by fusing them with another remarkable trait in More, where Richard so thirsted for the crown that he 'thoughte euerye daye a yeare tyll it were atchyeued'.[45] Much of the energy in both texts arises from the tension between protracted formal speeches and swift actions, like dispatching one's enemies before dinner. Some of the killing was More's invention, for instance the part of Richard in Clarence's death, but as Churchill points out, Shakespeare did not have to expand this hint, it was there fully developed in the *Mirror*, as well as the prophecy on G, ready for use.[46] More does not thematize Richard's ill-fated birth, nor the unnatural monster's slurs on the legitimacy of half his family. He does, however, bring out the villain's mimicking of true virtue and his inversion of the heroic theme, significant traits that will find their way to the stage.

Monstrosity takes on radically opposed meanings in narrative and play, however alike evil incarnate seems in both. It is extraneous to nature in the *History*, has no known origin, no rational cause, but bursts suddenly upon a happy community, through the accident of the King's death, and contaminates what was before a healthy organism. Shakespeare's evil is very much a part of nature, our nature. Some of the revulsion it inspires is for the distorted mirror Richard presents to his accusers. His is a collection of all their moral deformities. Where they, like More, compare him to the ugliest animals in nature, he stresses that he is all the more human for his cruelty, and therefore 'no beast'. He is more cold-blooded than any

---

[43] 'Iste rex Ricardus diebus suis ultra modum crudelis trienno & parum ultra ad instar Antechristi regnaturi regavit. Et sicut Antechristus in futuro in maxima sublimitate sua confundetur.' *Historia Regum Angliae*, ed. Thomas Hearney (Oxford, 1716), 218. On the symbolic meaning of each monstrosity, see Marienstras, 'Of a Monstrous Body', in Maguin and Willems (eds.), *French Essays*, 153–74.

[44] More ii. 7; xv. 322.

[45] More 25. Haste is repeatedly stressed, 46, 49, 51, 52, 54, 57, 68, 86 . . .

[46] Churchill, *Richard the Third up to Shakespeare*, n. 243. William Baldwin's Tragedy of 'George Plantagenet, Duke of Clarence', *Mirror*, xviii. 176–375.

of them, but his very absence of feeling makes him rather less vicious than, say, Margaret. There is not one of his crimes which they have not committed before: lies, perjury, betrayal, usurpation, murder, sacrilege. He goes one step further when he brings all sins to the extremest degree of incest, aiming to kill and re-engender his own flesh in the same brutal conflation of life and death as his own birth:

> *Eliz.* Yet thou didst kill my children.
> *Rich.* But in your daughter's womb I bury them,
>   Where in that nest of spicery they will breed
>   Selves of themselves, to your recomforture.   (IV. iv. 427–30)

This morbid autogenesis signs the biological doom of evil, echoing Anne's earlier curse, 'If ever he have child, abortive be it.'

There is a lighter side, and a faintly medieval flavour, to More's humour, when he discusses women who 'commonly not of malice but of nature hate them whome theire housebandes loue', or the lustful King marrying his enemy's wife, who 'many time had praied full hartly for his losse. In which god loued her better, then to graunt her her bone.' His grimmest wordplay is practised at the expense of his hero, 'not letting to kisse whome hee thoughte to kyll', who decides to rid himself of his nephews, 'as though the killing of his kinsmen, could amend his cause, and make him a kindly king'.[47] In the play, not only More's talented oratory, but More's sardonic humour, his enjoyment of the ludicrous, his killing puns, his verve are transferred to Richard, who uses them to break up the rigid patterns of rhetoric favoured by his antagonists. Not just for comic relief, but because they are Richard's best asset in making accomplices, audience included. Here again, the Greek precedent may help us with its interpretative keys. Among the dominant features of the *saturikon* that made the fourth part of a tetralogy were the satyrical chorus's interactive exchanges with the public. To Tony Harrison, who resurrected the form in his *Trackers of Oxyrhynchus*, it caused a liberating discharge after the tragedies.[48] If we relish Richard's humour at the expense of edifying figures, along with his debunking of stiff rhetoric, there is no atonement for the fear and pity we are brought to enjoy through his mediation. As Nicholas Brooke notes, he must bow at the end to the human need for ceremony and cyclical rites.[49]

The smiling villain returns under many guises in Shakespeare's plays, most tragically in *Hamlet*, whose hero likewise puns on kin and kind. But his murderous uncle is no jester, whereas Richard makes us laugh with him, often at the expense of his unpitied victims. It is by some flaw in their nature that they open themselves to his tricks. The only one who is a proper match for him is his nephew and namesake, young York, whom he finds 'a perilous boy, | Bold, quick, ingenious, forward, capable', though ironically enough, he fails to spot their affinity: 'He is all the

[47] More 7, 65, 8, 83.
[48] See his preface to the 2nd edn. of *Trackers of Oxyrhynchus* (London, 1991), p. xi. To Patricia Easterling, though, this concept of 'relief' leaves aside the properly tragic part of the *tragikè didaskalia*.
[49] Nicholas Brooke, *Shakespeare's Early Tragedies* (London, 1968), 50–79; 'Reflecting Gems and Dead Bones: Tragedy versus History in *Richard III*', in C. B. Cox and D. J. Palmer (eds.), *Shakespeare's Wide and Universal Stage* (Manchester, 1984), 104–16.

mother's, from the top to toe.' The others are too compromised, or arrogant, or stupid, or full of hatred, to inspire much emotion. Step by step, with each new dupe, Richard lowers the level of what is laughable, and brings us down with him. The scene of Hastings's fall is emblematic. As cruel children follow their leader's choice of a comic butt, flattered and secretly relieved to enjoy the bully's favour, all abandon Hastings to his fate when Richard commands: 'The rest that love me, rise and follow me.' *Exeunt omnes.* 'The stuff of fascism', Richard Eyre unerringly detected, when he made it the basis of his 1990 stage production.[50]

Where More's villain never invites identification, our relation with the stage Richard is far more ambiguous. Not content with being, like Vice, the most diverting character of the cast, he exposes the others' appetites, hypocrisies, cowardice, ridicule, and involves the spectators in pleasurable complicity against them, followed by retroactive shame when they take the measure of what they have condoned. The limit of tolerance is crossed when murder and rape are attempted in the family circle on one's own children. It is our lingering sense of complicity which causes mixed emotions when Richard meets his fate. He has richly deserved it, but we enjoyed the benefit of his guilt by proxy, and the pious consort who defeat him leave us with a bitter taste of mockery.

3. POETIC LICENCE

Time convulsed

The brevity of King Richard's career combined with his impatient nature to inspire the narrators with a sense of dramatic urgency absent from the earlier reigns. Yet history, even as brief as Richard's, follows a more meandering course to its pregnant conclusion than so-called lifelike drama, so the chroniclers feel in duty bound to record government business, diplomatic affairs, skirmishes on the borders. More, and Shakespeare, have no such ties. The main difference between their concise horror-shows is that More's has no historical perspective; his Richard's misdeeds are set against the backcloth of Edward's merry old England, *in illo tempore.* Shakespeare's dynamic progress of evil allows no space for pleasant interludes. The period represented lasted fourteen years, from Henry VI's death in 1471 to Bosworth in 1485, but only the last two years of the Plantagenets are actually shown on stage, more precisely the end of the Yorks, executed in some ten decisive days. In Shakespeare's contracted scheme, the news of Clarence's death is the last blow to Edward, though historically he predeceased the King by five years. On the other hand, Margaret who died a year before Edward gets extra time as a sort of living ghost, her survival after her son's demise being, as in Hall's phrase, 'more lyke a death then a lyfe'. Richard's haste, repeatedly stressed by More, is connected on stage to his violations of nature's course. The tune is set from the first trochaic 'Now', the offbeat rhythm that crashes winter into summer, catching everyone on

---

[50] 'On Directing *Richard III*', in Goy-Blanquet and Marienstras (eds.), *Le Tyran*, 133–9.

the wrong foot. Like the upset seasons, his monstrous birth, his lameness, and the untimely deaths he precipitates are as many disruptions of proper measure.

Once the evil tyrant has conquered the crown, More's history is nearly done, and Vergil takes over. In the Italian's report, this phase is twice as long as the first one.[51] Nearly two years elapsed between the failed uprising in September 1483 and the Battle of Bosworth, 22 August 1485, during which Richmond nearly lost hope of ever setting foot in England. Shakespeare treats the whole period in one scene, where Richard attempts to win his rival's promised bride, while news from abroad blow hot and cold in quick succession. Richmond's navy is in sight, waiting to join forces with Buckingham, several parts of the country rise up in arms, but the rebellious forces are soon dispersed, and Buckingham taken prisoner. The elements seem to unite on Richard's side, just long enough to reveal his frayed temper. It is, however, the briefest of lulls. By the end of the scene, Richmond is safely landed.

On the face of it, Shakespeare did not feel called upon to sift facts from invention. Whatever his private doubts, he simply adds up all the crimes, real or supposed, credited to Richard, and all the tales about him. Where the chroniclers behave like More's London recorder, showing everything as no part their own but someone else's words—anonymous witnesses, gossipy eavesdroppers, 'them that much knew and litle cause had to lye', 'such as wer secrete wᵗ his chamberers'—there is no such mediation on stage. Richard commits all his alleged crimes in full view, all the hostile anecdotes are represented or given as facts, with just one critical reservation, the tale carried by little York, who asserts he learnt it from Richard's nurse. Another episode makes a similarly oblique comment on the value of hearsay: the Mayor's assurance to the comedians 'in rotten armour' that he has as good as witnessed Hastings's treason with his own eyes:

> But, my good lord, your graces' words shall serve
> As well as I had seen and heard him speak.   (III. v. 62–3)

This could be Shakespeare outMoring More. In the long run Richard's manipulations backfired on himself, thanks to other equally reliable testimonies. Apart from these light touches of scepticism, there is little support for a subversive reading of *Richard III* in the text, unless one reads between the lines. Shakespeare refrains from any critical assessment of the current orthodoxy, does not dramatize the chroniclers' conflicts of opinion, and allows us no privileged view of Richmond's intimate thoughts, talents, or political plans for the future.

The same liberty of design leads the playwright to transfer many details found in his sources from one situation or character to another, like the Queen's tearing of her hair for her husband instead of her children, in dramatic awareness that 'The loss of such a lord includes all harms.' Richard is deprived of his speech on sanctuary, but it is he who courts Queen Elizabeth for her daughter's hand, instead of wise messengers bearing gifts as in the chronicles. He is the character who benefits

---

[51] From Edward's death to the murder of his children, 173–90. From the onset of decline to the end of Richard, 190–227.

from most transfers, especially when he is endowed with the narrators' humorous wit or pious pieces of wisdom.

The amount of material borrowed from the sources is impressive, and generally well known thanks to the extracts appended to most editions of the play. It is equally rewarding to examine the full sum of what Shakespeare chose to ignore. The reasons for his omissions have to be imagined. A wish to avoid parallels with other plays on the same subject may be one, though on close analysis, the aim seems rather to avoid harping on overworn themes, weakening the central design, or treading dangerous political ground. Stage policy may have promoted Herbert on Bosworth field, caution may have kept Morton or Stanley away from centre stage. Like Vergil and More, Shakespeare wisely refrains from staging the coronation of Richard. The ceremonies shown so far have all been broken or subverted by some violent transgression. In this case, it is clear from the sources reporting it that the whole nobility was present, and that none complained, nor challenged the title of Richard. And clearer still that Richmond took arms against an anointed king.

Unlike his sources, Shakespeare shows himself well able to resist the temptation of ornaments. He cuts mercilessly into Hall's verbosity, ignores most of his prosopopoeiae or demotes them to brief reports. The final act gives the leaders short symmetrical orations to their armies, in reverse order to Hall's. Richard's remorseless speech comes last, and is followed by his last tyrannous deed, the command to execute young George Stanley, which is uttered in one breath with his invocation to 'fair Saint George'. More's finer rhetoric fares no better. The argument in sanctuary, Buckingham's oration to the Londoners, are reported in abridged form. The confrontation at Stony Stratford comes as a piece of news brought by messenger; the only point that remains from the long narrated episode is the Prince's vain defence of his Woodville kin.[52] Although the play gives more room to the women than the *Henry VI* series, nothing remains of the communications between the Countess of Richmond and Queen Elizabeth, whose precious daughter remains invisible. Anne departs without being allowed her last interview with Richard. Vergil represents their son's death as the first stroke of divine justice, but Shakespeare never mentions the existence of this child, although filiation holds a central place in the whole series. His structural design of crime and punishment goes far beyond private sorrow. It excludes parallels with other princes of Wales who died too young to fulfil their promise.

For similar reasons, blood must not be too lavishly shed, Shakespeare having probably learnt from his experience of Senecan banquets that fear and pity diminish as piles of corpses mount. It was Deborah Warner's main concern and difficulty on directing *Titus Andronicus*, where four bodies have to fall in under a minute, to pre-empt laughter and make each death hurt.[53] In *3 Henry VI* emotion reaches a peak at Act I with Rutland's death, and cannot quite raise similar feelings for the Prince of Wales at the end, but *Richard III* shows new killing recipes, along with a

[52] More 19. *R3*, III. i. 4–16.

[53] See D. Goy-Blanquet, 'Titus Resartus', in Dennis Kennedy (ed.), *Foreign Shakespeare* (Cambridge, 1993), 43.

fastidious sense of timing. Against Horace's hierarchies, what passes show can only be touched by poetry, as is powerfully demonstrated in Clarence's dream. Richard is not present at his death, whereas in the *Mirror*, he leads the messy execution himself. The highest level of pathos is achieved not by showing, as in the *True Tragedy*, but by narrating the death of the young princes. The narration is twice removed from the deed, since the murderers reported it to a remorseful Tyrrel, who tells us how his paid villains 'Wept like two children in their deaths' sad story'. We noted above, having first watched then heard the story of Rutland's death, how Shakespeare tested which mode could best draw tears from the audience.[54] One last temptation he resisted, but his rival did not, is the defilement of Richard's dead body. In the *True Tragedy*, Richmond himself sends it on its shameful parade through the streets. Shakespeare ends retaliations with the tyrant; there is no posthumous vengeance on his corpse.

The centrality of Richard to the thematic structure entails the suppression of many parasitic details. Anne had all the makings of a romantic heroine—married off by Warwick to their former enemy at the age of 15, orphaned and widowed four months later, kidnapped by Clarence to prevent her wedding with Richard—but none of this material serves.[55] There is also much more in the narratives about Clarence than either plot or character uses. He was apparently eaten up by envy, probably had evil designs on the crown long before Richard, and committed a long list of offences before he was finally impeached of treason for rather obscure motives. Mancini reports his open hostility to the Queen and her family, who brought about his fall. According to Commynes, he had spread rumours that the King was a bastard. His stage nightmare omits all memory of his former betrayal of the Yorks, to concentrate on the crimes he committed for ungrateful Edward's sake. As to Richard's part in his murder, More is the only foundation: according to the more reliable Mancini, Richard was overcome with grief when he died.[56]

After three plays where the title role shone by defect, *Richard III* shows the paradoxical emergence of a hero. Many enticing side-tracks are thus left unexplored; the disruption of the commonweal has progressed far ahead of ancillary disloyalties. There is no trace of More's amused comment that Queen Elizabeth was once in the service of Margaret and prayed God heartily to defeat the Yorkists. The enemy from outside is no longer to be feared; the point stressed now is the rivalry between her family of upstarts and the rest of the court. Where the chroniclers spend a large number of pages on the diplomatic relations abroad, and a few on home affairs, the play says nothing of government business—Edward is presumably too ill, and Richard's reign ends almost as soon as it begins. In the chronicles he frequently calls for troops to dictate his will, and their threatening presence is constantly felt. On stage he seldom uses armed force, though he seems to have spies everywhere, plus

---

[54] *R3*, IV. iii. 8. *3H6*, I. iii; I. iv. 150–1, 169–74.

[55] She and her sister Isabel were the rich heiresses of the Warwick lands, over which their York husbands fought ruthlessly. See *Third Continuation of the History of Croyland*, 469–70.

[56] More 7. Hall 326, 369. Mancini, *The Usurpation of Richard III*, 77. On the connection with the prophecy, see Ramsay, *Lancaster and York*, ii. 422.

an endless supply of messengers who report Richmond's progress on a triumphant tide of supporters. All the Earl's setbacks are omitted, as well as his pledges to different women, his mistrust of Dorset, whom he left hostage to the French King, and his not so glorious rescue by William Stanley's troops when he was fighting a losing duel with Richard.[57] His friends all shine with virtue and reflected glory, Stanley first, who is cleared of any suspicion of double dealing.

The seeds of history

If Shakespeare used only a small portion of what he read about Richard's life and times, his memory seems to have registered, or deliberately stored, elements for which he found a use later. The bastard Dunois's refusal of the Coucy inheritance, the conflicting demands on the Exeter citizens, among other notes, inspired similar dilemmas in *King John*.[58] The Classical ironies stressed by More in the tale of Hastings's fall, the hubris that leads him on stage to scorn all signs and warnings, will be more fully developed in *Julius Caesar*, enhanced by one additional detail which does not serve here: a knight came to Hastings's house that morning before he was up, 'as it were of curtesy to accompany hym to the counsaile, but of trouth sent by the protector to hast him thitherward'.[59] Decius Brutus fulfils this part on the morning of Caesar's assassination, reinterpreting all the omens that might have prevented the tragedy.

The shared parentage of Richard and Falstaff with the Vice of moralities makes them distant cousins in humorous cynicism, while Henry IV's disguises on the battlefield seem a development of Richard's angry lines,

> I think there be six Richmonds in the field;
> Five have I slain today instead of him.   (v. iv. 11–12)

The sources report nothing of the sort at Bosworth. This is not to suggest that Shakespeare paints Richmond as a budding Machiavel—indeed the personal psychology of the character plays no great part here—but that the need for stratagem and dissembling is a constant of supreme power, one that calls for further exploration. The issue will only be fully argued at Agincourt with 'A little touch of Harry in the night'. King Henry V's personal involvement in the fight, which redeems both his father's poor show and Richard III's destructive heroism, will then offer a dialectical solution, if a temporary one, to the conflicting demands of power.[60]

At the beginning of the play, Richard complains that his occupation's gone, and bitterly resents 'this weak piping time of peace' where his physical disgraces show up against the courtly background of amorous pleasures. Shakespeare does not develop Gloucester's recorded opposition to the peace treaty with France, but still

[57] Vergil 24. Hall 409. Holinshed 433.

[58] Hall 144–5. Holinshed 298. *King John*, I. i. 150–81, II. i. 300–481.

[59] Cf. *Julius Caesar*, II. i. 202–11, II. ii. 65–107. More 51. In Hall 361, this knight is identified as the ubiquitous Thomas Howard.

[60] *1H4*, v. iv. 24–37. *H5*, Chorus IV. 47, IV. i. 244–90. On Henry V's exorcism of the past, see Goy-Blanquet, 'Sad Stories', 149–50.

makes him the last of the great medieval warlords, as appears in his final oration to his army. We have reached what critics called the Indian summer of English chivalry but, again, the full implications of this will come out more clearly in the following histories, when Prince Hal points out the limitations of Hotspur's archaic code of honour, and its potential risk to the commonwealth. Shakespeare's views on the subject place him far ahead of his contemporaries, when a majority of middle-class law-abiding citizens could enjoy revenge tragedies without worrying over the form of civil disobedience they advertised. How to execute an unreachable enemy, that was the question. Why or whether it should be done was not a dramatic issue. No revenge play before *Hamlet* seriously questions the ethics of blood duty; and yet, even before the genre reached its height of popularity, the clash of private and public values, with its measure of waste, was reflected in the eyes of a visionary Henry VI.

There is method in Shakespeare's imagination. It seems clear that his political insight progressed, through the histories, to the Roman plays and beyond. That having come to a dead end with the advent of the Tudors, he receded to the earlier Plantagenets to explore those 'mysteries of State' which the reigning dynasty protected fiercely against inquisitive writers. That having lifted the cloak of 'divine' monarchy in *Henry V*, he again went further back, beyond the Christian theocentric world, to pursue his enquiry into the workings of power. *Richard III* is connected by structure and theme not only to the other British or Roman histories, but to the whole tragic universe of Shakespeare. Macbeth shares many features with Richard, like him a worthy warrior fashioned by occasion into a murderer, unable to enjoy sleep after his regicide, who finds too late his reign is sterile. Both gaze into the void with devastating lucidity as they understand there is no turning back, and nothing to expect from the future. In the two plays, the commonweal is a living organism threatened by a no less lively disease, which loses virulence once it has triumphed, from lack of nourishment, and is expelled by a conjunction of restorative energies. In *Richard III*, the image is emblematized by Richard himself, spurred on by an insatiable appetite, obsessed with food, who must drink blood before he can enjoy dinner, and eats himself away, 'gnaws his lip', when he has consumed everything within reach.

Discontent, voiced in Richard's first line, is to Peter Brook the key word of the play. Antony Sher described the part he performed so memorably as 'the character actor's Hamlet'.[61] Theatre wisdom does not err when it detects a relationship between the two figures. Some of Richard's features already point in the direction of the sharp-witted malcontent hero and his usurping uncle, the smiling villain Claudius. Kings' games in Denmark are focused on what takes place behind or under the stage, in unlit spaces hiding not only revengeful ghosts, but manipulators and their tools, spies or killers. It takes a troop of genuine actors, player king and queen, to expose the political scene as the lying face of the theatre. But the oppositions in both plays reach more intimate depths. Apart from thematic similarities,

---

[61] Brook's answer to Al Pacino in *Looking for Richard*. Sher, *Year of the King*, 81.

Richard opens the way to Hamlet by interiorizing, if briefly, the *agon* and its arena. Each part of the first Plantagenet sequence, we saw, marks a new level of experimentation, and each level coincides with a progressive closure of the dramatic *locus*. The end of Part 3 prepared the emergence of a central character, 'myself alone'. The conflict between ever more intimate enemies logically leads to the *Spaltung* of the tragic hero, the inner fight of Richard with his private ghosts. 'Conscience is but a word that cowards use', he shouts, gathering his shattered will to don his armour, after the experience of division brought on by his nightmare. 'Richard loves Richard' is a desperate stance against the split which the reading of the Quarto accentuates: 'I and I'. The Folio 'I am I' simply reasserts the unity, the identity of self threatened by his accusing conscience, but the split is there as well, in the will to fly from the murderer—'What, from myself?'—in the imaginary debate between the hated and the loved selves. Richard knows he is in 'So far in blood that sin will pluck on sin', but quickly dismisses the thought to throw himself into the battle. He ends alone, having ventured on the shady side of consciousness to the limits of human experience, 'The undiscovered country from whose bourn I No traveller returns.'

Richard III is not an exact fit in the tetralogic sequence, as the anti-Tillyardian school amply demonstrated. It is oblivious of past deeds, the dramatic progression shows gaps, and the characters do not all conform to their earlier image. Shakespeare proves no more bound by his own creation than by More's or any other source. There is nonetheless an overall structure in the first cycle of histories. Since the death of the victorious Henry V, the dramatic space has shrunk with each phase, until it holes up in the spider's castle. The tragic structure tried out in the preceding play lacked a central character: he now comes on his cue. The centring of the action around a negative hero crowns a double evolution, the last stage of Shakespeare's apprenticeship, and the advent of an evil which has conquered the whole kingdom by stages. It is now summed up in a fiendish character, free from all human bonds, necessarily alone. By successive refinings, the conflict that opposed English and French, high and low born, father to son and brother to brother, is about to divide the very conscience of the subject.

Rival brothers

If large sections of the chronicles are ignored, sometimes a mere hint finds unexpected developments. Hastings's first spell in the Tower is Shakespeare's invention: it was suggested by the episode of his encounter with a pursuivant likewise named Hastings, which reminds him of an earlier meeting with the same man in the same place, at a time when thanks to the attacks of the Woodville clan 'he was for yᵉ while (but it lasted not long) farre fallen into yᵉ kinges indignacion, & stode in gret fere of himselfe'.[62] Hence his rejoicing at the thought that they must be executed that very day, a coincidence which is another invention, More's, too good to be ignored. Vergil's stress is on past guilt and the rewards of sin, where More plays up

---

[62] More 51. Hall 361. *R3*, III. ii. 99–100, 103. The pursuivant, hailed with a 'Well met Hastings' in Q, remains unnamed in F.

the Classical tricks of fate and the misinterpretation of oracles which lead men to their ruin. From such discrete hints and ironies, Shakespeare builds up a consistent web of unnatural symmetries, an artistic design so fused with the plans of alleged numinous powers that one can no longer tell which is which. There is only one dying speech in the sources, spoken by Vaughan at Pomfret, more in anger than remorse. In the play, the balance between faults and curses on one side, confessions and expiation on the other is almost perfect. Almost, for Margaret sees but the meanest half of the design. The crowning symmetry comes at the end, also drawn from the reports on the battle, in the duel of Richmond and Richard between their parallel tents.

Some of the most memorable scenes have even less basis in the chronicles. Admittedly, the citizens' anxieties for the future, young Edward's princely concerns for the past, even the vindictiveness of Clarence's children and the Duchess of York could more or less be inferred from the context, but the wooing of Lady Anne, the unhistorical presence of Margaret, the murderers' pangs of conscience, and the ritualized visits of the ghosts to both tents all testify to Shakespeare's imaginative resources. It cannot be just coincidence if a majority of these have parallels in other poets' works on the same subject.

Women play a major part in *Richardus Tertius* and the *True Tragedy*. Queen Elizabeth is shown in both plays lamenting her husband's death, conducting arguments to keep her younger son in sanctuary with her, and finally triumphant through her daughter's wedding to the conqueror. Both plays develop the character of Jane Shore. Both are heavily moral in celebrating the downfall of a tyrant, and no less heavily Senecan in rhetoric, dreams, ghosts, horrific murders, and various revenge ingredients—two features which critics of the Tillyardian school found dominant in Shakespeare's *Richard III*, and used as a basis for providentialist readings of the completed tetralogy. It now remains for their detractors to build up a counter-theory integrating these troublesome signs of a higher order.

Richardus Tertius was designed as a sort of trilogy, three 'Actiones' in five acts, meant to be performed on three separate evenings. Whether or not Shakespeare used it is still a point of division between critics.[63] Legge's play has two wooing scenes, one of which shows Richard courting his niece Elizabeth with extravagant flourishes. If it gave Shakespeare the idea for his duel with Anne, there the likeness ends, for the bombastic flame of Legge's Richard fails dismally with the lady. He confesses he spilt her brothers' blood but does not claim it was for love of her, and when he offers his breast to naked swords, it is a rhetorical phrase, not a direct challenge to her to kill him with his own. Maybe both playwrights found the idea elsewhere, in Seneca for instance, who is the most likely source, relayed by *The Mirror for Magistrates*, of one feature common to all revenge tragedies, the ghosts.[64]

---

[63] Churchill, Dover Wilson, Bullough think he did, Taylor and Jowett among others think they overstate the case.

[64] *Hercules Furens* in Jasper Heywood's translation for Bullough 236–7, 313–17, or in the Latin version according to Harold Brooks, '*Richard III*: Unhistorical Amplifications. The Women's Scenes and Seneca', *Modern Language Review*, 75 (Oct. 1980), 721–37. Jowett traces Richard's gambit of offering his sword to *Hippolytus*.

Jowett is entirely right when he notes that it grounds the play 'in the fundamental and violent dramatic tropes of the Senecan world', but that *Richard III* is definitely not a Senecan play. One could argue that Seneca's, like the chroniclers', is but one of the perspectives on the historical past, the one closest to Margaret's negative capability. And that all these points could also be found in Gascoigne's *Jocasta*: the curse of a ghostly figure who hovers in the background, stichomythian fencing, and a weeping chorus of 'four Thebane dames'.

The parallels with the *True Tragedy* are more intriguing, and the question of influences not so easily settled, as it rests again on priority.[65] A much debated suggestion was that Shakespeare avoided showing material dramatized elsewhere, like the murder of the princes which is a prominent scene in *True Tragedy*, because of Greene's recent charge of plagiarism.[66] These issues naturally entailed fresh arguments about dates of composition, and whether *Richard III* was written before or after Greene's Parthian shot. It seems beyond hope now to reconstruct the history of the anonymous play. As far as can be judged from the badly corrupted text that has survived, a close reading of both plays rather suggests an open competition between their authors, a rivalry of the kind imagined by the film *Shakespeare in Love* between Alleyn's and Burbage's theatres. That they knew, and possibly vied with, each other is attested by Hamlet's ironical apostrophe to the players: 'The croaking raven doth bellow for revenge' parodies a speech in *True Tragedy*, saluted by Muriel Bradbrook as the most prodigious piece of epiphora in the English drama.[67] Tit for tat, the croaking raven might be the upstart crow's retaliation on a clumsy plagiarist. Or a proud claim to have improved the original. Either way, it sounds like a self-conscious appraisal of their relative merits. Beside occasional phrases, the playwrights' selections of material show similarities which cannot all be explained by their tapping of the same sources, namely *The Mirror*. Of course, as Antony Hammond reminds us, 'the very lines which strike one as reminiscent of *Richard III* may be precisely that: copyist's or performer's recollections of the Shakespeare play, which had no place in the original text.' Though why, if *True Tragedy* came later, they should lift such a memorable phrase as 'A horse! A horse! My kingdom for a horse!' to flatten it into 'A horse, a horse, a fresh horse' defies understanding. Yet another bad case of ham actors and drunken compositors.

It is worth noting that the scenes on which the two playwrights meet, or wink at each other, are those with no historical basis. The *True Tragedy*, with approximately 2,300 lines divided into twenty-one scenes, is shorter by a third than *Richard III*. Its sum of historical material is also much less, though in a few instances it is closer to the chronicles, reproducing Stanley's answer that he has sons to spare, and giving

---

[65] Churchill, Dover Wilson, Bullough, Honigmann, Smidt, Jowett, Lull think *True Tragedy* was written first and find similarities. Emrys Jones and Hammond stress the differences. For a reassessment of *True Tragedy*, see Maguire, *Shakespearean Suspect Texts*, 317–18, and her opinion that in its extant version it may have served as source, 374 n. 54.

[66] Dover Wilson's suggestion, ed. *Richard III*, p. xxxi, was refuted by Kenneth Muir, *The Sources of Shakespeare's Plays* (London, 1977), 35

[67] *Themes and Conventions of Elizabethan Tragedy* (Cambridge, 1935), 99–100. *Hamlet*, III. ii. 248. *The True Tragedy of Richard III*, ll. 1892–3.

Richmond the command to draw Richard's corpse naked through the streets. This Richmond, more fragile and humane than Shakespeare's, is audibly disappointed with his stepfather's waverings, but duly thanks him for his share in the victory, glossing over the fact it was actually William Stanley who saved him. Richard is the more glamorous of the two, thanks to a Page who magnifies his deeds in a *chanson de geste* sung between the acts. The play gives large space to characters and episodes that Shakespeare did not use, Mistress Shore, Princess Elizabeth, the betrayal of Humphrey Banister. In many cases, what one author shows the other reports, and vice versa. *True Tragedy* represents the arrest of the Woodvilles at Stony Stratford, the argument with the Queen in sanctuary, the penance of Shore's wife, the death of the princes, the capture of Buckingham, the engagement of Richmond with Elizabeth, and the reuniting of Stanley with his son George, but narrates the execution at Pomfret, Buckingham's oration in Guild Hall, the offer of the crown to Richard, the suit to the Queen for her daughter's hand, Richard's nightmare, and his ghostly visitors. The courting of Queen Elizabeth is done by messengers as in the sources, but as in *Richard III* her consent remains in doubt.

The features connecting the two plays are of various kinds. Richard's soliloquies and asides in *True Tragedy* show the same willingness to confide in the audience. On his first entrance, he informs the public that he is determined to win the crown and has already taken steps with this aim in view. If he has removed logs like Clarence or Henry VI, it is not to be deprived of his due by mere children—here a touch anticipating Falstaff:

> Why what are the babes but a puffe of
> Gun-powder? a marke for soldiers, food for fishes,
> Or lining for beds . . .   (iii. 376–7)

Then we have three anxious characters, reflections of More's rumorous narrative, who discuss the uncertainties of the future. Several domestic scenes follow: Edward's dying attempt to reconcile his friends; the Prince's vain protest in defence of his Woodville uncle; Queen Elizabeth's laments and fears for her children's safety; young York's efforts to comfort her, eliciting a debauchery of antanaclasis on a par with Shakespeare's loudest fireworks:

> *Yorke.* May it please your grace.
> *Queene.* A my son, no more grace, for I am so sore disgraced, that without Gods grace, I
>   fall into dispaire with my selfe . . .   (ix. 809–11)

The climax of these private encounters is the meeting of the children with their murderers. The scene has no equivalent here in *Richard III*, but does share some significant points with the killing of Clarence: the princes' sombre mood, the murderers' dialogue with their victims, and the argument between them, one showing reluctance, the other chiding him for his faint-heartedness. Also noteworthy for similarities is Buckingham's last speech, which mixes remorse, accusations, curses, and a recollection of all he had done for Richard's sake, Richmond's welcome to his supporters, Richard's guilt-ridden soliloquy, with its evocation of a prisoner at the bar:

> My fearefull shadow that still follows me,
> Hath sommond me before the severe judge,
> My conscience witnesse of the blood I spilt,
> Accuseth me as guiltie of the fact ...   (xiv. 1403–6)

The Ghost of Clarence, crying revenge at the opening of the *True Tragedy*, is the only ghost to appear on stage; the others come as one lot in Richard's account of his nightmare, which begins in a life-weary tone close to Henry V's, or even Hamlet's,

> The hell of life that hangs upon the Crowne,
> The daily cares, the nightly dreames,
> The wretched crewes, the treason of the foe,
> And horror of my bloodie practise past,
> Strikes such a terror to my wounded conscience,
> That sleepe I, wake I, or whatsoever I do,
> Methinks their ghoasts comes gaping for revenge,
> Whom I have slaine in reaching for a Crowne ...   (xviii. 1874–81)

gathering momentum for the record-breaking epiphora of Hamlet's reminiscences. The King refuses to fly, though he knows all is lost: 'Downe is thy sunne, Richard, never to shine again.' Two long scenes follow his death. In the first, Report wonders how he may find 'the certain true report of this victorious battell fought to day' but cannot complain that rumour is full of tongues, since the Page gives him an exact account, reliable as to facts, yet highly encomiastic of 'worthie Richard that did never flie, but followed honour to the gates of death'. O for a muse of fire! In the last scene, Richmond thanks everyone around, including Stanley, receives the crown from his stepfather, and from the Queen mother the hand of fair Elizabeth who informs him she will obey her parents' wish and be his, in a position not unlike that of Princess Katharine after Agincourt. An epilogue celebrates the joining of the two houses, with a list of their descendants down to the then reigning Elizabeth, who is fused with her namesake as 'the meanes that civill wars did cease'.

To the above catalogue may be added a group of other parallel scenes which have more basis in the chronicles: Richard's conversations with Buckingham, their plans to part the Prince from his Woodville kin, the trap laid for Hastings, the Page's part as go-between, Catesby's staunch loyalty, the command to execute George Stanley and his reprieve, Richmond's private meeting with Stanley, whose reticence does not go down as well as in Shakespeare's version, Richard's request of a horse, refusal to flee, and death in single combat against Richmond. All in all, the sum of comparable features deserves a moment's consideration. And unless it is argued that by 1594 Shakespeare had written not only the first but the second historical sequence, as well as *Hamlet*, he must be the one who stored up odd old ends from *True Tragedy*, not the reverse; the anonymous author seems to have heard more of Marlowe's mighty lines than Shakespeare's, judging by the Tamburlainian flavour of his Richard's rants. Of course Shakespeare too had heard Marlowe, and both Richards commune with Faustus in their exclusion from divine grace. Acknowledgement of these influences by no means detracts from the poet's creative imagination, but may throw some light on its workings. To consider that it makes his poetry less original would be as silly as to pay homage to the author of a banal call for a horse as the true inventor of the famous phrase. There is a world of difference, a kingdom, between the two lines.

We come to the last major source of all Tudor histories. Critical opinion has often varied as to the extent of Shakespeare's debts to the *Mirror* in this play. All agree, though, that he found next to nothing in the 'Tragedie of Richard'. The most catching detail about it is the closing prose comment, probably in retort to inside criticism of the author's lame verse, 'the meeter was mysliked almost of all', but since King Richard never kept measure in any of his doings, 'it were against the *decorum* of his personage, to vse eyther good Meter or order', a notion Shakespeare abundantly exploited, beginning with his vigorous opening trochee and jumbled seasons, 'Now is the winter…'[68] However, he certainly did not endorse the implicit criteria of Baldwyn's decision to let this mediocre piece 'pass therefore as it is, though to good for so yll a person'; both *3 Henry VI* and *Richard III* show enough concern for the need to derive aesthetic pleasure from ugliness to classify him as a true Aristotelian in this regard.

The 'Tragedie of Clarence' lent more elements, the actual part of Richard in his death, which More simply evoked as a possibility, and the phrase 'New Christned' which the stage Richard wittily links up to the prophecy on 'G'. Sackville's Induction to the complaint of Buckingham, generally admired for its hallucinating journey across Acheron, probably served for Clarence's dream. The moral lessons taught in the other stories have some little echo in the dialogue. That of Hastings, a pedestrian versification of More's prose via Hall, illustrates the rewards of treachery, and stresses that the proclamation was written before he was even accused. Where Edward repents 'his surfeting', in the play it is Richard who moralizes the King's illness, deploring that 'he hath kept an evil diet long'.[69] Rivers denounces social climbers and worldly greeds, and Shore's wife the evils of forced marriage. Collingbourne speaks up for the ancient liberties of poets. These pointed lessons do not touch central issues of *Richard III*, though the *Mirror*'s ghosts may well have suggested the pattern of dying confessions. Its main themes of guilt, remorse, and punishment have an overall relevance to the play, though often with different applications: 'Shakespeare seems to have been stimulated by the rhetoric while eschewing the content,' as Hammond aptly puts it, whose scrupulous research brought up little more than specific verbal echoes from the Tragedies.[70] Apart from such pinpoint borrowings, others more general like the endurance of the past through ghostly survivors, the fall of ambitious rulers, and the doctrine of submission to God's deputies on earth have some common ground with the mental universe of the play, but none of its complexities or historical depth.

---

[68] 'Richard Plantagenet, Duke of Gloucester', 'To the Reader', 371.
[69] Tragedy xix, 'How king Edward through his surfeting and vntemperate life, sodainly died'. *R3*, I. i. 140.
[70] Hammond 89.

Motiveless malignity

'If God exists', Woody Allen once said, 'let's hope he has a good excuse.' Michelet rightly detected in the figure of the witch a crystallization of medieval despair, frustrated anger, hatred rather than denial of God.[71] Witchcraft and the cult of Satan reflected the established order with exactly symmetrical inversions, thus confirming its validity. These symmetries, like the ones which structure the play, have ancient roots, all but lost in the dark origins of Christianity. Coleridge had diagnosed Iago's as 'motiveless malignity', in the absence of any cause strong enough to measure with his destructive work. In the modern view, Richard would rather seem to suffer from an excess of motives. The reason of his villainy has been abundantly dissected by critics armed with Freudian or Lacanian concepts— deformity, mother's rejection, Oedipal emulation of his father. They make great sense, especially to the actors who have to create a psychological coherence for the character. To Early Modern historians and playwrights, however, for whom evil creatures were facts as unavoidable as war and plague, the question of motives was probably of less concern than the origin of evil, and the fact that it was allowed to prosper in God's creation.

The difficulty was unknown to pagan philosophers. Plato's material world was the creation of a demiurge; the division of tasks between two principles, one good, associated with light and spirit, the other bad, linked with matter and darkness, easily accounted for the presence of evil in nature. In Manichean doctrine, evil resulted from a weakness of God, an incapacity to master it. Arguing against this 'weakness', Augustine insisted God was not simply omniscient but almighty as well, infinitely bounteous and the maker of all things[72]—an insoluble contradiction, for how could God be both merciful and just? almighty, yet allow evil to triumph on earth? good, and let evil destroy innocent victims? If God created all things, he must be partly responsible for their evil ways, so why withhold forgiveness of sins he could have prevented? The answer, free will, made the contradiction even worse. Men were able to know good from evil, and free to choose between them, but needed the help of God's grace to make the right choice. Being predestined, not predetermined, they could use their will to place divine love above all other delights. Evil had a place in God's plans, as both a consequence of sin and a means of atonement through the sinner's suffering.[73]

Since God, the perfect One, produced all the forms in the cosmos, evil could only be explained as a deficiency, the absence of good, rather than something created. For the Neoplatonists, who did not believe in Creation, the universe was a whirl of elements held together by divine love, a concept drawn from Plotinus. The Pseudo-

---

[71] Jules Michelet, *La Sorcière: The Witch of the Middle Ages*, trans. Lionel J. Trotter (London, 1863).

[72] See Étienne Gilson, *History of Christian Philosophy in the Middle Ages* (London, 1955), 69–81. John M. Rist, *Augustine* (Cambridge, 1994), ch. VII, 'Evil, justice, and divine omnipotence'.

[73] Augustine, *The City of God*, xiv, xxviii, xiii. xiii, xiv. iii, xi.

Denys and most theologians after him use this theory as the basis of their argument, but still have to justify God's arbitrariness in refusing to save all sinners. Boethius treats the conflict between determinism and free will in terms similar to Augustine's central paradox, but he has no philosophical answer to the problem of evil. His hellenic culture leads him to imagine a scale of beings increasingly degraded as they move away from God and deeper into matter; he holds that all creatures are good and that only moral evil, the result of human free will, exists in nature. The medieval chroniclers, whose providentialist views were somewhat less consistent than Augustine's, shared Boethius' difficulty in reconciling God's perfection with the manifest presence of evil in the world.[74] They, too, hesitated between the independence of man's will and the power of the planets. One may be surprised to meet Fortune serenely speeding along the ways of the Lord in sixteenth-century chronicles, but one need not seek the humanists' influence in this strange combination: Boethius had already accommodated Fortune with its Classical trappings into the divine scheme, and engendered the Providence popularized by the chroniclers.

Following Plato, Augustine, Denys, Boethius, among others, who equate evil with non-being, the position defended by the Lateran Council in 1215 clarifies a process strikingly close to the one dramatized in *Richard III* and *Macbeth*: evil having no essence can be the source of nothing. It can diminish good but not consume it, or else nothing would remain for evil to reside in, so that it would destroy itself. An absolutely evil being would be a contradiction in terms, hating and cancelling his own essence. Could he but find anything to love and cherish in himself, then he would not be completely evil—the limit touched on the edge of Richard's night.[75] In his *Summa Theologiae*, the most consistent attempt of the age to conciliate theology and philosophy, Thomas Aquinas finds it difficult to reconcile the reality of natural evils with divine goodness, and admits they are the best argument against the existence of God. The Rhineland mystics, no less impregnated with Denys's Neoplatonism, argued that evil was necessary to the perfection of the world: it was part of the deity, its creature and instrument as well as its antagonist. Augustine had opened the way when he praised antithesis as the most beautiful of figures, both in the writing of the Bible and in that of Creation. Hall uses it at the onset of Richard's reign, to justify the space given to an evildoer, 'for contrary set to contrary is more apparaunt, as whyte ioyned with black, maketh the fayrer shewe'.[76]

In the *Daemonologie* which is contemporary with *Richard III*, King James explains that we actually need Satan 'as Gods hang-man'.[77] The Devil is given large powers to fulfil his mission: he may sometimes read parts of the future, perform magic tricks, even take on the appearance of a holy man to trap unbelievers, but he

---

[74] Thomas Aquinas was well aware of their differences when he used Boethius' theses to argue against Augustine's. *The Summa Theologica*, ed. Benziger Brothers (New York, 1947) I. vi. 2–4; I, xlix. 65. *Commentary on the De Trinitate of Boethius*, ed. A. Maurer (Toronto, 1953). On evil as a privation of goodness, *Summa*, I. xlviii. 1 and 3. See Courcelle, *La Consolation de Philosophie*, 318.

[75] Jeffrey B. Russell, *Lucifer: The Devil in the Middle Ages* (Ithaca, NY, 1984), 189–90.

[76] *City of God*, XI. xviii, quoting Corinthians 6: 7–10. Hall 374.

[77] James I, *Daemonologie*, in *Minor Prose Works of King James VI & I*, ed. J. Craigie and A. Law (Edinburgh, 1982), the preface, p. xx.

is incapable of creating anything, the mark which distinguishes his from God's powers. There is much to be learnt from this creature:

For since the Deuill is the verie contrarie opposite to God, there is no better way to know God, then by the contrarie; as by the ones power (though a creature) to admire the power of the great Creator: by the falshood of the one to consider the trueth of the other, and by the injustice of the one to considder the Iustice of the other: And by the cruelty of the one, to considder the mercifulnesse of the other: And so foorth in all the rest of the essence of God, and qualities of the Deuill. (II. vii. 38)

His Majesty understood the value of symmetries, however little style he may have learnt from rhetoric classes.

The chroniclers had no better weapons than this patchy philosophical equiment to harmonize the brute facts of life to theological orthodoxy. The symptoms of evil fill their pages, challenging their farragoes of suitable concepts to account for the frequent reversals of conjuncture. Their first concern is political rather than theological orthodoxy. We saw Hall doing his utmost with causes borrowed from ill-assorted doctrines to justify God's strange ways of treating good and bad kings. Neither he nor his colleagues waste time on Richard's motives, nor harbour doubts that he was part of God's mysterious plans: Antichrist, scourge, or limb of the devil, it all comes to the same in the end, with a well-deserved punishment dealt by almighty Providence. None of these pious men seems surprised that God should sacrifice innocent children to execute his judgements.

Consciously or not, the various hypotheses elaborated by earlier generations meet on the back of Richard, who hides a medley of folkloric and religious ingredients in his hump. Typically, he inverts the duality principle, blames his monstrous body on the Heavens, his crooked mind on Hell.[78] The Neoplatonist belief that divine love held the world together lends support to his own excuse for villainy: Love forswore him in his mother's womb and corrupted frail Nature with bribes. When Richard proclaims himself 'determinèd to prove a villain', he sums up the ensuing fight between his and a superior determination.[79] The stage character exists somewhere between free will and determinism, an incompleted nature, sterile, deprived of love 'which grey beards call divine' and of sun, God's or the Devil's hangman, Antichrist, Lucifer himself, the ultimate engagement in virtuous serfdom. Richard's avowed heredity may be traced back to Old Vice, but his choice to do wrong anticipates Milton's Satan, the negative spirit of Goethe's Faustus, the vertigo and utter loneliness of Sartrian liberty:

For freedom to cause giddiness it must choose in the theocratic world to be infinitely in the wrong. In this way it becomes *unique* in a world entirely directed towards Good; but it must adhere completely to Good, must preserve and reinforce it in order to retain the power of plunging into Evil.[80]

---

[78] 3H6, v. vi. 78–9.
[79] See Janis Lull's fine commentary on determinism, 5–17.
[80] Jean-Paul Sartre, *Baudelaire*, trans. Martin Turnell (London, 1949), 70. On the direct line running from the Old English Lucifer to Milton's Satan, see Russell, *Lucifer*, 134–8.

If Evil fights for Good, it is not to accomplish God's plans, but to preserve man's absolute freedom to choose Evil, in the way Milton, consciously or not, chose the side of Satan.

Enter the Devil

Shakespeare's creatures are cut to custom, in a manner skilful enough by now to accommodate the required historical information, and yet endow them with persuasive humanity. So persuasive that spectators will loudly admire Richard's 'incredible' seduction of Lady Anne, without stopping to consider whether Shakespeare managed to make the unlikely scene credible enough. Obviously he did, as none doubt the very existence of the monster, let alone his seductive talents. Laurence Olivier set the bar higher by conquering Anne over the body of her dead husband. With or without this alteration, spectators have no doubt Richard could do it. Some unfamiliar with the play come out believing he did. As appears from our trek through the chronicles, this monster is a thing of shreds and patches, or more properly fragments of texts and codes. The process is akin to the one described by Antony Sher in his building up of the part:

I sketch Richard's head from this morning's thoughts. Interesting how the melting-pot works—the drawing has the bulk of Lion's Head; Klaus Kinski's eye; and a harelip from the Coetzee book I've been reading here, *Michael K.* Of course there's no way I could look like this . . . But I love the thickness of this face; in a way, going back to the original Laughton image. With Brando's Godfather thrown in. (76)

Unlike More's creature, which springs from nowhere and has no near equivalent in the whole living world, Shakespeare's synthetic villain is a convincing addition of all too human traits. More's assertion that, unless reports lied, 'nature changed her course in his beginning' grows into an image of nature in the throes of childbirth spitting forth this undigested lump. There is not just an ethical but a cosmic dimension to Richard's monstrosity, his mountainous back, and arms like withered shrubs: 'It is in one sense time itself that has given birth to Richard, the chaos of civil war breeding the "unlicked bear whelp" whose only future is savage destruction.'[81]

Shakespeare's construct is built on the two main conflicting versions of the tyrant he found unblended in Hall. Thomas More recounts by analepsis Richard's activities before the death of his brother, to suggest that the usurpation was planned well before Edward's demise. In Vergil's history, Richard distinguishes himself first as a warrior devoted to the family cause, who gives no early signs of an unnatural ambition. Where Hall makes no attempt to smooth out the seams, the change in Shakespeare's character observes both psychological probability and dramatic necessity. Richard takes his cue from Edward's first lessons in individualism, soon relayed by Clarence, when he repudiates all affinities at the end of *3 Henry VI*: 'I have no brother, I am like no brother.' His desire to prove his father's elect reappears

---

[81] Berry, *Patterns of Decay*, 71.

somewhat skewed in *Richard III* when he has it rumoured that he is the only legitimate son/sun of York.

Thus the contradictory aspects of the character are the end result of both an individual and a collective process. Richard's ordeal, inseparable from the revenge tragedies of the civil war, becomes the national tragedy, by an ultimate perversion of feudal heroics. The sanguinary tyrant incarnates the final stage of a warrior nobility who drew away step by step from their civic ideal, and no longer feel bound to any master or duty but self-aggrandizement. His monstrous generation magnifies one of the rumours reported by More, that he was born 'not vntothed', and ties it up to another physical trait, told by Vergil, that 'he dyd contynually byte his nether lyppe'. Henry VI's dying intuition that he came 'to bite the world' recurs in the next play, recalled first by young York, and by the ogre's demand for Hastings's head before dinner. At the end of the process, having devoured all, he must sup upon himself—the pointed 'see, he gnaws his lip' echoes his nephew's wonder that 'he could gnaw a crust at two hours old'—and in his turn 'drop into the rotten mouth of death'.[82] An unprecedented version of the Senecan banquet, with time the devourer looming above Richard. Time's labours show a maturing process outside the grasp of the characters, a rebellion of nature against the usurper. In Wilbur Sanders's view,

'Providence' may still be an appropriate term for it, but it is a Providence which has emerged out of the natural, an enactment of universal moral law, not a mere proclamation of it; and it grows out of the soil of human life, rather than descending supernaturally from above.[83]

Satan can shift his shape to suit his purpose. When he takes a human form, he appears frequently monstrous and deformed, and lame because he fell from Heaven. He is also a skilled and persuasive debater. Many features of Richard's legend thus combined to establish him as a creature from Hell, first his nickname, Dickon, which was one of the popular names for the Devil, and his emblem, the boar, one of the Devil's many disguises. The North, from where Richard came and regularly sent for troops, was the domain of darkness, as the cardinal point on the left or sinister side of a church; on the medieval stage, north was the direction of Hell. Russell notes that the wide popular belief in the Devil formed the root of 'the witchcraze which was at its height in England at precisely the time that Shakespeare was at his'; a convergence of satiric trends in literature 'laid the basis for the replacement of the medieval Devil with Shakespeare's human villain, in whom evil is restricted to the individual human personality'.[84]

In folk tales, the Devil is associated with a host of animals, many of which are echoed by the characters' stock of insults—wolf, dog, spider, ape, basilisk, toad, tiger, phoenix, owl, raven. In the chronicles, Richard is often associated with some of these, wolf or tiger, but more frequently with the serpent or snake, the Devil's

---

[82] More 7. *3H6*, v. vi. 53–4. *R3*, III. iv. 76, 93–4; II. iv. 28; IV. ii. 28; IV. iv. 2.

[83] *The Dramatist and the Received Idea*, 103–4.

[84] Russell, *Lucifer*, 67–70, 244, 261, enumerates all these features, but does not mention Richard III. Robert Muchembled, *Une histoire du diable: XIIe–XXe siècle* (Paris, 2000), notes that the Devil has survived best in Anglo-Saxon countries, while the Latin ones treat him with derision.

shape in Eden. John Rous, followed by More, compared him with the Antichrist who, in medieval lore, is sometimes an incarnation of Satan, sometimes his son, or the leader of Satan's armies. Antichrist is the exact opposite of Christ, man and Devil as Christ is man and God; they will face each other at the world's end when he fights his last desperate battle against God.[85] In the play, Bosworth evokes Armageddon, while Richmond identifies himself with the mower of Doomsday, promising

> To reap the harvest of perpetual peace
> By this one bloody trial of sharp war.   (v. ii. 15–16)

This concludes the long chain of vegetal and cyclical metaphors running through the whole tetralogy. After the gory agriculture practised in the Wars of the Roses, one last bloody ritual will restore the land to its peaceful corn and vine growing. Far from dissolving the moral exemplum into timeless myth, Berry notes, Shakespeare anchors it into the historical reality of fifteenth-century England, thus providing his audience with an interpretative key to their troubled past: 'It is not as allegory that the Apocalypse informs *Richard III*, but as an underlying cultural myth, an archetypal presence that joins the play's conception of time to the larger structures of Christian history.' Richard embodies the violent century that fostered his coming: 'Henceforth he will dominate the world as a true distillation of the anarchic tendencies of the society that brought him into being.'[86] Born before his term, hurried on by a devouring urge, impatient of decorum, he upsets the rhythm of the calendar, limps ahead of the beat, interrupts devotions, and packs off his victims to Heaven without decorousness. For want of a better ceremonial, semi-clandestine rites, litanies of suffering and curses develop, led by Margaret who trusts that time will destroy her enemies as it did her. Being too corrupt herself to see beyond the slaking of tribal hatreds, her view of the future is mortgaged by the identical recurrence of punitive crimes. Her peace-loving husband, so despised for his passive gentleness, could alone transcend the closed system of revenge and offer the hope of a cure for the future.

Before the promised pacification, the kingdom undergoes the long agony foretold by Henry. If the providential arrival of Richmond appears a form of obligatory homage to the reigning dynasty, it proceeds nonetheless from a perfectly coherent moral vision which will be developed in the later works. The dynamics of evil eventually produces antibodies: troubled nature, after a long spell of fever, assembles its forces for a bloodletting purification. Richmond here anticipates Macduff. A new character in this stage-soiled cast, innocent of all past crimes, he is the symbol as well as the agent of national reconciliation. He neither resolves the ambiguities of the monarchic function, nor the moral impasses signalled by the dramatic conflicts of obligation. The action stops on the threshold of the present.

---

[85] See R. K. Emmerson, *Antichrist in the Middle Ages* (Manchester, 1981).
[86] *Patterns of Decay*, 95, 71.

Women and children first

The episodes freest from historical guidelines all involve characters who usually take little space on the world's main stage: women, children, ghosts, and paid murderers. The other contemporary plays on the subject also give more room to these characters than the chronicles. Whether Shakespeare parodies or avoids their patterns, he inserts his second roles in an entirely new thematic structure. The greater attention paid to women in the recent scholarly works and stage productions has shown them to be Richard's most resolute antagonists. The rest of the characters have some strength but not much variety, less even at times than in the sources. The merciless trimming to size fits them into the design at the cost of many original features. Clarence's shady friends, Hastings's loyalist plotters, the messengers running back and forth between the Queen and Margaret Stanley, Morton's network of spies, are not allowed to compete with the main schemer. There are no villains to supplant him either: Clarence, the paid murderers, Catesby, More's cowed citizens, all come out far less abject than in the sources. Instead of playing a double game, Dorset is back in arms even before Richmond lands, and fights on his side at Bosworth, which saves Richmond from leaving him behind as hostage, an act for which he gives Queen Elizabeth some rather long-winded excuses in the *True Tragedy*. Shakespeare's Dorset is the only one to escape the fate promised him by Margaret, while Richmond emerges cleaned from memories of his rambling years in France and all inglorious acts of war.

Women. Lady Anne appears but briefly in *Richardus Tertius* and *The True Tragedy*. Her part in Shakespeare's play is largely his creation, even though her marriage and hasty remarriage were facts, both results of the casualties of war. She was a childhood friend, and the daughter of a dead enemy, whose alliance presented no political advantage for Richard. Why he married her, Professor Emrys Jones rather shamefacedly admits to Al Pacino he does not know. There is no satisfactory explanation of this historical fact, at least none fitting the characters as they are sketched in the play, and no need to rehearse here all the psychoanalytical probes into Richard's or Anne's darker impulses. This scene, one of the world's greatest hits, fully demonstrates the scope of Richard's talent—he can win any woman against all odds, despite his earlier excuse that he 'cannot prove a lover'—and Shakespeare's—a poet after Aristotle's heart, able to convince with the most unlikely impossibility.

Anne thus wins a place in the feminine concert of woe, resentment, and curses. Her apostrophe to Richard, 'Foul devil ... thou hast made the happy earth thy hell', shows even before Margaret's masterclass in rhetoric an instinctive knowledge of its basic principles: make the object of hatred uglier, and the loss greater, than they were. She cannot have known this 'happy earth' which her own family's feuds had begun to ravage before she was born. Richard's retort to her insults, that he knows no touch of pity and therefore is no beast, exposes the conventional cast of her mind by his colder appraisal of humanity. When he gambles on the fact that she would not strike a kneeling enemy, she has already lost their duel by spitting at him, a breach of decorum so against her rigid conformism that she cannot forgive herself.

Queen Elizabeth does not give in so easily when she is rebuked by her stepmother for her unseemly show of despair. Like Anne, she manages quite a good rhetorical argument for her 'act of tragic violence', which prepares the public for her better resistance to Richard. The Duchess, perhaps the most blood-curdling of the wounded mothers, curses both herself for giving birth to a hell-hound and Richard, who seems to lose all stamina after her onslaught. The blind hatred of the curses sometimes misfires and turns back on their authors, but there is no denying their destructive force. Margaret's most significant role is to unite these antiphonal moans into a mounting, ultimately triumphant psalmody. A living ghost of the past, she knits the almighty alliance of the quick and the dead.[87]

To many directors, especially film directors, Margaret remains the heavy mother of the cast. They find it difficult to hold together Richard's caustic one-liners and her rhetorical litanies; Barton/Hall's *Wars of the Roses*, which played down the power of incantation in favour of political forces, allowed her only a marginal role. Yet Richard himself mimicks the style, for instance with his triumphant couplet

> Was ever woman in this humour wooed?
> Was ever woman in this humour won?

capped with a terse

> I'll have her, but I will not keep her long.   (I. ii. 231–3)

To cut the rhetoric is to lose the point made by Richard when he debunks his opponents' set patterns, deftly completes Margaret's curse with her own name, or mocks the churlish blessing of the Duchess:

> Amen. And make me die a good old man,
> That is the butt-end of a mother's blessing;
> I marvel that her grace did leave it out.   (II. ii. 109–11)

It also glosses over the fact that the programme of retribution is in progress, as Sam Mendes's ghostly Margaret recalled with each new death; and that Richard's irony, pleasing as it is to modern scepticism, is no match for it.

The single-mindedness of these women, the potential force of their protest, their incantatory rituals, are probably more deeply felt now, and better understood, than ever before. Directors of the past decades have gradually paid more attention to the 'wailing queens' as they are often called, unlike their predecessors' cutting policies which sacrificed women and children first. This evolution reflects not so much the influence of feminist studies as the pregnant images of those mad mothers who have demonstrated in all parts of the world against the murderers of their sons, and inspired Richard Eyre's feminine chorus. In his and Michael Boyd's RSC production, the deprived mothers were the driving force behind the less vindictive men.

---

[87] See Lull's parallel with the three Marys in the Resurrection plays, 9–12.

Children. After Margaret, Clarence's 'mawkish' children are often the next victims of a director's knife. Unlike Edward's lot, they cannot be made to sound natural; their expressions of sorrow are too stiff to be believed, and there is nothing in the text to remind us of their subsequent fate, though an Elizabethan audience would no doubt remember that both died under the Tudors. Yet Shakespeare took pains, without any historical basis, to invent a part for them, which his own company did not so easily dispense with, since they appear in both Q and F versions of the text. As often happens with Shakespeare, this 'unnecessary' scene helps to clarify his dramatic design. It brings one important piece of news: the King is dead. Clarence's children have been questioning the Duchess of York about their father's fate when Queen Elizabeth enters 'with her hair about her ears', one of the few authorial stage directions in the whole canon. Her show of grief is immediately censured by her haughty mother-in-law: whatever the motive, this is no way for a queen to behave. Elizabeth parries with the argument that the death of the King means tragedy for all his people, a tired cliché which in this instance is even truer than she herself thinks.

The scene then develops into an antiphonal threne, to which the children bring a sense of equal justice as strong as their elders: since she did not mourn their father, they will shed no kindred tears for her husband. But she has tears enough of her own not to need their sympathy. Her Woodville relatives, who have remained silent through these laments for the York brothers, now offer their condolences. The action makes no progress, the only hint of a move forward is Rivers's concluding advice, to send for her son the Prince immediately. What is most significant in this otherwise unremarkable passage is that there is very little dialogue and no communion at all between the members of the bereaved family. The quartet section rings changes on the words 'father', 'mother', 'widow', 'orphan', 'dear', 'loss', using symmetry, repetition, isocolon, anaphora, and so on, to create a concord of discords: all sing the same words but refuse to join in unison.

This is the first of a string of lamentations which runs through the whole play, up to the ghosts' final descant. It is immediately echoed in the following scene, where the citizens' concerns are less markedly stylized but run along much the same lines. News of the King's death and anxiety about the future. The minority of the heir. Rivalries at court. A surfeit of uncles, one of them dishonest. Ominous signs of coming storms. And proverbial wisdom: fear is everywhere but in God we trust. This straightforward piece is ostensibly a choric pause, one that helps throw some light on the royal family's rhetoric. Reduced to essentials, the courtly threne says little more than the citizens' simpler speeches. The King is dead, the Queen desperate, the Duchess has only one son left, who is treacherous.

The separate, nearly antagonistic expressions of sorrow show that the divisions between Yorks and Woodvilles have already infected the children with their rancour, a highly recurrent pattern in the tetralogy where crime and vengeance run in a seemingly endless vicious circle. The citizens' burden is 'What will become of England?' The Queen's is 'What will become of me?' If Dorset's answer is submission to God's will, Rivers's advice to the 'careful mother' is entirely practical: she has lost a king, but has another ready at hand to look after her. He takes up the word Dorset used, 'comfort', to signify both consolation and material comfort. This personal, self-centred variant of 'The King is dead, long live the King' is summed up in the perfect word-for-word symmetry of his concluding antithesis:

> Drown desperate sorrow in dead Edward's grave
> And plant your joys in living Edward's throne.   (ii. ii. 99–100)

Apart from highlighting the characters' frailties, the scene provides a useful reference mark in the development of grievances that will culminate in the ghosts' curses, eventually causing Richard's breakdown. One can certainly sympathize with directors who feel unmoved by Shakespeare's skilful display of thematics and cannot see their way to giving them flesh. It is nonetheless a key, at least a useful clue, to the overall pattern of the play. The four minor characters will soon leave the stage, while the two women remain to endure the worse losses still in store for them. They have a long way to go before impotent rage and private sorrow learn to unite in overwhelming harmony against their torturer.

A long chain of children enrolled in their parents' feud have died since young Talbot lost his life under his father's eyes in the last honourable campaign of the sequence, serving the King who was little more than a child himself. The next generation of young noblemen destroyed each other in tribal wars, dragging with them troops of anonymous sons and fathers. Rutland was the first victim in a series of cold-blooded murders, followed by the Prince of Wales, and Edward's children. Clarence's own were removed out of sight by their loving uncle. Neither their ulterior fate nor the existence of Richard's son have a place in this design. Each untimely death contributes to the main pattern of waste and extinction. Stanley's concern lest 'tender George | Be executed in his father's sight' is very unlike his attitude in the chronicle, but effectively recalls this bloody sequence until young Stanley's miraculous escape breaks the pattern and the heavy sense of doom created by Margaret's curses. Richmond, the hopeful child of Henry's prophecy, arrives in time to rescue Elizabeth, the only Plantagenet child to survive unscathed.

The theme of filiation links nature to politics, private to public affairs, individual to common weal, throughout the cycle. The name of Plantagenet reverberates through each part with a new chain of associations—name, fame, family, blood, title, claim, clan, feud, plant, root, uproot, trees, branches, bastard slips, thorns— all seeds of the roses picked in the garden of *1 Henry VI* to defend York's good name. Vergil's comment, that the York family became self-destructive once they were rid of all their enemies, is here concentrated on Richard, who creates havoc in family ties from his monstrous birth onwards. The accusations of bastardy which traditionally served to insult the rival party are turned by him against his own clan. Not content with disowning all family ties, or murdering his own blood, he seeks to ravish women whose relatives he has killed, and claims to replace or re-engender their lost ones, abolishing all proper distance in an incestuous replay of his own birth-in-death. Anne's curse on his abortive child does not so much evoke their own future son, suppressed for obvious thematic needs, as a cluster of popular beliefs in the sterility of monsters, which prevents all of Shakespeare's tyrants from fathering heirs.[88]

Ghosts. The world of *Richard III* is pointedly shown from the start as being a superstitious one, where a man may land in jail on the vaguest prophecy. Even a hardened sceptic like Richard is prepared to take an Irish bard's warnings on trust. An accusation of witchcraft of the kind alleged against Hastings was no laughing matter, either then or in the reign of Elizabeth. Ghosts generally have a difficult time on the modern stage, but whether or not we believe in them, the point is that Richard's contemporaries, and Shakespeare's, probably did. A long literary tradition confirmed both their credibility and their practical utility. In *The Mirror*, they bear witness to the fact that old sins cast long shadows, and deliver moral messages marked with the stamp of superior authority. In revenge plays like *The Spanish Tragedy*, as mediators between this and the other world they are also able to convey useful information buried in the past. The challenge for a director is to animate on stage a universe where their existence is at least contingent. Some can be dismissed as figments of a feverish brain or guilty conscience; others have a life of their own, and cannot be wholly bound up within Hamlet's or Richard's mind. In *Richard III* they must be the figments of two brains at least, expressing hidden guilt and hidden desire. They appear to both sleepers under juxtaposed tents, balancing threat and promise in equal doses. The dead victims of Richard add to the various functions of literary ghosts their prominent part in the ritual concert of avengers. The ghosts' ballet concludes the choreographic pattern set up by the avengers of Part 3.

Here the modern directors' problem with ghosts is doubled by the rhetorical cast of the scene: these ghosts cannot be made naturalistic! In the earlier plays, evidence of a world beyond appeared mostly through prophetic hints of the future, often in disguised and misguiding form, and in visible signs of shady origin, like the fiends conjured up by Joan or the Duchess of Gloucester. Richmond's troops are self-proclaimed 'Ministers of chastisement'. As if in answer to Margaret's incantatory summons, the host of the dead surround their executioner to the unanimous cry of 'Despair and die'. The link from Joan the witch to Margaret has often been stressed by critics, and by directors who have the same actress play both parts. Other continuities could be stressed as well, for instance between Joan, giving her blood to drink in exchange for victory, and the doomed victims who negotiate the protection of their family against their life with the grisly God of their fantasies, Clarence, or the Woodvilles:

> And for my sister and her princely sons,
> Be satisfied, dear God, with our true blood,
> Which, as thou know'st, unjustly must be spilt. (III. iii. 21–3)

All of Richard's victims find some comfort in the thought that God is bound to execute the rest of Margaret's programme:

---

[88] See Ernest Jones, *On the Nightmare* (London, 1949). Jean Céard, *La Nature et les prodiges: L'Insolite au XVIe siècle en France* (Geneva, 1977). Philip K. Bock, *Shakespeare and Elizabethan Culture: An Anthropological View* (New York, 1984).

Grey. Now Margaret's curse is fall'n upon our heads,
   When she exclaimed on Hastings, you, and I
   For standing by when Richard stabbed her son.
Riv. Then cursed she Richard,
   Then cursed she Buckingham,
   Then cursed she Hastings. O remember God,
   To hear her prayer for them, as now for us.   (III. iii. 14–20)

This divinity has much in common with the barbaric gods of pagan mythologies. Buckingham imagines him as enjoying a joke at the expense of his mortal creatures:

That high All-Seer which I dallied with
Hath turned my feignèd prayer on my head
And given in earnest what I begged in jest.   (v. i. 20–2)

Margaret congratulates him on the murder of the young princes, sitting the mourners on church pews for the blackest of black masses:

O upright, just, and true-disposing God,
How do I thank thee, that this carnal cur
Preys on the issue of his mother's body
And makes her pew-fellow with others' moan.   (IV. iv. 55–8)

The rituals of *Richard III* cannot be dissociated from rhetoric, which has taken on such overtones of political manipulation in the past century that it seems impossible now to hear its cadences without instinctively dismissing them as mendacious. This is to shut out the other function of rhetoric, which is to make the truth manifest. Indeed, apart from Richard, the majority of characters, Buckingham, Clarence, Margaret, Anne, are quite capable of twisting facts to suit their argument, but the audience is usually warned if a particular orator cannot be trusted, proof enough that not all eloquence is deceitful. In Reboul's view, since all discourse, sincere or not, is manipulative, all teaching worth the name must begin by exposing its own rhetoric, to prevent its own misuse.[89] The moral dilemma concerning rhetoric is not mendacity but power. Richard claims, as Henry V and other manipulative speakers will do after him at great length, that he is a man of few words, more skilled in fighting than in courting favour. Having done so, he takes control of the situation, as Henry will. The device of the humility topos is as old as rhetoric itself, and part of the ambivalence finely analysed by the philosopher Paul Ricœur.

For Thomas More, the problem is indeed not a matter of lies; the power is not in words but in weapons, in the constant presence of armed soldiers near the rostrum. People are too scared to protest, but it is plain that no one is persuaded or misled by those persuasive speeches. The long prosopopeiae of Elizabeth and Buckingham on sanctuary are virtuoso exercises in the clear exposition of an argument. Their styles are identical, her bad faith as patent as his, and neither speech reveals much of the speaker's personality. More is sensitive to the dramatic quality of their conflict over possession of the child, but does not use the speeches to explore their psychology,

---

[89]   Olivier Reboul, *La Rhétorique* (Paris, 1993).

even less to expose the paradoxical nature of eloquence. He sees no need for a humility topos, never attempts to hide his own mastery of rhetoric, nor wonders about its mesmerizing power. The risk is that it might miss its aim—establish the sincerity of the orator—by lighting up the artificiality of the performance. Yet its efficiency must be worth a try, since our modern politicians still attempt the gamble again and again, on TV audiences increasingly immune to their wiles. Shakespeare is the first to dramatize its founding ambiguity, and to stress that its art disappears under the mask of sincerity, nothing in the speech itself distinguishing a sincere from a lying orator. The test can only be in the confrontation of words with deeds, and ultimately in the theatre, which can create the confrontation by contracting historical time, and have the truth of it now.

The chroniclers call on God, Fate, Fortune, or Chance indiscriminately to try and make sense of facts. If their narratives have any shape at all, it is that of the pageant, king after king after king and year after year of eventful histories, which Shakespeare edits ruthlessly, cutting sharp angles into these flat uncomic strips to create perspective. The choric figures of 1 and 2 *Henry VI* disappear with the collapse of their morally intelligible universe, leaving but choreography to make sense of Part 3. The rhetorical devices effect a 'mise en ordre des passions', an artificial order imposed on an increasingly upset world to make it visible to the eye, keep it articulate by an imaginative effort. Each tableau re-enacts the central drama, each pattern is broken as soon as perceived. In the last play of the sequence, it is Richard who designs the patterns that he plans to destroy, while his victims turn the full catalogue of tropes to unexpected functions. Brian Vickers finds these patterned speeches vigorous but static: 'the early poetry displays its rhetoric stiffly', Richard like Shakespeare is manipulating the feeling via the rhetoric, from outside, 'Nature has not yet digested the Art'.[90] If the young Shakespeare is 'peacocking', to use Peter Stein's word, displaying his own talent behind Richard's, he like his character shows off to show up. His stiff rhetoric is for *monstratio*, not demonstration, a test of the power of art to represent truth.

Revenge, we saw in 3 *Henry VI*, demands symmetries. Hatred takes on the shape of *Ubi sunt*, and multiplies anaphoras in a roll call of the dead. Stichomythias, antitheses, oxymorons express an Augustinian vision of the world as a dramatic fight between Good and Evil. Against these mighty rhetorical engines, Richard with his gleeful mimicry embodies all the transgressions they resist. His enjoyment in breaking ponderous measure, bigoted ceremonies, and old rhetorical moulds is communicative until it recoils on him. The minor amendments to the sources we have been through suggest that the fight is between two equally dubious procedures. From the edge of the stage where Margaret stands at the beginning, the rhetoric of revenge works itself up in the women's wailing speeches, gradually occupies the centre, calls up the dead, and with these old stiff models succeeds in crushing Richard, the last solitary artist of disorder.

---

[90] Brian Vickers, 'Shakespeare's Use of Rhetoric', in S. Schoenbaum (ed.), *A New Companion to Shakespeare Studies* (Cambridge, 1971), 95.

Murderers. The carriers of moral lessons are so discredited that there are none but professional murderers left to recall the Christian doctrine of remorse and forgiveness. Richard has the largest number of references to conscience in the play. All the others' words of repentance are at best attrition, regrets for the consequences of their faults, mixed with furious appeals to Heaven to punish other sinners as mercilessly as themselves. Richard's sanctimonious answers to their fulminations do not just expose blind hypocrisies, they are a twisted reminder of norms which have been increasingly flouted through the disorders of civil war, just as his self-portrait is an exact negative of the virtuous monarch. The inversion of Christian ethics is so radical that the paid killers' sense of duty turns crime into a moral obligation. Conscience, a muted voice heard by Clarence in his sleep, grows into a life-size, wholly undesirable, character in the murderers' exchange:

> 2 M. 'Tis a blushing, shamefaced spirit that mutinies in a man's bosom. It fills a man full of obstacles . . . It is turned out of towns and cities for a dangerous thing, and every man that means to live well endeavours to trust to himself and live without it.
> 1 M. 'Tis even now at my elbow, persuading me not to kill the duke.   (I. iv. 132–9)

They are the ones who remind Clarence that he has broken every rule he now urges them to observe. After the first betrayal of his brothers, the breach of his promise to Warwick did not clean his record but added one more perjury to his account.

The gamekeepers of *3 Henry VI* had pointed out to King Henry the limits of allegiance: with the changing reigns, what was fealty yesterday is treason today. Conscience, the great corrupter of a man's soul, tempts self-respecting cut-throats away from their duty when moral courage commands them to do the job they were paid for. Yet these natural philosophers feel unease at the clash of principles developed in their argument with Clarence. Like the assassins of Edward's children, they are the first to express genuine remorse for their deeds. Their poor dregs of conscience are all that has survived from the wreck of holy Henry's kingdom. As men who stand on what is considered the last rung of humanity, they measure the depths to which their society has descended, moments before a new, equally radical turn is taken in the opposite direction, once the absolute in crime has conquered all.

Richard embodies the terminal phase, not the origin, of the disease in the commonweal. It is he who tests the other characters' integrity, challenging them to defy their own codes. Anne is wooed 'in her heart's extremest hate', yet he wins her, 'Having God, her conscience, and these bars' against him. As Barbara Everett points out in Al Pacino's film, there are limits that the most hardened criminals will never cross. They must forsake Richard and he must lose. Once the disagreements are buried with the dead, new models of correct behaviour emerge ready for public adulation. All rally around Richmond with almost audible relief at being able to tell unerringly good from evil, and cement new bonds in a common hatred of the wrongdoer.

Laurence Olivier fought Richard's last battle so fiercely that his assistants had to remind him from the wings: 'Hey, Larry, you're supposed to *lose* this one!' Some part of us no doubt would like him to win. The play's formal symmetries seem to many critics regressive after the chiaroscuro that bathes *Henry VI*. It is no wonder, in our world of many-shaded greys, if we feel let down by a conclusion of sharply contrasted black and white. Yet the play is disquietingly attuned to today's feelings, when whole towns are seen to share in self-righteous revulsion, monitored and amplified by the media, against law- or code-breakers. The recent orgies of mourning for young victims, the hue and cry against their abusers, have shown the resilience of archetypal exorcisms in societies starved of communion rites, and may well give fresh relevance to Shakespeare's histories. When Michael Boyd's actors asked the audience to cry 'Long live Richard, England's worthy King!', they were certainly prepared to incorporate silence or adverse reactions into their act, but perhaps not, at least in the first performances, for the enthusiastic response they got instead. The same spectators would have cried 'Long live Henry' with equal enthusiasm at the end, had they been asked to. There is no escaping the fact that *Richard III* does conform to dominant ideology. The play does not just imply that good and evil are complementary, as in early Christian philosophy. Its crude contrasts reflect the malleability of orthodoxy, right and wrong exchanging places in the public mind with a chilling ease that will be explored more freely in *Julius Caesar*.

Conclusion: A World to Bustle in

By the end of *Richard III*, Shakespeare has all the tools of his profession well in hand. He has worked his way through the chronicles to the front of the Elizabethan stage, learning the crafts of history, literature, and court politics as he went, testing new genres and new techniques with each play. There may be breaks or unconformities in the story, but comparison with its sources indicates a continuous development in thought process and artistic design. The four parts of the first historical sequence each mark a major step in the advancement of drama and the edification of his audience. Having moved from the heavily didactic chronicle play to the austere elegance of the Classical formulas, Shakespeare sets the Ancient masters to school with the first successful integration of themes, forms, language, and character of the Elizabethan stage. With a helping of More's black humour, he achieves the mixture of genres that will produce Falstaff and mark a number of his later plays—an innovation on *Henry VI*, which has very little comedy in it, apart from ambiguous rustics like Joan of Arc or Jack Cade. He will continue to experiment with form till the end of his career, working fashions, traditional modes, and mechanisms to their limits. When he follows practice or obeys set rules, it is to try how far they can be bent to an original purpose. The will to exceed technical complexities leads him to double improbable pairs of twins, use but one-third of the time unit allowed by the neo-classics or, to quote Northrop Frye, borrow some unlikely story somewhere and add six impossibilities to the plot.

Far from opposing history to tragedy, the dramatic construction of *Henry VI* manages the transitions from a collective viewpoint embracing centuries to a human temporality, bounded in the shell of one man's life. Part 1 carves out a strong if rather crude pattern in the episodic chronicle, alternates group scenes and close-ups to expose the main cause of failure abroad, with a longer view of history than the Elizabethan writers who explore it for instant remedies of every ailment. How much of the play is Shakespeare's remains difficult to assert on the faith of internal or external data. The qualitative leap taken with Part 2 is equally dubious evidence that he did not write most of Part 1. It is wide, but no wider than between Parts 2 and 3, or between the trilogy and *Richard III*. However large or small his share may have been, editors generally grant him the tragic death of Talbot, which seals the first phase of the national tragedy and fits it into the larger design of the sequence. The play shows genuine confidence in British mettle, traces of which still inspire the Bastard of Falconbridge's guarantee of success 'If England to itself do rest but true'. If.

There is no trace left of nationalistic pride in Part 2, nor confidence in England's virtue and merits, but an increasing doubt as to the chances of a Christian ruler in the world of politics. The plotting reveals both the scheming guile of the voracious plotters, and the playwright's mastery of *sustasis*. The selection of material shows as much assurance as in Part 1, and more thrift. Instead of racing through large chapters of narrative, Shakespeare concentrates on the relevant period and extracts a strict causal chain from the chronicler's loose logic. Characters show hidden complexities and grow into convincing human or inhuman beings. As the angle of vision shifts from high to low estates, the staging of a popular rebellion opens new areas of dramatic conflict.

Part 3 drives revenge tragedy to its limits by confronting this home-grown exotic genre with the records of the nation's still smouldering past. The wounds of civil wars upset all levels of the social edifice, giving topical urgency to the Aristotelian formula, violence in the family ties. Time becomes a major dramatic agent in the design of perspective—a double agent, when the historical enquiry displays the ambivalent making/writing of history that will raise Henry V's Chorus above pro- saic mendacity, just as the raw facts themselves unfold under our beMused eyes. *Richard III* shows the spectacular ascent of character to a crowning position, in a development unforeseen by the fathers of Greek tragedy. As Richard takes the plot in hand, for the first time Shakespeare looks for the keys of political action and the mainsprings of history down into the coils of the human will. Hamlet is there, simply dying to be born.

The misfortunes of *Henry VI* have shattered the ideal image of monarchy. The tyrant's progress follows from the King's self-denial of princely violence, but *Richard III* offers no clear answer to the dilemma of power: Providence interrupts the debate by sending Richmond. The restoration of order by a peerless knight has all the look of a return to the heroic tradition, but in fact prudently returns heroics to the legendary past: Richmond claims kinship with St George, not with the too recent and too real Henry V, just as, under the Tudors, the chivalric codes ceased to govern the exercise of power, and took an increasing part in its representation. Shakespeare uses anachronism 'positively and functionally',[1] with allusions to Machiavel, one anachronism that can hardly be blamed on his absent-mindedness, and with a second set of histories that draws even closer to the 'mysteries of State' protected by his Queen's majesty. Throughout this double sequence, the distinc- tions and discontinuities are clear between yesterday and today; Shakespeare's analogies stress similitude only to highlight change. History acts as a check on the artifical virtuosity of the theatre, and tests its ability to stage reality. Only on stage could it be whispered that in truth the King was naked.

At this point, Shakespeare draws closer to Plato than to Aristotle in his will to make truth and beauty ideally meet. Like many of his fellow playwrights, he gives fair notice to the audience that the theatre is the place of counterfeit. As Plato

---

[1] Northrop Frye, *A Natural Perspective: The Development of Shakespearean Comedy and Romance* (New York, 1965) 20–1.

warned against the sophists, the most eloquent of poets exposes the slipperiness of language and the manipulations of rhetoric. Shakespeare visibly understood the Classical aesthetics, which so many of his contemporaries confused with ethics, yet in the last analysis he is the one who reconciles these two ends of art. His own references to Classical culture free themselves from their traditional associations. What his characters perceive in the turns of fortune's wheel is their own powerlessness, their limited vision of the universe, and the relentless harrowing of time, as the tragic hero begins to understand he cannot call back yesterday.

Both Henriads end, like tragedies, among a heap of corpses, and like comedies, with a wedding and the promise of a renewed society. As in Greek drama, the hero's claim that he has conquered the dark forces of the past seems to be 'rather expressing a hope, making an appeal that remains full of anxiety even amid the joy of the final apotheosis'.[2] The orthodox conclusion of *Richard III* puts a provisional stop to fertile lines of thought opened up by *Henry VI*. The dynamics of regicide produces Macbeth, 'Bellona's bridegroom', in yet another dark tale of origins to the present monarchy. Richmond, Macduff, old Hamlet, Edgar, all fight armed combats to secure the crown, always in legitimate duels against varying degrees of evil, or so their supporters tell us. The persistent motif of the duel is staged at the opening of *Richard II*, only to be defused. The King must be killed nevertheless, and his blood shed to sprinkle the growth of the new dynasty, as in the most archaic succession rites. The political rift is tentatively healed by the Machiavellian surgery of Henry V, whose cloak of ceremony briefly unveils the figure of the Tudor monarch, 'Our Empress'. Despite the setting in an earlier reign, all the signs show that we are moving on forward, as England matures away from the superstitious world of *Henry VI*. Where Richard ominously entered life as one enters death, Glendower's tales of his prodigious birth fail to raise the least shudder, only a ripple of laughter. Ordeals give way to law courts. Meanwhile the countryside cultivates a life of its own at safe distance from the court and its battlegrounds. The agony of medieval sacred monarchy, and its civic reconstruction in a reign when 'miracles are ceas'd', reinterpret the primitive murder of the father as the rites of passage into adulthood of a nation. Plantagenet with its vegetal images of growth weaves the human, dynastic, archaeological, mythical history of the realm.

Shakespeare seems to be holding the rein on his poetic imagination until he has measured its validity against the sober matter of history, the trial of truth, and the will to know where we come from. Having passed this crucial test, the scene moves on to pre-Christian Antiquity. *Hamlet* explores the Nordic underground of the British imagination, as strong a contrast as that offered by the sedate Renaissance castle of Elsinore, above its labyrinth of casemates where a colossal Holger Danske sits slumbering, his broadsword across his knees, ready to wake up from his millenary trance, says the legend, if peril threatens. In *Julius Caesar*, the origin of Empire is again a form of regicide, committed on a morally dubious yet charismatic figure, and political engineerings unhampered by the pieties of Augustinian philo-

---

[2] Vernant and Vidal-Naquet, *Myth and Tragedy*, 10.

sophy. Shakespeare's farewell to Rome, in *Cymbeline*, shows Britain triumphant over a corrupted Italy, nobly paying tribute to its Latin past.

Shakespeare is not our contemporary, and yet no dramatist today has replaced him on our horizon, no essay in politics has superseded his parliament of voices. Where medieval philosophy only conceived of evil as an absence of good, the major historical revolution of the Protestant Renaissance was its recognition of evil as an active force, which drove Marlowe to peer into the metaphysical void of *Doctor Faustus*, perhaps the most haunting expression of a new modern angst. Shakespeare stands on the edge of this void. He captures a world lost to us at the moment of its collapse, and seizes in one dramatic image the tensions at work, the scattered pieces, and the man watching the explosion. Where Marlowe makes us feel the horrendous waste, and the answering silence of theology, Shakespeare's dialectical view of history stages a contest of destructive and dynamic forces, wavering between the tragedy and the comedy of life. The touchstone of drama is reversal, the lesson of history is reversibility.

Bibliography

This bibliography is restricted to works with direct bearing on the present study.

ALLEN, JOHN W., *A History of Political Thought in the Sixteenth Century* (London, 1957).

ANGLO, SYDNEY, *Spectacle Pageantry and Early Tudor Policy* (Oxford, 1969).

ARISTOTLE, *Poetics*, in *The Basic Works of Aristotle*, ed. Richard McKeon (New York, 2001).

—— *La Poétique*, text, trans., and notes, Roselyne Dupont-Roc and Jean Lallot (Paris, 1980).

ARTAUD, ANTONIN, *The Theatre and its Double*, trans. Victor Corti (London, 1993).

AUGUSTINE, *Confessions*, trans. Henry Chadwick (Oxford, 1991).

—— *The City of God against the Pagans*, Latin and English, ed. W. MacAllen Green (Cambridge, Mass., 1957–72).

—— *The City of God: John Healey's Translation of 1610*, ed. R. V. G. Tasker (London, 1967).

BACON, Sir FRANCIS, *The History of the Reign of Henry VII*, ed. Jerry Weinberger (Ithaca, NY, 1998).

BAKER, HERSCHEL, *The Race of Time: Three Lectures on Renaissance Historiography* (Toronto, 1967).

BALDWIN, T. W., *William Shakspere's 'Small Latine & Lesse Greeke'* (Urbana, Ill., 1944).

BALDWIN, WILLIAM, et al., *The Mirror for Magistrates*, ed. Lily B. Campbell (Cambridge, 1938).

BARTHES, ROLAND, 'L'Ancienne Rhétorique', in *Communications*, 16 (Paris, 1970).

—— 'Introduction to the Structural Analysis of Narratives', in *A Barthes Reader*, ed. Susan Sontag (London, 1982), 251–95.

BARTON, JOHN, with HALL, PETER, *The Wars of the Roses, Adapted from 'Henry VI Parts I, II, II' and 'Richard III'* (London, 1970).

BATE, JONATHAN, *Shakespeare and Ovid* (Oxford, 1993).

BERRY, EDWARD I., *Patterns of Decay: Shakespeare's Early Histories* (Charlottesville, Va., 1975).

BEVINGTON, DAVID M., *Tudor Drama and Politics: A Critical Approach to Topical Meanings* (Cambridge, Mass., 1968).

BLANPIED, JOHN W., *Time and the Artist in Shakespeare's English Histories* (Newark, Del., 1983).

BLOCH, MARC, *The Royal Touch: Sacred Monarchy and Scrofula in England and France*, trans. J. E. Anderson (London, 1973).

BOCK, PHILIP K., *Shakespeare and Elizabethan Culture: An Anthropological View* (New York, 1984).

BODIN, JEAN, *Method for the Easy Comprehension of History*, trans. Beatrice Reynolds (New York, 1945).

BOETHIUS, *Chaucer's Translation of Boethius' 'De Consolatione Philosophiae'*, ed. Richard Morris (London, 1868).

BOLTON, WHITNEY F., *Shakespeare's English: Language in the History Plays* (Cambridge, Mass., 1992).

BOURDIEU, PIERRE, *Language and Symbolic Power*, trans. G. Raymond and M. Adamson (Cambridge, 1991).

Bowers, Fredson, *Elizabethan Revenge Tragedy, 1587–1642* (Princeton, 1971).

Bradley, David, *From Text to Performance in the Elizabethan Theatre: Preparing the Play for the Stage* (Cambridge, 1992).

Brooke, Nicholas, *Shakespeare's Early Tragedies* (London, 1968).

—— 'Reflecting Gems and Dead Bones: Tragedy versus History in C. B. Cox and D. J. Palmer (eds.), *Richard III*', in *Shakespeare's Wide and Universal Stage* (Manchester, 1984), 104–16.

Bullough, Geoffrey (ed.), *Narrative and Dramatic Sources of Shakespeare*, vol. iii (London, 1966).

Bury, John B., *The Idea of Progress: An Inquiry into its Origin and Growth* (London, 1932).

Certaine Sermons or Homilies Appointed to be Read in Churches in the Time of Queen Elizabeth I (1547–1571): A Facsimile Reproduction of the Edition of 1623, ed. M. E. Rickley and T. B. Stroup (Gainesville, Fla., 1968).

Champion, Larry S., *The Noise of Threatening Drum: Dramatic Strategy and Political Ideology in Shakespeare and the English Chronicle* (Newark, Del., 1990).

Chrimes, S. B., Ross, C. D., and Griffiths, R. A. (eds.), *Fifteenth-Century England 1399–1509: Studies in Politics and Society* (Manchester, 1972).

Churchill, George B., *Richard the Third up to Shakespeare* (Berlin, 1900).

Clemen, Wolfgang H., *A Commentary on Shakespeare's Richard III*, trans. Jean Bonheim (London, 1968).

Colley, Scott, *Richard's Himself Again: A Stage History of Richard III* (London, 1992).

Commynes, philippe de, *Memoirs of Philippe de Commynes*, ed. Samuel Kinser, trans. Isabelle Cazeaux (Columbia, SC, 1973).

Courcelle, Pierre, *La Consolation de Philosophie dans la tradition littéraire: Antécédents et postérité de Boèce* (Paris, 1967).

Curtius, Ernst R., *European Literature and the Latin Middle Ages*, trans. Willard R. Trask (London, 1953).

Daniel, Samuel, *The Civil Wars*, ed. Laurence Michel (Newhaven, 1958).

Darras, Jacques, *Nous sommes tous des romantiques allemands: De Dante à Whitman en passant par Iéna* (Paris, 2002).

Day, Gillian, *King Richard III* (London, 2002).

Derrida, Jacques, *Dissemination*, trans. Barbara Johnson (London, 1993).

Driver, Tom F., *The Sense of History in Greek and Shakespearean Drama* (New York, 1960).

Dumézil, Georges, *The Destiny of a King*, trans. Alf Hiltebeil (Chicago, 1973).

Dupont, Florence, *L'Insignifiance tragique* (Paris, 2001).

Eliot, T. S., 'Dante', in *Selected Essays* (London, 1999).

Emmerson, Richard K., *Antichrist in the Middle Ages: A Study of Medieval Apocalypticism, Art and Literature* (Manchester, 1981).

Fabyan, Robert, *The New Chronicles of England and France*, ed. Sir Henry Ellis (London, 1811).

Ferguson, Arthur B., *Clio Unbound: Perception of the Social and Cultural Past in Renaissance England* (Durham, NC, 1979).

Foxe, John, *The Acts and Monuments of John Foxe*, ed. Revd George Townsend (New York, 1965).

Frye, Northrop, *A Natural Perspective: The Development of Shakespearean Comedy and Romance* (New York, 1965).

Fussner, Frank S., *The Historical Revolution: English Historical Writing and Thought, 1580–1640* (Westport, Conn., 1976).

—— *Tudor History and the Historians* (New York, 1970).

GARBER, MARJORIE, *Shakespeare's Ghost Writers: Literature as Uncanny Causality* (New York, 1987).

GASCOIGNE, GEORGE, and KINWELMERSH, FRANCIS, *Jocasta, a Tragedy*, adapted from L. Dolce's translation of Euripides, in *Complete Works of G. Gascoigne*, ed. J. W. Cunliffe (Cambridge, 1907).

GENTILLET, INNOCENT, *Anti-Machiavel*, ed. C. Edward Rathé (Geneva, 1968).

GEOFFREY of MONMOUTH, *The History of the Kings of Britain*, trans. Lewis Thorpe (Harmondsworth, 1966).

GILLINGHAM, JOHN, *The Wars of the Roses: Peace and Conflict in Fifteenth-Century England* (Baton Rouge, La., 1981).

—— (ed.), *Richard III: A Medieval Kingship* (London, 1993).

GILSON, ÉTIENNE, *History of Christian Philosophy in the Middle Ages* (London, 1955).

GOLDING, ARTHUR, *Ovid's Metamorphoses: The Arthur Golding Translation of 1567*, ed. John F. Nims (Philadelphia, 2000).

GOODMAN, ANTHONY, *The Wars of the Roses: Military Activity and English Society, 1452–97* (London, 1981).

GOY-BLANQUET, DOMINIQUE, *Le Roi mis à nu: Histoire d'Henry VI, de Hall à Shakespeare* (Paris, 1986).

—— *Shakespeare et l'invention de l'histoire* (Brussels, 1997).

—— *William Shakespeare: Richard III* (Paris, 1999).

GRAFTON, RICHARD, *The Chronicle of Iohn Hardyng . . . Together with the Continuation of Richard Grafton*, ed. Henry Ellis (London, 1812).

—— *A Chronicle at Large and Meere History of the Affayres of England*, ed. Henry Ellis (London, 1809).

GREENBLATT, STEPHEN, *Renaissance Self-Fashioning: From More to Shakespeare* (Chicago, 1980).

GREENE, ROBERT, *Greene's Groat's Worth of Wit*, facsimile reprint (Menston, 1969).

GRIFFITHS, RALPH A., *The Reign of King Henry VI: The Exercise of Royal Authority, 1422–1461* (London, 1981).

GROSS, CHARLES (ed.), *A Bibliography of English History to 1485, Based on the Sources and Literature of English History from the Earliest Times to about 1485* (Oxford, 1975).

GURR, ANDREW, *The Shakespearean Stage 1547–1642*, 3rd edn. (Cambridge, 1992).

HALL, EDWARD, *The Union of the Two Noble and Illustre Famelies of Lancastre and Yorke. Hall's Chronicle*, ed. Henry Ellis (London, 1809).

HAMMOND, P. W., and SUTTON, ANNE F., *Richard III: The Road to Bosworth Field* (London, 1985).

HANHAM, ALISON, *Richard III and his Early Historians, 1483–1535* (Oxford, 1975).

HANKEY, JULIE (ed.), *William Shakespeare, 'Richard III': Plays in Performance* (London, 1981).

HARRISON, TONY, *Trackers of Oxyrhynchus*, 2nd edn. (London, 1991)

HARTOG, FRANÇOIS (ed.), *L'Histoire d'Homère à Augustin: Préfaces des historiens et textes sur l'histoire* (Paris, 1999).

HATTAWAY, MICHAEL, *Elizabethan Popular Theatre* (London, 1982).

HAY, DENIS, *Annalists and Historians: Western Historiography from the Eighth to the Eighteenth Centuries* (London, 1977).

HEUSCH, LUC DE, *The Drunken King, or the Origin of the State*, trans. Roy Willis (Bloomington, Ind., 1982).

HEYWOOD, THOMAS, *Pleasant Dialogves and Drammas, Selected ovt of Lucian, Erasmus, Textor, Ovid, &c.* (London, 1637).

HINCHCLIFFE, JUDITH, *King Henry VI, Parts 1, 2, and 3: An Annotated Bibliography*, Garland Shakespeare Bibliographies 5 (New York, 1984).

HINMAN, CHARLTON (ed.), *The Norton Facsimile: The First Folio of Shakespeare* (New York, 1968).

Historiae Croylandensis Continuatio, in *Ingulph's Chronicle of the Abbey of Croyland*, trans. H. T. Riley (London, 1854).

Historie of the Arrivall of Edward IV in England, ed. John Bruce (London, 1938).

HOBBES, THOMAS, 'Of the Life and History of Thucydides', preface to his translation of *Eight Bookes of the Peloponnesian Warre*, in *The Collected English Works of Thomas Hobbes*, vol. viii, ed. Sir William Molesworth (London, 1843).

HODGDON, BARBARA, *The End Crowns All: Closure and Contradiction in Shakespeare's History* (Princeton, 1991).

HOLINSHED, RAPHAEL, *Holinshed's Chronicles of England, Scotland and Ireland*, ii: *1066–1399*, iii: *1399–1553*, ed. Henry Ellis (London, 1807–8).

HOLLANDA, FRANCISCO DA, *De la peinture: Dialogues avec Michel-Ange*, trans. S. Matarasso-Gervais (Aix-en-Provence, 1984).

HORACE, *The Art of Poetry: An Epistle to the Pisos*, English and Latin, trans. George Colman (New York, 1976).

HORROX, ROSEMARY, *Richard III: A Study in Service* (Cambridge, 1989).

HORTMANN, WILHELM, *Shakespeare on the German Stage: The Twentieth Century* (Cambridge, 1998).

HOWARD, JEAN E., and RACKIN, PHYLLIS, *Engendering a Nation: A Feminist Account of Shakespeare's English Histories* (London, 1997).

ISER, WOLFGANG, *Staging Politics: The Lasting Impact of Shakespeare's Histories*, trans. David H. Wilson (New York, 1993).

JACKS, PHILIP J., *The Antiquarian and the Myth of Antiquity: The Origins of Rome in Renaissance Thought* (Cambridge, 1993).

JACKSON, RUSSELL (ed.), *The Cambridge Companion to Shakespeare on Film* (Cambridge, 2000).

JACOB, E. F., *The Fifteenth Century, 1399–1485*, ed. Sir George Clark (Oxford, 1993).

JACQUOT, JEAN, ' "Le Théâtre du monde", de Shakespeare à Calderón', *Revue de littérature comparée*, 31 (1957), 341–72.

—— 'Histoire et tragédie dans *Henry VI*', in Jacquot (ed.), *Le Théâtre tragique* (Paris, 1962), 161–78.

JAMES I, *Daemonologie*, in *Minor Prose Works of King James VI & I*, ed. James Craigie and A. Law (Edinburgh, 1982).

JONES, EMRYS, *The Origins of Shakespeare* (Oxford, 1977).

KANTOROWICZ, ERNST H., *The King's Two Bodies: A Study in Mediaeval Political Theology* (Princeton, 1957).

KASTAN, DAVID S., *Shakespeare and the Shapes of Time* (Hanover, NH, 1982).

—— *Shakespeare after Theory* (New York, 1999).

KEEN, MAURICE, *Chivalry* (Newhaven, 1984).

KEETON, GEORGE W., *Shakespeare's Legal and Political Background* (London, 1967).

KELLY, HENRY A., *Divine Providence in the England of Shakespeare's Histories* (Cambridge, Mass., 1970).

KENNEDY, DENNIS, *Looking at Shakespeare: A Visual History of Twentieth-Century Performance* (Cambridge, 1993).

—— (ed.), *Foreign Shakespeare: Contemporary Performance* (Cambridge, 1993).

298 *Bibliography*

KENYON, JOHN PHILIP, *The History Men: The Historical Profession in England since the Renaissance* (London, 1983).

KERRIGAN, JOHN, *Revenge Tragedy: Aeschylus to Armageddon* (Oxford, 1996).

KIERKEGAARD, SØREN, *The Concept of Irony, with Constant Reference to Socrates, Together with Notes of Schelling's Berlin Lectures*, ed. and trans. Howard V. and Edna H. Vong (Princeton, 1989).

KINGSFORD, CHARLES L., *English Historical Literature in the Fifteenth Century* (Oxford, 1913).

KNOX, JOHN, *The First Blast of the Trumpet against the Monstrous Regiment of Women*, in *John Knox on Rebellion*, ed. Roger A. Mason (Cambridge, 1994).

KOTT, JAN, *Shakespeare our Contemporary*, trans. Boleslaw Taborski (London, 1964).

KYD, THOMAS, *The Spanish Tragedy*, ed. D. Bevington (Manchester, 1996).

LAROQUE, FRANÇOIS, *Shakespeare's Festive World* (Cambridge, 1991).

LATHROP, HENRY B., *Translations from the Classics into English from Caxton to Chapman, 1477–1620* (New York, 1967).

LEFORT, CLAUDE, *Le Travail de l'œuvre: Machiavel* (Paris, 1986).

LEGGATT, ALEXANDER, *Shakespeare's Political Drama: The History Plays and the Roman Plays* (London, 1988).

LE GOFF, JACQUES, *Time, Work and Culture in the Middle Ages*, trans. Arthur Goldhammer (Chicago, 1980).

The Life and Death of Jack Straw, ed. Kenneth Muir and F. P. Wilson (Oxford, 1957).

LEVINE, NINA S., *Women's Matters: Politics, Gender, and Nation in Shakespeare's Early History Plays* (Newark, Del., 1998).

LINDENBERGER, HERBERT, *Historical Drama: The Relation of Literature and Reality* (Chicago, 1975).

LUCIAN, *How to Write History*, trans. K. Kilburn, in *The Works of Lucian*, Greek and English, ed. A. M. Harmon (London, 1913), vol. vi.

LYDGATE, JOHN, *The Fall of Princes*, ed. H. Bergen (London, 1924).

MACHIAVELLI, NICCOLO, *The Discourses*, trans. Leslie J. Walker (London, 1975).

—— *The Prince*, ed. Quentin Skinner and Russell Price (Cambridge, 1988).

McKELLEN, IAN, with LONCRANE, RICHARD, *William Shakespeare's 'Richard III': A Screenplay* (London, 1996).

MAGUIN, J.-M., and WILLEMS, MICHÈLE (eds.), *French Essays on Shakespeare and his Contemporaries: 'What would France with us?'* (Newark, Del., 1995).

MAGUIRE, LAURIE E., *Shakespearean Suspect Texts: The 'Bad' Quartos and their Contexts* (Cambridge, 1996).

MANCINI, DOMINIC, *The Usurpation of Richard III*, ed. C. A. J. Armstrong (Oxford, 1936).

MARCUS, LEAH, *Puzzling Shakespeare: Local Reading and its Discontents* (Berkeley, 1988).

MARIENSTRAS, RICHARD, *New Perspectives on the Shakespearean World*, trans. Janet Lloyd (Cambridge, 1985).

——and GOY-BLANQUET, DOMINIQUE (eds.), *Le Tyran: Shakespeare contre Richard III* (Amiens, 1990).

MARIN, LOUIS, *Portrait of the King*, trans. Martha M. Houle (Basingstoke, 1988).

MARLOWE, CHRISTOPHER, *'Tamburlaine the Great', and 'The Massacre at Paris'*, ed. Edward J. Esche (Oxford, 1998).

MARTINDALE, CHARLES, and MARTINDALE, MICHELLE, *Shakespeare and the Uses of Antiquity* (London, 1990).

MIOLA, ROBERT S., *Shakespeare and Classical Tragedy: The Influence of Seneca* (Oxford, 1997).

MONSTRELET, ENGUERRAND DE, *La Chronique d'Enguerran de Monstrelet, 1400–1444*, ed. L. Douët d'Arcq (Paris, 1857–62).

MOORE, JAMES A. (ed.), *Richard III: An Annotated Bibliography*, Garland Shakespeare Bibliographies 11 (New York, 1986).

MORE, THOMAS, *The History of King Richard the Thirde*, a facsimile of Rastell's 1557 edition, ed. W. E. Campbell, in *The English Works of Sir Thomas More* (London, 1931), vol. i.

—— *The History of King Richard III*, in *The Complete Works of St Thomas More*, ed. Richard S. Silvester, vol. ii (New Haven, 1963).

——*A New Text and Translation of Historia Richardi Tertii*, ed. Daniel Kinney, in *The Complete Works of St. Thomas More*, vol. xv (New Haven, 1986).

MOULTON, IAN F., ' "A Monster Great Deformed": The Unruly Masculinity of Richard III', *Shakespeare Quarterly*, 47 (1996).

NORTON, THOMAS, and SACKVILLE, THOMAS, *The Tragedy of Ferrex and Porrex*, in *Two Tudor Tragedies*, ed. William Tydeman (London, 1992).

ORGEL, STEPHEN, and KEILEN, SEAN (eds.), *Shakespeare and History* (New York, 1999).

PICCO, FRÉDÉRIC, *La Tragédie grecque: La Scène et le tribunal* (Paris, 1999).

PLUTARCH, *Plutarch's Lives of the Noble Grecians and Romans*, trans. from Jacques Amyot by Thomas North, ed. George Wyndham (London, 1895–6).

POOLE, REGINALD L., *Medieval Reckonings of Time* (London, 1918).

POTTER, LOIS, 'Bad and Good Authority Figures: *Richard III* and *Henry V* since 1945', *Shakespeare Jarhbuch* (1992), 39–54.

POWICKE, F. M. (ed.), *Handbook of British Chronology* (London, 1961).

PRAZ, MARIO, ' "The Politic Brain": Machiavelli and the Elizabethans', in *The Flaming Heart* (New York, 1958).

PRIOR, MOODY E., *The Drama of Power: Studies in Shakespeare's History Plays* (Evanston, Ill., 1973).

PUGLIATTI, PAOLA, *Shakespeare the Historian* (New York, 1996).

—— 'Shakespeare's Historicism: Visions and Revisions', in Jonathan Bate, Jill Levenson, and Dieter Mehl (eds.), *Shakespeare and the Twentieth Century* (Newark, Del., 1998), 336–49.

RACKIN, PHYLLIS, *Stages of History: Shakespeare's English Chronicles* (Ithaca, NY, 1990).

RALEGH, Sir WALTER, *The History of the World*, in *The Works of Sir Walter Ralegh*, ed. William Oldys and Thomas Birch (Oxford, 1829).

RAMSAY, JAMES H., *Lancaster and York: A Century of English History, A.D. 1399–1485* (Oxford, 1892).

RICŒUR, PAUL, *The Rule of Metaphor: Multi-disciplinary Studies of the Creation of Meaning in Language*, trans. R. Czerny et al. (London, 1986).

——*La Mémoire, l'histoire, l'oubli* (Paris, 2000).

RIGGS, DAVID, *Shakespeare's Heroical Histories: 'Henry VI' and its Literary Tradition* (Cambridge, Mass., 1971).

RIST, JOHN M., *Augustine* (Cambridge, 1994).

ROLLE, DIETRICH, 'The Concept of Tragedy in Plays and Theoretical Treatises of the Elizabethan Era', in Ulrich Horstmann (ed.), *Kunstgriffe: Festschrift für Herbert Mainusch* (Frankfurt am Main, 1989).

ROPER, WILLIAM, *The Lyfe of Sir Thomas Moore, Knight*, ed. Elsie V. Hitchcock (London, 1935).

ROSS, CHARLES D., *Richard III* (London, 1981).

ROUS, JOHN, *Historia Regum Angliae*, ed. Thomas Hearney (Oxford, 1716).

RUSSELL, JEFFREY B., *Lucifer: The Devil in the Middle Ages* (Ithaca, NY, 1984).

RUTTER, CAROL C., *Documents of the Rose Playhouse* (Manchester, 1999).

SALADIN, J.-C., *La Bataille du grec à la Renaissance* (Paris, 2000)

SALINGAR, LEO, *Shakespeare and the Traditions of Comedy* (Cambridge, 1974).

SANDERS, WILBUR, *The Dramatist and the Received Idea: Studies in the Plays of Marlowe and Shakespeare* (Cambridge, 1968).

SCOT, REGINALD, *The Discoverie of Witchcraft*, ed. M. Summers (New York, 1972).

SENECA, *Seneca, His Ten Tragedies Translated into English, Edited by Thomas Newton, Anno 1581*, trans. Jasper Heywood et al., ed. C. Whibley, pref. T. S. Eliot (London, 1927).

SHAKESPEARE, WILLIAM, *King Henry VI, Parts I, II, III*, ed. A. S. Cairncross, the Arden Shakespeare (London, 1957–64).

—— *King Richard III*, ed. Antony Hammond, The Arden Shakespeare (London, 1983).

—— *The First Part of King Henry VI*, ed. M. Hattaway (Cambridge, 1990).

—— *The Second Part of King Henry VI*, ed. M. Hattaway (Cambridge, 1991).

—— *The Third Part of King Henry VI*, ed. M. Hattaway (Cambridge, 1993).

—— *King Henry VI, Part I*, ed. Edward Burns, Arden Third Series (London, 2000).

—— *King Henry VI, Part II*, ed. Ronald Knowles, Arden Third Series (London, 1999).

—— *King Henry VI, Part III*, ed. John D. Cox and Eric Rasmussen, Arden Third Series (London, 2001).

—— *The Tragedy of King Richard the Third: Parallel Texts of the First Quarto and the First Folio with Variants of the Early Quartos*, ed. Kristian Smidt (Oslo, 1969).

—— *The First Quarto of King Richard III*, ed. Peter Davison (Cambridge, 1996).

—— *King Richard III*, ed. Janis Lull (Cambridge, 1999).

—— *Richard III*, ed. John Jowett (Oxford, 2000).

SHER, ANTHONY, *Year of the King: An Actor's Diary and Sketchbook* (London, 1985).

SIDNEY, PHILIP, *The Defence of Poesie*, in *The Complete Works of Sir Philip Sidney*, ed. Albert Feuillerat (Cambridge, 1923).

SMITH, Sir THOMAS, *A Discourse of the Commonweal of this Realm of England: A Compendious or Briefe Examination of Certayne Ordinary Complaints*, ed. Mary Dewar (Charlottesville, Va., 1969).

—— *De Republica Anglorum: The Maner of Gouernement or Policie of the Realme of England* (Menston, 1970).

STOWE, JOHN, *Chronicles of England from Brute unto the Present Yeare of Christ 1580* (London, 1580).

SUTTON, A. F., and HAMMOND, P. W. (eds.), *The Coronation of Richard III: The Extant Documents* (Gloucester, 1983).

TASWELL-LANGMEAD, THOMAS T., *English Constitutional History: From the Teutonic Conquest to the Present Time*, rev. T. F. T. Plucknett (London, 1946).

TAYLOR, MICHAEL, *Shakespeare Criticism in the Twentieth Century* (Oxford, 2001).

THOMAS AQUINAS, *The Summa Theologica*, ed. Benziger Brothers (New York, 1947).

—— *Commentary on the De Trinitate of Boethius*, ed. A. Maurer (Toronto, 1953).

TILLYARD, E. M. W., *Shakespeare's History Plays* (London, 1944).

The True Tragedy of Richard the Third, to which is Appended the Latin Play of Richardus Tertius by Dr. Thomas Legge, ed. Barron Field (London, 1844).

VAN LAAN, THOMAS, *Role-Playing in Shakespeare* (Toronto, 1978).

VELZ, JOHN D., *Shakespeare and the Classical Tradition: A Critical Guide to Commentary 1660–1960* (Minneapolis, 1968).

VENET, GISÈLE, *Temps et vision tragique: Shakespeare et ses contemporains* (Paris, 1982).

VERGIL, POLYDORE, *Three Books of Polydore Vergil's English History, Comprising the Reigns of Henry VI, Edward IV, and Richard III*, ed. Henry Ellis (London, 1844).

—— *The Anglica Historia of Polydore Vergil*, ed. and trans. Denys Hay (London, 1950).

VERNANT, JEAN-PIERRE, and VIDAL-NAQUET, PIERRE, *Myth and Tragedy in Ancient Greece*, trans. Janet Lloyd (New York, 1988).

VEYNE, PAUL, *Writing History: Essay on Epistemology*, trans. Mina Moore-Rinvolucri (Manchester, 1984).

WALPOLE, HORACE, *Historic Doubts on the Life and Reign of King Richard the Third*, ed. P. W. Hammond (Gloucester, 1987).

WATSON, DONALD G., *Shakespeare's Early History Plays: Politics at Play on the Elizabethan Stage* (London, 1990).

WEIMANN, ROBERT, 'Shakespeare on the Modern Stage: Past Significance and Present Meaning', *Shakespeare Survey*, 20 (1967).

—— *Shakespeare and the Popular Tradition in the Theater* (Baltimore, 1978).

—— 'Performance-Game and Representation in *Richard III*', in Edward Pechter (ed.), *Textual and Theatrical Shakespeare: Questions of Evidence* (Iowa, 1996), 66–85.

WELLS, STANLEY, and TAYLOR, GARY, *William Shakespeare: A Textual Companion* (Oxford, 1987).

WILSON, RICHARD, *Will Power: Essays on Shakespearean Authority* (New York, 1993).

WOOD, CHARLES T., *Joan of Arc and Richard III: Sex, Saints and Government in the Middle Ages* (Oxford, 1988).

WRIGHTSON, KEITH, *English Society, 1580–1680* (London, 1982).

ZEEVELD, GORDON W., *Foundations of Tudor Policy* (Cambridge, Mass., 1948).

Index

Characters appear under their most frequent and least confusing designation (thus: Richard III, Humphrey of Gloucester, Duchess of Gloucester) or under the family name when their separate identities are not essential (Somerset, Mortimer). Anonymous characters are regrouped by functions, for instance bishops and cardinals under 'churchmen'.